HIKING NORTH CAROLINA

A GUIDE TO MORE THAN 500 OF NORTH
CAROLINA'S GREATEST HIKING TRAILS

FOURTH EDITION

Randy Johnson

FALCONGUIDES

GUILFORD, CONNECTICUT

To my mother and father.
My dad—
for taking me to my first mountaintop.
My mom—
for teaching me to appreciate it.

FALCONGUIDES®

An imprint of The Rowman & Littlefield Publishing Group, Inc.
4501 Forbes Blvd., Ste. 200
Lanham, MD 20706
www.rowman.com

Falcon and FalconGuides are registered trademarks and Make Adventure Your Story is a trademark of The Rowman & Littlefield Publishing Group, Inc.

Distributed by NATIONAL BOOK NETWORK

Copyright © 2016 The Rowman & Littlefield Publishing Group, Inc.
This FalconGuides edition 2020

Photos by Randy Johnson unless otherwise noted
Maps by The Rowman & Littlefield Publishing Group, Inc.

British Library Cataloguing in Publication Information available

Library of Congress Cataloging-in-Publication Data available

ISBN 978-1-4930-4600-3 (paper: alk. paper)
ISBN 978-1-4930-4601-0 (electronic)

∞™ The paper used in this publication meets the minimum requirements of American National Standard for Information Sciences—Permanence of Paper for Printed Library Materials, ANSI/NISO Z39.48-1992.

The author and The Rowman & Littlefield Publishing Group, Inc. assume no liability for accidents happening to, or injuries sustained by, readers who engage in the activities described in this book.

CONTENTS

THE HIKES
Mountains

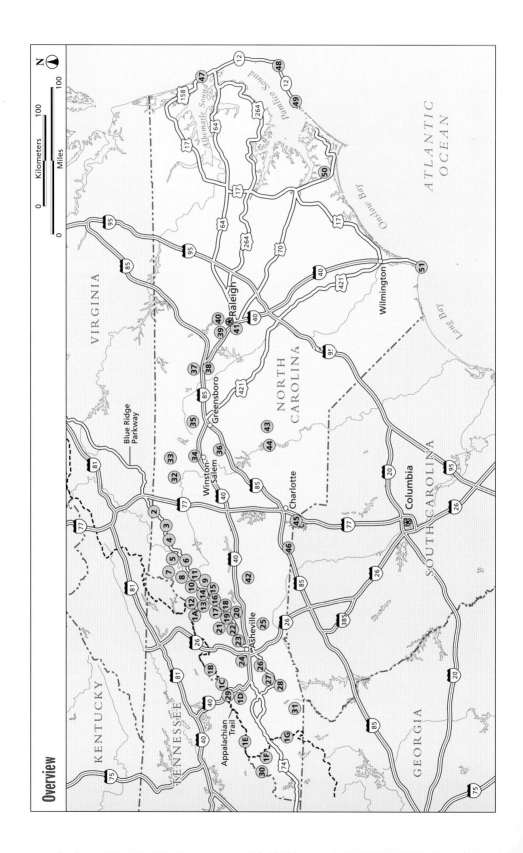

ACKNOWLEDGMENTS

My involvement with trails has been long and life-transforming—which brings me to you. My fondest hope is that readers of this book will encounter inspiration, if not in these pages then in the places they take you. Thank you for helping make this book, and my life in the outdoors, possible.

If you have a reaction to share, a correction to make, a question to ask, please visit me at www.randyjohnsonbooks.com. You'll find much to interest you on the site.

Credit for any book goes way beyond the writer. Working with rangers, managers, and other park employees is the best thing about writing a trail guide. Dedicated, enthusiastic, and—in most cases—woefully underpaid, they work tirelessly to help hikers more deeply appreciate the state's special places. When you meet them on the trail, please take time to thank them.

I'm also indebted to those who've shaped my path in this outdoor life. Hugh Morton's encouragement helped me create my own job at Grandfather Mountain and work for preservation and public access to the mountain's backcountry. Among many people at Grandfather, I'm grateful for help from Harris Prevost, Winston Church, and Grandfather's one-time trail manager Steve Miller. And without the added volunteer effort of many close friends including Ken Johnson, Robert Branch, Steve Owen, Gerry McDade, Jeep Barrett and others, I would not have been able to establish the mountain's trail management program. That's a story I tell in what's been called the definitive book on the mountain, *Grandfather Mountain: The History and Guide to an Appalachian Icon*. In recent years, as task force leader for the Grandfather Mountain to Blowing Rock portion of North Carolina's Mountains-to-Sea Trail, it's been my privilege to work with countless volunteers, including Jim Hallsey, John Lanman, Drew Koehler, and many young students from Appalachian State University's Delta Sigma Phi fraternity.

Those above and many other people have encouraged me to explore my own potential as I made the backcountry a backdrop for my life. This book celebrates the love we share for wild places.

INTRODUCTION

North Carolina is one of the United States' premier places to hoist a pack and hit the trail. Our national forests—from the Nantahala and Pisgah in the west, to the Uwharrie in the middle of the state, and the Croatan on the coast—rank near the top in hiker days of trail activity. Pisgah was the first national forest in the East.

North Carolina's national parks, the Great Smoky Mountains and Blue Ridge Parkway (both partially in neighboring states), are, respectively, the nation's most popular national parks and the most visited units of the national park system—quite an accolade as the National Park Service turned 100 in 2016. Many people haven't even heard of another North Carolina part of the national park system, Greensboro's Guilford Courthouse National Military Park. The battle fought there in 1781 saved the American Revolution, and the park's trails do it justice.

That's just the start of North Carolina's natural and historical outdoor appeal. Its long coastal arc of sand, called the Outer Banks, is as outstanding as any barrier island chain in the continental United States. Two national seashores, national wildlife refuges, even a key Nature Conservancy parcel, preserve the best for walkers. There's even the sandy streets of a ghost town to wander. And it's all reached by an atmospheric system of state ferries.

The people of North Carolina have a remarkable record of activism when it comes to parks and trails. The state park system is full of parks where the people led and preservation followed. That achievement reached a major milestone in 2016, when North Carolina's state park system celebrated its own centennial. The first state park, Mount Mitchell, was authorized in 1915 by Governor Locke Craig and dedicated in 1916 to save the last virgin forest on eastern America's highest peak. Since the mid-1990s, the state's Parks and Recreation Trust fund has added new state natural areas and parks, such as Grandfather Mountain, Elk Knob, Gorges, and more, while funding trail construction and rehabilitation and building new visitor centers and exhibits. Funding has ebbed and even been threatened since the recession due to increasingly polarized state politics. Sadly that means challenges for an agency that draws ever more people to parks while state tourism continues to grow, based in large part on North Carolina's richness in natural resources. But trail proponents are doing their best to preserve the state's environment and the flow of park revenue—some of which makes its way to counties and cities where trails and greenways are still expanding.

Increasing numbers of North Carolinians, and even citizens of other states, aim their own private donations and activism at organizations that protect and fund the state's nationally significant parks. That includes a host of local, regional, and national land trusts that are buying up the state's beauty spots an acre at a time. If you haven't joined one of these groups, symbolized so aptly by The Nature Conservancy, now is the time to do it. They range from the Friends of the Great Smoky Mountains (friendsofthesmokies.

In many parts of the mountains, the Appalachian Trail leads hikers to Canada—or at least to the Canadian forest zone.

org) and the Great Smoky Mountains Association (smokiesinformation.org) to the Blue Ridge Parkway Foundation (brpfoundation.org) and Friends of the Blue Ridge Parkway (friendsbrp.org). There's a "friends group" for state parks (ncfsp.org) and even groups for individual parks or groups of parks. Many of these organizations are mentioned in this book. Some have North Carolina vanity license plates you can buy to help funding.

Trail aficionados volunteer all over the state; some are building the Mountains-to-Sea Trail, which will literally link the Smokies to the Outer Banks. The idea for this nationally significant statewide trail got its birth in 1977 through the passion of people like state trail planner Jim Hallsey and Secretary of Natural Resources Howard Lee, who proposed the idea in a now-famous speech. The effort floundered for a while, but that changed in the 1990s when late trail pioneer Allen de Hart and others launched the increasingly professional Friends of the Mountains-to-Sea Trail. The route has been designated as a unit of the state park system; today, two-thirds of the trail is in place and urban areas are stepping up to preserve land and encourage a path likely to offer an unparalleled mix of wild settings and trail town experiences that include lodging and dining (https://mountainstoseatrail.org/). Visit the Friends' website to order or download the latest guidebooks.

Trails aren't just being built in North Carolina, they're being invented. In 2013 the Asheville-based Blue Ridge Parkway Foundation received a presidential award for devising the brilliant idea of turning trails all over the state—and the country—into engaging interpretive paths. The group chooses an easy portion of an existing trail, adds signing and interpretive brochures, and lures families into the woods to boost fitness and fun. The TRACK Trail program has exploded in North Carolina (and across the nation), in part because of an Internet component that encourages kids to bag as many trails as they can. That contribution to the state's trail culture doesn't even include the millions of dollars the Foundation has generated for the Blue Ridge Parkway itself. Find TRACK Trails listed under many categories in the Trail Finder near the end of this book. Most are just for hiking but others feature boating and biking. Visit the program's website to find more (kidsinparks.com/).

When you fuse the distinctive appeal of the Southern Appalachians with the sultry beauty of the Piedmont in the middle of the state, then factor in the islands and estuaries that border the Graveyard of the Atlantic, it's obvious that North Carolina spans a second-to-none, mountains-to-sea spectrum of scenic beauty (now linked by trail!). Here's your introduction to the great state of hiking in North Carolina.

THE REGIONS

Like most southeastern states, North Carolina comprises three regions: the mountains, the Piedmont, and the coastal plain.

Its mountains are a massive, complex jumble of topography. The North Carolina–Tennessee border splits the Great Smoky Mountains, and lesser ridges spill in all directions from that nearly 7,000-foot central spine. South of the Smokies, smaller ranges cover hundreds of square miles. North of them, the Allegheny Front continues along the state's northern border; eastward, the Blue Ridge Mountains peel off as the front range of the Appalachians. At places such as Grandfather Mountain, this latter group towers nearly a vertical mile over the western Piedmont. North of Asheville, a range called the Black Mountains soars to the East Coast's highest summits. On these and other lofty peaks, Canadian-zone forests alternate with crag-capped, alpine-like meadows. Much of this mountain land is federally owned.

The Piedmont of North Carolina—a name that means "at the foot of the mountains"—runs from the base of the Blue Ridge Mountains to the fall line, that drop-off where streams tumble to the coastal plain. Piedmont topography varies: Rippling foothills on the west become noticeably flat on the east. A profusion of flowering shrubs and trees grow in this "flatland" forest where man-made lakes often provide outstanding trail destinations.

Below the Blue Ridge, trails generally undulate through woodlands, but many Piedmont state parks boast one of the state's most distinctive and interesting geographical features—monadnocks, or isolated single summits. Crowders Mountain (west of Charlotte) and Pilot Mountain (north of Winston-Salem) are fine examples. (The latter's field trip educational materials for grades 9–12 cover these "mountains away from the mountains" and how they were formed.)

There are also modest Piedmont mountain ranges. The tops of the Uwharrie Mountains, northeast of Charlotte, reach heights of just 1,000 feet. Northwest of Charlotte, at nearly 3,000 feet, the South Mountains are the loftiest of the flatland summits. When the summer heat wanes, these Piedmont ranges make it easy for the state's urbanites to take a hike in the mountains without driving hours west. And they extend the hiking and backpacking season into winter, when the state's highest peaks are bitterly cold and snowy. Individual entries reveal more.

The Coast region, or coastal plain, is indeed the flattest part of North Carolina. Its distinctively sandy soils run to the beaches and bays. In Croatan National Forest, the largest federal tract here, trails wander into cypress forests and onto saltwater marshes. Barrier islands may be the best part of far eastern North Carolina. From north to south, paths explore dunescapes and ponds, saltwater marshes and ancient maritime forests. Trails dot private lands all along the coast and wander through resorts or state and national wildlife preserves, as well as Cape Hatteras and Cape Lookout National Seashores.

THE SEASONS

North Carolina's climatic contrasts create a range of options that is nothing short of wonderful. While summer hikers enjoy near-tropical temperatures on the coast and in the Piedmont, mountain-goers find cool walks. In winter it's possible to enjoy temperate outings in the east while, on the same day, people are snowshoeing and cross-country skiing in the mountains. The choice is yours. All you need is a close eye on the weather.

North Carolina's mountain climate is remarkably diverse due to the varying elevations in the western part of the state. The southern mountains, from Asheville south of the Great Smoky Mountains to the state's southwestern tip, have a milder climate. Average summer days there will be around 80°F. Summer temperatures (June through August) in southwestern mountain valleys can be hot: up to the low 90s. In the higher northern mountains, which include the high Great Smokies and reach north to the Virginia border, normal summer days peak in the mid-70s; the hottest days will reach the mid-80s. Summer nights in the north dip to the mid-50s and mid-60s. On the highest peaks in both areas, summer days can be downright chilly. Misty conditions can drop temperatures to the 50s and 60s. The coolest summer nights can dip to the upper 40s at higher elevations. Part of the cool of North Carolina's loftiest peaks is due to the fact that they are home to a kind of temperate rain forest. You will encounter sunny periods there, but generally summer is a time for daily thunderstorms and, possibly, sustained periods of wet weather.

That changes in early fall. In September and October, days become drier, and temperatures cool on the highest peaks. The first light snow often dusts summits in October. Autumn color is best by October 15 in the northern mountains and by October 25 in southwestern sites. Fall color lasts into early November in the lowest valleys, and warm, summerlike spells often delight November hikers. By late November and early December, the area often sees its first snowfall.

Hikers and skiers looking for snow should visit the mountains in January, February, and early March. Ample snowfall often covers the trails, with temperatures dipping below 15°F at night and, during surges of cold, staying below freezing for days at a time. Extremely high winds, arctic temperatures, and deep snow can make these mountains as challenging as those in New England. But the snow doesn't stay all winter. Coverage fluctuates with the weather; for a guide, turn to the 2019 second edition of my 1986 "cult classic" (I'm told) regional ski book, *Southern Snow: The New Guide to Winter Sports from Maryland to the Southern Appalachians* from the University of North Carolina Press. There's also the Weather Channel on TV or the web (weather.com), or newer more local Internet weather sites like Ray's Weather, which has been accurate in predicting and reporting on mountain microclimates.

Spring may be the least-appealing season in the mountains. Snow and rain are frequent, as is mud during March and April. When the area dries to warm, clear days, flowers bloom profusely—in early May in the south, by late May in the north. Budding trees don't reach the highest peaks until early June, and the spectacle of blooming rhodo-dendron explodes across the highest elevations by the third weekend in the month (see Craggy Gardens and Roan Mountain for more).

In the Piedmont, summer (late May through September) can be very hot and sticky, with daytime temperatures ranging from the mid-80s to high 90s. Thunderstorms are frequent, though not as prevalent or cooling as in the mountains. The northern Pied-mont can be as much as 5 degrees cooler, and at times cloudier, than the southern Piedmont.

Fall (October through November) is wonderful in the midsection of the state. The summer heat is gone, though Indian summer days can still reach the 80s. Autumn color peaks by November 15, but colorful forests and invigorating weather can last late into the month. Piedmont mountain parks, greenways, and lakeshore trails are best at this time of year.

Winter (December to March) often yields bright, dry, and crisp days. Rain usually falls here when the mountains receive snow. Very little snow falls on Piedmont trails; when it does, it's gone in a day or so.

Spring is another premier time to hike the Piedmont. It can be rainy, but flowers bloom by mid-March. By April, near-summer warmth produces explosive blossoms. May has more of the same, with summer temperatures arriving late in the month.

Gray's lily is one of the rare flowers that mountain hikers glimpse on the South's "bald" summits.

The coastal plain and the shore are a world apart. Summer at the coastal parks and on Outer Banks trails is hot and sunny in spades. But like subtrop-ical areas elsewhere, onshore breezes and thundershowers can make the trails (and camping) attractive for acclimatized hikers (but not me!). Those who are least attracted to hot weather should consider the shoulder seasons of spring and fall. My favorite months at the beach are April, May, September, and October. From late September to mid-November (hur-ricane season), the ocean is warm, and lower humidity days (mid-70s to mid-80s) are perfect for walking, not to mention swimming. Spring is sim-ilar, except ocean-water temperatures aren't inviting until late May.

On the coast, the north-to-south range in climate is as noticeable as it is in the mountains. Warmer, sunnier days occur earlier and stay later on the southernmost beaches, a pattern reflected in the fact that flora and fauna on those strands is similar to areas much farther south.

BEING PREPARED

Given North Carolina's varied climate and geography, there is no substitute for adequate planning. This section covers the most important elements involved in preparing for a safe, enjoyable outing; hikers should also check the information included in the overviews and details of each trail entry. The following are general tips and hiking advice—an orientation—to FalconGuides and this book.

Selecting a Trail

When you are deciding which one of the hikes from *Hiking North Carolina* to take, your first step is matching the trail with your level of ability. Hikes listed in this book are described as easy, moderate, or strenuous, with "moderately" and "extremely" modifying those terms. Generally, regardless of length, an easy trail has a graded or benched treadway, meaning that the tread has been excavated, like a mini road grade, to permit predictable footing. An easy hike is relatively level, meaning that its grade, or rate of rise, is gradual and consistent. A moderate trail involves a rougher, rockier treadway and fluctuations in the rate of rise, though the climb is usually gradual. Strenuous trails are steep overall or in places, require substantial exertion, and often have uneven footing or necessitate the use of ladders or climbing over rocks. When a trail is said to "slab around a peak," it means that it avoids a summit, generally keeping to a level grade at one elevation.

Add these basic terms to the descriptions in the trail entries. For instance, the Nuwati Trail on Grandfather Mountain (rated moderately easy) is considered untaxing because of gradual grades. Nevertheless, the text mentions that the trail has rocky footing, a fact that hikers will need to consider.

Trail entries often use the terms "loop" or "circuit" to describe a recommended hike. In general a loop is a single trail that leaves a trailhead, splits at some point, then returns the hiker to the initial path and trailhead (often called a "lollipop loop"). A circuit is a hike that originates on one trail but turns onto another trail to return to the same starting point. Either of these hikes resembles a circle of sorts. The entry also often specifies elevation gain.

Mileages are given for most hikes, often with "about" appended to them. This is done where seemingly reliable data conflicts with other information, such as park brochures or official publications. All mileage information should be considered a best estimate. Certain kinds of terrain make it difficult to measure with certainty exactly how long a trail is. In addition, the varying levels of experience that hikers bring to the trails make mileage information less meaningful. Certainly, you don't want to set off on a 10-mile hike when a 2-mile hike is what you have in mind; nevertheless, trail descriptions and ratings are often more valuable than simple mileage figures.

To further inform your trail choices, I've included entries that suggest ways for inexperienced or less physically fit hikers to sample longer, more strenuous trails. Most entries, for instance, suggest places to turn around or alternative routes that avoid the most difficult terrain. Still, a person in very poor condition could find an easy-rated trail to be a challenging hike, so the trail descriptions in this book are subjective. If you are considered overweight, do no regular exercise, or are unsure of foot, create your own hike rating system: Expect an easy hike to feel moderately difficult, and a moderate hike to be strenuous. The nice thing is that, with consistent exercise, your rating system will change.

How to Use the Maps

The maps in this book that depict a detailed close-up of an area use elevation tints, called hypsometry, to portray relief. Each gray tone represents a range of equal elevation, as shown in the scale key with the map. These maps will give you a good idea of elevation gain and loss. The darker tones are lower elevations; the lighter grays are higher elevations. The lighter the tone, the higher the elevation. Narrow bands of different gray tones spaced closely together indicate steep terrain, whereas wider bands indicate areas of more gradual slope.

Maps that show larger geographic areas use shaded, or shadow, relief. Shadow relief does not represent elevation; it demonstrates slope or relative steepness. This gives an almost 3-D perspective of the physiography of a region and will help you see where ranges and valleys are.

Don't Forget High Tech: The Web and GPS

The first edition of this book was the first North Carolina trail guide to feature websites and discuss the value of the Internet for hikers. This edition offers even more focused and useful sites. Today, the nature-loving legion of hikers are among the most likely demographic to be online. Be sure to keep in touch with the exploding trove of information about hiking to be found on the web, especially for the latest on campground rates, new trails, storm closures, and more, including trail maps and apps for specific parks. I hope this book's overview makes the overwhelming, and at times unreliable, Internet free-for-all a little more accessible.

High tech has also taken to the trails with the Global Positioning System, or GPS. The maps in this book are already compatible with the Universal Transverse Mercator (UTM) system of coordinates used by GPS units. That is intended to encourage experimentation with GPS units and their capacity to pinpoint your location on the maps in this book or to overlay GPS "waypoints," or locations on your hike, onto computer-based topographical maps. With one of a number of available computer topo map products, it's easy to print out great maps before a hike, to record the entire route of your hike on a map when you return, and even to find your way to desired locations.

That latter capacity has led to "geocaching." All over the state, GPS enthusiasts have established hidden caches of diverse items, including a log of visitors. Finding them is fun—kind of like a backcountry scavenger hunt. Log onto geocaching.com to find your way into this world. Or try ncgeocachers.org. And be sure to check out FalconGuides on route finding and using GPS.

What to Carry

Since the first edition of this book, improvements in outdoor gear have gone from evolution to revolution.

The leap to lightweight trail gear in the 1970s dropped World War II–era backpacking loads from 60 pounds to 40. Another major morph is ongoing. Ultralight gear means overnight loads can now be as light as 20 pounds. All kinds of high-tech hiking items are part of the trend—a real plus whether you're a youngster just starting out or a baby boomer getting back to the woods with new hips.

Overnight gear tells the tale. Inflatable and closed cell sleeping pads, and the adapter that turns them into luxe camp seats, just add about a pound. Stoves, like MSR's lightest models, have dropped into the realm of mere ounces. Cook kits and utensils are titanium—and virtually weightless.

For hikers, fabrics are a big part of the story. The newest are extremely lightweight, breathable, and waterproof. Only a single layer is now needed for tents (no fly), packs, and rain jackets (welded seams have eliminated thread holes, and waterproof zippers have done away with the extra weight of zipper flaps).

Weight isn't all that's changed. Many packs have built-in hydration systems that permit you to drink through a tube, doing away with the need to carry a water bottle.

If you avoid the tendency to carry the kitchen sink, outdoor adventure has never been more accessible. The website backpackinglight.com is a great place to start.

The shortest, easiest nature trail in this book requires the hiker to carry nothing more than a camera or binoculars. But hikers who venture farther into fields or forests will want to carry a few basics.

A small backpack or fanny pack holds the essentials: a water bottle (or hydration system), a snack or extra food, spare clothing, and other protective items (sunscreen, insect repellent, sunglasses, a hat, and a rain jacket). Be sure to have a small first-aid kit (bandages, antiseptic, extra-strength aspirin/acetaminophen, moleskin for blisters). Check out adventuremedicalkits.com for a great selection. Take this book (or relevant photocopied pages), the recommended hiking maps, and any trail permits required.

Clothes

Choose clothes that are comfortable and protective.

In summer, anywhere in the state, shorts and T-shirts are a must. But climate, insects, or poisonous plants can intervene. On the coast or in the Piedmont, you may find it necessary to have a hat, long-sleeved T-shirt, and long, loose pants (perhaps with zip-off legs) because of sun, bugs, or vegetation. A heavier version of the same outfit can be worn in the mountains' cooler conditions. And remember, a high-altitude sun can burn as much as at the beach. The latest trail shorts and T-shirts are virtually weightless, dry fast, have antimicrobial properties that eliminate odor, and are even sun protection formula (SPF) rated.

When choosing clothing, the best policy is to be prepared for the worst weather the season and place can deliver. This means being flexible and dressing in layers. However lightly clothed you find yourself in summer, be prepared for rain and wind. The best choices are jackets made of new high-tech synthetic fabrics. You'll have to throw a little money into this effort, but it's worth it.

Whether you are reveling in cold salt spray in summer or climbing into a Blue Ridge snowstorm, your waterproof outer layer of clothing (shell jacket and pants) is your first line of defense. Under that, wear layers—how many varies by season. Synthetic fabrics, such as polypropylene, that are warm even when wet, are the best choices. Polypropylene T-shirts, long underwear, and fleece jackets and pants are indispensable for cold weather.

You'll need major insulating garments in North Carolina's winter mountains. The choice for insulation is, again, synthetic fills that won't lose their insulating value when wet. Nevertheless, waterproof fabrics are bringing down back in vogue.

Footwear

On easy trails, a sturdy pair of walking or running shoes will do. But on moderate or more difficult hikes—or even easy hikes with rocky footing—you'll depend on hiking boots.

The newest-generation boots are light and relatively inexpensive compared with the heavy, costly leather boots associated with the 1970s backpacking boom. The new boots boast waterproof fabrics and various kinds of nonskid soles. They add comfort, safety, and enjoyment to any hike, making them a worthwhile purchase for even a casual hiker.

But boots may not be the only kind of shoe a serious hiker or backpacker will need. Winter hikers will need more than a three-season, lightweight boot. Rather than avoid paths that cross streams without bridges, consider carrying a pair of aqua shoes, which slip over bare feet, or sport sandals for wading. The Crocs style of foam slip-on is almost weightless and makes a great camp shoe after a day on the trail.

The ultimate item you'll want to carry isn't in your pack but in your head: knowledge. The information contained in this book is timely and extensive, but no single trail guide can do it all. Prepare yourself by seeking out the variety of resources available to those who enjoy the outdoors, perhaps including courses in CPR and first aid. Read Falcon-Guides and other books on survival, route finding, mountaineering, backpacking, and additional outdoor topics.

Weather Dangers

Owning or carrying the proper clothing isn't enough. Be sure to don your high-tech garments *before* you become thoroughly wet or chilled.

Hypothermia results when lack of food and/or exposure to severe weather prevents the body from maintaining its core temperature. With the dramatic cooling effects of wind and rain, it can occur at any time of year, even at temperatures well above freezing. To prevent exposure, stay dry and protected with the right clothing—especially a hat, since up to 70 percent of lost heat can emanate from your head. Don extra clothing when you stop for a rest, before you get chilled. Drink plenty of fluids (in winter, just breathing robs you of moisture). Adequately fuel yourself with food. Nibble energy foods (such as trail mix, sandwiches, and hot soups). Set up camp earlier to accommodate an inexperienced or less physically fit member of your party. The best way to treat hypothermia is to stop it before it starts, but if you can't, do not ignore the uncontrollable shivering and, later, the slow and slurred speech, stumbling gait, clumsiness, and seeming disorientation of a hypothermic hiker. Take immediate action to shelter and refuel anyone with these symptoms. If the victim is uncooperative, or unconscious, use a sleeping bag to sandwich the lightly dressed hiker between two similarly dressed helpers.

Frostbite is another danger. Frozen flesh often results from severe cold, and its first sign is reddened skin. Next, the frozen site—often toes, fingers, or portions of the face—will turn white or gray. The best prevention is to stay warm so that your extremities receive the blood flow they need. If you can avoid it, do not venture into extreme conditions or exposed areas where windchill factors are below minus 20°F. In severe conditions, hikers should monitor one another's faces and suggest shelter when the need arises. Do not rub frozen skin or slap frozen extremities together. When an area with severe frostbite begins to thaw, expect severe pain; use aspirin or acetaminophen on the way to medical assistance.

In summer, a hiker's major danger is lightning, especially on exposed mountaintops. Lightning is a complex combination of charges that bounce from cloud to ground and

Reaching Mount Mitchell's summit in winter isn't easy, but for those who do, the peak's 100-plus inches of annual snowfall offer a very "un-Southern" experience.

back. Suffice it to say, take shelter at the first sign of lightning. Other lightning safety tips include move off ridgetops; seek shelter in a group of smaller trees rather than under one tall one; rest in a low, dry area (but not a gully or near a pond, where water can conduct the current); avoid overhangs or small caves where ground current might pass through you. In a lightning storm, it's best to sit in the open below surrounding high points and atop a rock that is detached and thus insulated from the ground. To further insulate yourself, crouch low or kneel on top of your pack or sleeping pad.

Heat stroke and heat exhaustion are summer equivalents of hypothermia. North Carolina boasts more than its share of hot hikes, so carry and drink plenty of fluids if you're sweating heavily. Avoid hiking in the hottest part of the day; to cool off, slip into one of the trailside pools so often mentioned in this book's hike descriptions. If you feel dizzy and drained, heat exhaustion may be the culprit. Relax, drink fluids, and let your body recover. Heat stroke is the more extreme condition: Rather than being damp and drained, you'll be dry and feverish—dangerous signs that the body has given up its attempts to cool itself down by perspiring. If things get this bad, immediately cool the affected person with cold, wet compresses. Administer water to resume hydration.

Trailside Pests

Winter weather largely eradicates North Carolina's most bothersome bugs, reptiles, and plants. But spring, summer, and fall are different matters.

In mild and hot weather, wasps, hornets, and bees of various kinds are found across the state. Take every precaution to avoid contact with concentrations of bees. Be cautious when you see a large number of bees around fruit and flowers; be on the lookout for nests hanging from limbs, in hollow trees or logs, or on the ground. If you notice heightened activity and presence of bees, move away. And don't act like a flower. You can't avoid sweating, which attracts some bees, but don't entice them with perfume or scented body-care products.

Most stings are minor and easily treated. Simply scrape an embedded stinger out with a knife blade (squeezing it out releases more venom into your bloodstream). A paste made of water and unseasoned meat tenderizer that contains papain (a papaya enzyme) can neutralize bee venom; baking soda paste does not. Some stings are not so simple. When a person is allergic to bee stings or stung enough times, the danger of anaphylactic shock and even death can be great. Around one hundred people die from bee stings each year in the United States. An over-the-counter antihistamine that contains diphenhydramine (such as Benadryl) can help control mild allergic reactions. Serious toxic reactions and anaphylactic shock can set in immediately or after some delay. If you know you are allergic to bee stings, always carry an epinephrine syringe bee sting kit—and be sure your companions know where it is and how to use it.

Ticks are another source of potentially deadly bites. North Carolina's hot Piedmont and coastal forests are favorite habitats for ticks, especially in late spring through summer. Hikers on the state's highest mountains are less likely to encounter ticks, especially where spruce and fir forests prevail. Lyme disease is one serious malady carried by ticks; Rocky Mountain spotted fever is another. North Carolina is infamous for the latter. Both diseases can take up to two weeks to gestate before symptoms develop. Among the signs are arthritis-like joint pain, high fever, and/or a circular rash.

The best defense against ticks is three-pronged. First, use a tick and insect repellent that contains N, N-diethyl-3-methylbenzamide, more widely known as DEET. Second, whether you use chemicals or not, wear long-sleeved shirts and long pants, and avoid walking through tall grass, brush, or dense woods. Third, frequently check yourself for ticks, especially at night and when you finish a hike. Focus on armpits, ears, scalp, groin, legs, and where clothes, such as socks, constrict the body. It takes a while for ticks to attach and transmit disease, so you have a good shot at preventing infection if you find ticks early.

If a tick becomes embedded in your skin, use a bit of repellent or rubbing alcohol or a hot, extinguished match to encourage it to back itself out. If you must use tweezers to remove a tick, grasp the head to avoid squeezing toxins into the wound. And don't hesitate to pull a little bit of your skin out with it so that mouthparts do not remain.

Flies can also be a problem in many areas of North Carolina. In spring (mid-April to mid-June), hikers on the state's highest peaks can be troubled by the same tiny blackflies that pester North Country hikers in Minnesota and Maine. More often hikers here see common houseflies and horseflies; the latter seem particularly vicious at the coast. The best defenses are to be sure to carry and use insect repellent, keep food and garbage covered or stored elsewhere when picnicking and camping, and cover your body. Consider wearing a repellent-coated cap or treated garments. The latest garments from L.L.Bean and other brands include bug-banning technology.. These clothes work and diminish the amount of chemicals needed to survive summer.

Mosquitoes are prevalent in the state, especially on cool mountain evenings and on trails that pass coastal marshlands. In the latter locations, mosquitoes can be voracious. For most comfort, hike the buggiest locations, such as coastal marshes, in fall and winter; at other times, do not fail to carry and use repellent with DEET, because nothing else will do. And keep high-tech clothing with insect-repelling technology in mind.

North Carolina also has plant pests. Poison ivy, poison oak, and poison sumac are all found here, though the highest peaks are free of these troublesome plants. All produce contact dermatitis—rash and watery blisters that appear from 12 to 48 hours after skin rubs against the plant resin. The outbreak usually runs its course in ten days, but isolated cases can be severe or cause allergic reactions. Learn to identify these plants (remember "leaves of three, let it be"), and be wary of wading through brush in shorts.

If you realize you just touched one of these poisonous plants, remove and isolate contaminated clothing until it can be washed at home. Flush the affected skin with water but no soap; your skin's natural oils will temporarily protect you. Cover rash areas with calamine lotion. See a physician if face, genitals, or more than 25 percent of your body is affected.

Snakes rank high on the list of hiker fears. Indeed, North Carolina's venomous vipers range from the timber rattlesnake and copperhead (found across the state except for the highest peaks) to the cottonmouth moccasin, usually confined to the warmest, wettest coastal sites east of Raleigh. Luckily, of the 20,000 people a year who are bitten by venomous snakes in the United States, only 6 to 15 die. The low death rate is due to several factors: The venom of these species is relatively slow-acting; almost half of all snakebites do not include the injection of venom; and antivenin is widely available at hospitals.

All the above kinds of snakes are generally heftier than nonvenomous snakes and have triangular or arrow-shaped heads and vertically slit pupils (versus tube-shaped heads and round pupils on nonvenomous snakes). To avoid snakebites, don't reach blindly behind logs and rocks, inspect wooded sites where you plan to sit, and watch where you step.

Snakes play a role in nature, so don't harm them. Your best bet is to be observant and able to recognize venomous snakes before they can bite. All too often, snakes such as the nonvenomous northern water snake, found widely in the state, are killed in cases of mistaken identity.

If bitten, be able to report what kind of snake attacked. Observe your wound: The bite of a pit viper includes two or more prominent fang marks, while the bite of a harmless snake usually leaves two rows of indentations and no big holes. If you can, use a commercial snakebite kit within 3 minutes of the bite. Immediately remove all watches and rings, which may cause constriction from swelling, and do not make incisions with a knife or try to suck out the venom. Do not use tourniquets, cold water, or ice packs, since these heighten the possibility of gangrene. Instead, loosely splint and immobilize the affected limb; with a pen, mark on the victim to record the time and spread of swelling. If you are within 20 minutes of the trailhead, carry the victim (or permit him or her to walk slowly, with frequent rests) to a vehicle for immediate transfer to a hospital. If hiking alone, walk as calmly as possible back to your car for help. Hikers who are far from a trailhead should send a companion for help and wait for emergency personnel to return with antivenin. Many trails in this book have good cell phone service.

Most other animals in North Carolina are harmless to hikers. The exception is the rarely seen black bear. Most of the time, a backcountry glimpse of one of these reclusive mammals features its rear end sprinting away. If you have a sudden encounter with a nearby bear, especially a mother with cubs, steadily and calmly back away. Leave the area. Do not run or climb a tree, since this may provoke a chase—and you cannot outrun a bear. Stand your ground in a charge: Bears often bluff these.

The most problematic locations for bear encounters are in popular campsites, where marauding bears forage through garbage. There they can be aggressive, especially if you approach while they are enjoying food. Stay away. The best defense against such encounters with bears—and with skunks and other animals, even mice—is to keep your food away from camp. Safely hang bagged food by tossing a rope over a tree limb, tie on your food container, run it up into midair away from the trunk, and secure the rope's other end where you can reach it. Be aware, bears are coming into increasing contact with campers in the Great Smokies, nearby national forests, and at Appalachian Trail shelters. Always check ahead on park and forest websites to be aware of shelter and campsite closures or restrictions (which can include mandatory use of bear canisters or on-site food cables).

The other animal threat is a microscopic one. The ingestion of waterborne pests can cause a variety of backcountry infections. Perhaps the best known is *giardia lamblia*, but an *E. coli* infection can be deadly. Hikers have even contracted Type A hepatitis from drinking untreated water in the "wilderness." Giardia victims may not feel the effects for days or weeks, but you should see a physician if you develop foul-smelling gas, loss of appetite, bloating, stomach cramps, or nausea. Unfortunately, even pristine-looking streams may contain these and other disease-producing agents. All hikers should carry water from treated sources, including commercially bottled drinks, or treat the water they use.

Do not disinfect water with Halazone, chlorine, or iodine. Boiling water for at least 5 minutes (before adding food or flavoring) will kill the tiny cysts that cause giardiasis. Do that, and campers can feel safe preparing hot foods with water from streams and springs. Boiling can cause drinking water to taste flat, though, so either pour it back and forth between clean containers to restore its oxygen content or add flavorings.

All the above water issues make drinking from trailside springs increasingly problematic, so be sure to filter all your drinking water. The best bet is to purchase a portable water pump filter purifier from an outdoor store or travel catalog. The smallest water purifiers weigh only ounces! These devices make it relatively safe to drink from most backcountry water sources.

ZERO-IMPACT HIKING

Everyone's heard the dictum "Take only pictures, leave only footprints." Well, even footprints are a problem in many popular wilderness areas—causing soil compaction and erosion. Nevertheless, damage to the environment can be minimized.

The basic idea of zero-impact hiking and camping is to minimize any evidence of your presence. That starts with staying on defined trails and restricting your outings to a small party of people. Intelligent strategies for protecting trails, such as not shortcutting switchbacks, also mean you won't brush directly through poison ivy or step on that snoozing copperhead. It's bad form to hike into the woods in a group of eight or more, because anywhere you choose to picnic or camp will be overwhelmed. Groups of four to six people are best, in part because they can more easily find campsites and deal with emergencies. Larger groups are noisier; most people prefer quiet or a natural noise level in the backcountry. Whatever the size of your party, try to keep your noise level down, especially when camping in the vicinity of others. Noise travels in the damp after dark. There's no excuse for loud conversation or rowdy behavior after 9 p.m.

The other obvious no-no is littering, the number-one trail pollution problem. The motto "Pack it in, pack it out" has become the basic credo of backcountry travel. Too many people still lug food and drink into the woods in heavy containers, then leave the bottles and cans behind when they're empty. Pack properly, using lightweight plastic, and you won't be tempted to jettison the refuse. Also, bag refuse immediately to avoid attracting bugs and animals. And consider picking up litter left by others. It sets a good example.

Everyone generates waste in the woods, so proper disposal is another element of zero impact. At popular parks and trails, use the restrooms before hitting the trail. While hiking or camping, use proper methods of disposal to keep urine, feces, soap, and garbage out of water sources; these cause the increasing pollution of streams and springs. To make a "cat hole" for body waste, use a tiny trowel to remove a cap of sod (keep it intact) and dig a hole at least 6 inches deep in organic soil (damp but not wet), at least 200 feet from surface water, trails, campsites, or other places people congregate. This is your "toilet." Use natural toilet paper such as leaves, or pack out toilet paper in a plastic bag. After using your pit, mix soil into the waste to hasten decomposition, then cover with the sod cap. When urinating, avoid hitting plants; instead go into mineral soil or sand. Choose a sunny spot to hasten evaporation.

Camping impacts the environment in ways that hiking does not. Hikers who intend to camp should read up on clean camping: How to choose a campsite, the safety and environmental benefits of carrying a camp stove, and many other topics are addressed in several fine publications. A touchy topic for campers is how to keep your body and equipment clean without polluting streams and lakes. Some camping purists choose not to bathe in the backcountry; others wouldn't camp if they couldn't get clean. The best way to wash and not pollute nearby drinking water is to carry a large pot or bucket of water at least 200 feet from the water source. Lather minimally with biodegradable soap, rinse, and then disperse and dilute any suds on the ground with more water.

To brush your teeth, go the same distance away and use the smallest amount of paste possible. Disperse it by spitting, and rinse away residue with water. The Leave No Trace organization is the ultimate source for guidelines on clean camping. Be sure to visit them at lnt.org.

HIKING WITH DOGS

Woodsy forays with Fido are rewarding experiences. There's nothing like sharing the exercise and camaraderie of the great outdoors with your four-legged friend. But be aware that dogs can be a headache for other hikers and for park managers.

Sadly, not everyone out there loves dogs (or, at the very least, your dog). It can be a frightening, frustrating experience to see an unleashed animal charging down a trail at you, especially if you're a parent with children or another pet owner with your dog on a leash. Remember, these hikers have rights too. They're out there to enjoy the peace and quiet of the wilderness. Irresponsible pet owners can find themselves in instant conflict with others, especially at campsites.

Some owners see it as part of the fun for their dog to run free. If that's you, your best bet is to find a fenced field (without grazing livestock) or a dog park. It's not fair to intimidate or annoy other hikers. Most important, wild areas are too fragile for this kind of recreation.

Many national parks prohibit dogs because their territorial instincts can complicate life for wildlife populations already trying to survive in shrinking natural areas. While out of sight of their owners, dogs that run free dig up animal dens, even kill wildlife, and leave their scent (not to mention piles of poo) on the trail.

There are real virtues to using a leash. Many dogs get permanently lost in wild areas, severely injured in encounters with wildlife, or hurt in falls. Keeping your dog on a leash can even enhance your awareness of nearby wildlife.

If there is a leash law at the park you visit, please obey it. Unleashed dogs increase the possibility that your dog will be banned from your favorite park. Beyond all that, you could be fined.

HIKING WITH KIDS

Hiking is a wonderful way to instill a love of the outdoors, an enjoyment of physical fitness and exercise, and less-tangible values of environmental and personal responsibility in young people.

You don't have to wait until a child is 10 years old to take him or her out into the woods. Many of the easiest hikes in this book are great for kids. Trail descriptions highlight paths suitable for toddlers on their first unaided woods walks, family hikes, beginner backpacking trips, and saunters with the elderly and physically challenged. Sample some of these, but don't expect to make the entire hike or reach that intended campsite. Be flexible with tiny hikers. Let them set the pace.

Many parents purchase sophisticated child-carrier packs that include a pouch for kid items. These increase your mobility, but remember to avoid tree limbs and other obstacles. Also, children often fall asleep in these packs, and few have a way to stabilize a sleeping hiker's head. Be prepared to use a scarf, pillow, or other item to cushion the napping kid. Work this out in advance of a longer hike.

Cool-weather hiking with children poses more challenges. Since children in backpacks aren't active, it is easy for them to become cold, especially in winter. Don't overdo winter hikes and cross-country ski trips. Carry hot drinks or soup in a thermos; nothing is better if a child becomes cold. Be aware that just bundling a child in urban-style outerwear may not keep her or him warm. There is no substitute for effectively layered, high-quality clothing. Foam-lined, heavily insulated boots with polypropylene or wool socks and substantial mittens should also be basic requirements. Children who have a bad experience will not be enthusiastic about hiking in the future.

Focus on comfort and safety. Items such as sunscreen, hats, insect repellent, and topical anesthetic for bug bites or sunburn are some of the ingredients of a successful family hike.

BACKCOUNTRY ETIQUETTE

You can enhance your safety and limit human conflict in the backcountry, just as you can have zero impact on the environment. Backcountry conflict arises in many ways. Hikers have tempers too.

Camping is a touchy topic. Many serious campers cope with darkness by going to sleep; when nearby tenters build a giant bonfire and party until midnight, the result can be unpleasant. Avoid such conflicts by choosing your site well. Know your preferences. Choose an isolated campsite if you are a wilderness purist; choose a car-accessible campground or other appropriate place if you're taking the neighborhood kids on their first camping trip. With a little forethought and consideration, you can minimize conflicts among users.

Trails have their own form of etiquette. Unless it's unsafe to do so, step aside when other hikers approach, even if you have the right-of-way. Be diplomatic at all times. If the chemistry in a given situation is wrong, be the first to back down and move on. And be a sensitive dog owner (see Hiking with Dogs above).

Criminal violence is rare on trails, but it makes the news, and instances of robbery and rape seem to be increasing. For that reason, be friendly but reasonably wary. Backcountry users have much in common, and the camaraderie of the woods, especially the Appalachian Trail, can cause some people to treat everyone they meet as if they were old friends. But it is far better to keep an urban sense of security about you, which means not leaving your pack and other gear unattended, not volunteering valuable information about yourself or your belongings, and avoiding suspicious people.

Do not hike alone; if you do, don't hesitate to say you're with a group of friends just down the trail. Dress conservatively, don't flaunt expensive equipment or jewelry, and don't leave valuables in your vehicle. The number-one crime associated with hiking is the trailhead auto break-in. When your trek begins at an isolated trailhead, consider parking at a nearby business and arranging to be shuttled. This book points out some of those spots.

No matter what, let a responsible party know where you are going, your intended route, and when you plan to return. Religiously comply with hiker registration and user permit systems, which exist at many North Carolina parks and preserves. These function as a safety net and, where fees are collected, support the maintenance and management of the trails you've come to enjoy.

Enjoyment is, after all, what trails are all about. There's the exercise, the good times you share with those who accompany you, and the scenic views, both vast and intimate. You'll savor the sound of wind as it rushes over a forest and be astounded by the way dense vegetation suddenly gives way to a dramatic vista. You will discover how sweat and hard work reap rewards. It's no wonder that Henry David Thoreau and many other soul-searchers have found that walking facilitates the thinking process. Hiking has a way of leading your mind to new insights as surely as it leads you to new settings. May you, and those you hike with, find both.

Please contact the author of this guidebook, to forward corrections or to explore added content and updates, by visiting randyjohnsonbooks.com.

Map Legend

40 (Interstate shield)	Interstate Highway	∧	Cave
64 (US shield)	US Highway	†	Cemetery
90 (State shield)	State Highway	(graduation cap)	College/University
2000 (Secondary State shield)	Secondary State Highway	—	Dam
192 (Forest Road shield)	Forest Road	⊕	Hospital
(double line)	Local Road	▬	Inn/Hotel
= = = = =	Unpaved Road	!	Gate
—+—+—+—	Railroad	(lighthouse)	Lighthouse
•—•—•—•	Utility/Power Line	⚒	Mine
▬▬▬▬▬	Featured Trail	♣	Park (Small)
- - - - -	Trail	Ⓟ	Parking
·············	Off-Trail Hike	⤬	Pass/Gap
‖‖‖‖‖‖	Boardwalk/Steps	▲	Peak/Summit/Spot Elevation
- - - - -	Ferry Route	(picnic)	Picnic Area
—··—··—	State Line	(ranger)	Ranger Station/Headquarters
(curved line)	Small River/Creek	(restaurant)	Restaurant
(marsh symbol)	Marsh/Swamp	(restrooms)	Restrooms
(oval)	Body of Water	∴	Ruins
(thick line)	National/State Forest/Park	(viewpoint)	Scenic View/Viewpoint
(dashed line)	National Monument/Wilderness Area	(shelter)	Shelter/Cabin
(thin line)	State/Regional Park	(ship)	Ship/Ferry Boat
(gray line)	Miscellaneous Park	⌐°	Spring
(amphitheater)	Amphitheater	(stables)	Stables
(bluffs)	Bluffs	(tower)	Tower
(boat ramp)	Boat Ramp	○	Town
⌣	Bridge	①	Trailhead
■	Building/Point of Interest	⊢——⊣	Tunnel
▲ (A)	Campground	(viaduct)	Viaduct
▲	Campsite	❓	Visitor/Information Center
⊛	Capital	(waterfall)	Waterfall

MOUNTAINS

1 APPALACHIAN TRAIL

Each spring, hundreds of people hoist heavy packs onto their backs and strain down a misty trail, intent on accomplishing the most difficult task of their lives: going the length of the Appalachian Mountains. The footpath links a tree-covered mountaintop in Georgia and a rock-capped summit in central Maine. The trail winds for 300 miles across western North Carolina, home to some of its highest elevations and most spectacular scenery. Nearly 85 years old, the Appalachian National Scenic Trail (AT) was the first organized recreational avenue to wilderness. Today there are many long-distance trails, but none equals the AT.

When first proposed in 1921 by regional planner Benton MacKaye (Mc-KIE), the idea for a cross-Appalachian trail was labeled "an experiment in regional planning." Actually, it was a philosophical experiment too, intended to dilute the hold that industrialism had on modern life. The AT would preserve the East's wilderness while offering the laboring masses an uplifting escape from the manufacturing economy. Many people recognized that the unspoiled Appalachians—so different from other denuded and eroded lands—were at stake. And trail enthusiasts liked the idea of the path itself.

Creating the AT was a large task. Within two years of MacKaye's first article proposing the AT, the major trail organizations, including fledgling groups in the South, had endorsed the plan and built the first sections of the AT in New England. In 1925 a meeting held in Washington, DC, formally created the Appalachian Trail Conference Incorporated, forerunner of the organization that manages the path today; the conference's name was changed to the Appalachian Trail Conservancy (ATC) in 2005. At these early stages, MacKaye's philosophical bent still shaped the trail's future; he announced at the conference that "the trailway should 'open up' a country as an escape from civilization. . . . The path of the trailway should be as 'pathless' as possible."

In the late 1920s that's exactly how it was. The original route plan led from Cohutta Mountain in Georgia, across the Great Smoky Mountains, to Grandfather Mountain in North Carolina, through southwestern Virginia, across the Blue Ridge Mountains at what is now Shenandoah National Park, and on to its northern terminus at Mount Washington in New Hampshire. With railroad imagery fostered by MacKaye, the trail's "main line" described above would link to various "branch lines." In the South, feeder trails were meant to reach Birmingham and Atlanta, funneling jaded urban workers into the refreshing green corridor of renewal. North Carolina's Mountains-to-Sea Trail and the Bartram Trail, and Vermont's Long Trail, are examples of branch lines that did come about.

In reality, the AT was built largely out of existing trails in the North and through unexpected devotion from trail clubs and the USDA Forest Service in the South. The Southern Appalachian section was finished quickly, surprising New Englanders, who felt sure their region's trail clubs would be the most active. The Southerners helped build other sections too: The Potomac Appalachian Trail Club was instrumental in completing the trail through Maine to Mount Katahdin.

During AT construction, nearly 600 miles of the Skyline Drive and the Blue Ridge Parkway were built, claiming dozens of miles of the AT's early route. Many trail clubs opposed building those roads. Luckily, the Civilian Conservation Corps (CCC) was enlisted to revise the route and build some of the three-sided lean-to shelters that line the trail. Nevertheless, Appalachian Trail Conference chairman Myron Avery called the scenic roads a "major catastrophe in Appalachian Trail history." Today, we nod at Avery's assertions. Although the Parkway boasts wonderful hiking opportunities, its leg-stretcher hikes do not a wilderness experience make. (See this author's Blue Ridge Parkway trail guides.)

The trail, in any form, became a symbol. Long before wilderness preservation was ever achieved in the East, diehard trail builders helped protect remnants of a wild heritage. By 1937 the first version of the trail was complete. Thousands of minor catastrophes and positive changes have happened since then. The bad events range from hurricanes to commercial development of private land, all claiming portions of the trail. The good occurrences come too, since at each time of loss, a new generation of trail enthusiasts has stepped in and carved a new path. The extension of the trail to Mount Katahdin, originally a branch site rather than a terminus, was one of thousands of changes that qualify the AT as a living entity. It was Myron Avery who said that the AT was the trail of which it could never be said, "It is finished—this is the end!"

The Appalachian Trail started as, and remains, an effort spearheaded by the public. But the Appalachian Trail Conservancy also enlisted the support and cooperation of the national parks, national forests, state parks, and other agencies and individuals. Since 1938, when a minimum width was established for the trail corridor through federal land, the extent of cooperation between AT enthusiasts and the government has been astounding. In 1968 the AT became the first National Scenic Trail under the landmark National Trails System Act, which gave control to the Appalachian Trail Conference. It also authorized the acquisition of 1,000 miles of trail in private hands, by eminent domain if necessary. But acquisition of land was slow. After pressure from the trail community, an Appalachian Trail bill passed Congress in the late 1970s that has substantially sped up land acquisition along the route. Today, almost all of the path is in public ownership.

The trail has elevated some isolated mountain burgs into backcountry boomtowns. Hikers bring thousands of dollars into towns lacking mainstream tourist attractions. Hot Springs, North Carolina, is one place swelled by trail traffic that has been named an official AT "Trail Town." So is Roan Mountain, Tennessee. "The Appalachian Trail passes within 5 miles of 105 towns," says Brian King, Appalachian Trail Conservancy spokesman. "Many of those towns see the trail as their primary tourist attraction. Just the money spent on gas, food, and lodging is a significant transfer of wealth from urban areas to the Appalachians."

Maintenance of the path never wanes and is accomplished through the efforts of dozens of organizations affiliated with the Appalachian Trail Conservancy. The conservancy boasts 40,000 members and thirty-one affiliated clubs. Many times each year, volunteers toil long hours in the task of maintaining their portions of the footpath and any of nearly 300 overnight shelters on the route. All told, about 6,000 volunteers work each year on the path.

Because of such necessary efforts, the heart of the most populous part of the United States is today a forest trail. This premier hiking path is a world-class adventure covering about 2,200 miles. Only 500 or so people a year finish the complete hike over the loftiest mountains in eastern North America. In fact, those who have accomplished the entire feat number fewer than 10,000. Millions of hikers hit the trail annually, for a short stroll, a summit hike, or a multi-night backpacking trip. The Appalachian Trail in North Carolina is a wonderful string of day hikes. The best are presented below.

The perils of the trek might be unimaginable to sedentary Americans. If the sheer physical task weren't arduous enough, equipment and its failures pose other problems. If

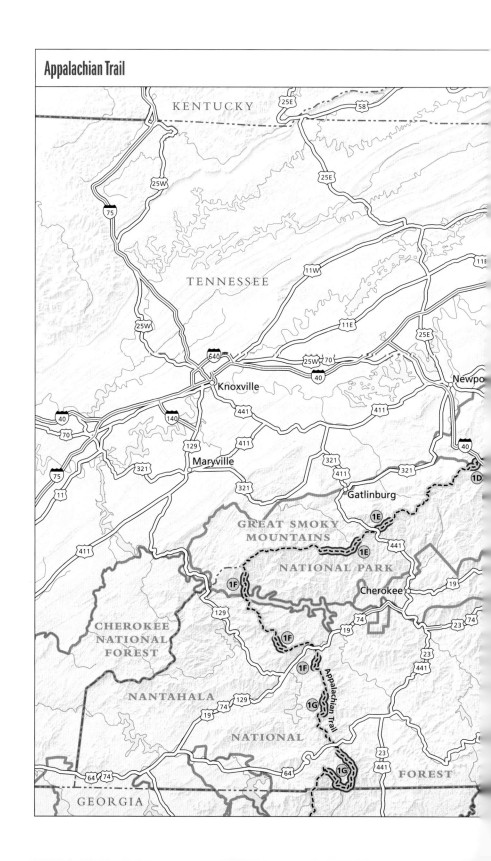

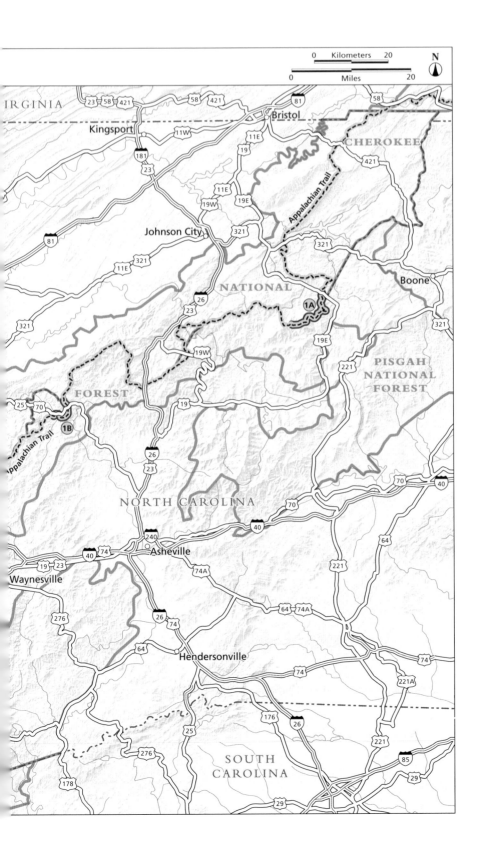

In many parts of the North Carolina mountains, stone chimneys are all that remain to remind us of early settlers.

you've ever had a blister from new hiking boots, imagine having boot problems as you walk 10 or more miles daily. Even when a hiker's boots are comfortable, they wear out or fall apart on the trek, often at the least opportune time. That kind of roulette plagues everything a hiker relies on, from a backpacking stove to a tent to a sleeping bag.

The end-to-end AT hiker ultimately discovers that the human body is just another piece of equipment bound to fail. Most people find a three- or four-day backpacking trip to be an ample undertaking; imagine walking for an entire summer. An end-to-end hike on the AT is a Herculean undertaking. And not everybody makes it.

Luckily, even an AT day hike is rewarding. Within North Carolina alone, hikers pass through tree-covered, modest mountains that conjure the Appalachians of stereotype. They see their share of poverty in these stark, rugged hills. But they also see some of the East's grandest, most spectacular views. And there is mud, cold summer rain, stinging spring snow, and just about everything else a mountain climate can deliver, including awesome solitude and pockets of virgin wilderness.

Almost a century after the trail was begun, the philosophical uplift that MacKaye hoped for has taken place. Our current outdoor lifestyle and environmental conscious-ness are traceable in part to the existence of the Appalachian Trail and the wildlands that enclose it. The path's enduring grandeur inspires generation after generation of hikers. Perhaps more than any other recreational facility in the world, the Appalachian Trail symbolizes the power of nature to work wonders in the hearts and minds of those who take the time to wander in the woods.

Besides becoming a member of the ATC, a worthwhile step to consider, North Caro-linians also support many other groups that nurture the state's parks, forests, and seashores. Many of these organizations offer a fun way to fund them—buy a license plate! Attractive custom plates are available, and each generates funds for the organization. The author's own Appalachian Trail Conservancy AT plate reads "CLMB."

HOW TO USE THE AT MILEAGE LOG

The mileage log and entries that follow are more than a list of landmarks on the Appala-chian Trail in North Carolina. Included are detailed recommendations for day hikes and backpacking trips that are among the best in North Carolina and the East. Also included are suggested side trails and circuits, including one wheelchair-accessible trail, so be sure to scan this important section. Mileages are given for recommended hikes, but just grab a pencil and calculator to customize the log for hikes of your choice.

N to S	S to N	
0.0	324.2	Trailhead on US 19E, between Roan Mountain, TN, and Elk Park, NC (location of Station at 19-E hostel)
0.6	323.6	(spring, former Apple House Shelter gone)
3.0	321.2	Doll Flats (campsites, spring)
5.4	318.8	Hump Mountain
6.3	317.9	Bradley Gap
7.6	316.6	Little Hump Mountain
9.2	315.0	Yellow Mountain Gap/0.3-mile blue-blazed side trail east to campsites at the former location of Overmountain Shelter, closed due to struc-tural problems. A spring is on left of trail near shelter site.
11.1	313.1	Stan Murray Shelter (old Roan Highlands Shelter)
12.9	311.3	Grassy Ridge side trail
14.1	310.1	Round Bald
14.8	309.4	Carvers Gap, TN 143, NC 261

1A SOUTHERN BALDS

WHY GO?

The section of the Appalachian Trail that enters North Carolina starts in the north and immediately crosses the meadow-covered mountaintops called the Southern Balds (see Roan Mountain for more detail on the balds). This is the most-alpine scenery in the region, with great backpacking and day-hiking opportunities. See map 1A on page 13.

THE RUNDOWN

General location: Between Bakersville and Elk Park

Distance: Round-trip day hikes from Carvers Gap: 1.4 miles to Round Bald; 2.8 miles to Jane Bald; 3.8 miles to Grassy Ridge Bald. Round-trip hikes from Yellow Mountain Gap: 3.2 miles to views near Little Hump Mountain; 8 miles to Hump Mountain (10.8 miles from US 19E).

Difficulty: Moderately strenuous to nearby mountaintops; very strenuous for lengthy day hikes or a backpack of the entire ridgetop, especially north to south

Maps: USGS Carvers Gap, Elk Park, and White Rocks Mountain; Appalachian Trail Conservancy AT map and guide

Elevation gain: 2,200 feet south to north

Water availability: A water fountain and restroom are located 1.8 miles from Carvers Gap at the Roan Mountain Gardens forest service station, open late spring through early fall. There's a modern pit privy at Carvers Gap. Nearby water sources are in the community of Roan Mountain and Roan Mountain State Park. Near the Elk Park Trailhead, the Station at 19-E hostel can provide water. Water is also available at springs along the route.

For more information: Appalachian Ranger District, 632 Manor Road, Mars Hill 28754; (828) 689-9694; appalachianrd@fs.fed.us. Appalachian Trail Conservancy: appalachiantrail.org.

FINDING THE TRAILHEADS

 There are three AT trailheads. To reach the Elk Park Trailhead from Boone, go though Linville and Newland (or Banner Elk) to reach US 19E. Go 0.9 mile west of the state line to a small parking area on the left (GPS: 36.177425/-82.011778).

To reach Carvers Gap, stay west on US 19E past the Elk Park Trailhead, then turn left on TN 143 in the town of Roan Mountain. Carvers Gap's roadside parking lot and privy are 14 miles from that junction (GPS: 36.106415/-82.111234). From Asheville and more southerly areas, take NC 261 from Bakersville about 14 miles to Carvers Gap.

The Yellow Mountain Gap Trailhead is on US 19E south of Elk Park. Between Elk Park and Newland, take US 19E south toward Spruce Pine from the junction with NC 194. Go south past Minneapolis to a right on Roaring Creek Road at 8.6 miles. Keep right at all the forks to reach the trailhead below Yellow Mountain Gap, at about 5 miles (GPS: 36.117029/-82.048951).

Parking overnight along US 19E is not recommended, but it's easy to arrange for pickup and drop-off from the nearby Station at 19-E, a hostel and brew pub 0.9 mile east of the AT trailhead on 19-E (www.thestationat19-E.com, 575-694-0734). Winter access to the Carvers Gap and Roaring Creek Trailheads can be complicated by deep snow; they are a low priority for plowing.

THE HIKES

The white-blazed Appalachian Trail traverses the entire ridge, sticking closely to the state line all the way. The trail is well marked, but the open terrain can provide substantial route-finding challenges in snow, fog, and rain. Use caution and take adequate maps. Expect unusual weather year-round. Though cool days are the norm in summer at these heights, high-altitude sun can be punishing, so take a hat and sunscreen.

Backpackers who intend to walk this section of the trail end to end should hike from south to north, since the trail descends in that direction from Carvers Gap (5,512 feet) to Elk Park (2,880 feet). Though graded, the steep 5-mile climb from Elk Park to Hump Mountain rises 2,700 feet, more than the entire elevation gain going north from Carvers Gap to Elk Park. From either direction, hikers find campsites plentiful in the grassy gaps lining the trail.

From Carvers Gap, cross the road and fence toward the grassy meadows of Round Bald. The recently rerouted trail switchbacks through scenic spruces to meadows and views in all directions atop Round Bald (5,826 feet), a summit resembling the broad end of an egg. This is a short 0.7 mile from Carvers Gap.

The trail descends to open Engine Gap at 1 mile, ascends to a rock outcrop at 1.3 miles, and reaches the Jane Bald summit (5,807 feet) at about 1.4 miles (nice turnaround points for a shorter view hike).

When the AT slides left, a side trail reaches Grassy Ridge, a bald summit with spectacular views at 6,000 feet. Continuing left, the AT plummets past a spring on the right at about 2 miles. The trail reaches a spur of Grassy Ridge then drops steeply left to Low Gap (5,000 feet) and Stan Murray Shelter at 3.7 miles. A side trail south of the ridge leads 100 yards to a spring.

The trail climbs over Elk Hollow Ridge then descends to Buckeye Gap. Hikers cross a nearly 5,000-foot summit with nice views at 4.8 miles. Bear right off the main ridge. At 5.6 miles the trail drops into Yellow Mountain Gap (4,682 feet). The Overmountain Victory Trail (OVT), a National Historic Trail, crosses the AT here. This is the route of colonists who defeated British colonel Patrick Ferguson's forces at the 1780 Battle of King's Mountain in South Carolina, a pivotal step in winning the Revolutionary War. To the right, the road-width colonial trace descends in about 0.7 mile to the Roaring Creek Road (NC 1132), another popular starting point. A blue-blazed side trail leads right from just below the gap to a spring and campsite, former location of the Overmountain Shelter, closed in 2019 as structurally unsound. Parking is about 0.7 mile southwest of the gap on Roaring Creek Road via a gated forest road that parallels the OVT.

Leaving Yellow Mountain Gap, the trail ascends a steep meadow and gradually enters a woods road, bearing right. Follow the AT along the woods then left as it bears away from the trees into a meadow past a large rock outcrop to Little Hump Mountain (5,459 feet) at 7.2 miles. Descending, it passes through a small gap between the two peaks of Little Hump—a great campsite with a spring. It climbs again to the second peak then descends gradually into Bradley Gap (4,960 feet) at 8.5 miles.

Leaving Bradley Gap, the trail ascends the open summit ridge of Hump Mountain, an occasionally rocky, alpine-feeling 1-mile hike to the peak (5,587 feet) at 9.4 miles. The all-encompassing views include Mount Mitchell, Roan Mountain, Grandfather Mountain, and Virginia's highest summits, Mount Rogers and Whitetop. Meadows sweep away, interspersed with crags. Returning to Yellow Mountain Gap and then to Roaring Creek Road from here is a 10-mile round-trip.

After humping it up from Yellow Mountain Gap, the view of Hump Mountain is worth a pause.

From Hump Mountain, the route to US 19E has changed substantially in the past decade or so. The AT heads east from the summit on a new section of trail, actually an old vehicle route across the bald top, completed in the early 1980s. The trail turns left, enters the woods, then starts a graded descent back west (past a nice view of Elk Park). It slabs into the open meadows of Doll Flats, a good campsite, at 11.8 miles. From Doll Flats the new trail leads northwest, down a narrow ridge, under a power line, and then switchbacks into Wilder Mine Hollow at 12.7 miles.

The trail follows a road across a stream through the Wilder Mine area, where iron ore was mined in the late nineteenth and early twentieth centuries, and where rock was quarried in the 1950s. (**Caution:** The mineshafts are dangerous; keep out!) Continuing on the road, the trail crosses the stream to pass the former site of Apple House Shelter at 14.2 miles.

Hikers will turn left from the road and pass an old railroad bridge support where the narrow-gauge Eastern Tennessee & Western North Carolina Railroad used to run between Johnson City, Tennessee, and Boone, North Carolina, from the late 1800s to its demise in a 1940s flood. The line carried ore from the Wilder Mine and another massive operation nearby at Cranberry, North Carolina. A trail bridge spans Buck Creek, the lowest stream along the trail, and an old driveway rises left to the edge of US 19E at 14.8 miles. A day hike or overnight backpacking trip from here to Hump Mountain, a 10.8-mile round-trip, would be rewarding but extremely strenuous. This trailhead is not a recommended place to leave your car unattended (see above: The Station at 19-E offers shuttle service).

The Appalachian Trail winds south over Roan Mountain from Carvers Gap. For more on this section, see the Roan Mountain hike later in this book.

N to S	S to N	
14.8	309.4	Carvers Gap, TN 143, NC 261
16.5	307.9	Roan High Knob Shelter
17.4	306.8	A side trail to Roan High Bluff, the Cloudland Trail, starts nearby at a USFS fee station parking lot.
18.4	305.8	Ash Gap
21.4	302.8	Hughes Gap
23.6	300.6	Little Rock Knob
24.7	299.5	Clyde Smith Shelter

This shelter was named for the late AT trail volunteer Clyde Smith. See Grandfather Mountain and Hi-Balsam Shelter for more about his life and work.

N to S	S to N	
25.8	298.4	Campsite
26.6	297.6	Greasy Creek Gap
29.4	294.8	Campsite
30.9	293.5	Iron Mountain Gap, TN 107, NC 226
33.8	290.4	Cherry Gap Shelter
34.9	289.3	Low Gap
37.1	287.1	Unaka Mountain
38.1	286.1	FR 230
38.7	285.5	Deep Gap/ Groundhog Creek Shelter
39.7	284.5	Beauty Spot Gap
40.2	284.0	Beauty Spot
41.4	282.8	FR 230
42.5	281.7	Indian Grave Gap
46.6	277.6	Curley Maple Gap Shelter
49.5	274.7	Jones Branch Road
50.7	273.5	Chestoa Pike
50.8	273.4	Nolichucky River; Chestoa Bridge, Erwin, TN
54.7	269.5	Temple Hill Gap
57.1	267.1	No Business Knob Shelter
57.3	266.9	Spring
61.4	262.8	Ogelsby Branch
62.0	262.2	Spivey Gap, US 19W
62.5	261.7	Campsite
64.0	260.2	High Rocks
64.3	259.9	Whistling Gap

66.3	257.9	Little Bald
67.3	256.9	Campsite
67.7	256.5	Bald Mountain Shelter
68.6	255.6	Big Stamp
68.9	255.3	Big Bald
69.7	254.5	Spring
71.7	252.5	Low Gap
73.1	251.1	Street Gap and Road
74.7	249.5	Springs
75.4	248.8	Sams Gap, Flag Pond Road, US 23, I-26 (highest interstate highway in eastern America; 3,800 feet)
77.2	247.0	High Rock
77.8	246.4	Hogback Ridge Shelter
79.0	245.2	Rice Gap
80.0	244.2	Big Flat
80.6	243.6	Frozen Knob
83.4	240.8	Rector Laurel Road
83.9	240.3	Devil Fork Gap, NC 212
85.7	238.5	Campsite
86.6	237.6	Flint Mountain Shelter
89.5	234.7	Shelton Graves
89.8	234.4	Spring
91.1	233.1	Big Butt Mountain
93.0	231.2	Jerry Cabin Shelter
95.5	228.7	Big Firescald Knob
96.5	227.7	Blackstack Cliffs
96.7	227.5	White Rock Cliffs
96.8	227.4	Spring
98.5	225.7	Camp Creek Bald, side trail to fire tower
99.8	224.4	Little Laurel Shelter
103.1	221.1	Log Cabin Drive
104.7	219.5	Allen Gap, NC 208, TN 70, water
106.9	217.3	Spring
108.4	215.8	Spring Mountain Shelter
110.1	214.1	Hurricane Gap
111.2	213.0	Rich Mountain Fire Tower side trail
113.5	210.7	Tanyard Gap, US 25/70
114.5	209.7	Campsite
116.1	208.1	Pump Gap
118.0	206.2	Lover's Leap Rock
119.4	204.8	US 25/70, NC 209; Hot Springs, NC

Appalachian Trail—Southern Balds (1A)

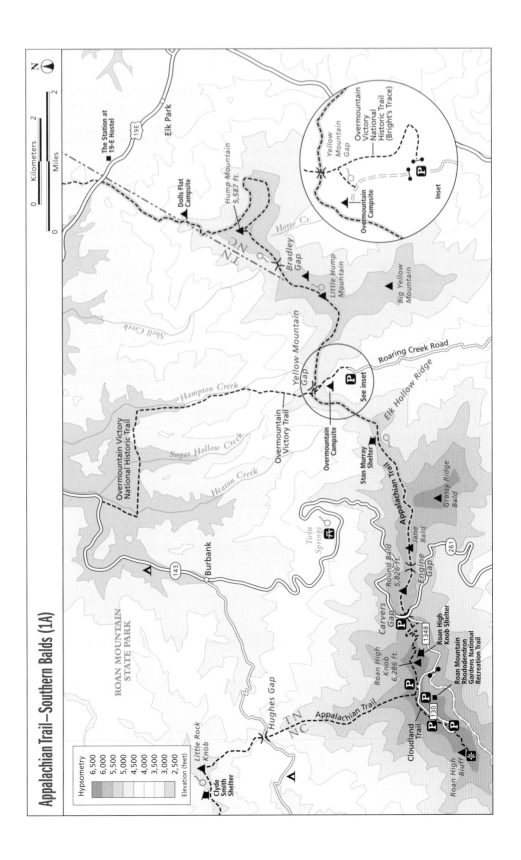

Hot Springs is an AT "Trail Town" with a choice day hike and overnight backpack trip on the trail. Like Damascus, Virginia, this is a tiny mountain burg with growing popular culture cachet where end-to-enders pick up supply mailings. Hot Springs is a nice place to visit for AT devotees, in part because the town has a rich history as a thermal spa. Hikers can take advantage of the popular "cure" at Hot Springs Resort and Spa, a soak in 100°F water (828-622-7676). The facility has a campground, cabins, spa services, and more (nchotsprings.com).

The hiking possibilities just east of town are wonderful additions to the AT. To avoid the hike out of downtown, park at the Silvermine Trailhead. To reach it, go east from Hot Springs on US 25/70 across the French Broad River Bridge and immediately go left and under the bridge on SR 1304. Turn left at the first intersection and follow the signs to the trailhead for several circuit hikes. The short, steep hike to Lover's Leap Rock is a circuit with spectacular views down to the French Broad from a legendary rock ledge. Walk back down the access road to the Nantahala Outdoor Center and follow the AT left along the French Broad River. The AT climbs over steep switchbacks to a spur onto Lover's Leap viewpoint. Beyond the view, take the orange-blazed Lover's Leap Trail left, go left again when the trail combines with the Pump Gap Trail, and descend to your car at about 1.6 miles. You could also hike up the combined Pump Gap/Lover's Leap Trail and go left along the AT to the first crossing of the Pump Gap loop. Going left there and back to your car makes a 4-mile circuit. This is also good in reverse, reaching Lover's Leap from a less-trafficked direction.

To cut the crowds, lessen the grade, lengthen the walk, and possibly make an over-nighter out of it, start at the Silvermine Trailhead and hike up the orange-blazed Lover's Leap Trail. Go left on the Pump Gap Trail at the first switchback above the parking lot. The Pump Gap Trail forks; both branches reach the AT. Take the right fork (the "first crossing" mentioned above), the easiest climb to the AT, and take a left. Go left on the other branch of the Pump Gap Trail and back to your car for a 3-mile hike. To com-pletely avoid the AT, do the loop above but cross the AT, descend beyond, then climb back to cross the AT and descend the other side of the loop for a nearly 6-mile loop.

N to S	S to N	
122.6	201.6	Deer Park Mountain Shelter
126.0	198.2	Garenflo Gap (2,500 feet)
128.5	195.7	Big Rock Spring
130.1	194.1	Bluff Mountain (4,686 feet)
132.5	191.7	Walnut Mountain Shelter
133.8	190.4	Lemon Gap, SR 1182, TN 107
137.4	186.8	Roaring Fork Shelter
139.2	185.0	Max Patch Summit (4,629 feet)
140.0	184.2	Max Patch Road, SR 1182

Appalachian Trail—Hot Springs Area (1B)

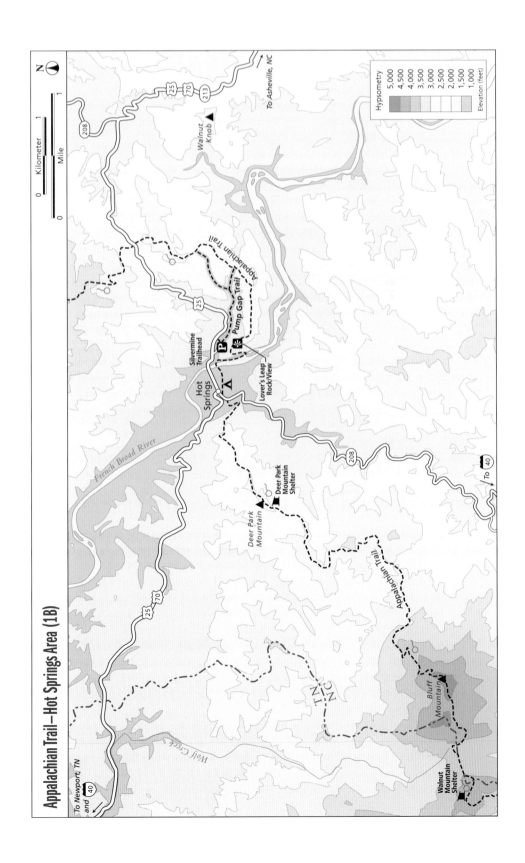

Max Patch is one of the state's most outstanding balds and a perfect day hike. The view from the top (4,629 feet) is noteworthy because Mount Mitchell and high peaks rise on one side and the rippled Smokies bulk massively on the other.

The purchase of Max Patch by the forest service in September 1982 eliminated a 3.8-mile AT section that followed a dusty public road. A new, scenic portion of the AT was built over the peak in 1984.

Instead of hiking up and back on the AT, new trails (opened in 1995) permit a 1.4-mile moderate circuit loop over the summit. Leave the lot on the old road grade trail that rises to the left. At the AT, turn right and go over the summit at 0.7 mile. Turn right at 1.1 miles on a gravel road back to the parking area at 1.4 miles. To make this an over-nighter at the Roaring Fork Shelter (or at its tent sites—no camping is allowed on the bald), take the hike above but go left on the AT in 0.5 mile. The shelter side trail goes right at 2.1 miles (water is 0.1 mile ahead on the AT). Return from here over the summit for a 5-mile round-trip. There's also a 2.4 mile circuit over the peak that uses horse trails.

By far the easiest way to reach the trailhead is to leave I-40 about 39 miles west of Asheville at the Harmon Den exit (exit 7). Turn right onto FR 148, Cold Springs Road. Follow that to the first major junction in about 6 miles and go left (there are signs on the way). Stay left where the next road goes right, and follow NC 1182 for just under 2 miles to the parking area on the right, just beyond where the AT crosses the road at the gap. The preferred map for this hike is the *USDA Forest Service Harmon Den Trail Map.*

N to S	S to N	
142.7	181.5	Brown Gap
145.6	178.6	Deep Gap, Groundhog Creek Shelter (2,900 feet)

Between Brown and Deep Gaps, in the Harmon Den area, the AT, Rube Rock, and Groundhog Creek Trails form a triangular circuit hike of about 10 miles. This hike lies in the 1920s-logged Cold Springs Creek drainage, the tract to the west as you drive up Max Patch Road. A CCC camp was set up in the area, and much of the current route of the AT between Max Patch and I-40 was built between 1936 and 1938.

To reach the start of this hike in Brown Gap, leave I-40 about 39 miles west of Asheville at the Harmon Den exit (exit 7). Turn right onto FR 148, Cold Springs Road. In 3 miles make the first left on FR 148A at the Harmon Den parking area; drive to the top of the ridge where the AT crosses the road, about 1.2 miles from the turn (where there's a parking area and toilets). From Hot Springs go south on NC 209 for 7.2 miles and turn right onto SR 1175. Go 5.3 miles to a right turn onto SR 1181. Follow that to a T junction with SR 1182 and go left. Take the next right, FR 148 (Cold Springs Road). Follow FR 148 to the next right onto FR 148A at the parking area, and drive to the AT at the top of the ridge.

This is an unusual walk because the hike starts high (on the AT), descends to a low point, climbs back to a high point, and then descends to the trailhead. Follow the AT west out of Brown Gap; at 0.6 mile go left on the Rube Rock Trail. The rugged, steep path descends to the junction with the Groundhog Creek Trail. On the way, the trail joins FR 358A. Turn right on the road (a left goes back to Brown Gap), and after 0.5

Appalachian Trail–Max Patch Area (1C)

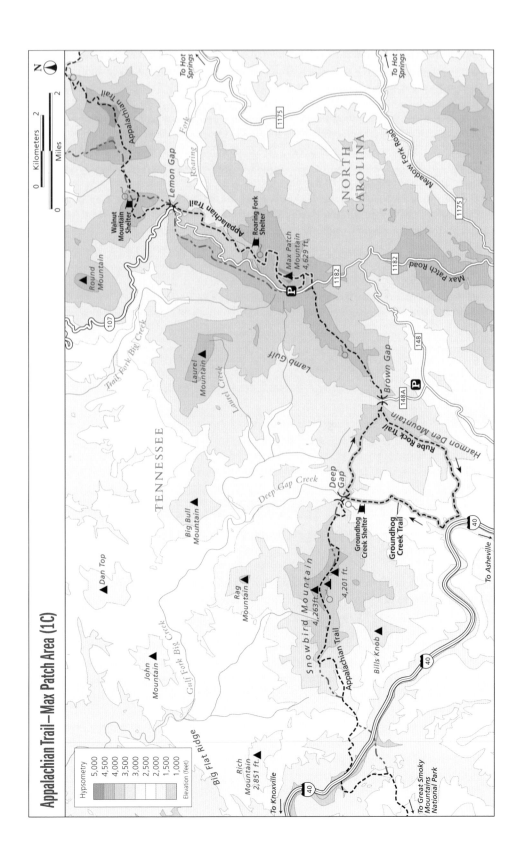

mile go left on the woods path again. The trail follows Rube Rock Branch. About 1,800 feet below the AT, the Rube Rock Trail turns onto an old railroad grade and parallels I-40 before reaching a T junction with the Groundhog Creek Trail, 5.1 miles from the start of the hike.

To the left, the Groundhog Creek Trail leads to a unique trailhead: I-40 (where parking is illegal). Turn right and follow the logging grade uphill along Groundhog Creek to the AT, 2.3 miles and 1,000 feet above. The Groundhog Creek Shelter is located at 7.2 miles. The AT is 0.2 mile farther, at 7.4 miles. Turn right on the AT. Brown Gap is 2.9 miles ahead, a round-trip of 10.3 miles.

A nice out-and-back summit backpack takes the AT south past Deep Gap to a fine campsite 4.9 miles from Brown Gap and 0.5 mile from the summit of Snowbird Mountain and its awesome view of the Smokies (a 10.8-mile round-trip).

N to S	S to N	
147.6	176.6	Campsite
148.1	176.1	Snowbird Mountain
149.6	174.6	Spanish Oak Gap
150.5	173.7	Painter Branch
152.8	171.4	Green Corner Road
153.3	170.9	I-40 underpass
153.7	170.5	Pigeon River (1,400 feet), Tobes Creek Road, Waterville Road
153.9	170.3	State Line Branch
155.2	169.0	Davenport Gap, NC 284, TN 32; eastern boundary of Great Smoky Mountains National Park

1D GREAT SMOKY MOUNTAINS NATIONAL PARK

Also see the general entry for the Great Smoky Mountains National Park on pages 181 to 197. If you're camping you'll need a permit and that section overviews the detailed regulations on pages 181 and 182.

From the area of Davenport Gap, on the northern side of the park, one of the AT's best hikes is Mount Cammerer (5,025 feet), site of an old Yosemite-style fire tower, rare in the East, that was built by the CCC in the 1930s. The tower was in jeopardy of being lost to time and weather on this peak until the summer of 1995, when it was repaired and rededicated. Today hikers can use its catwalk to enjoy a panoramic view. This is one of many fire towers being restored and attracting new interest among hikers.

The strenuous hike can start at the AT trailhead (5.8 miles one way), but the National Park Service recommends starting at nearby Big Creek Ranger Station to avoid auto break-ins and vandalism. Take I-40 West from North Carolina into Tennessee and leave the interstate at exit 451, Waterville. Turn left under the interstate then left again to cross the Pigeon River. Make another left, then a right, on Waterville Road. Stay on Waterville

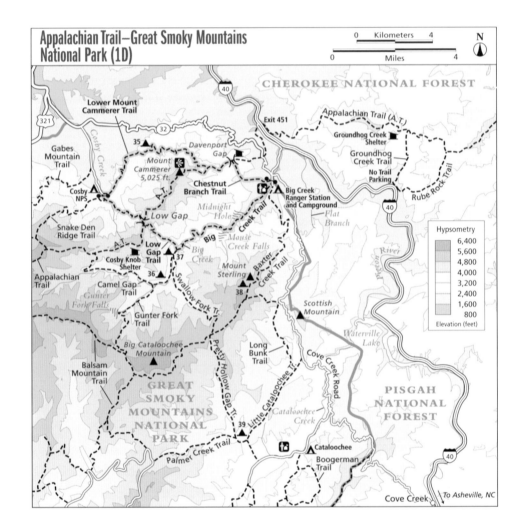

Appalachian Trail–Great Smoky Mountains National Park (1D)

Road for 2 miles to a crossroads in the village of Mount Sterling. Davenport Gap is 1.2 miles or so to the right. Straight across the intersection, it's 0.2 mile to parking at Big Creek Ranger Station and the start of the Chestnut Branch Trail.

Taking the Chestnut Branch Trail, you reach the AT in 2 miles (the Davenport Gap Shelter is 1 mile to the right). Going left, the Lower Mount Cammerer Trail intersects on the right at 2.9 miles. Just past the Lower Mount Cammerer Trail on the way up, a side trail branches left to a spring at 3.2 miles; another is located on the right at 4.8 miles, just beyond an uphill site used by the CCC. At 5.3 miles the Mount Cammerer Trail leads right 0.6 mile to the tower, built by the CCC, restored in 1996, and one of the country's classic fire lookouts. This is an 11.8-mile round-trip for day hikers.

For those who want to camp, the Davenport Gap Shelter is only 3 miles into the hike; the Cosby Knob Shelter is 2.8 miles beyond the side trail to the Cammerer tower, or 8.1 miles from the trailhead.

The 7.8-mile Lower Mount Cammerer Trail, which links the AT to Cosby Campground in Tennessee, is a wonderful return route for a 21.6-mile circuit backpack trip.

To make this circuit, turn right on the Low Gap Trail at 7.5 miles, just beyond Mount Cammerer and before Cosby Knob Shelter. The Low Gap Trail descends in 2.5 miles to the Lower Mount Cammerer Trail. Follow that back to a left on the AT and then go right on the Chestnut Branch Trail back to your car for a three-day backpack trip. If you make the above circuit hike, designated backcountry campsite #35 is a good second-night campsite on the Lower Mount Cammerer Trail.

Another option is to go left from Low Gap beyond Mount Cammerer. Descend on the Low Gap Trail to backcountry campsite #37, and from there return to the ranger station parking on the Big Creek Trail (this requires a short roadside walk) for an approximately 18-mile backpacking trip.

N to S	S to N	
156.1	168.1	Davenport Gap Shelter
157.1	167.1	Chestnut Branch Trail
158.3	165.9	Spring
159.9	164.3	Spring
160.4	163.8	Mount Cammerer side trail
162.5	161.7	Low Gap Trail
163.2	161.0	Cosby Knob Shelter
163.8	160.4	Cosby Knob
167.1	157.1	Snake Den Ridge Trail
169.0	155.2	Mount Guyot side trail
169.1	155.1	Guyot Spring
169.7	154.5	Guyot Spur (6,300 feet)
170.9	153.3	Tri-Corner Knob Shelter
171.9	152.3	Mount Chapman
173.4	150.8	Mount Sequoyah
176.1	148.1	Pecks Corner Shelter
177.4	146.8	Bradleys View
180.7	143.5	Porters Gap, the Sawteeth
182.6	141.6	Charlies Bunion
183.5	140.7	Icewater Spring Shelter (thru-hikers only)
183.8	140.4	Boulevard Trail
186.5	137.7	Newfound Gap, US 441

1E GREAT SMOKIES' NEWFOUND GAP AREA

Newfound Gap, though a truly popular place to start a hike, is nevertheless the best way to reach a few of the Smokies' most spectacular viewpoints. Heading east, strenuous day hikes reach three awesome views: The Jumpoff, Charlies Bunion, and The Sawteeth.

Newfound Gap is on US 441, 16 miles south of Gatlinburg, Tennessee, and 20 miles north of Cherokee, North Carolina. Leaving the gap, the trail is impressively graded; it was one of the first built-from-scratch sections of the AT, artfully excavated by the CCC. The trail slides gradually from gap to gap and reaches the Boulevard Trail at 2.7 miles. This is an evergreen ridge that leads 5.3 miles to the summit of Mount LeConte (6,593 feet).

The LeConte Lodge, open late March into November, is the closest thing in the South to the alpine huts of Europe—which is why reservations are not easy to get. (See the Great Smokies chapter for more details.) There is also a shelter on Mount LeConte. The summit provides great views of the main ridge of the Smokies along the North Carolina border.

Catch it on a real "Smokies day" and the Spruce-Fir Nature Trail is an eerie ebb and flow of fog and mist.

To reach The Jumpoff (6,100 feet), go left on the Boulevard Trail at 2.7 miles and in 0.1 mile turn right. The trail crosses 6,150-foot Mount Kephart and at 3.2 miles reaches a clifftop view looking down more than 1,000 feet. The round-trip hike is about 6.5 miles.

One of the most scenic sections of the Smokies is next. Continuing north on the AT past the Boulevard, the trail reaches the start of a fire-denuded ridge crest at 3.6 miles. At 3.8 miles in the heart of this area are the two peaks that make up Charlies Bunion, a great picnic spot for a roughly 8-mile round-trip hike. A trail to the left starts a loop of the two peaks. Extending the hike another 1.9 miles one way creates a nearly 12-mile round-trip that permits a traverse of the Sawteeth, a serrated spine with its own alpine feel.

N to S	S to N	
188.2	136.0	Indian Gap
191.0	133.2	Mount Collins Shelter
193.2	131.0	Mount Love
194.4	129.8	Clingmans Dome

If you drive to Clingmans Dome, the Spruce-Fir Nature Trail is an easy interpretive hike on the left, 2.6 miles from the turnoff on US 441. The 0.5-mile nature trail (buy a brochure at the trailhead) that once wandered the lush Canadian Zone forest now showcases an ecosystem decimated by a variety of environmental problems (for more information see the Mount Mitchell section). This is a great trail to snowshoe or cross-country ski to when the road is closed December 1 to March 31 (expect deep snow). That harsh climate is another factor impacting the forest.

The path may be paved, but the hike to Clingmans Dome will have you breathing hard and raving about the view.

The easiest hike from the Clingmans Dome parking area (7.6 miles west of Newfound Gap on the Clingmans Dome Road) is the 0.7-mile paved trail to the spiraling, grandiose view tower atop the peak, at 6,643 feet the highest in Great Smoky Mountains National Park. The entire park spreads out before you. Notice the bulk of Mount LeConte. This is the western terminus of North Carolina's Mountains-to-Sea Trail. There's an information station at the parking lot.

A good day hike from the same area is the popular trip to Andrews Bald. Its open meadows are more modest than others in the Smokies and nearby Roan Mountain, but worth the trip nonetheless.

The trail to Andrews Bald, called the Forney Ridge Trail, leaves the west side of the dome parking area at the start of the paved path to the top. It drops steeply 0.2 mile to a junction on the right with the Clingmans Dome Bypass Trail (it reaches the AT in 0.6 mile). Keep left and pass the Forney Creek Trail on the right at just over 1 mile. Stay left on Forney Ridge Trail through high-elevation forest, ferns, and moss that have been adversely affected by pollution. You'll emerge onto Andrews Bald, with nice views over the Nantahala National Forest to the south, at about 1.8 miles. The round-trip is about 3.6 miles and rated strenuous, in part for the rockiness of the trail.

Silers Bald is another good hike from the parking lot at Clingmans Dome. The hike is much longer and more strenuous, but two backpacking shelters permit overnighters. Take the Clingmans Dome Bypass Trail from the parking lot and go left on the AT at

Appalachian Trail—Great Smokies' Newfound Gap Area (1E)

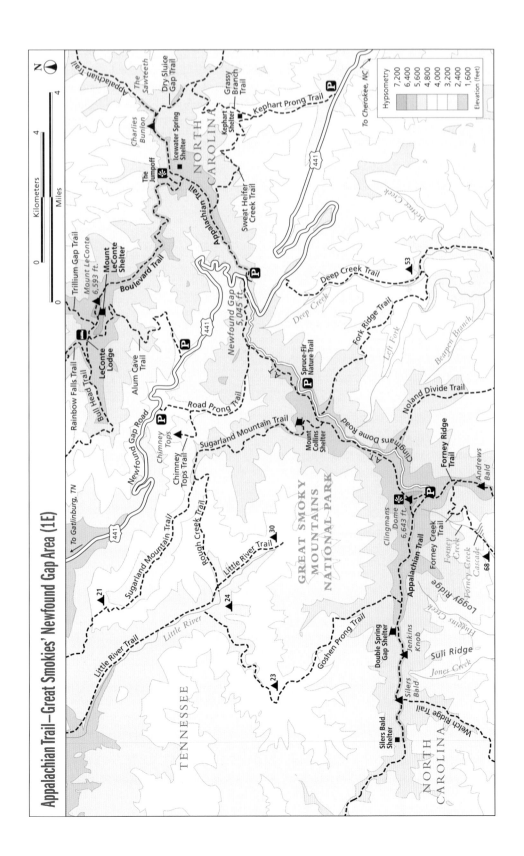

about 1 mile. Pass the Double Spring Gap Shelter at 3.5 miles and spectacular views of upcoming Silers Bald from Jenkins Knob at 4 miles (a nice turnaround point for an 8-mile round-trip). Cross the alpine crags of the Narrows and reach Silers Bald at 5.4 miles, the park's largest, most spectacular meadow-covered peak. Silers Bald Shelter is another 0.2 mile, just past a trail that leads right 100 yards to a spring.

N to S	S to N	
197.3	126.9	Double Spring Gap Shelter
198.8	125.4	Silers Bald
199.0	125.2	Silers Bald Shelter
202.0	122.2	Buckeye Gap
204.6	119.6	Sams Gap
204.8	119.4	Derrick Knob Shelter
205.1	119.1	Chestnut Bald
205.9	118.3	Sugar Tree Gap
208.3	115.9	Mineral Gap
209.0	115.2	Beechnut Gap
209.3	114.9	Thunderhead (east peak)
209.9	114.3	Rocky Top
211.1	113.1	Spence Field Shelter via Eagle Creek Trail, Bote Mountain Trail
214.0	110.2	Russell Field Shelter
214.8	109.4	Little Abrahams Gap
216.2	108.0	Devils Tater Patch
216.8	107.4	Mollies Ridge Shelter
218.2	106.0	Ekaneetlee Gap
219.6	104.6	Doe Knob
221.9	102.3	Birch Spring Gap Shelter
223.1	101.1	Shuckstack
226.5	97.7	Lakeview Drive West
227.1	97.1	Little Tennessee River, Fontana Dam; southern boundary of Great Smoky Mountains National Park
227.5	96.7	Fontana Dam Visitor Center

1F STECOAH AREA

North from Fontana Dam (at 480 feet, the highest dam in the East), the AT offers a strenuous hike to the top of Shuckstack, climbing 2,300 feet in 4.4 miles, for a 8.8-mile day hike. A 14-mile backpacking circuit uses the Lost Cove and Lakeshore Trails. To reach the trailhead, take NC 28 West from Bryson City. About 11 miles past Stecoah, turn right onto NC 1245 (about 2 miles east of Fontana Village). Pass the Fontana Dam Visitor Center (May to November, 9 a.m.–7 p.m. daily), cross the dam, and go right to the AT parking area (GPS: 35.460530 / –83.811118). Just across the dam, a road goes left to a great view of the dam and powerhouse. The road across the dam can be closed when heightened national security alerts are in place. An alternate route follows the road below the dam.

The trail crosses Little Shuckstack to Shuckstack at 4.4 miles. An old access road rises a short distance to a fire tower with good views of the Smokies' crest. Backpackers can make a 13-mile circuit by descending to Sassafras Gap at 3.7 miles and going right on the Lost Cove Trail. Pass backcountry campsite #91 at about 5.7 miles to a left on the Lakeshore Trail at about 6.4 miles. Campsite #90 is on the lakeshore in 0.3 mile. Backtracking along the Lakeshore Trail's 5.2 miles makes a circuit that ends with glimpses of rusting old vehicles along parts of a pre-dam access.

N to S	S to N	
227.9	96.3	Fontana Dam Shelter
229.1	95.1	NC 28; Fontana Dam
231.4	92.8	Campsite
231.8	92.4	Walker Gap/Yellow Creek Trail
233.2	91.0	Black Gum Gap
234.6	89.6	Cable Gap Shelter
235.5	88.7	Yellow Creek Gap, Yellow Creek Mountain Road (SR 1242)
237.9	86.3	Cody Gap
238.7	85.5	Hogback Gap
240.5	83.7	Brown Fork Gap
240.7	83.5	Brown Fork Gap Shelter
242.1	82.1	Sweetwater Gap
243.1	81.1	Stecoah Gap, Sweetwater Creek Road, NC 143

From Stecoah Gap (GPS: 35.358266 / –83.717873), the AT makes a nice day or overnight hike to Cheoah Bald and the Sassafras Gap Shelter. The strenuous hike has awesome views atop the grassy, 5,062-foot summit, about 5.5 miles. To reach the trailhead, go northeast from Robbinsville about 8.6 miles on NC 143, or go northwest of Franklin on NC 28. Just past Stecoah, turn left on NC 143 and reach the trailhead at about 3 miles.

Leaving the gap, the trail switchbacks and gains the ridge crest in the first 0.5 mile. It passes through Simp Gap at about 2 miles. At Locust Cove Gap, 3.1 miles, a spring is 500 feet to the right. Hit the summit of the bald and a view trail left at about 5.5 miles from the start. Beyond the peak the trail dips along a sharp ridge and leads to Sassafras Gap at 6.7 miles. A spring and a shelter are off to the right. The great view and shelter make this a worthwhile 13.4-mile overnighter.

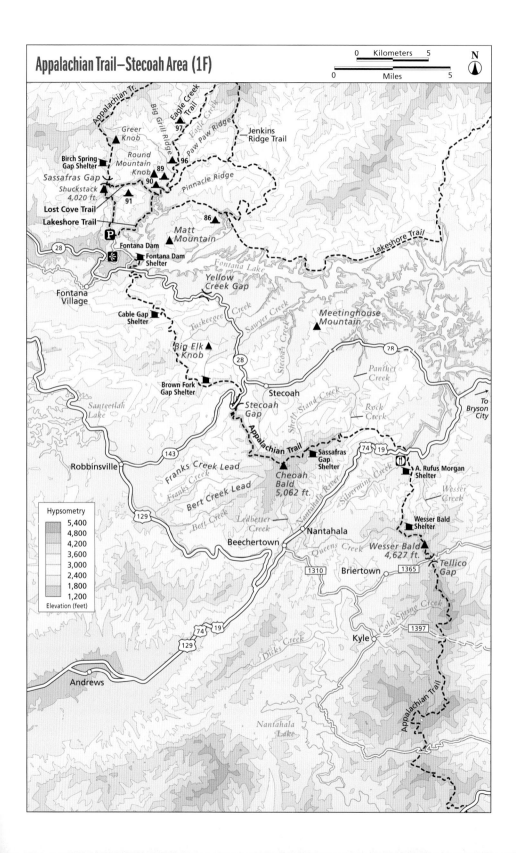

Appalachian Trail–Stecoah Area (1F)

Kilometers

Miles

N

Appalachian Trail

Eagle Creek Trail

Big Grill Ridge

Paw Paw Ridge

Eagle Creek

Jenkins Ridge Trail

97

Greer Knob

96

Round Mountain Knob

89

Birch Spring Gap Shelter

90

Sassafras Gap

Shuckstack 4,020 ft.

91

Pinnacle Ridge

Lost Cove Trail

Lakeshore Trail

P

86

Matt Mountain

Lakeshore Trail

Fontana Dam

28

Fontana Dam Shelter

Fontana Lake

Yellow Creek Gap

Fontana Village

Tuskeegee Creek

Sawyer Creek

Stecoah Creek

Meetinghouse Mountain

78

Cable Gap Shelter

Big Elk Knob

28

Panther Creek

To Bryson City

Brown Fork Gap Shelter

Stecoah

Stecoah Gap

Santeetlah Lake

Appalachian Trail

Shell Stand Creek

Rock Creek

143

Franks Creek Lead

Franks Creek

Bert Creek Lead

Cheoah Bald 5,062 ft.

Sassafras Gap Shelter

74 19

A. Rufus Morgan Shelter

Robbinsville

Santahala River

Silvermine Creek

Wesser Creek

129

Bert Creek

Ledbetter Creek

Nantahala

Wesser Bald Shelter

Beechertown

Queens Creek

Wesser Bald 4,627 ft.

Tellico Gap

1310

Briertown

1365

1397

Hypsometry

Elevation (feet)
5,400
4,800
4,200
3,600
3,000
2,400
1,800
1,200

Cold Spring Creek

Kyle

74 19

129

Dicks Creek

Andrews

Nantahala Lake

Appalachian Trail

N to S	S to N	
245.2	79.0	Simp Gap
246.2	78.0	Locust Cove Gap
248.6	75.6	Cheoah Bald
249.8	74.4	Sassafras Gap Shelter
250.7	73.5	Swim Bald
253.6	70.6	Grassy Gap
255.1	69.1	Wright Gap
256.7	67.5	US 19, Nantahala River; Wesser, NC, Nantahala Outdoor Center
257.5	66.7	A. Rufus Morgan Shelter
260.8	63.4	Jumpup Lookout
262.4	61.8	Wesser Creek Trail, Wesser Bald Shelter
262.5	61.7	Spring
263.2	61.0	Wesser Bald View tower
264.6	59.6	Tellico Gap, SR 1365

The short, strenuous climb from Tellico Gap to a refurbished fire tower on Wesser Bald is a memorable day hike that can also be an overnight trip. To reach the trailhead, go northeast from Andrews or southwest from Bryson City on US 19/129. Just south of the Nantahala Gorge and the town of Nantahala, turn east along the Nantahala River on SR 1310. At 5 miles turn left onto SR 1365 and park in Tellico Gap at 4.1 miles (GPS: 35.268205 / -83.572312). From Franklin go west on US 64 for 3 miles and turn right at a "Wayah Bald" sign. Take the first left onto Wayah Road (SR 1310). Pass Nantahala Lake and Kyle and turn right at a sign that reads "Tellico Gap."

The trail leaves the gap and rises beside a gated gravel road that also reaches the fire tower. The trail attains a crag at the peak (4,627 feet) at 1.4 miles, and a side trail leads to an observation deck on a fire tower (a 2.8-mile round-trip). A campsite is located at 2 miles; 0.1 mile beyond, a trail leads to a spring. At 2.2 miles a short trail leads left to the Wesser Bald Shelter, built in 1994. The shelter, nearby campsites, and a fine spring make this a good overnight backpack trip, especially at off times of the year. From the shelter, a nice view at Jumpup is another 1.6 miles.

N to S	S to N	
266.0	58.2	Spring
266.3	57.9	Side trail to Rocky Bald Lookout
267.5	56.7	Copper Ridge Bald Lookout
268.2	56.0	Cold Spring Shelter
269.4	54.8	Burningtown Gap, SR 1397
271.7	52.5	Licklog Gap
273.0	51.2	Wayah Shelter
273.5	50.7	Campsite/ Bartram Trail
273.9	50.3	Wayah Bald

1G WAYAH BALD/ STANDING INDIAN

Incredible Wayah Bald (5,200 feet) is reached by road and is an easy barrier-free trail. The AT and Bartram Trail meet on its summit. A paved, 0.3-mile trail leads from the parking area to the top of the mountain. To reach the peak, take US 64 West from Franklin. In 3 miles turn right at the "Wayah Bald" sign. Take the first left on Wayah Road (SR 1310). Go 9 miles to Wayah Gap and turn right onto gravel FR 69. The parking area near the Wayah Bald tower is 4.3 miles from there (GPS: 35.178834 / -83.562459). The original summit tower, a CCC-built National Historic Landmark, burned during the record-setting 2016 wildfire season. It was rebuilt with community involvement and is still dedicated to John B. Byrne, a former Nantahala National Forest supervisor who suggested the 81-mile route for the AT through this part of the forest.

N to S	S to N	
275.8	48.4	Wine Spring/Bartram Trail
276.3	47.9	FR 69

The AT south from Wayah Gap to Siler Bald is a nice hike. The trail leaves the road just east of the gap and passes the Wayah Crest picnic area. At 1.7 miles, a blue-blazed side trail goes left, the first leg of a loop that passes Siler Bald Shelter (at 0.6 mile) and returns to the AT 0.5 mile farther south. The entire side trail is 1.1 miles. Where the first trail goes left to the shelter, a 0.2-mile spur leads right to expansive views on the summit of Siler Bald (5,216 feet). The entire day hike, including the bald and shelter loop, is 3.7 miles.

N to S	S to N	
276.8	47.4	Wilson Lick Ranger Station
278.1	46.1	Wayah Gap, SR 1310
279.8	44.4	Siler Bald Shelter
282.0	42.4	Panther Gap
282.9	41.3	Swinging Lick Gap
283.1	41.1	Campsites
284.0	40.2	Winding Stair Gap, US 64; Franklin, NC
287.1	37.1	Wallace Gap, Old US 64
287.7	36.5	Rock Gap, Standing Indian Campground

Standing Indian Campground and the Wayah Ranger District Backcountry Information Center is one of the best hiking destinations in North Carolina's southwest mountains. It is one of the few places where you can actually make a loop hike on the AT.

There are short day hikes in the area, including the Big Laurel Falls Trail. This family day hike begins on FR 67, 5 miles past the backcountry information center, and leads 1 mile round-trip to a waterfall. The easy walk follows an old railroad grade. At the split, the right fork leads to the waterfall.

The best of the more-rugged day hikes is a 5-mile out-and-back from Deep Gap to spectacular views at Standing Indian Peak. There are also circuit hikes, including a 25-mile circle from the backcountry information center. This is one of the best places on the AT to get a multiday feel for the trail and be able to park your car in a safe spot.

Fantastic scenery ups the appeal of this area. This section is among the most scenic on the entire nearly 2,200-mile route. Many of the hikes lie in the Southern Nantahala Wilderness, a 24,000-acre tract in North Carolina and northern Georgia. The preferred map for hikes in this area is the forest service's Southern Nantahala Wilderness/Standing Indian Basin trail map.

The shortest day hike leaves Deep Gap, not the information center. To find the trailhead, turn from US 64 onto FR 71 about 12 miles south of Franklin (less than 0.5 mile south of the Macon and Clay County line). FR 71 reaches Deep Gap (4,341 feet) in 6 miles. This hike is strenuous, but part of it follows an old logging grade. The AT passes Standing Indian Shelter at 0.8 mile. At 2.4 miles a side trail reaches a spring on the left. In another 300 feet, the Lower Ridge Trail crosses, dropping left to Standing Indian Campground in 4.2 miles and leading right in 600 feet to the vista from the 5,499-foot summit of Standing Indian. The round-trip is 5 miles.

All of the hikes below start at the backcountry information center beside Standing Indian Campground. To reach it, drive 10 miles west of Franklin on US 64 and turn left onto the Wallace Gap Road (Old US 64). In 2 miles turn right onto FR 67 toward Standing Indian Campground to reach the backcountry information center in another 2 miles (GPS: 35.075994 / -83.528509). A perfect overnight backpacking trip climbs from the Kimsey Creek Trail, traverses a portion of the AT over Standing Indian, and returns on the Lower Ridge Trail for a 10.8-mile hike. Leave the information center on the blue-blazed Park Creek Trail and cross the bridge into Standing Indian Campground. Go right on the Park Creek Trail and take the first blue-blazed trail leading left.

This hike is moderately strenuous, climbing gradually along a trout stream. At 4.2 miles it turns along the AT and at Standing Indian (about 6.7 miles) goes left down the switchbacking Lower Ridge Trail to the information center. This circuit has an elevation gain and loss of about 2,000 feet.

Another circuit just north of the Kimsey Creek/Lower Ridge hike climbs the Park Creek Trail to Park Gap and descends back to the information center on the Park Ridge Trail for a 10-mile hike. To make this circuit follow the blue-blazed trail away from the information center and go right on the Park Creek Trail after crossing the Nantahala River. The trail follows the river, passing left turns to the Kimsey Creek and Park Ridge Trails. Portions of the trail lie on an old railroad grade used during extensive logging in the 1900s. The trail passes a log dam at about 1 mile and turns left from the river and ascends Park Creek at about 1.5 miles. On the way up the mossy stream, a connector trail goes left to the Park Ridge Trail. A left here shortens the circuit to 5.4 miles. At Park Gap, about 6 miles, go left onto the Park Ridge Trail and descend past the connector and back to the parking area at 10 miles. The elevation gain and loss on the hike, which tops out at 4,200 feet, is about 850 feet.

The lengthiest hike in the area, and the finest AT experience, starts at the information center and goes east or west. To the east it climbs the 2-mile Long Branch Trail, traverses the AT between Glassmine Gap and Standing Indian, and descends on either the Long Branch or Kimsey Creek Trail. The hike is about 24.2 miles. Using Lower Ridge Trail, the hike is about 21.5 miles. There are many campsites along the way (Beech Gap, Betty

Creek Gap, and Mooney Gap), and three shelters (Standing Indian, Carter Gap, and Long Branch Shelter). One of the best views on the entire hike is at Albert Mountain (5,250 feet). An interpretive sign describes the Coweeta Experimental Forest, visible below.

N to S	S to N	
287.8	36.4	Rock Gap Shelter
290.3	33.9	Glassmine Gap
291.3	32.9	Long Branch Shelter
293.7	30.5	Albert Mountain
294.0	30.2	Bear Pen Trail, FR 67
294.5	29.7	Bear Pen Gap
295.0	29.2	Spring
295.3	28.9	Mooney Gap, FR 83
296.2	28.0	Betty Creek Gap
298.9	25.3	Ridgepole Mountain
299.9	24.3	Carter Gap Shelter
300.3	23.9	Timber Ridge Trail
301.4	22.8	Coleman Gap
303.1	21.1	Beech Gap
306.0	18.2	Lower Ridge Trail, Standing Indian Mountain
307.5	16.7	Standing Indian Shelter
308.4	15.8	Deep Gap, FR 71
310.5	13.7	Wateroak Gap
311.4	12.8	Chunky Gal Trail

The Chunky Gal Trail offers a nice AT-related day hike. The trail leaves the AT heading west, crosses Chunky Gal Mountain, and ends at Tusquitee Bald on the Rim Trail in 22 miles. The best way to hike part of the trail is to start on US 64 (about 17 miles west of Franklin) and hike the 5.5 miles from there to the AT over Chunky Gal Mountain (with nice views at 4.8 miles). The 11-mile hike is strenuous, with plentiful ups and downs between Glade Gap and the AT.

For a nice overnight backpacking trip from here, hike south on the AT another mile and spend the night at Muskrat Creek Shelter. The round-trip backpack trip is 13 miles. Chunky Gal Mountain got its name from an Indian legend: A chubby girl fell in love with a boy from a different tribe. When he was banished by her parents, she followed the boy into the wilds.

N to S	S to N	
311.6	12.6	Whiteoak Stamp
312.4	11.8	Muskrat Creek Shelter
313.3	10.9	Sassafras Gap
314.7	9.5	Sharp Top
315.2	9.0	Bly Gap
315.3	8.9	North Carolina–Georgia Line
317.2	7.0	Rich Cove Gap

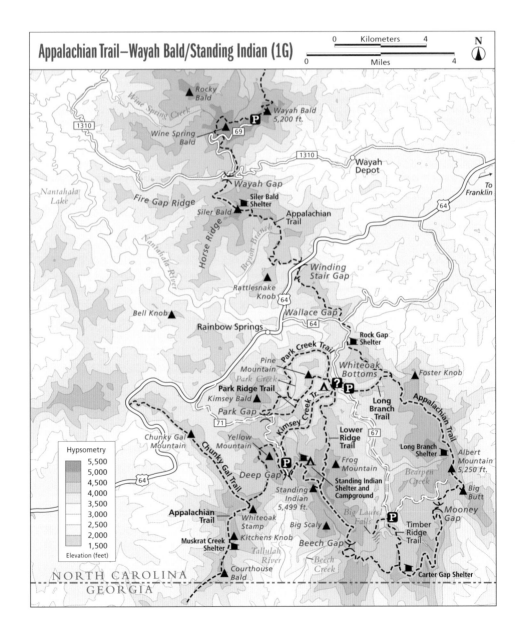

Appalachian Trail–Wayah Bald/Standing Indian (1G)

0   Kilometers   4

0   Miles   4

N

Rocky Bald

Wine Spring Creek

1310

Wayah Bald 5,200 ft.

P

69

Wine Spring Bald

Wayah Depot

1310

Nantahala Lake

Wayah Gap

Fire Gap Ridge

Siler Bald Shelter

64

To Franklin

Siler Bald

Appalachian Trail

Horse Ridge

Bryson Branch

Nantahala River

Winding Stair Gap

Rattlesnake Knob

64

Bell Knob

Wallace Gap

64

Rainbow Springs

Rock Gap Shelter

Park Creek Trail

Pine Mountain

Whiteoak Bottoms

Foster Knob

Park Creek

Kimsey Creek Tr.

Park Ridge Trail

Kimsey Bald

P

Long Branch Trail

Appalachian Trail

Park Gap

71

Lower Ridge Trail

67

Chunky Gal Mountain

Yellow Mountain

Long Branch Shelter

Albert Mountain 5,250 ft.

Chunky Gal Trail

Frog Mountain

Bearpen Creek

64

P

Deep Gap

Standing Indian 5,499 ft.

Standing Indian Shelter and Campground

Big Butt

Appalachian Trail

Whiteoak Stamp

Big Scaly

Big Laurel Falls

P

Mooney Gap

Timber Ridge Trail

Muskrat Creek Shelter

Kitchens Knob

Beech Gap

Tallulah River

Beech Creek

Carter Gap Shelter

Courthouse Bald

Hypsometry
| Elevation (feet) |
| 5,500 |
| 5,000 |
| 4,500 |
| 4,000 |
| 3,500 |
| 3,000 |
| 2,500 |
| 2,000 |
| 1,500 |

NORTH CAROLINA

GEORGIA

317.4	6.8	Campsite
318.4	5.8	Blue Ridge Gap
319.0	5.2	As Knob
319.7	4.5	Plumorchard Gap Shelter
320.9	3.3	Bull Gap
322.4	1.8	Cowart Gap
323.1	1.1	Campsite
324.2	0.0	Dicks Creek Gap, US 76

2 CUMBERLAND KNOB RECREATION AREA

Cumberland Knob is where construction of the Blue Ridge Parkway started on September 11, 1935. This is the high road's first recreation area. At 2,860 feet, Cumberland Knob isn't a spectacular peak, but the 1,000-acre enclave includes a nice day hike. The primary facilities are a large picnic area and a comfort station.

A small cemetery reminds visitors that life was hard a century ago in these mountains. A sign tells of a 16-year-old mother-to-be who asked for permission to be buried here under an apple tree. The landowner said OK, thinking her death was far off. Rebecca Smith Moxley died soon after her baby was born.

The shortest hike here wanders over the top of Cumberland Knob. From the Woodland Trail sign in front of the now-closed information station, go hard right onto the Cumberland Knob Trail past the graveyard and up the paved path along the picnic tables near the parking lot. Emerge at the summit on the right side of an old stone-and-log shelter with a shake roof and fireplace. Turn left across the front of the shelter, descend gradually to the Gully Creek Trail, and go left back to the woodland trail sign (a 0.4-mile loop).

GULLY CREEK TRAIL

WHY GO?
The Gully Creek Trail explores a topographically intriguing watershed.

> **THE RUNDOWN**
>
> **General location:** Northwest North Carolina near Sparta
> **Distance:** 2.5-mile loop
> **Difficulty:** Strenuous
> **Maps:** USGS Cumberland Knob, VA/NC. Download a parkway handout map of Linville Falls trails at the "Brochures" link on the Blue Ridge Parkway's website (see below).
> **Elevation gain:** 820 feet
>
> **Water availability:** Picnic area has water May through October. Treat stream water before using.
> **For more information:** Blue Ridge Parkway, 199 Hemphill Knob Rd., Asheville 28803-8686; (828) 271-4779; (828) 298-0398 (recorded information and mailing requests); nps.gov/blri

FINDING THE TRAILHEAD

Exit the Blue Ridge Parkway at milepost 217.5, less than 2 miles south of the Virginia–North Carolina border, to the Cumberland Knob Recreation Area. Park near the old information station in the picnic area (GPS: 36.553924 / -80.907362).

The Blue Ridge Parkway got its start at Cumberland Knob, and many motorists express their support with North Carolina's distinctive Blue Ridge Parkway Foundation license plate.

THE HIKE

From the vista side of the information station (there's a nice view of Pilot Mountain), head left at the Woodland Trail sign to start the Gully Creek Trail; as you near the picnic loop, turn right downhill on the paved trail.

The trail dips off the ridge, and you soon leave the rhododendron on many switchbacks down the dry ridge to Gully Creek. Beyond, the green fields of farms lie 1,000 feet below.

The trail switchbacks repeatedly on the sunny southeast side of the ridge, a growing stream continually blocking the trail's route. When Gully Creek tumbles in from the left, cross it for the first time at 0.5 mile on rocks. There's a bridge, many waterfalls, and more crossings before you finally rise away from the stream at 1.2 miles. Off to the left, pines cap the portal where Gully Creek escapes into the Piedmont.

The trail rounds the apex of the ridge at 1.4 miles and, bam, the lush and mossy rhododendron and hardwood ecosystem on the wetter, colder, more northerly slope gives way to the dry and sunny southeastern-side forest of mountain laurel and pine. A carpet of needles scents the air.

The trail makes a steepening climb along the ridge then slides off to the right along the top of a drainage under the bulk of Cumberland Knob. At 2.2 miles, the Cumberland Knob Trail goes left 0.2 mile to the historic picnic shelter atop the knob. Stay right; the trail becomes paved near the parking area.

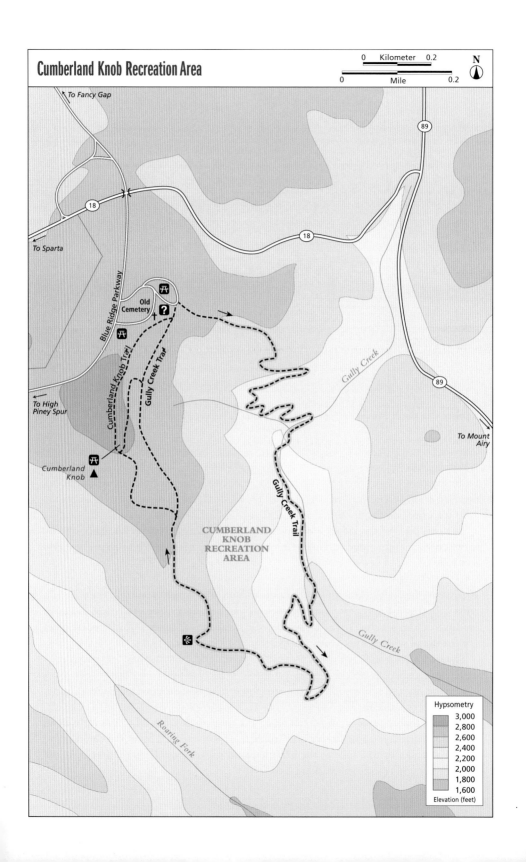

Cumberland Knob Recreation Area

0   Kilometer   0.2

0   Mile   0.2

N

To Fancy Gap

89

18

18

To Sparta

Blue Ridge Parkway

Old Cemetery

To High Piney Spur

Cumberland Knob Trail

Gully Creek Trail

Gully Creek

89

To Mount Airy

Cumberland Knob

Gully Creek Trail

CUMBERLAND KNOB RECREATION AREA

Gully Creek

Roaring Fork

Hypsometry

	3,000
	2,800
	2,600
	2,400
	2,200
	2,000
	1,800
	1,600

Elevation (feet)

From the Virginia line to the Great Smokies, the Blue Ridge Parkway is one-stop shopping for great hikes.

KEY POINTS

0.0   Start near the information station.

0.5   Cross Gully Creek.

0.9   Small falls at creek crossing.

1.2   Leave Gully Creek.

1.4   Dramatic change in vegetation.

2.2   Left goes to Cumberland Knob; keep right.

2.4   Another left to Cumberland Knob; keep right.

2.5   Arrive back at the parking area.

3 STONE MOUNTAIN STATE PARK

WHY GO?

Stone Mountain State Park is a more than 14,000-acre parcel that combines the park's namesake summit below the Blue Ridge Parkway and a 370-acre satellite tract above the Parkway on Bullhead Mountain (a grandstand on the hawk migration). Spectacular Stone Mountain is a light-gray granite dome that rises 600 feet above the surrounding forests. A variety of similar domes are visible in the park, all part of a 25-square-mile pluton, a large blob of igneous rock formed underground.

Over the 350 million years since its formation, erosion has exposed sections of the dome. Weathering has pockmarked the summits and cracked and creased the faces. The best example of this is the Great Arch, a huge crack down the mountain's main face and a favorite climb for rock climbers attracted to this world-class climbing destination. Hikers find great views from the peaks and dramatic cascades on plentiful streams. The biggest is Stone Mountain Falls, a 200-foot drop over—what else?—a dome.

Trout-fishing is a major attraction, with 20 miles of streams designated high-quality trout waters, including the waters of Bullhead Creek. There are two wheelchair-accessible fishing platforms along the East Prong of Roaring River.

Like many other North Carolina state parks, Stone Mountain was preserved through citizen interest and action. Conservation efforts started in the 1960s and included the donation of 418 acres by the North Carolina Granite Corporation, owner of much of the surrounding land. The park was dedicated in 1969, and Stone Mountain was designated as a National Natural Landmark in 1975. Besides having some of North Carolina's best scenery, there's interesting history too. The Hutchinson Homestead is a major interpretive

Besides being a great place to camp, the Widow's Creek Trail is one of the park's most scenic paths.

site, with a mid-1800s house, barn, and outbuildings that were wonderfully restored in 1998. A road permits access for the disabled.

Park facilities expanded in 2006. Just past the park office (with its visitor center exhibits), the campground was greatly enlarged to ninety sites and modernized. It's open year-round, has hot showers, and sites are reservable on the park's website or at 877-7-CAMP-NC (722-6762). The steep and dangerous start of the Stone Mountain summit loop trail near Hutchinson Homestead (the "Lower Trailhead parking") was rebuilt with nice stable steps and switchbacks. A major new trailhead for that hike was also built on the left just past the campground (the "Upper Trailhead parking"). The trail from that new lot also ties into a preexisting loop trail access from a nearby picnic area. That gives hikers three separate places to park and really spreads out hiker traffic, whether you're making an up-and-down hike to the summit or tackling the entire circuit. That means the busy old main trailhead near Hutchinson Homestead is now best used for hikes to the homestead, loops of Wolf and Cedar Rocks, and the lower waterfalls. The 3-mile Widow's Creek Trail has six backcountry campsites for backpackers, among the best in any state park.

THE RUNDOWN

General location: Between the Blue Ridge Parkway and the town of Elkin

Distance: A loop of the entire Stone Mountain Trail is about 4.5 miles from the recommended Upper Trailhead. From the Lower Trailhead, the two lowest waterfalls are out-and-back walks of 4 miles (and 4.6 miles to the base of Stone Mountain Falls). The best-kept-secret Wolf Rock/Cedar Rock circuit is 2.8 miles. An out-and-back walk to the view of Stone Mountain from the main trailhead is just more than 1 mile. From the picnic area, the summit of Stone Mountain is 2.3 miles (4.6 miles round-trip). The hike is a little less from the new trailhead. The round-trip to the top of Stone Mountain Falls is about 1.6 miles from the picnic area (a bit less from the new trailhead). The round-trip hike to the farthest campsite on the Widow's Creek backpacking trail is 6 miles. The Mountains-to-Sea Trail runs 6 miles from Widow's Creek Trail to the Blue Ridge Parkway's Devil's Garden Overlook. Widow's Creek Falls is a stroll from the roadside.

Difficulty: Strenuous for the Stone Mountain summit from the picnic area or new trailhead, moderate to the top of Stone Mountain Falls. From the Hutchinson Homestead Trailhead, moderately strenuous to the lower waterfalls and for the Wolf Rock circuit. Moderate for the Widow's Creek Trail. Easy for the short walks to views of Stone Mountain, to Widow's Creek Falls, and the Hutchison Homestead TRACK Trail.

Maps: USGS Glade Valley. Download a trail map at the park's website (see below).

Elevation gain: 425 feet to Stone Mountain from the picnic area and new trailhead; 2,074 feet to the Parkway on Widow's Creek Trail/ Mountains-to-Sea Trail

Water availability: Water is available at the park office/visitor center, at the picnic area, and at main trailhead restrooms year-round. Treat water from streams.

For more information: Stone Mountain State Park, 3042 Frank Pkwy., Roaring Gap 28668; (336) 957-8185; ncparks.gov/ Visit/parks/stmo/main.php; e-mail: stone.mountain@ncparks; mountainstoseatrail.org/.

The park's GPS coordinates are 36.3873/-81.0273. From Elkin, go north from I-77 on US 21. In about 11 miles, turn left onto SR 1002. Trip your odometer, and turn right at 4.6 miles on the John P. Frank Parkway to reach the Stone Mountain State Park entrance at 7 miles and the visitor center just beyond. Before the park entrance, SR 1100 comes in from the right. This is a good access route to or from the Blue Ridge Parkway for hikers on the Mountains-to-Sea Trail. The road leads to US 21 just below the crest of Roaring Gap.

The park office is on the right at 7.8 miles. Directly across the road on the left is the picnic area (GPS: 36.379094/-81.029687). Continuing on the park road, the Upper Trailhead is a short distance on the left (GPS: 36.383959/-81.027974). At 10.3 miles, the Lower Trailhead parking for Hutchinson Homestead and Stone Mountain Loop Trail is also on the left. From there, a spur road leads higher, permitting access for the disabled to the restored pioneer farm and view of the cliffs. Parking areas for Widow's Creek Falls and Widow's Creek Trail (GPS: 36.395429/-81.068407) are 0.9 mile and 1 mile farther on the right.

THE HIKES

The easiest starting points for a 4.5-mile round-trip of Stone Mountain are the picnic area and a nearby new Upper Trailhead just beyond the campground. Both trailheads are 400 feet higher than the Hutchinson Homestead's Lower Trailhead.

Follow the trail signs through the picnic area on the blue-blazed Stone Mountain Connector and descend gradually to cross Big Sandy Creek into open meadows near the junction with the trail from the Upper Trailhead. The trail rises left to a junction by the chimney of a long-gone mountaineer's cabin at 0.5 mile. Go right on the orange

The Stone Mountain summit is covered with a verdant carpet of sedge.

circle–blazed, road-width Stone Mountain Trail on a rocky tread in a spectacular chestnut oak and pine forest with an open, grassy understory. The slight arc of the ridge gives little hint of the drop-offs that surround you. Step off left for the view at the top of the first big dome.

The trail rises out of the next gap straight up the very steep edge of the dome on the right side of the mountain. (*Caution:* This heart-pumping climb could be tricky in wet or icy conditions.) Back again in the superb, parklike setting of the summit forest, leftward trails lead to views. At the top of Stone's biggest dome (about 2.3 miles), dead trees are weathered like driftwood and the elements seem ready to rip the soil layer from its tenuous hold on the rock. The dome gets steeper the farther down you stray. The jingle of rock-climbing gear wafts up from the face. Retrace your steps to your car for a 4.6-mile hike (a little less to the new trailhead).

On the way back to the picnic area, if you turn right at the chimney, it's 0.3 mile to the top of 200-foot Stone Mountain Falls (a side trip that adds 0.6 mile to the summit hike). If you just hike from the picnic area to the top of the falls, it's a 1.6-mile hike (a little less from the Upper Trailhead). *Caution:* Fatalities have occurred here—stay within the elaborate railings of the upper viewing area. A gargantuan flight of wood steps descends to the base of the falls—but the bottom and two other falls might be a better hike from elsewhere (covered below).

The Lower Trailhead near the Hutchinson Homestead is another recommended starting point. From this lower parking area, a central path runs up the valley below the towering face of Stone Mountain—the bottom of the Stone Mountain Loop Trail. Leave the parking area beside the restrooms and soon the orange circle–blazed upper Stone Mountain Loop goes left (4.5 miles total in either direction). Continuing, the easy trail crosses a small stream and passes a right turn to the Wolf Rock Trail. Past the disabled parking area at the Hutchinson Homestead, a few trails go left to the wonderfully interpreted early settler site. This easy 0.4 mile hike from the bottom (0.8-mile round-trip) is now the park's TRACK Trail. One of the four interpretive brochures insightfully contrasts the 1850s Appalachian lifestyle to modern times.

Just beyond, at about 0.6 mile (1.2 miles round-trip), there's a meadow with benches and stunning views of the mountain. The Great Arch climbing route soars above (bring your binocs or telescope and watch the climbers). A plaque designates the park as a National Natural Landmark. The climber's path crosses the meadow to the cliff.

Continue on the wide main trail for a moderate hike to the park's lowest cascades, Lower and Middle Falls. The Cedar Rock Trail goes right (more later); the main trail makes four easy stream crossings, passes plentiful ferns, and shrinks to a footpath on the way past huge chunks of rock exfoliated from the domes above. Head right on the blue circle–blazed Middle Falls/Lower Falls Trail at about 1.5 miles and hop the first stream. The trail to Middle Falls goes right to the top of the falls not far beyond. This is the easiest round-trip, at 3.6 miles.

Back on the main trail, go right to Lower Falls. A wider stream crossing is next, then a road grade descent to the falls. Add a rock hop to the base of the cascade and you might want to bring water shoes. Round-trip with both falls is about 4.2 miles.

The park's biggest cascade is just 0.3 mile beyond the turnoff to Lower Falls. Continue and the main trail gets smaller and ascends the boardwalk steps up and then down to the base of Stone Mountain Falls. Round-trip here is 3.6 miles (4.8 miles including Lower Falls). You could head up the huge flight of wood steps and on to the summit of Stone

For my money, a hike of the Cedar Rock Trail is the choice for great views of Stone Mountain and more solitude. Note the Great Arch climbing route arcing up the face to left of center.

Mountain for a strenuous 3.9-mile hike (7.8 miles round-trip). The picnic area and Upper Trailhead parking areas mentioned above are easier starting points.

One of the best-kept-secret hikes at Stone Mountain is the circuit over Wolf and Cedar Rocks. This hike is much less popular than Stone Mountain, but it offers similar spectacular views that include Stone Mountain itself. Just past the Stone Mountain view on the main trail, go right at about 0.6 mile on the gradual, red circle–blazed Cedar Rock Trail. Go right again at 0.6 mile where the white-square blazed Black Jack Ridge Trail goes left (this side trail omits views and lengthens the hike by 1.4 miles). Not far ahead, the first dome offers great views of Stone Mountain. Continue to emerge onto a second dome amid more awesome vistas. Watch the blazes on the rock here—they bear left and down the rock, not to the right, level and across.

Entering the woods, go right at 1.6 miles on the red-blazed Wolf Rock Trail where the Black Jack Ridge Trail comes back in on the left. The trail climbs past an old farm structure, through grassy woods similar to those atop Stone Mountain. At a junction at 1.8 miles, go left to great views from massive Wolf Rock, where it's easy to find your own private perch. Back on the main trail, continue past an impressive stone wall on the right. The trail bears right and begins a steep descent that eventually veers left down switchbacks to the main trail at 2.6 miles. A left leads back to your car for a 2.8-mile round-trip hike.

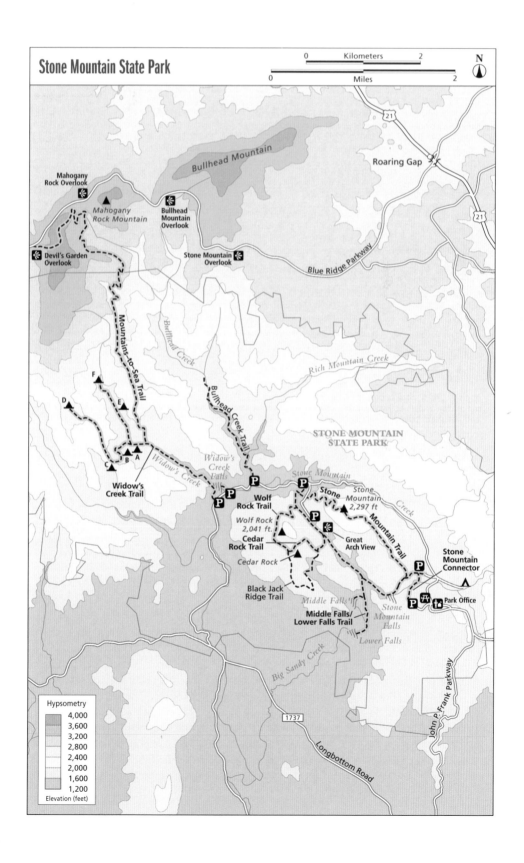

Stone Mountain State Park

Kilometers
0   2

Miles
0   2

N

Mahogany Rock Overlook

Bullhead Mountain

Roaring Gap

Mahogany Rock Mountain

Bullhead Mountain Overlook

Devil's Garden Overlook

Stone Mountain Overlook

Blue Ridge Parkway

Bullhead Creek

Rich Mountain Creek

Mountains-to-Sea Trail

Bullhead Creek Trail

STONE MOUNTAIN STATE PARK

F

D   E

A

C   B

Widow's Creek Trail

Widow's Creek Falls

Widow's Creek

Stone Mountain

Wolf Rock Trail

Stone Mountain 2,297 ft.

Stone Creek

Mountain Trail

Wolf Rock 2,041 ft.

Cedar Rock Trail

Cedar Rock

Great Arch View

Stone Mountain Connector

Black Jack Ridge Trail

Middle Falls

Stone Mountain Falls

Park Office

Middle Falls/ Lower Falls Trail

Lower Falls

Big Sandy Creek

1737

John P. Frank Parkway

Longbottom Road

Hypsometry

	4,000
	3,600
	3,200
	2,800
	2,400
	2,000
	1,600
	1,200

Elevation (feet)

In early 2020, new sections of the Mountains-to-Sea Trail in Stone Mountain State Park permitted hikers to traverse the entire park, one section connecting the Window's Creek Trail and the main Lower Trailhead parking. Hikers see this sign climbing the MST up to the Parkway.

Another less-traveled path that some guidebooks omit is the Widow's Creek Trail to the park's six backcountry campsites, one of the best places to backpack in a North Carolina state park. This superb, 3-mile out-and-back hike is peopled mostly by campers (please respect the privacy of their sites). The trail starts flat then climbs up and over a steep ridge to join Widow's Creek (the popular, short roadside path to the falls is below and off to the right). After that climb, it crosses the stream repeatedly on bridges. Streamside site A has its own personal waterfall. The trail splits, with the dead-end right branch leading quickly to sites E then F, the latter perfect for streamside silence and solitude. Drier sites B, C, and D are on the steeper left branch. Reaching site D won't be easy for beginners.

A portion of the Mountains-to-Sea Trail adds a nice dimension to the park. That path branches from the Widow's Creek Trail 1 mile from the trailhead and before the backcountry campsites. The park says it's 6 miles to the trailhead at Devil's Garden Overlook on the Blue Ridge Parkway, or 6.6 miles from the Widow's Creek Parking area, almost 13 miles round-trip. This trail is a little-traveled round-trip that really lets you take the measure of the Blue Ridge as it rises 2,000 feet to the Parkway. The hike up toward the Parkway would be a nice second-day hike on a three-day stay at the park's backpack campsites. Another option would be to spot a car in Stone Mountain State Park and hike downhill from the Parkway to your Widow's Creek Trail campsite. When you drop your car at the park, grab your backcountry campsite permit (best sites—A, E, and F) in advance and head up to the Parkway in a second car. Campsites must be chosen and paid for at the Widow's Creek Trailhead.

4 DOUGHTON PARK

The Blue Ridge Parkway's Doughton Park rears up to bulging meadows and dramatic headlands. The ridge that carries the Parkway encircles Basin Cove, a watershed more than 2,000 feet deep. This isolated, 6,000-acre backcountry is one of only a handful of places on the Parkway where backpacking is permitted.

The once-thriving valley community was first settled after the Civil War and abandoned after a flood in 1916. At easy-to-reach Wildcat Rocks, look over the edge into Basin Cove at century-old Caudill Cabin, a tempting hiking destination in the center of the 30-mile trail system. Hikers also encounter old chimneys, foundations, fences, and fields being reclaimed by forest. Backpackers need a free camping permit to use the designated backcountry campsite. At milepost 238.5, don't miss rustic Brinegar Cabin.

Doughton has a picnic area and campground. You can reserve sites at Doughton Park Campground (336-372-8877) in advance by using the recreation.gov website or calling (877) 444-6777. Sadly, the park's concession-operated restaurant and twenty-four-room Bluffs Lodge have been shuttered in recent years. Thanks to the Blue Ridge Parkway Foundation and funds from the public, the state, and the Appalachian Regional Commission, interior and exterior renovations are nearing completion on the restaurant which is expected to open as early as 2020.

FODDER STACK AND WILDCAT ROCKS

WHY GO?
An easy paved trail to a view of Caudill Cabin and a rugged but short scramble to a spectacular crag both start from the same trailhead.

THE RUNDOWN

General location: Northwestern North Carolina south of Sparta
Distance: 0.3 mile out and back for Wildcat Rocks; 2 miles round-trip for Fodder Stack
Difficulty: Moderate for Fodder Stack
Maps: USGS Whitehead. A Doughton Park handout map includes all the hikes below and is available online at the "Brochures" link on the Blue Ridge Parkway's website (see below), the ranger station (milepost 245.5), and campground contact kiosk.
Elevation gain: Negligible
Water availability: Water fountains are available at developed facilities May to October; treat stream sources before using.
For more information: Blue Ridge Parkway, 199 Hemphill Knob Rd., Asheville 28803-8686; (828) 271-4779; (828) 298-0398 (recorded information and mailing requests); nps.gov/blri; mountainstoseatrail.org/

Even if you don't hike to Caudill Cabin, a glance from this overlook at the building far below presents an image of Appalachian isolation.

FINDING THE TRAILHEAD

Leave the Blue Ridge Parkway at milepost 241.1. Bear left at the turn to the lodge. Park in the farther lot (GPS: 36.430291/-81.175220).

Wildcat Rocks is the craggy outcrop beyond the lodge where a stone wall surveys the watershed. A paved path begins in front of the lodge. Instead head to the second parking lot near the start of the Fodder Stack Trail and take the paved path to the right. Some people picnic on the sunny rocks.

Nearby Fodder Stack is a lump that juts from the main ridge and stands on its own above steeply dropping terrain. This family hike veers left off the back of the parking lot and down to a bench with great views. The trail then follows the craggy ridgeline and ends with a little loop on the summit of Fodder Stack. In the leafless seasons, the surrounding expanse of openness creates a stunning feeling of being out in the middle of it all.

KEY POINTS

0.0   Start from the second parking lot. Take trail to right to Wildcat Rocks.

0.3   Return to Fodder Stack Trail.

0.4   Bench with a view of Caudill Cabin.

0.8   Rocky crag on right with nice view.

1.3   Bench at summit view.

2.0   Arrive back at the parking lot.

BLUFF MOUNTAIN TRAIL

WHY GO?

Any stretch of this yellow-blazed 7.5-mile roadside path is worth a wander. The entire route is now part of the Mountains-to-Sea Trail (MST). Two hikes feature a stunning view from the trail shelter atop the crest of Bluff Mountain at 3,796 feet.

THE RUNDOWN

General location: Northwestern North Carolina south of Sparta
Distance: 1.6 miles out and back from Alligator Back Overlook; 0.6 mile out and back from the Doughton Park Picnic Area
Difficulty: Moderate to Bluff Mountain from Alligator Back

Overlook; easy from the picnic area; other stretches easy to moderate
Maps: See information for online handout map above.
Elevation gain: 320 feet from Alligator Back Overlook; 50 feet from picnic area

FINDING THE TRAILHEAD

Alligator Back Overlook is at milepost 242.4 (GPS: 36.421039/-81.190113). Access Doughton Park Picnic Area from milepost 241.1 (GPS: 36.421575/-81.183319).

Through much of Doughton Park, the Bluff Mountain Trail is the Mountains-to-Sea Trail as it alternates between meadows and woodsier sections.

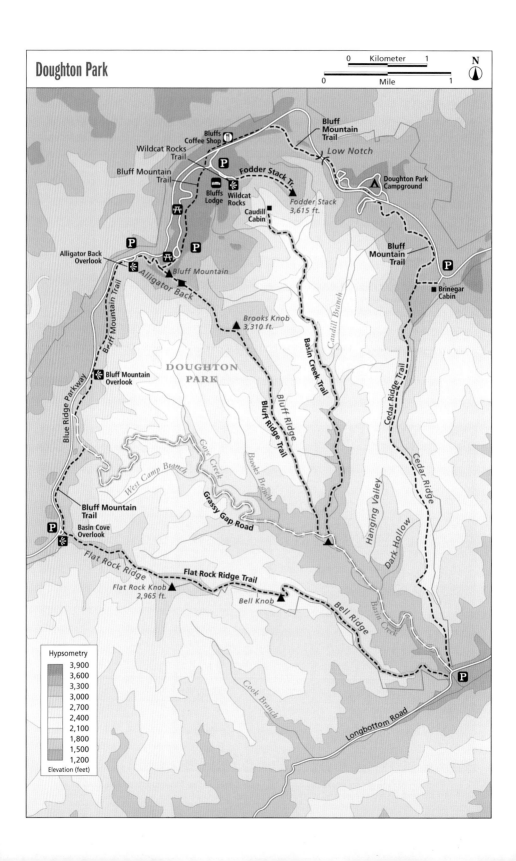

Doughton Park

0 Kilometer 1

0 Mile 1

N

Bluffs Coffee Shop

Bluff Mountain Trail

Low Notch

Wildcat Rocks Trail

Bluff Mountain Trail

Doughton Park Campground

Fodder Stack Tr.

Bluffs Lodge

Wildcat Rocks

Fodder Stack 3,615 ft.

Caudill Cabin

Bluff Mountain Trail

Brinegar Cabin

Alligator Back Overlook

Alligator Back

Bluff Mountain

Caudill Branch

Bluff Mountain Trail

Brooks Knob 3,310 ft.

DOUGHTON PARK

Basin Creek Trail

Bluff Mountain Overlook

Bluff Ridge

Blue Ridge Parkway

Cove Creek

Brooks Branch

Bluff Ridge Trail

Cedar Ridge Trail

West Camp Branch

Hanging Valley

Cedar Ridge

Dark Hollow

Bluff Mountain Trail

Grassy Gap Road

Basin Cove Overlook

Flat Rock Ridge

Flat Rock Ridge Trail

Bell Ridge

Basin Creek

Flat Rock Knob 2,965 ft.

Bell Knob

Cook Branch

Longbottom Road

Hypsometry

| 3,900 |
| 3,600 |
| 3,300 |
| 3,000 |
| 2,700 |
| 2,400 |
| 2,100 |
| 1,800 |
| 1,500 |
| 1,200 |

Elevation (feet)

THE HIKE

The arching "alligator back" is one of Doughton Park's most inspiring roadside sights. The cliffs and crags promise great views, and actually reaching the peak is worth the walk.

From Alligator Back Overlook, descend and go left onto the Bluff Mountain Trail/MST. The path breaks into steep sections of log steps before emerging onto crags with dramatic views. Past the views, soon turn right onto the red-blazed Bluff Ridge Trail (left, the Bluff Mountain Trail/MST goes to the picnic area). Not far beyond is the three-sided trail shelter atop Bluff Mountain (no camping).

KEY POINTS

0.0   Start at Alligator Back Overlook.

0.2   Trail starts to climb.

0.5   Spectacular clifftop views.

0.6   Turn right onto Bluff Ridge Trail (from picnic area, turn left at 0.2 mile).

0.8   Reach trail shelter view (0.3 mile from picnic area). Return the way you came.

1.6   Arrive back at the starting point (0.6 mile from picnic area).

The shelter and nearby clifftop make one of the Parkway's best easy hikes from the end loop of the picnic area. Take the path through the expansive meadow; in about 0.2 mile, turn right to the rocky clifftop then return and stay straight on the Bluff Ridge Trail to the shelter. Retrace your steps.

The rest of the Bluff Mountain Trail/MST is best strolled out and back from your choice of starting points—it's one of those "transportation" paths that link roadside facilities.

ONE WORTHWHILE START STANDS OUT:

Brinegar Cabin. Leave the end of the cabin's parking area and take the trail up the hill. Turn right in about 0.2 mile where the Cedar Ridge Trail goes left into Basin Cove. There are nice meadow views at about 0.4 mile for a turnaround (an 0.8 mile round-trip). It's also just over a mile from the Brinegar Cabin to the park's campgrounds, so campers could hike to Brinegar and back for round-trip hikes of 2.8 or 2.2 miles (from the tent and RV campsites, respectively).

BASIN COVE CIRCUIT HIKES

WHY GO?

The Flat Rock Ridge Trail–Grassy Gap Fire Road circuit is the easiest Basin Cove loop hike and one of the best moderate backpacking trips on the Blue Ridge Parkway. It can include a side trip to Caudill Cabin.

THE RUNDOWN

General location: Northwestern North Carolina south of Sparta
Distance: 11.1 miles for the Flat Rock Ridge Trail-Grassy Gap Fire Road circuit; 8.7 miles for the Bluff Ridge Trail-Grassy Gap Fire Road route; 13 miles for the Bluff Ridge Trail-Flat Rock Ridge Trail circuit
Difficulty: Strenuous (largely due to distance)
Maps: See information for online handout map above.
Elevation gain: 1,800–1,900 feet

FINDING THE TRAILHEADS

From the Blue Ridge Parkway, park at Basin Cove Overlook (GPS: 36.390807/-81.199823) at milepost 244.7 (less than a mile from the ranger office at milepost 245.5, where camping permits are available). Bluff Mountain Overlook is at milepost 243.4 (GPS: 36.408531/-81.195604).

THE HIKES

Basin Cove is perfectly configured for circuit hikes or backpacking trips. The Bluff Mountain Trail/MST gradually parallels the Parkway along the upper rim of Basin Cove, and four trails plunge in and join at the base.

Many hikes are possible; just look at the map. Unfortunately, the Cedar Ridge/Bluff Ridge circuit requires 4 miles of roadside walking on Bluff Mountain Trail—not exactly backcountry but very scenic. And the required campsite is not well positioned for the northern route. The best circuit, especially for backpackers, is on the southern end of Doughton Park—a counterclockwise loop of the Flat Rock Ridge Trail and Grassy Gap Fire Road.

From the Basin Cove Overlook, descend steeply; in 0.1 mile go right on the Flat Rock Ridge Trail where Bluff Mountain Trail/MST goes left. The Flat Rock Ridge is rugged, with frequent ups and downs, but it's well maintained and has the best views (one is at the 2-mile mark) of the routes into the valley.

Exit onto Longbottom Road at 5 miles; go left across the bridge and then left again on the easy streamside Grassy Gap Fire Road past a Doughton Park backcountry sign. Pass the Cedar Ridge Trail on the right and cross a new trail bridge (sponsored by the Piedmont Outing Club and Blue Ridge Parkway Foundation). The designated campsite (nice picnic spot for hikers) is on the left at 6.7 miles. The camping area's eight sites will accommodate up to forty people (maximum group size is twenty). Water should be treated or boiled and all trash packed out. Quiet hours are from 10 p.m. to 6 a.m. Pick up a permit at the ranger station noted above or at the campground contact station during the warmer months. Pass the campsites and, after a long gradual rise, go left on the Bluff Mountain Trail at 11.7 miles. This makes a premier three-day camping trip—a hike to Caudill Cabin on day two and an easy fire road walk back to the Parkway on day three.

KEY POINTS

- **0.0** Start at Basin Cove Overlook.
- **0.1** Go right on Flat Rock Ridge Trail where the Bluff Mountain Trail goes left.
- **2.0** Ridgetop view.

5.0   Left on Grassy Gap Fire Road.

6.7   Pass campsite—or set up a tent.

10.1   Left on Bluff Mountain Trail.

11.1   Arrive back at the trailhead.

The shortest circuit (and perhaps the best day hike without camping gear) starts at the Bluff Mountain Overlook (milepost 243.4). Stroll north on the Bluff Mountain Trail before the climb to the Bluff Mountain Shelter at 1.9 miles. Then descend the steep and forested Bluff Ridge Trail 2.8 miles to the campsite—4.7 miles from the start. That leaves an easy return leg of 5 miles on the fire road and 0.6 mile on the Bluff Mountain Trail for a day hike of 10.3 miles.

The most rugged loop—done clockwise, the easier way—starts at the Basin Cove Overlook and travels north on Bluff Mountain Trail. Turning right, it descends Bluff Ridge Trail to the campsite for a 6.4-mile first leg. Then it follows the Grassy Gap Fire Road to Longbottom Road, where two right turns reenter the woods on the Flat Rock Ridge Trail, the uphill hike with the easiest switchbacks and best views (for a 13-mile round-trip).

CAUDILL CABIN

WHY GO?

This is the easiest way to get to Doughton Park's most isolated and evocative spot—the 100-plus-year-old, 20- by 20-foot cabin where Martin Caudill raised fourteen children. The cabin was restored by the Parkway in 2001 with the help of modern-day Caudill relatives Lenny and Larry Caudill, both of whom still visit the old homeplace. The brothers have placed a family history folder inside for visitors (no camping, please). Campers who spend two nights at the backcountry campsite have the easiest hike to the cabin on day two. Check out my YouTube video "Hiking the Blue Ridge Parkway: Historic Caudill Cabin."

THE RUNDOWN

General location: South of Sparta
Distance: 10 miles out and back
Difficulty: Strenuous (largely due to distance)

Maps: See information for online handout map above.
Elevation gain: 1,400 feet

FINDING THE TRAILHEAD

At Parkway milepost 248, go east (downhill) on NC 18. At 6.2 miles, turn left onto Longbottom Road. At 4 miles, stay left on Longbottom Road. Three miles from that turn, park on the right just past a bridge across Basin Creek (GPS: 36.375212 / -81.144729). The Grassy Gap Fire Road enters the woods directly across the road from the parking area; the Flat Rock Ridge Trail does the same on the far side of the bridge.

The Caudill family visits "their cabin." Brothers Larry Caudill (bottom) and Lenny (top) return from doing a little maintenance on their ancestor's dwelling with Lenny's son Alex (middle).

THE HIKE

The heart of Basin Cove, including Caudill Cabin, is most easily reached from below the Parkway. Follow the green-blazed easy and wide Grassy Gap Fire Road for 1.7 miles along Basin Creek. You'll soon pass the Cedar Ridge Trail on the right and cross a new trail bridge. There's a second pair of trail junctions (both on the right) at 1.7 miles, where the 2-acre camping area borders the creek on the left.

At this junction turn right onto the blue-blazed Basin Creek Trail, an old wagon road. Over the 3.3 miles from this junction to the cabin, the grade makes a dozen wet crossings of Basin Creek or tributaries (I'd bring Crocs or water shoes). You'll pass a millstone in the creek on the first steep stretch, then a few old chimneys. There's a waterfall with a swirling cold-water whirlpool to soak in at 2.5 miles. The old grade deteriorates, passes another nice chimney, and ends in a grassy clearing at the cabin, 3.3 miles from the campsite and 5 miles from your car. Wildcat Rocks and Fodder Stack tower above. Imagine living in such a hardscrabble place. On your hike down, pause beside the trail at the campsite to find Alice Caudill's grave; she was one of many killed in the 1916 flood that turned the Basin Cove community into a ghost town.

Notice this millstone in Basin Creek as the Basin Creek Trail starts its climb to Caudill Cabin.

KEY POINTS

0.0   Start at Longbottom Road.

1.7   Turn right at campsite from Grassy Gap Fire Road onto Basin Creek Trail.

2.4   Pass first old chimney.

3.6   Pass another chimney.

4.2   A waterfall tumbles down Basin Creek.

5.0   Reach Caudill Cabin. Return the way you came.

10.0 Arrive back at the trailhead.

5 MOUNT JEFFERSON STATE NATURAL AREA

WHY GO?

A scenic motor road comes close to reaching Mount Jefferson's almost 5,000-foot summit. The drive to the park's upper parking area is worth the trip even if you don't hike, with impressive vistas at 2.2 miles (Sunset Overlook) and 3.2 miles (Jefferson Overlook). Scattered below are the pastoral farms of a county known for the state's only cheese factory and the New River, a National Wild and Scenic River, with riverside campsites along canoe routes through nearby New River State Park.

Rising 1,600 feet above surrounding terrain, dramatic Mount Jefferson was designated a National Natural Landmark in 1975. Like nearby Elk Knob, this is a geologically and botanically unique amphibolite mountain.

The mountain was renamed Mount Jefferson in 1955, ostensibly to honor Thomas Jefferson's father. The previous name, dating from 1810, was a racial slur that no state park needs. In that vein, it's said that the overhanging crags obvious along the Rhododendron Trail sheltered runaway slaves traveling to Ohio on the Underground Railroad.

Like so many others in North Carolina's park system, 541-acre Mount Jefferson State Natural Area was proposed and secured for park status by citizens raising their own funds. Picnicking and hiking are the park's primary recreational activities. The picnic area is located in a beautiful summit forest an easy stroll from the upper parking area. It has nineteen sites with water, restrooms, a picnic shelter, and grills.

THE RUNDOWN

General location: Rural Ashe County near Jefferson

Distance: 2.2-mile summit circuit; 4-mile round-trip on the Mountain Ridge Trail

Difficulty: Moderate for Lost Province Trail; strenuous for the others

Maps: USGS Jefferson. Download a trail map at the park's website (see below).

Elevation gain: 400 feet for the summit loop of the Rhododendron and Lost Province Trails

Water availability: Water is available from summit picnic area restrooms and water fountains during warm months.

For more information: Mount Jefferson State Natural Area, 1481 Mount Jefferson State Park Rd., West Jefferson 28694; (336) 246-9653; ncparks.gov/Visit/parks/moje/directions.php; e-mail: mount.jefferson@ncparks.gov

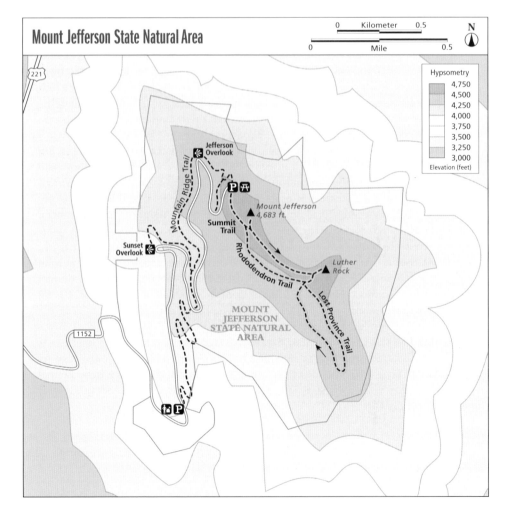

Mount Jefferson State Natural Area

Hypsometry
| Elevation (feet) |
| 4,750 |
| 4,500 |
| 4,250 |
| 4,000 |
| 3,750 |
| 3,500 |
| 3,250 |
| 3,000 |

Jefferson Overlook

Mount Jefferson
4,683 ft.

Summit Trail

Mountain Ridge Trail

Sunset Overlook

Rhododendron Trail

Luther Rock

Lost Province Trail

MOUNT
JEFFERSON
STATE NATURAL
AREA

221

1152

FINDING THE TRAILHEAD

The park is easily reached from US 221, the Robert G. Barr Expressway. Go north of the US 221/Business 221 junction at West Jefferson, and in 1.3 miles turn right on Mount Jefferson State Park Road. Go straight at a stop sign and begin a winding ascent that enters the park 1.4 miles from US 221 and reaches the summit parking area and trailhead at 3.6 miles (GPS: 36.404676/-81.465308).

THE HIKES

The 0.3-mile Summit Trail, 1.1-mile Rhododendron Trail (the park's interpretive TRACK Trail), and the 0.75-mile Lost Province Trail create two worthwhile loops at the top of the mountain. The 2.2-mile circuit hike includes a great view at Luther Rock and scattered interpretive signs. Leave the upper parking lot on a rocky road grade to the Mount Jefferson summit. The trail ascends through a picnic area, often amid the hiss of high-elevation breezes. At 0.1 mile, side trails go right 50 feet to restrooms (a sign here dispenses TRACK Trail brochures). In another 150 feet at a junction, the return of the Rhododendron Trail comes in on the right.

Continuing left up the grade, the road climbs steeply, switchbacking left to a trail junction where the Rhododendron Trail goes right. Go left to a radio tower (former site of a North Carolina Forest Service fire lookout) where a sign on the uppermost crag says the peak is 4,683 feet. Head out on the Rhododendron Trail and immediately note one of those interesting "shelter rock" overhangs below the trail on the left—presumably a hiding spot used 160 years ago by African Americans escaping slavery. This is easy, undulating ridgetop walking, with some rocky spots, through a rich forest of diverse tree species, among them northern red oak, sugar and mountain maples, and yellow birch.

Take the left to Luther Rock for open views from an outcrop of mica gneiss. Just below is the town of Jefferson, with its early-1900s county courthouse. Just above and to the right of town, Virginia's second-highest peak, Whitetop, is on the left, and Mount Rogers, the highest (5,729 feet), is on the right. Backtracking, take a left and steeply descend the Rhododendron Trail onto the sunny side of the mountain amid mountain ash, white ash, and basswood. Take another left to loop the Lost Province Trail. Rejoining the Rhododendron Trail, this virgin oak–chestnut forest has three distinct levels. The forest floor is relatively open, punctuated with wildflowers such as white bee balm and jack-in-the-pulpit. A mature canopy of trees towers above a mid-story of beautiful Catawba rhododendron. The effect is quite dramatic, especially between June 10 and July 1, when many shrubs and flowers bloom. The tunnel-like trail reemerges on the descending road from the fire tower just above the restrooms.

The park's newest addition is the Mountain Ridge Trail, a strenuous 2-mile ascent from the park headquarters to the summit lot. The rugged trail's many stone steps let hikers take the measure of the mountain. Never very far from the summit road, the trail stops at both viewpoints on the drive to the top and connects to both ends of the long summit parking lot.

6 E. B. JEFFRESS PARK

One of the Blue Ridge Parkway's best self-guiding interpretive trails and a number of historic structures make E. B. Jeffress Park a truly worthwhile stop for hikers. One of the Parkway's smallest roadside recreation areas (600 acres) memorializes E. B. Jeffress, the 1933 chairman of the North Carolina State Highway and Public Works Commission who helped route the Parkway through North Carolina rather than Tennessee.

CASCADES TRAIL

WHY GO?
This tree-focused interpretive nature trail leads to a cascading waterfall.

THE RUNDOWN

General location: About 20 miles north of Blowing Rock
Distance: 1-mile loop
Difficulty: Moderate
Map: USGS Maple Springs
Elevation gain: 170 feet
Water availability: Water fountain at trailhead May through October. Treat stream water before using.

For more information: Blue Ridge Parkway, 199 Hemphill Knob Rd., Asheville 28803-8686; (828) 271-4779; (828) 298-0398 (recorded information and mailing requests); nps.gov/blri.ncmst.org.

FINDING THE TRAILHEAD

Park in the Cascades parking area at Parkway milepost 271.9 (GPS: 36.245555/-81.458016). The trail goes left at the restroom building. A picnic area surrounds the opposite end of the parking lot, where the Tompkins Knob Trail ties in.

THE HIKE
This loop shows off the ecological community that teeters on the escarpment of the Blue Ridge. The path starts out paved as it wanders the crest of cliffs overlooking the Piedmont (best when the leaves are down). You'll marvel at the meadow-covered farming community suspended on lower mountains just below the Blue Ridge.

Keep right where the loop splits to dip down across a bridge over Falls Creek (closed and likely to be replaced at press time). Descend to the right from there to two rock wall–encircled overlooks where the waterfall leaps over the edge. (Signs say deaths have occurred here—stay behind the barriers.) Retrace your steps back from the brink to the bridge but stay right to follow the stream as it tumbles through a quiet valley on its way to the falls. Along the way, the Mountains-to-Sea Trail veers right to head north. It's appropriate that trees are the subject of the trail's twenty interpretive plaques. Between

Flame azalea and rhododendron bloom during the same late-May time frame on the Cascades Trail and at Tompkins Knob.

the drier cliff side and the well-watered stream drainage, hikers encounter many of the trees that populate Blue Ridge forests.

KEY POINTS

0.0   Start at the Cascades parking area.

0.05 Go right where loop splits.

0.3   Cross log bridge over stream and go right at junction.

0.4   Upper falls view, with lower platform 150 feet below.

0.5   Bear right at junction.

0.9   Bear right at final junction to parking lot.

1.0   Arrive back at the parking area.

TOMPKINS KNOB TRAIL

WHY GO?

This trail through a whispering white pine forest inspires real appreciation for early mountain residents.

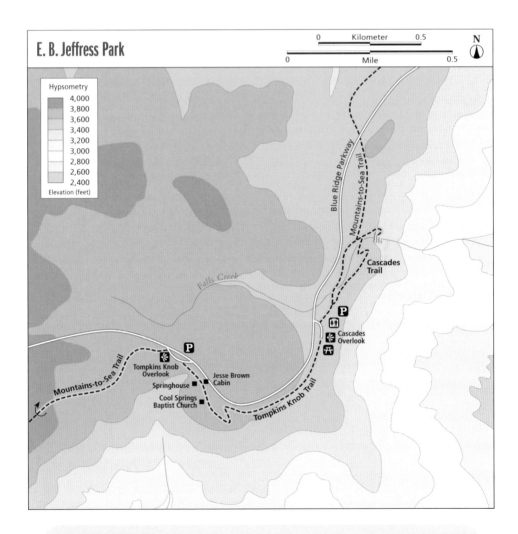

E. B. Jeffress Park

Hypsometry

Elevation (feet)
4,000
3,800
3,600
3,400
3,200
3,000
2,800
2,600
2,400

Blue Ridge Parkway

Mountains-to-Sea Trail

Cascades Trail

Falls Creek

Cascades Overlook

Tompkins Knob Overlook

Jesse Brown Cabin

Springhouse

Cool Springs Baptist Church

Mountains-to-Sea Trail

Tompkins Knob Trail

THE RUNDOWN

General location: About 20 miles
north of Blowing Rock
Distance: 0.6 mile one way

Difficulty: Easy
Map: USGS Maple Springs
Elevation gain: Negligible

FINDING THE TRAILHEAD

Park at Tompkins Knob parking area (GPS: 36.244276 / -81.465850), milepost
272.5, and take an immediate left from your car along and into the woods.

THE HIKE

This pleasant path offers a choice between a stroll to three interesting historic structures
and a longer walk to the picnic area at the nearby parking area for the Cascades Trail.
Best bet—start here and turn the Cascades Trail into an even longer hike. The link north
between these two overlooks is now part of the Mountains-to-Sea Trail and makes this
one of the MST's best day hikes.

Leave the overlook left on the short stroll to Jesse Brown's Cabin, a late nineteenth-century residence near Cool Spring, a lofty seepage trickling out of the ground to your right. Notice how the logs funnel water through the sagging springhouse. The cabin has an impressive fireplace, and the "Baptist church" up the gradual hill is just a shelter used when circuit-riding preachers were on hand. No living-history happens here, just quiet aplenty to imagine life more than a hundred years ago.

Head left at the church and descend gently all the way to the Cascades Trail parking and picnic area under inspiring white pines. This could also be a nice out-and-back from the Cascades parking area to the cabins (1.2 miles round-trip). Better yet, start from the Tompkins Knob parking area and hike to the Cascades, turning the 1-mile waterfall walk into a really pleasant 2.4-mile hike.

All the above hikes can be busy on a weekend, so if solitude is the goal, take the MST south not north. Leave Tompkins Knob overlook to the right across the grass and enter the woods on a gradual, wonderfully scenic section of the MST through white pines and needle-covered forests. Turn around when you want to return from nowhere.

KEY POINTS

0.0 Start at the Tompkins Knob parking area

0.15 Pass between Jesse Brown's cabin and springhouse.

0.2 Enter the woods beyond Cool Springs Baptist church.

0.25 Pass first bench.

0.5 Second bench.

0.6 Arrive at E. B. Jeffress Park Picnic Area and Cascades Trail parking.

From Elk Knob, it's not unusual to look north and see snow dusting Mount Rogers (right) and Whitetop, Virginia's first and second highest peaks.

7 ELK KNOB STATE PARK

WHY GO?

Elk Knob is one of North Carolina's newest state parks, saved from the prospect of second-home development by The Nature Conservancy and local residents. Elk Knob is one of many high peaks north of Boone in what's called the Amphibolite Mountains for their unique geological composition. Amphibolite is a metamorphic rock that is rich in nutrients and supports many rare plants. Elk and adjacent Snake Mountain rise to more than 5,500 feet, the equal of peaks south of the Boone area like Beech Mountain, the East's highest town and ski resort, and Hump Mountain, on the Roan Highlands part of the Appalachian Trail. In 2019, North Carolina designated a future hiking route from Boone to West Jefferson over these lofty and spectacularly meadow-covered mountains as the Northern Peaks State Trail.

Elk itself sits on that high ridge near the Tennessee border, a favored snow location, one reason the park encourages winter sports fans to bring snowshoes and Nordic skis. The park proudly states, "We strive to keep the park open in extreme winter conditions when many other parks are forced to close. This allows for unprecedented State Park access."

The park's facilities include an administrative office, a picnic area, and a 1.9-mile Summit Trail to 5,520-foot Elk Knob built with the help of hundreds of volunteers. The easy yellow diamond–blazed Beech Tree Trail, the park's interpretive TRACK Trail, is a 1-mile loop around the picnic area. The red diamond–blazed Maple Run Trail (0.5 mile) is another easy loop. The 2-mile, orange diamond–blazed moderate to strenuous Backcountry Trail leads to pack-in campsites.

THE RUNDOWN

General location: About 10 miles north of Boone
Distance: 1.9 miles one way
Difficulty: Moderately strenuous
Maps: USGS Zionville. Download a map at the park's website (see below).
Elevation gain: About 1,000 feet

Water availability: In season at park office
For more information: Elk Knob State Park, 5564 Meat Camp Rd., Todd 28684; (828) 297-7261; ncparks.gov/Visit/parks/elkn/main .php; e-mail: elk.knob@ncparks.gov

FINDING THE TRAILHEAD

Take NC 194 north of Boone for 4.3 miles and go left on Meat Camp Road, SR 1335. In 5.5 miles, turn right into the park in the gap between Elk Knob and Snake Mountain. The office is on the left, but keep right for the Summit and Beech Tree Trail parking area (GPS: 36.331687 / -81.689179).

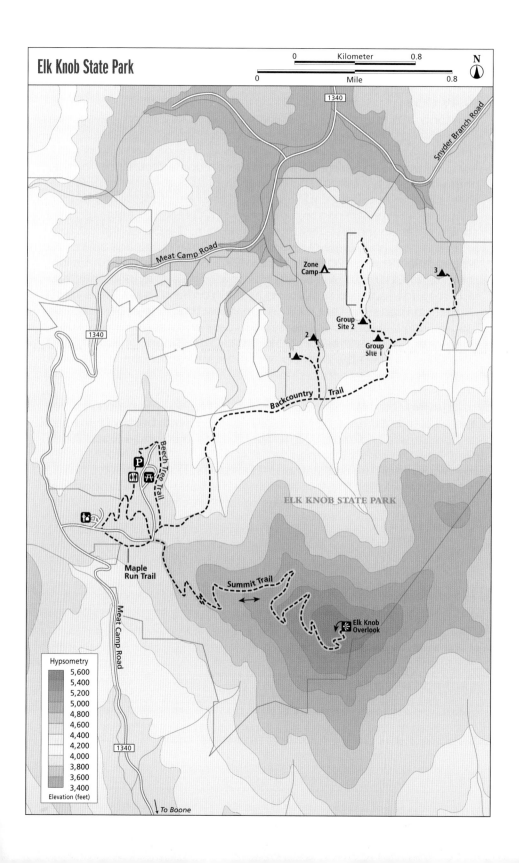

Elk Knob State Park

Kilometer
0   0.8

Mile
0   0.8

N

1340

Snyder Branch Road

Meat Camp Road

Zone Camp

3

1340

Group Site 2

Group Site 1

2

1

Backcountry   Trail

Beech Tree Trail

P

Maple Run Trail

ELK KNOB STATE PARK

Summit Trail

Meat Camp Road

Elk Knob Overlook

Hypsometry
5,600
5,400
5,200
5,000
4,800
4,600
4,400
4,200
4,000
3,800
3,600
3,400
Elevation (feet)

1340

↓ To Boone

The stone masterpiece of Elk Knob's Summit Trail was a labor of love for countless volunteers.

THE HIKE

Elk Knob's well–graded Summit Trail climbs at a relaxing rate of rise that turns 1,000 feet of elevation gain into a moderately strenuous hike. In switchbacks, the blue diamond–blazed trail offers benches made of stone or wood for resting. Impressive rock steps and paved portions of the path weave up the south slope and then cross to the north face through wildly wind-shaped forest (where snow might be found in April). The trail often crosses a steep old road grade that was once the route to the top.

The stunted summit forest offers views in many directions, all informed by interpretive plaques that point out distant peaks. Elk is equidistant between Mount Mitchell to the south, the highest peak in North Carolina and the East, and Mount Rogers and Whitetop to the north, the loftiest summits in Virginia. Other distinctive landmarks lie to the south, including massive Grandfather Mountain and two major ski areas, Beech and Sugar Mountain resorts, still striped with white slopes late into spring. Keep your eye on this area as conservationists seek to preserve these summits. The future Northern Peaks Trail will be one of North Carolina's premier hiking destinations.

8 THE BOONE AREA

The granola-inclined college town of Boone is the hub of what's called the High Country corner of northwestern North Carolina. The area has been popular as a resort since the 1880s, when the lowland rich first fled summer heat to spark tourism in the mountains. They came for the South's coolest summer temperatures and still-popular hostelries like Blowing Rock's Green Park Inn and the chestnut bark–covered luxury of Linville's historic Eseeola Lodge. Today the appeal includes a trio of wineries.

The inns and shops of Main Street in the town of Blowing Rock epitomize the appeal of High Country tourist towns. The Blowing Rock, a crag with a great view and an Indian legend, bills itself as "North Carolina's first travel attraction." Other area burgs include Linville, at the base of Grandfather Mountain, one of the United States' first planned resort communities. Banner Elk license plates call it the ski capital of the South in recognition of Beech and Sugar Mountains, the state's biggest ski resorts. Both are towns. Beech is the highest municipality in the East (5,506 feet), home to the cool and scenic Emerald Outback trail system, great for hiking, mountain biking, snowshoeing, and cross-country skiing (emeraldoutback.com). Another plus is the new Rocky Knob Park in Boone (the Pump Track portion is a cycling TRACK Trail). Mountain bikers predominate, but hikers are welcome to this top-notch new trail destination.

The Blue Ridge Parkway courses through the region, where facilities include Julian Price Memorial Park (milepost 296.9), a major picnic area and campground memorably sited beside Price Lake. Linville Falls also has a campground and a large picnic area (milepost 316.4). There's also a campground at Crabtree Meadows (milepost 339.5). Don't forget camping in the Pisgah National Forest. Black Mountain is a classic campground nestled at the base of Mount Mitchell.

Far below Grandfather Mountain in a dirt road–laced region flanking the Wilson Creek Gorge, Mortimer Campground sits on the site of a 1930s Civilian Conservation Corps camp. Reserve sites in advance at all the above campgrounds online at recreation. gov or by calling (877) 444-6777. The summit state park at Mount Mitchell (milepost 355) also has a restaurant and small tent camp area (highest in the East).

Environmental awareness is easy to cultivate on this stretch of the Parkway. The Museum of North Carolina Minerals (milepost 330.9) is one of the best geology exhibits anywhere. Just off the Parkway, Grandfather Mountain's Nature Museum and environmental wildlife habitats are first-rate. Mount Mitchell also has a nature museum. Just a few miles east of the town of Linville Falls on US 221 is Linville Caverns—North Carolina's only commercial cavern.

Museum-quality crafts are also in evidence. Between crafts for sale in Moses Cone Park's Manor House (milepost 294) and the stunning original works of art available in the Folk Art Center near Asheville (milepost 382), you'll be astonished at the vibrancy of Appalachian handcrafts. The High Country is a high point of the North Carolina mountain experience.

BOONE GREENWAY

WHY GO?

This isn't your average urban linear park. The largely Appalachian State University–owned property is an almost backcountry watershed tucked between neighborhoods. From many places along the greenway, surrounded by forest, green summits, and a remarkably clean mountain stream, you'd almost forget you're surrounded by a town of 20,000 people.

The fully accessible paved trail is mostly flat as it follows and crosses the South Fork of the New River through open meadows and colorful forests to the sound of rippling water. There's also a historic ruin, plentiful benches, picnic tables and shelters, as well as interpretive signing, great bird watching, flower viewing, and evidence of wildlife.

The town of Boone's 1986 comprehensive planning process built the original $100,000 path. It was dedicated in 1991 as the Lee and Vivian Reynolds Greenway in honor of the couple's beautification work. Dogs must be on-leash (and picked up after); in-line skaters and bikers should yield to walkers and runners.

THE RUNDOWN

General location: Boone
Distance: Basic length is 2.7 miles one way (5.4 miles out and back); satellite loops and connectors add another 1.6 miles. Adjoining natural surface trails create more options.
Difficulty: Easy
Maps: USGS Boone. Visit the town of Boone website (townofboone.net) and click "Town Parks & Greenways" to download a greenway map. Or grab a map at Watauga County's new state-of-the-art Parks and Recreation Complex.
Water availability: There are warm-weather water fountains available at Clawson-Burnley Park and the Watauga County Parks and Recreation Complex.
For more information: Watauga County Parks and Recreation Complex, 231 Complex Dr., Boone 28607; (828) 264-9511

FINDING THE TRAILHEADS

The best trailhead for the core greenway is the trail's midpoint at Clawson-Burnley Park (GPS: 36.205301/-81.650993). Turn off State Farm Road onto Hunting Hills Lane at the Watauga County Recreation Complex (on the left) and pass the former National Guard Armory (right) to turn left into Clawson-Burnley Park. Not far away, near Watauga Medical Center on Deerfield Road, there's parking for a paved loop that connects to the greenway (GPS: 36.201726/-81.650154). The most distant ends of the greenway permit the longest walks (or bike rides). The most urban greenway access is close to Walmart behind Southgate Shopping Center south of Blowing Rock Road (GPS: 36.198388/-81.660761). The most rural end of the greenway starts beside the Boone Wastewater Treatment Plant, not far from US 421. Head east out of town on US 421; 1.2 miles past the NC 194 junction, turn right just before the New River bridge onto New River Hills Road. Curve around with the river and turn left across a low water bridge at Casey Lane. Parking is on the right (GPS: 36.214457/-81.644661).

Gazing from the Boone greenway's bridges makes you wonder whether there's really a town nearby.

THE HIKES

Short loops are the easiest way to sample the trail. From Deerfield Road by the hospital, a landscaped 0.5-mile loop circles between Winkler's Creek and the South Fork of the New River. There's also a 0.5-mile loop that encircles a man-made wetland at Clawson-Burnley Park, a great destination in itself. Interpretive signs about Boone-area riverside flora and fauna make this a nice place for nature study and birding. There are wheelchair-accessible picnic shelters, roofed picnic tables, and many benches to soak up the scenery.

For a nice hike to a ruin, head north from Clawson-Burnley Park. Pass the wetlands to the covered bridge beyond; or go north a short distance on Hunting Hills Lane, cross the South Fork of the New River, and turn left along a beautiful white pine forested section of trail (with woodsy side paths). Either way, looping the covered bridge makes a nice 0.7-mile loop.

North of the covered bridge, the trail hugs the tree-lined riverbank (though you can shorten the walk by crossing the field). There's a second bridge at 1 mile, and just beyond on the left, an entire trail system of gravel or dirt paths called the Kennedy Trails connects back to ASU's athletic fields. A trail sign back at the covered bridge maps those trails (where access is just across the sports field).

Continuing north on the main greenway, there's a picnic spot at a historic dam site, about 1.3 miles from the complex. The stone ruin is a hydroelectric generation station

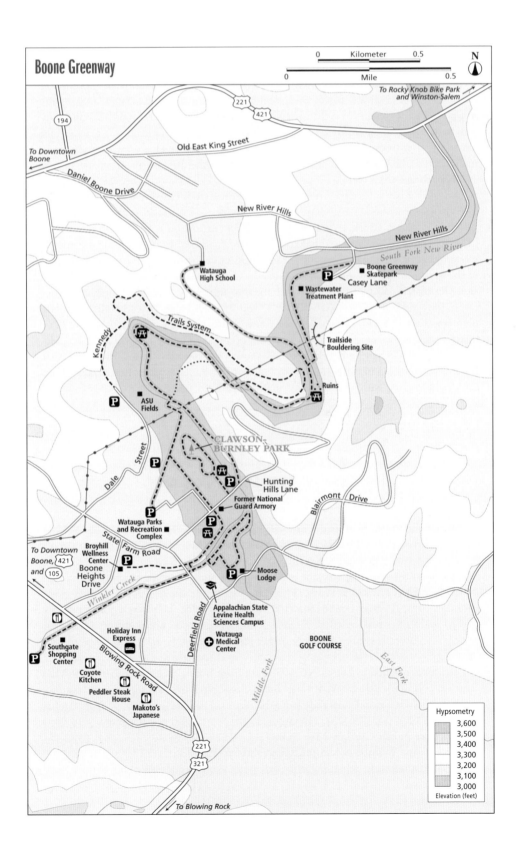

Boone Greenway

0   Kilometer   0.5
0   Mile   0.5

N

221
421

To Rocky Knob Bike Park
and Winston-Salem

194

To Downtown
Boone

Old East King Street

Daniel Boone Drive

New River Hills

New River Hills

South Fork New River

Watauga
High School

P

Casey Lane

Boone Greenway
Skatepark

Wastewater
Treatment Plant

Trails System

Kennedy

Trailside
Bouldering Site

P

ASU
Fields

Ruins

Street

Dale

CLAWSON-
BURNLEY PARK

P

P

Hunting
Hills Lane

Blairmont Drive

P

Former National
Guard Armory

P

Watauga Parks
and Recreation
Complex

State Farm Road

P

To Downtown
Boone, 421
and 105

Broyhill
Wellness
Center

Boone
Heights
Drive

P

Moose
Lodge

P

Winkler Creek

Deerfield Road

Appalachian State
Levine Health
Sciences Campus

Watauga
Medical
Center

Middle Fork

BOONE
GOLF COURSE

East Fork

Holiday Inn
Express

P

Southgate
Shopping
Center

Coyote
Kitchen

Peddler Steak
House

Blowing Rock Road

Makoto's
Japanese

221
321

To Blowing Rock

Hypsometry

3,600
3,500
3,400
3,300
3,200
3,100
3,000
Elevation (feet)

that produced Boone's first electricity from 1915 to 1924 for the Appalachian Training School, now Appalachian State University. The remains of an 11-foot-high wood dam are still visible in the river. Head back from here and it's a 2.6-mile walk. Continuing north, the main greenway passes a side trail left that runs 0.6 mile through a quiet side valley to Watauga High School (no trailhead parking), a nice streamside 1.2-mile out-and-back. Continuing north on the greenway, cross another bridge at 1.5 miles and follow the river through rhododendron and white pines past the town's wastewater treatment plant to the Casey Lane Trailhead. Starting there, the dam-site picnic area is an easy 1.2 miles round-trip.

The more urban side of the greenway lies southwest from Clawson-Burnley Park. Follow the greenway beside Hunting Hills Lane past the old National Guard Armory and go left to Winkler's Creek. A "trail cloverleaf" across the stream at State Farm Road links to the 0.5-mile roadside loop cited above on Deerfield Road. To reach the greenway's western end at Southgate Shopping Center, cross under State Farm Road. A right leads to the local hospital system's Broyhill Wellness Center, but go left to follow a bike lane along Furman Road. Not far from where the trail veers right off to the creekside, it goes under Blowing Rock Road (US 321/221) and exits on Pride Drive beside Southgate Shopping Center. Start at Casey Lane or Clawson-Burnley Park and it's an easy walk or bike ride to the shopping center for dinner at popular restaurants like The Peddler steakhouse, Coyote Kitchen, and Makoto's. Talk about a fun summer evening outing. Not far beyond where the trail turns right from Furman Road, the Holiday Inn Express offers the closest lodging with pedestrian access to the path.

VALLE CRUCIS COMMUNITY PARK

Every mountain traveler visits the historic Mast Store in the Vermont-like vale of Valle Crucis. The original, nearly 140-year-old Mast General Store was called "America's premier country store" by Charles Kuralt.

Just behind the old landmark, the Valle Crucis Community Park provides a nice leg-stretcher along the Watauga River. There are two picnic shelters in the 22-acre park, started in 1985. A paved 1-mile loop circles the grassy fields and passes a pond and wetland to parallel the rushing river. There are ample benches to watch anglers casting for trout in the river. Kids have a variety of playground apparatus, and there are restrooms on-site.

The park is reached by taking NC 105 south from Boone and making a right to Valle Crucis on NC 194. Pass the Mast Farm Inn, a classic place for lodging (themastfarminn.com), and not far beyond, turn right onto the dirt road just before the Mast Store Annex (GPS: 36.211238 / -81.776175). The original Mast Store is just past the annex (828-963-6511). Other North Carolina Mast Stores are located in downtown Boone, Asheville, Waynesville, and Winston-Salem (mastgeneralstore.com).

Consider supporting the nonprofit park with a tax-deductible contribution (vallecrucispark.com).

9 JULIAN PRICE MEMORIAL PARK

Julian Price Memorial Park is one of the scenic high points of the Blue Ridge Parkway. Its 4,200 acres contain a golden 47-acre lake, the Parkway's second-largest picnic area, and its largest campground, with superb lakeside camping. You can reserve sites at Price Park Campground in advance online at recreation.gov or by calling (877) 444-6777.

Price Lake is the park's centerpiece. Grandfather Mountain towers in the distance, the source of the lake visible as a bowl-shaped valley scooped out high on the peak. When the lake is frozen into jagged, jumbled sheets, access is still easy for winter hikers and cross-country skiers—the Park Service plows the road from the US 221/Holloway Mountain Road exit (milepost 298.6), easily reached from Blowing Rock.

In summer, canoes, rowboats, and kayaks dot the lake. Bring your own or rent at the park's boathouse at milepost 297 (no sails or motors).

GREEN KNOB TRAIL

WHY GO?
This loop hike combines towering trees, meadow-capped hilltops, and panoramic views.

THE RUNDOWN
General location: About 4 miles west of Blowing Rock
Distance: 2.1-mile loop
Difficulty: Moderate
Maps: USGS Boone. Download a parkway handout map of Price Park at the "Brochures" link on the Blue Ridge Parkway's website (nps.gov/blri). Maps are also available at the Price Park Campground kiosk.
Elevation gain: 460 feet

FINDING THE TRAILHEAD

Park at Sims Pond Overlook (milepost 295.9), 1.3 miles south of the US 221 exit near the town of Blowing Rock (GPS: 36.142480 / -81.719718).

THE HIKE
Cross the spillway bridge and dam of Sims Pond and turn left along the rhododendron-lined shoreline.

The trail rises along the feeder stream through a long grove of towering hemlocks, sadly now dying or dead due to the hemlock woolly adelgid. The trail rises above the stream as the *ka-thump* of cars can be heard above on the Sims Creek Viaduct.

At a bridge and bench (0.6 mile), a side path climbs steeply right to Sims Creek Viaduct Overlook (an alternate start). The trail steepens and rises out of the drainage to arc left into a broad meadow (follow concrete posts with blue directional arrows). Exit the meadow through a fat-man squeeze and dip into hardwoods past a weathered bench to a view of Price Lake and Grandfather Mountain. Descend more steeply down a scenic ridgeline route through woods and smaller meadows to another spectacular view at the bottom. Go left through a fat-man squeeze; a rhododendron tunnel brings you to the Parkway and the sound of cars. Walk left 150 feet to Sims Pond Overlook.

KEY POINTS

0.0   Start at Sims Pond Overlook.

0.6   Access trail to Sims Creek Viaduct Overlook.

1.0   Leave woods into first meadow.

1.4   Exit meadow near summit of Green Knob.

2.1   Arrive back at the overlook.

BOONE FORK TRAIL

WHY GO?
One of the Parkway's longer trails follows a scenic mountain stream with rocky plunges and deep pools. The first part of this hike in Price Park picnic area is an interpretive TRACK Trail where evidence of beavers is seen. Visit kidsinparks.com/price-memorial-park-picnic-area.

THE RUNDOWN

General location: About 4 miles west of Blowing Rock
Distance: 4.9-mile loop, with a 1.4-mile out-and-back TRACK Trail
Difficulty: Strenuous beyond the TRACK Trail

Maps: USGS Boone. Download a parkway handout map of Price Park at the "Brochures" link on the Blue Ridge Parkway's website (nps.gov/blri). Maps are also available at the Price Park Campground kiosk.
Elevation gain: 440 feet

FINDING THE TRAILHEAD

Turn into the Price Park Picnic Area at milepost 296.4; park in the first lot on the right, opposite the restroom (GPS: 36.139423 / -81.727161).

THE HIKE
Pass the restroom and cross Boone Fork Creek where a map sign marks the start of the loop. Grab a TRACK Trail brochure and go right along the creek past a boggy area favored by beavers. Obvious railroad ties in the rhododendron tunnel treadway mark this as the old railroad grade of the Boone Fork Lumber Company, which logged part of Grandfather Mountain (for more, see the author's award-winning book, *Grandfather Mountain: The History and Guide to an Appalachian Icon* from the University of North Carolina Press). At about 1 mile, the Mountains-to-Sea Trail (coming from ahead of you)

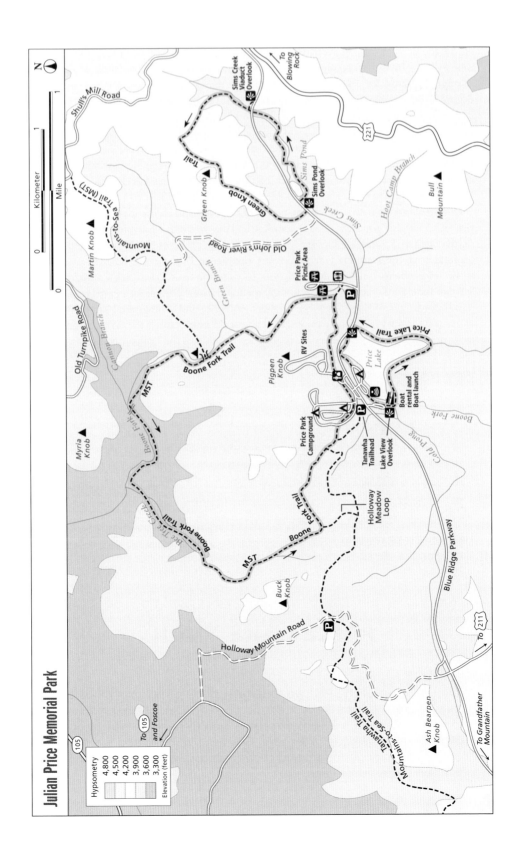

Julian Price Memorial Park

Hypsometry

4,800
4,500
4,200
3,900
3,600
3,300

Elevation (feet)

N

Kilometer

Mile

Shull's Mill Road

Sims Creek Viaduct Overlook

To Blowing Rock

Green Knob Trail

Green Knob

Sims Pond

Sims Pond Overlook

Martin Knob

Mountains-to-Sea Trail (MST)

Old John's River Road

Sims Creek

221

Hoot Camp Branch

Bull Mountain

Green Branch

Price Park Picnic Area

Camp Branch

Old Turnpike Road

Boone Fork Trail

RV Sites

Pigpen Knob

Price Lake Trail

Myria Knob

MST

Boone Fork

Bee Tree Creek

Boone Fork Trail

Price Park Campground

P

Tanawha Trailhead

Lake View Overlook

Boat rental and Boat launch

Price Lake

Boone Fork

Cold Prong

Boone Fork Trail

MST

Buck Knob

Holloway Meadow Loop

P

Holloway Mountain Road

To 105 and Foscoe

105

Blue Ridge Parkway

To 211

Tanawha Trail

Mountains-to-Sea Trail

Ash Bearpen Knob

To Grandfather Mountain

crosses the stream north on a long bridge. (Taking that right across the bridge, it's just 0.1 mile to Price Park's backcountry campsite; permit required from Price Park's developed campground kiosk or nearby Sandy Flats ranger office.) Continuing on the combined Boone Fork/Mountains-to-Sea Trail, the path passes a side trail to Hebron Falls, a popular sunning and swimming spot, then levels through woods and negotiates a ladder before turning sharply downhill to the stream and the best waterfall on the trail at 1.8 miles.

The trail repeatedly climbs up to, then down from, sections of old railroad grade; trestles once carried logging trains across the space between the grades. Switchback left out of the Boone Fork drainage at about 2.5 miles along Bee Tree Creek. After a bridge, the trail leaves the stream on a section of new trail built in 2013.

Passing beneath a rock outcrop, the new trail bears left and climbs into a meadow to a sign at 3.5 miles. Turn left across the meadow and descend into white pines to a junction on the right at 3.9 miles. Here the Mountains-to-Sea Trail turns right for Grandfather Mountain and the Tanawha Trail joins you. Continue on Boone Fork/Tanawha to a split at 4.1 miles where Tanawha turns off right to its terminus at Price Park Campground. Stay left through the campground, cross the road, and pass restrooms on a paved trail. The trail becomes gravel, passes between a ranger residence and campground kiosk (source of permits for the backcountry campsite) at about 4.5 miles, crosses the RV campground road, and descends into the meadow to the loop sign. Cross the bridge to your car.

KEY POINTS

0.0 Start at the Julian Price Memorial Park picnic area.

0.5 Extensive beaver activity across the stream.

1.0 Mountains-to-Sea Trail branches right to Moses Cone Park.

1.8 Rejoin Boone Fork near hike's biggest waterfalls.

2.5 Trail enters drainage of Bee Tree Creek.

3.9 Mountains-to-Sea and Tanawha Trail junction right from Grandfather Mountain.

4.1 Tanawha Trail goes right to campground terminus.

4.5 Pass ranger residence and campground kiosk.

4.9 Arrive back at the picnic area.

PRICE LAKE TRAIL

WHY GO?

A lakeside loop of the Parkway's largest body of water. An out-and-back walk here is Price Park's second TRACK Trail for hikers (also see Boone Fork Trail). Or bring, or rent, a boat. The first-ever paddlers TRACK Trail follows the lakeshore. Both the walking and water brochures are scavenger hunts and beaver activity is seen here too. Visit kidsinparks.com/price-lake.

Whether you're watching from the shoreline path or paddling through the pungent fall scents of campfire smoke, Price Lake's TRACK Trail is a golden pond autumn experience.

THE RUNDOWN

General location: About 4 miles west of Blowing Rock
Distance: 2.5-mile loop
Difficulty: Easy to moderate
Maps: USGS Boone. Download a parkway handout map of Price Park at the "Brochures" link on the Blue Ridge Parkway's website (nps.gov/blri). Maps are also available at the Price Park Campground kiosk.
Elevation gain: Negligible

FINDING THE TRAILHEAD

Either of two lakeshore overlooks is a potential starting point. The preferred start, Lake View Overlook, is reached by a spur road at milepost 297.2 (GPS: 36.135734 / -81.738382). Price Lake Overlook is at milepost 296.7 (GPS: 36.138982 / -81.732288).

THE HIKE

Leave the southern end of the Lake View Overlook by the trail map sign and descend a wheelchair-accessible ramp behind the boat rentals (the start of both TRACK Trails). The first 0.7 mile of this trail has been upgraded for wheelchair access to stream and lakeshore fishing spots. (Expect similar improvements on the rest of the trail.) The trail bridges Cold Prong then Boone Fork, the lake's main source, and crosses a boggy area on a boardwalk at about 0.7 mile. Turn around at a lakeside fishing deck opposite the

Even beginner cross country skiers can tackle the flat section of the Price Lake Trail south from Lake View Overlook.

boat launch for a 1.4-mile hike that's one of the best on the Parkway for the wheelchair-bound, very young hikers, and cross-country skiers.

From this point back to the Parkway, the trail around the longest arm of the lake is a woodsy and quiet walk punctuated by the hollow *thunk* of paddle on canoe or kayak. There's a new boardwalk and a bridge across a boggy area on the far end of the lake, where the trail crosses Laurel Creek to bear left back toward the Parkway (the walking Track Trail retraces its steps from here). A variety of rocks reach into the water, enticing boaters to land and anglers to cast, all with good views of Grandfather Mountain. Descend steps to the Parkway at 1.7 miles and go left across the dam through Price Lake Overlook. A paved path passes another lakeside fishing/view deck then enters campground Loop A—easily one of the premier places on the Parkway to set up a tent.

The trail bisects the campground past a restroom (2.2 miles) then skirts the campground amphitheater to reenter Lake View Overlook at 2.5 miles.

KEY POINTS

0.0   Start at Lake View Overlook.

0.7   Cross boardwalk and bridge to fishing deck.

1.0   Boardwalk signals left turn along final side of the lake.

1.7   Turn left along Parkway to cross dam.

2.2   Pass restrooms.

2.5   Arrive back at Lake View Overlook.

10 MOSES CONE MEMORIAL PARK

This park's 3,500 acres memorialize Moses Cone (1857–1908) who, with brother Cesar, amassed a fortune in North Carolina's post–Civil War textile industry in Greensboro. "Denim King" Cone built his Flat Top Manor mansion on the crest of the Blue Ridge. It's now home to the Parkway Craft Center, where artisans demonstrate their skills and rangers lead summer season tours of the long-closed upstairs of the house.

The rich estate's sprawling forests reach from hardwood- and hemlock-filled drainages at Bass and Trout Lakes to the meadow-covered peaks of Rich and Flat Top Mountains. It is one of the most beautiful and special places on the Blue Ridge Parkway.

More than 25 miles of road-width carriage paths wander lightly on the land, creating easy avenues for carefree strolls. At times, they corkscrew mysteriously—one section is called The Maze. These paths are perfect for family walks and become Nordic nirvana to cross-country skiers. (Snow hikers should help preserve smooth skiing conditions by starting a walker's path and not walking in ski tracks.)

In winter, portions of the Cone Park and adjacent Julian Price Park sections of the Parkway are plowed of snow between US 321 and Shull's Mill Road in the north and from US 221/Holloway Mountain Road to Price Lake in the south.

Cone Park attracts many horseback riders, so you'll find yourself stepping around reminders of equine passage. Bicycles, however, are prohibited on the trails. Within Cone Park's trail system, junctions are many and can be confusing. These recommended hikes carefully describe directions, but use the map to create more. The lakes of Cone and neighboring Price Parks are one of the mountains' best places for a "golden pond" experience. There's nothing like a lakeshore hike through a hissing breeze, fluttering leaves, and golden high-altitude summer light.

Consider the 0.7-mile Figure Eight Trail just behind the mansion that Moses and Bertha Cone shared with guests. Plaques introduce you to the forest and the culture of the local mountaineers. Impressive hardwoods, rhododendron, hemlock, white pine, spruce, and fir lend a northern feel. It's an easy cross-country ski trail.

FLAT TOP ROAD

WHY GO?
The best hike to Cone Park summit views.

THE RUNDOWN
General location: Just outside Blowing Rock
Distance: 5.6 miles round-trip
Difficulty: Moderate
Maps: USGS Blowing Rock. Download a parkway handout map of Cone Park at the "Brochures" link on the Blue Ridge Parkway's website (see below). Maps are also available at the Cone Manor House.
Elevation gain: 580 feet

In summer, breezy days in Cone Park's upland meadows come complete with waving grass and flowers.

Water availability: Water fountain at Cone Manor House. Stream water caution: extensive cattle grazing and horse traffic.
For more information: Blue Ridge Parkway, 199 Hemphill Knob Rd.,

Asheville 28803-8686; (828) 271-4779; (828) 298-0398 (recorded information and mailing requests); www.nps.gov/blri

FINDING THE TRAILHEAD

Park at the far end of the Manor House parking area (GPS: 36.149989/ -81.691726) and descend past the Carriage Barn on a wheelchair-accessible route to the gravel path below; go left.

THE HIKE

Flat Top Road is an out-and-back hike that climbs through meadows to spectacular views from a summit tower on Flat Top (4,558 feet).

Follow Flat Top Road left and under a Parkway tunnel to a junction; bear right (uphill) into woods. Enter more meadows at 0.9 mile; a spur leads left to graves where Cone and his wife lie sheltered by a grove of evergreens. Mrs. Cone lived four decades after her Moses's death, long enough to see her husband's grave broken into in 1924. The *Watauga Democrat* headline read "Ghouls Enter Grave of Moses H. Cone." Beyond the meadow, the road switchbacks just above cliffs then curves around the summit to reach a view tower at 2.8 miles (5.6 miles round-trip). Grandfather Mountain dominates the vista.

BASS LAKE LOOP

WHY GO?
A circumambulation of Cone Park's prettiest lake.

THE RUNDOWN

Distance: 0.8-mile loop from the lakeshore parking lot; 1.2-mile loop from the US 221 trailhead
Difficulty: Easy

Maps: USGS Blowing Rock. See information for online handout map above; map also available at Cone Manor House.
Elevation gain: Negligible

FINDING THE TRAILHEADS
Exit the Parkway at milepost 294.6 to US 221. Turn left and descend in about 1 mile to two trailheads. The first is a left turn on a paved road into the Bass Lake entrance for parking by lakeshore restrooms (GPS: 36.140976 / -81.686936). Just past that turn, the roadside Bass Lake parking slip is on the left (GPS: 36.138457 / -81.685640).

THE HIKE
In dry weather, this easy, scenic loop might be suitable for wheelchairs from the lakeshore parking area below US 221.

From the lakeside lot, pass the restrooms to the trail and go right to weave in and out along the shore amid maples past the 0.4-mile side trail to the parking slip on US 221. Head left across the dam, with Cone Manor House visible above. Across the dam, keep left as two trails go right. Continue left around the lake and back to the parking area for an 0.8-mile loop. Starting on US 221, hikers bear right past one junction and keep right to cross the dam. The added access distance makes this a 1.2-mile loop.

MANOR HOUSE CIRCUIT AND MAZE TRAIL

WHY GO?
The quintessential Cone Park day hike to the manor.

THE RUNDOWN

General location: Just outside Blowing Rock
Distance: 4.7-mile loop
Difficulty: Moderate

Maps: USGS Boone. See information for online handout map above; map also available at Cone Manor House.
Elevation gain: 420 feet

Exit the Parkway at milepost 294.6 to US 221. Turn left and descend in about 1 mile to the Bass Lake entrance (GPS: 36.140976/-81.686936). Go just past the entrance and park on the left in the roadside Bass Lake parking slip (GPS: 36.138457/-81.685640).

THE HIKE

The easy grade of this circuit hike is rated moderate because of its length. After a short descent from the roadside parking slip, go left at the first junction on Duncan Road and cross the paved road to the lakeshore parking area.

At 1.1 miles the road passes meadows below the manor house; then the Rock Creek Carriage Road goes left to Blowing Rock Stables. At 2.3 miles turn right onto the paved road that runs to the manor (2.6 miles).

Enjoy the mansion then bear right below the house and descend along the edge of the meadow on the initially paved Watkins Road. At 3.2 miles turn sharply right onto the Deer Park Road (Watkins Road goes left). Just past a meadow at 3.9 miles, the Apple Barn Connector goes left into The Maze. The historic Apple Barn, where Cone processed the prize-winning fruit from his estate, is a nice point of interest only 0.2 mile to the left (0.4-mile round-trip).

Continue downhill through stately white pines to the Bass Lake Loop Trail at 4.4 miles. Bear left across the bridge (avoid the hard left into The Maze), angle right across the dam, and then go left away from the lake. Turn left again to reach US 221 for a 4.7-mile hike. If you take the Apple Barn side trip, this is a 5.1-mile hike.

KEY POINTS

0.0 Start at the roadside Bass Lake parking slip.

0.1 Turn left onto Duncan Road.

1.7 Go right at junction; Rock Creek Carriage Road goes left.

2.3 Turn right onto paved road.

2.6 Reach Manor House.

3.2 Turn sharply right onto Deer Park Road.

3.9 Go right at junction with Apple Barn Connector.

4.4 Cross dam at Bass Lake.

4.5 Go left at junction across dam to leave lake.

4.7 Make last left up to parking lot, avoiding Duncan Road.

Both Bass Lake hikes pass entrances into the Maze Trail. To tackle that, park at either Bass Lake parking area and head to the dammed end of the lake and then turn right at the sign into The Maze. Hikers during summer are rarely sure where they are, so use this map and take no shortcuts.

The carriage path corkscrews around for 2.3 miles before reaching the Apple Barn at 2.6 miles. Do not go right at the Apple Barn onto Black Bottom Road. (See the map for more on this and Watkins Road, Cone's loneliest circuit hike.)

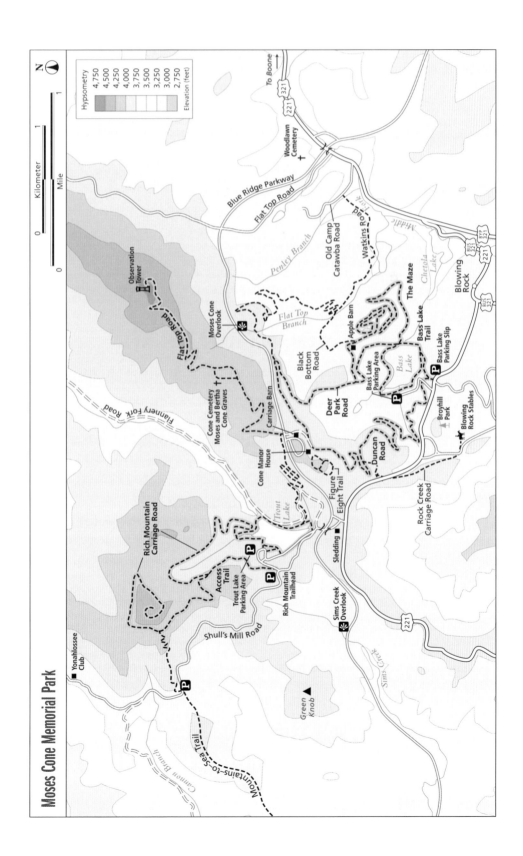

Moses Cone Memorial Park

Hypsometry

Elevation (feet)
- 4,750
- 4,500
- 4,250
- 4,000
- 3,750
- 3,500
- 3,250
- 3,000
- 2,750

N

Kilometer
0   1

Mile
0   1

To Boone

221 321

Woodlawn Cemetery

Blue Ridge Parkway

Flat Top Road

Penley Branch

Old Camp Catawba Road

Watkins Road

Middle Fork

Cherola Lake

Blowing Rock

BUS 321

BYP 321

221 321

BUS 321

Observation Tower

Flat Top Road

Moses Cone Overlook

Flat Top Branch

Black Bottom Road

Apple Barn

The Maze

Bass Lake Trail

Bass Lake Parking Slip

Deer Park Road

Bass Lake Parking Area

Bass Lake

Flannery Fork Road

Cone Cemetery
Moses and Bertha Cone Graves

Carriage Barn

Cone Manor House

Figure Eight Trail

Duncan Road

Broyhill Park

Blowing Rock Stables

Rock Creek Carriage Road

Rich Mountain Carriage Road

Trout Lake

Sledding

Access Trail

Trout Lake Parking Area

Rich Mountain Trailhead

Sims Creek Overlook

221

Yonahlossee Club

Shull's Mill Road

Green Knob

Sims Creek

Mountains-to-Sea Trail

Cannon Branch

Keep left another 0.2 mile to a T junction at 2.8 miles (here Deer Park Road leads right to the Manor House). Go left; at Bass Lake, 3.3 miles, bear right back across the dam. Go left to the US 221 parking slip, or stay along the shore if you started at the lower lot. Both hikes are 3.6 miles.

KEY POINTS

0.0   Start at the lakeshore lot. Walk counterclockwise around lake past the dam.

0.3   Turn into The Maze.

2.6   The Maze ends at the Apple Barn.

2.8   Turn left at T junction.

3.3   Bear left across Bass Lake dam, then head right along shore.

3.6   Arrive back at lakeshore lot.

RICH MOUNTAIN TRAIL

WHY GO?
The best hike to Cone Park's upland meadows, one option uses the Mountains-to-Sea Trail.

THE RUNDOWN

General location: Outside Blowing Rock
Distance: 5.2 miles out and back from the first trailhead; 3.6 miles out and back from the second trailhead
Difficulty: Moderate to strenuous

Maps: USGS Blowing Rock. See information for online handout map above; map also available at the Cone Manor House.
Elevation gain: 510 feet from first trailhead

FINDING THE TRAILHEAD
Both starts are on Shull's Mill Road, best reached from the US 221/Parkway junction 0.5 mile south of Cone Manor. Exit the Parkway at milepost 294.6 and take the first right on Shull's Mill Road (trip your odometer). Descend under the Parkway tunnel and bear left uphill to a trailhead on the right at 0.5 mile (GPS: 36.151772/-81.705153). The paved road downhill there is the exit (one way) for the Trout Lake parking area. For the Mountains-to-Sea Trail, drive another 1.3 miles and park on the left in the curve (GPS: 36.159649/-81.717901). The trail climbs steps up a bank across the road.

THE HIKE
Boone's baby-boomer locals used to call this Nowhere Mountain. By whatever name, Rich Mountain is a great hike or ski tour.

From the first trailhead on Shull's Mill Road, the carriage path access trail climbs steadily to a crest at about 0.6 mile. Bear left across the meadow on the upper part of

Cone Park's miles of atmospheric carriage roads are especially appealing when an autumn walk adds the rustling crunch of red and yellow leaves.

Rich Mountain Carriage Road. (Don't bear right; a lower section also descends to Trout Lake, a longer hike below.)

Beyond the meadow, the road passes a junction to the left with the Mountains-to-Sea Trail at 1.2 miles (cross the fence on a stile and it's 0.4 mile down to the second trailhead on Shull's Mill Road). Continuing, you leave the forest into a meadow at 1.7 miles. The trail corkscrews to the summit (4,370 feet) at 2.6 miles. Advanced hikers can wander the meadows going up or down—just avoid the obvious, eroding routes.

From the second trailhead, the steeper Mountains-to-Sea Trail climbs to the stile on the main path at 0.4 mile. Turn left—the peak is 1.4 miles distant, 1.8 miles from your car—for a 3.6-mile round-trip.

KEY POINTS

- 0.0   Start at the Rich Mountain Trailhead off Shull's Mill Road.
- 0.6   Bear left across the meadow onto Rich Mountain Carriage Road.
- 1.2   Mountains-to-Sea Trail goes left.
- 1.7   Enter summit meadow.
- 2.6   Reach the peak. Return the way you came.
- 5.2   Arrive back at the trailhead.

TROUT LAKE LOOP AND RICH MOUNTAIN CARRIAGE ROAD

WHY GO?

Trout Lake is far less visited than Bass Lake, and its shores are covered with an inspiring forest of towering hemlocks (sadly being killed by the hemlock woolly adelgid). This is a memorable lakeshore walk or ski trip.

THE RUNDOWN

General location: Outside Blowing Rock
Distance: 1-mile lakeshore loop; 2.6-mile circuit of lower Rich Mountain Carriage Road; 6.6-mile circuit to Rich Mountain summit

Difficulty: Easy for lake; moderate to strenuous for the longer walks
Maps: USGS Boone. See information for online handout map above; map also available at Cone Manor House.
Elevation gain: Negligible around lake; 610 feet to Rich Mountain

FINDING THE TRAILHEAD

Exit the Parkway at milepost 294.6 and turn right onto Shull's Mill Road. Pass through the Parkway tunnel and take the second, oblique right onto a one way road to the Trout Lake parking area (GPS: 36.152788 / -81.702959).

THE HIKE

From the edge of the Trout Lake parking area, take one of the two access trails that dip to the carriage road below and go right. Shortly take a left and walk the road you just drove in on. As you near Shull's Mill Road, turn left and dip into the woods again. At 0.5 mile reach Flannery Fork Road; go left to cross the dam. Stay left to continue through tall trees and glimpse a northern lakeshore scene. Avoid the major right turn at a small water impoundment; either of the next two side trails right leads uphill to the parking area for a 1-mile loop hike.

KEY POINTS

0.0   Start at edge of the Trout Lake parking area.

0.4   Carriage Road goes right; stay left.

0.7   At Flannery Fork Road, go left across the dam.

0.9   Rich Mountain Carriage Road goes right; stay left.

1.0   Arrive back at the parking area.

The proximity of Rich Mountain Carriage Road makes a more ambitious hike possible. To stroll beside the lake and explore the lower Rich Mountain Carriage Road, take a left from the parking area on the lakeshore for 0.3 mile. Go left at the first junction by the water enclosure on Rich Mountain Carriage Road. The trail passes through a gate

Moses Cone Park is a popular winter hiking and cross-country skiing spot. This stile links the steeper Mountains-to-Sea Trail from Shull's Mill Road with Cone Park's very skiable Rich Mountain Trail.

at 1.6 miles, soon exits the woods, and at 1.9 miles enters the meadow above the main Rich Mountain Trailhead on Shull's Mill Road. To the right, the road goes across the meadow to the summit.

Go left and down the carriage road access trail to Shull's Mill Road at 2.5 miles, then left on the parking area exit road (or cross that road and descend a portion of carriage road) to the Trout Lake parking area for a 2.6-mile hike. *Note:* If you go right at 3.9 miles to the summit of Rich Mountain then retrace your steps and descend to the Trout Lake parking area; it's a 6.6-mile circuit.

11 BLOWING ROCK

WHY GO?

The Glen Burney Trail makes it easy to leave your lodging on quaint village streets and descend into virgin timber and tumbling waterfalls. This trail has been in use since the earliest days of human habitation in the North Carolina mountains. Loggers used the path to commute through the Johns River Gorge between their homes on the heights to timber-harvesting operations at towns such as Edgemont. Formal trails were built in the late 1800s, when tourists first arrived to escape the hot flatlands of the South. Early guests at hotels such as the Green Park Inn, Blowing Rock's landmark hostelry, picnicked at Glen Burney Falls.

The scenic waterfall area the trail explores was donated to the town in the early part of the twentieth century. Portions of the trail were rebuilt with beautiful stonework by the CCC during the 1930s. Then public use was interrupted by vacation home development. A Sierra Club coordinated group of mid-1980s trail volunteers upgraded the path. The author and Kinney Baughman, a principal builder of Granfather Mountain's Profile Trail (along with Jim Morton) reopened Glen Burney in 1991 under conservation grants. The trail starts beside a beautiful downtown park complex that includes a lake, shoreline jogging, and barrier-free trails.

THE RUNDOWN

General location: Blowing Rock
Distance: 3 miles round-trip
Difficulty: Moderately strenuous
Maps: USGS Boone. Download a hiking map at http://www.townofblowingrocknc.gov/home/showdocument?id=1834.
Elevation gain: 800 feet

Water availability: Spring box on trail at falls view (treat); various places in town
For more information: Blowing Rock Chamber of Commerce, 132 Park Ave., Blowing Rock 28605; (828) 295-7851; www.blowingrock.com

FINDING THE TRAILHEAD

From the US 321 bypass in Blowing Rock, turn at the traffic light onto Sunset Drive toward downtown. At the traffic light facing the town park, turn left onto Main Street. In 0.1 mile turn right onto Laurel Lane. At the Wallingford Lane stop sign, in 0.2 mile, go straight and immediately turn left at 0.3 mile into the Annie Cannon Gardens Trailhead (GPS: 36.132529 / -81.680595).

THE HIKE

The venerable old Glen Burney Trail leaves the landscaped parking area, crosses New Years Creek, and follows the stream amid towering beech and hemlock on a level, road-width path.

Dipping left from the grade, the path descends a series of switchbacks into the gorge below. The trail passes a concrete-and-stone structure built in the 1920s, one of the first

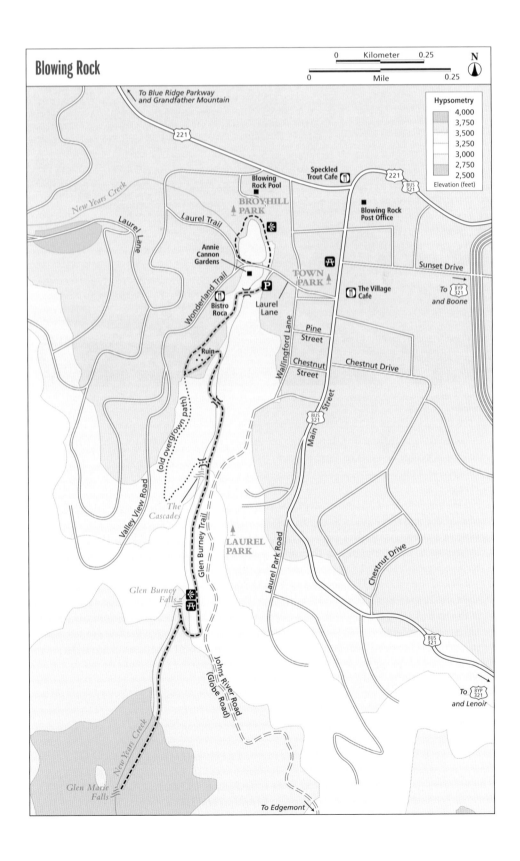

Blowing Rock

Kilometer

0   0.25

0   Mile   0.25

N

Hypsometry

4,000
3,750
3,500
3,250
3,000
2,750
2,500

Elevation (feet)

To Blue Ridge Parkway
and Grandfather Mountain

221

New Years Creek

Laurel Lane

Laurel Trail

Blowing
Rock Pool

Speckled
Trout Cafe

221

BUS
321

BROYHILL
PARK

Blowing Rock
Post Office

Annie
Cannon
Gardens

Wonderland Trail

P

Bistro
Roca

Laurel
Lane

Sunset Drive

TOWN
PARK

The Village
Cafe

To BYP
321
and Boone

Wallingford Lane

Ruin

Pine
Street

Chestnut
Street

Chestnut Drive

Main Street

BUS
321

(old overgrown path)

The
Cascades

Glen Burney Trail

LAUREL
PARK

Laurel Park Road

Chestnut Drive

Valley View Road

BYP
321

Glen Burney
Falls

Johns River Road
(Globe Road)

To BYP
321
and Lenoir

New Years Creek

Glen Marie
Falls

To Edgemont

Don't stray beyond the snowy view platform if you hike to Blowing Rock's Glen Burney Falls in winter.

modern sewage treatment plants in the mountains. Descend among towering hemlocks to cross a bridge and follow a graded, not very rocky treadway above the rushing stream. Emerge at The Cascades, about 0.8 mile from the parking area (a 1.6-mile round-trip hike).

Heading left down the stone steps, the trail skirts The Cascades, with nice views back toward the waterfall. At the next junction, go right past a trickling spring box and picnic table to an observation deck perched atop the falls. (People have died here, so stay within the railing to avoid slipping on the top of the treacherous falls.) This is a premier place to have a picnic, about 1 mile from the parking area.

Back at the junction, go right, away from the stream, to a fork. Left reaches a road; go right. After a steep descent on old stone steps, reach a T junction. Turn right to the pool at the base of Glen Burney Falls, or go left to Glen Marie Falls, 1.6 miles from the parking area. The trail to Glen Marie Falls switchbacks between views at the top (do not pass the old cable barrier), middle (great view—good turnaround spot), and bottom. Below that lies private property.

12 ELK RIVER FALLS TRAIL

WHY GO?

This spectacular hike leads to 65-foot Big Falls, more often called Elk River Falls, and its cliff-encircled pool.

THE RUNDOWN

General location: Elk Park
Distance: 0.5 mile out and back
Difficulty: Moderate (for steepness)
Map: USGS Elk Park
Elevation gain: 100 feet
Water availability: No water at the trailhead; hikers accessing the trail through the town of Elk Park can find water there.

For more information: Appalachian Ranger District, 632 Manor Rd., Mars Hill 28754; (828) 689-9694; e-mail: appalachianrd@fs.fed.us

FINDING THE TRAILHEAD

The trail is reached via back roads from the town of Elk Park, on US 19E near the North Carolina–Tennessee border. From Newland take NC 194, then US 19E, for 8.3 miles through Elk Park to a right turn onto SR 1303 (at an Elk River Falls sign). Measuring from this turn, go left at 0.3 mile onto Elk River Road, SR 1305. At 2.5 miles continue straight on SR 1305 as SR 1306 goes left across a bridge. Cross a bridge at 3.8 miles, enter the national forest at 4.1 miles, and reach the parking area at 4.3 miles from US 19E (GPS: 36.196963 / -81.969944).

THE HIKE

This short waterfall hike is tucked into an isolated tract of Pisgah National Forest near Tennessee. Area trailheads have had vehicle break-ins, so don't leave anything of value in your car. This yellow-blazed trail is a popular 0.5-mile round-trip saunter after church on Sunday for local families. The parking lot is lined with grills and picnic tables (no camping), and a scenic, fishable river flows by.

The Elk River Falls Trail leaves the north end of the parking lot, ascends a flight of steps, and then dips into a tall, streamside forest of hemlock and rhododendron along the Elk River. This is a level walk that passes a bench before reaching the head of the falls.

From here, daring—perhaps stupid—students from local colleges occasionally leap into the pool, a heart-stopping, body-thumping 65 feet below. Don't do it. A slip near the falls, without the right momentum, could kill, and it routinely does, so often that the fatalities regularly make the news. Stay off the rocks and descend the flights of steps beside the cliff face. At the bottom, the path leads out of the woods onto a rocky bar with a great view of a large pool and a horseshoe-shaped canyon hemmed in by sheer cliffs. The waterfall plummets straight down, creating a spectacular sight even during relatively dry periods. It also creates a truly turbulent plunge basin that, yep, you guessed it, has also caused drownings. If you're a daredevil for whom all that sounds like an excuse to tempt fate, local first responders kindly request that you pick a different hike.

13 ROAN MOUNTAIN

Roan Mountain has two major summits, both just under 6,290 feet, but that's just a small part of a massive ridge that extends to the northeast that makes up the namesake massif known as the Roan Highlands.

The Roan area is most synonymous with the grassy, alpine-appearing summits called the Southern Balds (see the Appalachian Trail section). Actually, balds come in two varieties—grassy and heath, the latter covered in dense, shrubby vegetation like rhododendron, mountain laurel, blueberries, and other heath-community plants. The mountaineers called them "slicks," and they look that way from a distance. They were also called "hells," and you'd know why if you ever bushwhacked through one.

The garden-like grassy mix of meadows and rhododendrons on Roan is artfully explained in one Native American legend. The tale holds that the Catawba Indians challenged the tribes of Earth to a great battle; the ensuing struggle denuded the summits. Where every Catawba brave fell, a rhododendron blossomed blood-red as a memorial. Appropriately, the red rhododendron found on these heights is the Catawba rhododendron.

The late-June rhododendron bloom is one of the Southern Appalachians' premier natural events, celebrated by festivals in North Carolina and Tennessee. Theories about the balds speculate that fires, perhaps created by Native Americans, claimed the trees and made the soil unsuitable for reforestation. There is sentiment also that the balds have been in existence for thousands of years—perhaps starting with fire and then being maintained by the grazing of buffalo and elk. Later, Appalachian mountaineers used them for grazing. A quarter-century ago, revegetation of the balds may have gotten a helping hand when the forest service acquired the land and grazing was curtailed.

By the mid-1980s, a conference was called to weigh the future of the balds and "the alarms really went off," says Paul Bradley, a former Pisgah National Forest district ranger for the area that includes Roan Mountain. "Scientists, forest service officials, and the public realized that if we didn't start doing something immediately, we'd lose the balds." A loss it would be. The Southern Balds shelter one of the greatest concentrations of rare plants in the Southern Appalachians.

The statistics were ominous. Of 2,500 bald acres on Roan and adjoining summits, 1,641 acres had started growing in. The reforestation appeared to be a natural process. Environmentalists usually averse to manipulating the environment joined the chorus of concern. Everyone agreed that activities like grazing were helping endangered species survive. Among those are sedges that add to the alpine look of the meadows. The forest service set out to maintain 1,000 acres of the balds and reclaim another 1,600. Today, grazing and mowing help that process.

The mountain has long attracted hikers. Early explorer and botanist Asa Gray called it "the most beautiful mountain east of the Rockies." In 1877 the first tourist accommodation was built on the peak. Between 1885 and 1915, the 166-room Cloudland Hotel attracted visitors, who rode trains to nearby stations and then took stagecoaches up the last 4 miles on a road now part of the Appalachian Trail (see the Cloudland Trail entry). The mountain was horribly logged, but it's hard to imagine that now.

Roan Mountain State Park, just below the peak, is a wonderful resource for hikers. The park has a tent/RV campground, rustic cabins, a pool, picnic sites, and natural history programming that culminates during the rhododendron festival and spring and fall naturalists' rallies. Through the 1980s the park maintained a cross-country ski center that eventually closed. Nevertheless, Roan averages about 130 inches of annual snowfall and easily offers the Deep South's best cross-country skiing and snow camping (hikers, and snowshoers, please don't walk in ski tracks). With an eye on the weather, it isn't difficult to go cross-country skiing in Dixie. For much more on winter recreation in the North Carolina Mountains and the South, see *Southern Snow: The New Guide to Winter Sports from Maryland to the Southern Appalachians* by Randy Johnson (randyjohnsonbooks.com). This updated, expanded second edition of the author's 1986 "cult classic" ski book was published in 2019 by the University of North Carolina Press.

RHODODENDRON GARDENS NATIONAL RECREATION TRAIL

WHY GO?
This easy, paved, wheelchair-accessible National Recreation Trail wanders through rhododendron gardens.

THE RUNDOWN

General location: Roan Mountain, near Carvers Gap on the North Carolina–Tennessee border
Distance: 1.2-mile round trip
Difficulty: Easy, partly barrier-free
Map: USGS Bakersville
Elevation gain: Negligible
Water availability: There is a water fountain at the trailhead contact station and a trailhead restroom open late spring through early fall.
For more information: Appalachian Ranger District, 632 Manor Rd., Mars Hill 28754; (828) 689-9694; e-mail: appalachianrd@fs.fed.us
Roan Mountain State Park: (423) 772-0190; tnstateparks.com/parks/about/roan-mountain

FINDING THE TRAILHEAD
The trail is reached from Carvers Gap on the North Carolina–Tennessee state line. From near Newland, North Carolina, go west into Tennessee about 5 miles on US 19E, then left on TN 143 in the town of Roan Mountain. From Asheville and more southerly areas, take NC 261 from Bakersville to Carvers Gap. From there a paved summit road leads up the mountain (SR 1348) . That road is open from Memorial Day to late September; a nominal fee is charged. After passing the fee station, avoid parking lot #1 on the right and go left a few tenths of a mile on a gravel road (FR 130). About 1.7 miles from Carvers Gap, pull into parking lot #2 on the left (GPS: 36.101881/-82.135092).

THE HIKE
The 1.2-mile Rhododendron Gardens National Recreation Trail forms three loops. It leaves parking lot #2 beside picnic tables and a small contact station with restrooms. The uppermost loop is a flat, barrier-free 0.3-mile paved trail that wanders through Canadian

The third week in June finds "the Roan's" rhododendron gardens in world-class bloom.

Zone forest to an observation deck with spectacular views of blooming rhododendron in season. Branching from the upper loop is a lower, 1-mile figure-eight trail through the rhododendron, the uppermost loop of which is also paved. This is the best wheelchair-accessible spruce-fir forest trail in the Southern Appalachians. It is rarely warm at this elevation and often quite chilly, even in summer. By mid-August, bees cling sluggishly to goldenrod swaying in chill breezes. Elderberry, blueberry, gooseberry, mountain ash, red spruce, and Fraser fir round out a forest that drips with the feel of the far north. On foggy days, wind-whipped mist and clouds ebb and flow. New England's highest peak, Mount Washington, is only 2 feet loftier than Roan Mountain.

Connections before and after the view deck link to the upper of the two lower loops. At the four-way junction below, continue down the lower loop through rhododendron accented by soaring black spikes of red spruce. Returning across the four-way junction, reenter the barrier-free trail and take the uppermost section of trail you missed back past the contact station to your car.

In winter this deeply snow-drifted area is an awesome and popular cross-country ski site that requires a nearly 2-mile ski up the gated road from Carvers Gap. A round-trip ski-tour is about 5 miles from Carvers Gap. The upper loop is suitable for beginners; the lower two require more snow and better turning ability.

CLOUDLAND TRAIL

WHY GO?
A high-altitude family hike leads through spruce-fir forest across the crest of Roan Mountain to Roan High Bluff. An Appalachian Trail (AT) section can be added.

THE RUNDOWN

General location: Carvers Gap
Distance: 3-mile round-trip, with a 1-mile option. Adding the AT section creates a 7.5-mile round-trip hike or ski.
Difficulty: Easy for the Cloudland Trail; strenuous for the AT addition
Maps: USGS Carvers Gap and Bakersville
Elevation gain: About 100 feet gained on the main hike; 900 feet with the AT
Water availability: There are warm-weather water fountains adjacent to the trailhead restrooms at the forest service's Cloudland parking/picnic area and at the Rhododendron Gardens contact station/restroom; both open early summer through early fall. Water is also available from a spring behind Roan High Knob shelter, just off the AT.
For more information: Appalachian Ranger District, 632 Manor Rd., Mars Hill 28754; (828) 689-9694; e-mail: appalachianrd@fs.fed.us

FINDING THE TRAILHEAD

See Rhododendron Gardens National Recreation Trail entry for getting to Roan Mountain.

For the AT, park along the fence line in Carvers Gap or in the tiny parking area with a modern vault toilet (GPS: 36.106414/-82.111224). For the Cloudland Trail, take the paved summit road (open Memorial Day to late September) up the mountain (SR 1348) from Carvers Gap past the fee station. Go right at 1.7 miles into parking lot #1, the main Cloudland Trailhead (GPS: 36.104361/-82.133122).

To reach several other Cloudland parking areas across the mountain's crest, go left at parking lot #1 on gravel FR 130. Pass the Rhododendron Gardens Trail on the left at 1.8 miles. Pass parking lot #3 on the right to enter the road's final loop. The last trailhead is at 2.3 miles, where the road curves back and the path quickly reaches Roan High Bluff (GPS: 36.096145/-82.139642).

THE HIKE

The walks—or great cross-country ski trips—described here explore lush evergreen forests. In summer, cool breezes hiss through the spruces and mist rolls across the meadows. In fall, evergreens contrast with electric mountain ash and yellow birch. Winter at these heights is often a fairyland of frost-feathered trees and deep drifts.

Start the Cloudland Trail at parking lot #1 with a wonderful view into east Tennessee. The wide trail enters the trees and climbs past a rightward side trail to a view. The yellow-blazed trail levels into the open past parking lot #2 and gradually descends along FR 130 through rhododendron to parking lot #3. Turn right just before reaching the lot; the trail parallels the lot to cross the road (about 0.7 mile) and bisect the end loop of FR 130.

Roan Mountain

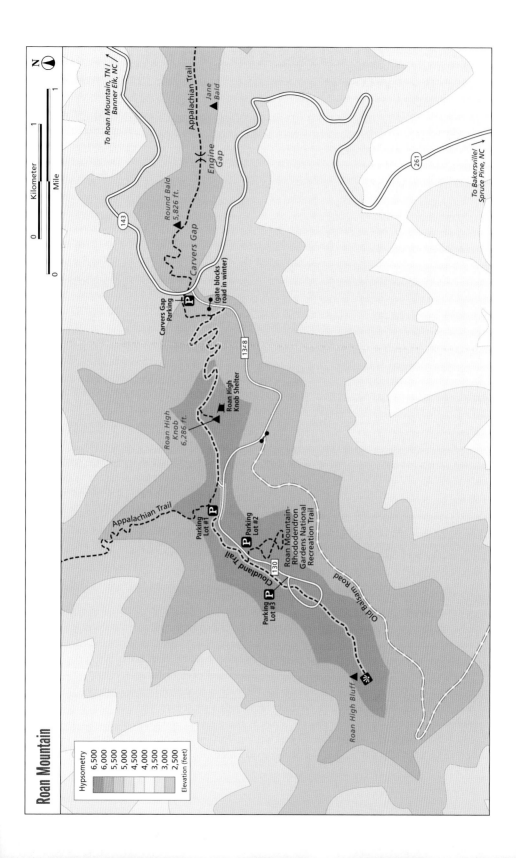

Hypsometry

Elevation (feet)
6,500
6,000
5,500
5,000
4,500
4,000
3,500
3,000
2,500

N

0   1   Kilometer
0   1   Mile

To Roan Mountain, TN /
Banner Elk, NC

Appalachian Trail

Jane Bald ▲

Engine Gap

Round Bald
5,826 ft. ▲

Carvers Gap

261

To Bakersville /
Spruce Pine, NC

143

Carvers Gap Parking P

(gate blocks road in winter)

13·8

Roan High Knob Shelter ▪

Roan High Knob
6,286 ft. ▲

Appalachian Trail

Parking Lot #1 P

Cloudland Trail

Parking Lot #2 P

130

Roan Mountain
Rhododendron
Gardens National
Recreation Trail

Parking Lot #3 P

Old Balsam Road

Roan High Bluff ▲

Carvers Gap, with easy access to the Appalachian Trail and Roan Mountain, is also a welcome to winter for Southerners in search of snow.

The last stretch of Cloudland beyond the FR 130 end loop is about 0.5 mile. This short, steeper, curvy section makes a moderate 1-mile round-trip hike or advanced ski to great views at an observation deck atop Roan High Bluff. Views reach down 4,000 feet to the valley and back to Roan High Knob (6,286 feet), the mountain's highest summit, accessible by the Appalachian Trail. See page 1 for a photo of this view point.

To lengthen the hike and include that summit, take the white-blazed AT into the woods near the privy at Carvers Gap. (If you're skiing, step around the Carvers Gap gate on the summit road, ski 100 yards uphill, and turn right on an AT access path that avoids the unskiable lower section.) The AT above is a road-width carriage path used in the late nineteenth/early twentieth century to ferry guests up to the Cloudland Hotel. It climbs gradually up switchbacks through verdant evergreen forest and crests at 1.5 miles, where a 0.1-mile side trail left reaches Roan High Knob shelter. The enclosed CCC-built cabin sleeps about eight. The AT dips beyond this crest to SR 1348, the road up Roan, in about 2 miles. Skiers should head higher on the summit road to connect to parking lot #1 and the Cloudland Trail. Hikers continue on the AT but before the trail descends steeply into Tennessee, bear left 0.2 mile to parking lot # 1 and the start of the Cloudland Trail.

The ski routes above, and adjacent trails, constitute some of the best cross-country skiing in the South. Search 'cross country ski Roan Mountain' on YouTube for the author's ski video.

14 TANAWHA TRAIL

Costly trail- and road-building techniques were required to minimize impact when the Blue Ridge Parkway finally crossed the fragile side of Grandfather Mountain. The road opened on September 11, 1987, and, with it, the Tanawha Trail, a crowning achievement of the Blue Ridge Parkway trail network.

Hikers won't fail to notice an astounding number of intricate stone stairways, rock-paved treadways, and laminated wood bridges (lowered by helicopter), all designed to minimize hiker damage to this scenic environment. The feds spent almost $750,000 on the 13.5 miles of trail between Beacon Heights, near Linville, and Price Park Camp-ground, near Blowing Rock.

In one spot, the road leaps away from the mountain on a multimillion-dollar, computer-designed space-age span called the Linn Cove Viaduct. The famous segmented bridge was built with each ensuing section affixed to the one before it—over thin air.

Perhaps the best views on the Tanawha Trail are from Rough Ridge, a high outcrop where boardwalks and handrails are required to keep the public from trampling the low, alpine-like vegetation, some of it rare and endangered.

The hikes described below focus on the grandest vistas from the trail, but hikers can hike the Tanawha end to end, and beyond, as this is now part of the Mountains-to-Sea Trail. Camping is permitted only at designated sites on the Parkway; to make a multiday trip possible, backpackers must camp in Grandfather Mountain State Park and at either Price Park Campground or the Price Park backcountry campsite (see the Boone Fork Trail entry in Price Park). (Reservations for either of the latter campsites are required from the campground check-in kiosk at Price Park.)

TANAWHA TRAIL HIKES ON GRANDFATHER MOUNTAIN

WHY GO?

A variety of easy hikes, one accessible to wheelchairs, lead to great views, including the Linn Cove Viaduct and two ways to scale the peak of Rough Ridge.

THE RUNDOWN

General location: Blue Ridge Parkway, near Grandfather Mountain
Distance: 0.3-mile round-trip for barrier-free trail; 1-mile round-trip to views of the viaduct. Another 0.3-mile hike reaches boardwalk views. An end-to-end walk of the trail section is 2.7 miles; round-trip hikes of 1.1 and 2 miles lead to the peak of Rough Ridge.
Difficulty: Easy and barrier-free for paved trail under viaduct; moderately strenuous for all others
Maps: USGS Grandfather Mountain. Download a parkway handout map of Tanawha Trail at the "Brochures"

link on the Blue Ridge Parkway's website (see below). Maps are also available at the Linn Cove Visitor Center. The Grandfather Mountain attraction hiking map shows the trail best and can be downloaded from the attraction's website (see below) or picked up free at the Grandfather Mountain attraction entrance. From the Linn Cove Visitor Center, go south 0.7 mile. Exit onto US 221 and go right 1 mile to entrance.

Elevation gain: 480 feet from Rough Ridge parking area to peak; about 540 feet from Wilson Creek Overlook

Water availability: May through September, the Linn Cove Visitor Center has water and restrooms. The Grandfather Mountain entrance has water year-round. Water is plentiful along the trail (treat before using).

For more information: Blue Ridge Parkway, 199 Hemphill Knob Rd., Asheville 28803-8686; (828) 271-4779; (828) 298-0398 (recorded information and mailing requests); nps.gov/blri

Grandfather Mountain, PO Box 129, Linville 28646; (800) 468-7325; (828) 733-2013; grandfather.com

FINDING THE TRAILHEAD

The trailheads are located on the Blue Ridge Parkway, just north of the US 221 entrance to the Parkway, 3 miles east of Linville and 12.6 miles south of US 321 in Blowing Rock. The Linn Cove Visitor Center trailhead is at milepost 304.4 (GPS: 36.090784 / -81.814063); Wilson Creek Overlook at milepost 303.6 (GPS: 36.100526 / -81.808748); Rough Ridge parking area at milepost 302.8 (GPS: 36.098359 / -81.797124).

THE HIKES

The easiest walk to a view of the Linn Cove Viaduct begins at the Linn Cove Visitor Center, where displays explain the technical and natural history behind this amazing portion of the Parkway. A paved and barrier-free trail winds from the far end of the parking lot for 0.15 mile to a viewpoint beneath the viaduct.

For the next-easiest viaduct walk, stay on the trail beyond the pavement to the level of the bridge and zigzag under cliffs, through a jumble of huge boulders, and amid towering hemlocks. The viaduct soars beside you, evidenced by the occasional *whoosh* and thump of a passing car. The trail leaves the Linn Cove stream drainage; at 0.5 mile at a sign, turn right amid rhododendron to a roadside boulder for an oft-photographed postcard view back at the bridge (1-mile round-trip).

From the viaduct, the Tanawha Trail undulates across the flank of the mountain to its scenic and popular highpoint at Rough Ridge. This cliff-bordered crag is popular with rock climbers, who call it Ship Rock. The sparse, alpine-like vegetation on the crest permits spectacular 360-degree views.

The most direct route to the summit of Rough Ridge is from the parking area of the same name. Ascend steps and decking to turn left and cross an arching wooden bridge (pets must be kept on leash). A right turn leads 4 miles north, around Pilot Knob and down through luxuriant spruces, past Boulder Field Overlook to Boone Fork Overlook.

The trail climbs Rough Ridge amid blueberry bushes and galax and then turns a corner, passes a fascinating stack rock formation, and wanders 200 feet of boardwalk designed to keep hikers from trampling the low vegetation. This may be the easiest Parkway path to an awesome view. From this boardwalk, just 0.3 mile from the parking area (0.6 mile round-trip), the view is remarkably similar to that from the summit—another

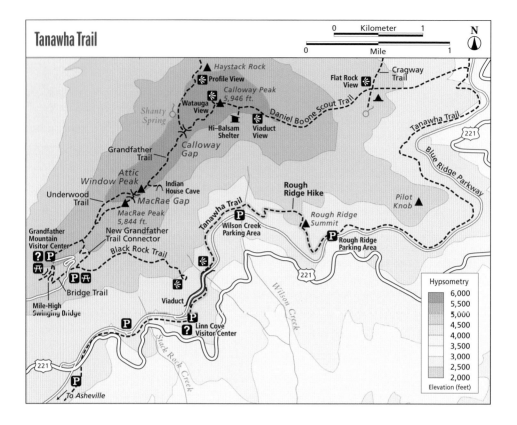

Tanawha Trail

Haystack Rock
Profile View
Calloway Peak
5,946 ft.
Watauga View
Shanty Spring
Hi-Balsam Shelter
Viaduct View
Grandfather Trail
Calloway Gap
Daniel Boone Scout Trail
Flat Rock View
Cragway Trail
Tanawha Trail
221
Blue Ridge Parkway
Attic Window Peak
Indian House Cave
Underwood Trail
MacRae Gap
MacRae Peak 5,844 ft.
Rough Ridge Hike
Pilot Knob
Grandfather Mountain Visitor Center
New Grandfather Trail Connector
Tanawha Trail
Wilson Creek Parking Area
Rough Ridge Summit
Rough Ridge Parking Area
Black Rock Trail
221
Bridge Trail
Mile-High Swinging Bridge
Viaduct
Wilson Creek
Linn Cove Visitor Center
Black Rock Creek
221
To Asheville

Hypsometry
6,000
5,500
5,000
4,500
4,000
3,500
3,000
2,500
2,000
Elevation (feet)

0.3 mile ahead up rocky, moderate switchbacks (1.2 miles round-trip). From either location, it's easy to watch a sunset and get back to your car quickly. This vista engulfs you. Above, the three highest summits of Grandfather Mountain reach a dramatic climax. From the highest, Calloway Peak (5,946 feet, farthest right), the Wilson Creek drainage drops like a chute past Rough Ridge (where you're standing), Black Rock Cliffs (to the south, above the viaduct), and Pilot Knob (behind you). Mount Mitchell lies left and south on the horizon. This is the greatest single rise of the Blue Ridge escarpment. The Piedmont flattens almost a vertical mile below the peaks, beyond the rippling corduroy of Pisgah National Forest.

For a longer hike that avoids the crowds, start at Wilson Creek Overlook and hike under the bridge and into the woods above the road. At the Tanawha Trail, go right and cross Wilson Creek. The trail dips below an outcrop within sight of the road and then climbs across boulder fields with towering trees and inspiring spring wildflowers. You'll reach a saddle where stone steps artfully surmount the crag-capped summit of Rough Ridge, about 1 mile from the Wilson Creek parking area (2 miles round-trip). If you left another car below at the Rough Ridge parking area, descend for a 1.6-mile hike. If you didn't leave a car there, return to your starting point. Or, descend to the Parkway and it's a still-pleasant 0.8-mile roadside walk back to Wilson Creek Overlook for a 2.4-miler.

15 GRANDFATHER MOUNTAIN STATE PARK AND ATTRACTION

Grandfather Mountain's public image has evolved over the years. Once almost exclusively seen as a tourist attraction owned by noted North Carolinian Hugh Morton, Grandfather has become synonymous with its spectacular backcountry. The Mile-High Swinging Bridge is still a popular attraction reached by car, but there have been plenty of changes since Morton passed away in 2006. The bulk of the mountain became a North Carolina state park in 2008, and tourist development transitioned to a nonprofit stewardship foundation in 2009. The mountain's now publicly owned highest peaks are laced with a wonderful network of trails that tower over the attraction. The once-ignored backcountry hiking network experienced a renaissance in the late 1970s when the author's fee-based hiking program reopened and reclaimed the trails that had been closed after a hiker died of hypothermia. Over the years, the pay-for-use trail system became an innovative example of wilderness management, and hiking and nature appreciation emerged as a now preeminent part of the Grandfather Mountain experience.

Growing scientific research has since revealed the mountain to be one of eastern America's premier natural areas. The mountain's 4,000 acres boast forty-three species of rare or endangered plants and animals, more than Great Smoky Mountains National Park. In 1993 Grandfather became the nation's only privately owned biosphere reserve designated by the United Nations. That's just the latest chapter in the mountain's long history—a stirring saga related in the author's 2016 book, *Grandfather Mountain: The History and Guide to an Appalachian Icon.*

It's a rocky climb up the Cragway Trail, but when you finally get to Top Crag, an all-encompassing view surveys the Boone Fork Bowl (right), Calloway Peak (above left), and the Piedmont far below. COURTESY OF VISIT NC.COM.

Hikers should keep in mind that the state park and the attraction are different entities with different policies (visit the park and attraction websites). Under state park management, the trail fees were ended, but a camping fee has been reinstated and campsite reservations are required in advance (877-722-6762 or reserveamerica.com). A day hiking permit is also required, but it's free and available at trailheads (except the rules are a little different on trails that start inside the attraction). The attraction closes at night, so the permit notes that no camping is permitted from there unless you are dropped off. Do not leave your car overnight inside the attraction, and be sure to return from your day hike by the noted time on the trail signs. Hikers walking into the attraction from the state park are not charged, but be aware that it's a very long day hike and there is no walking allowed on the road. Hikers reaching the attraction must expect to hike back or be picked up (their ride will be charged to enter).

Hikers should be alert to weather conditions at Grandfather Mountain. People have died on the mountain from exposure, lightning strikes, falls, and heart attacks. The mountain is known for snowy winters and year-round high winds.

TANAWHA TRAIL AND DANIEL BOONE SCOUT TRAIL TO CALLOWAY PEAK

WHY GO?

The Daniel Boone Scout Trail climbs to Calloway Peak. Two other view-packed trails also start on the Tanawha Trail from the Blue Ridge Parkway, one a nice beginning backpacking trip.

THE RUNDOWN

General location: Off the Blue Ridge Parkway, about 20 miles west of Blowing Rock

Distance: 7.2 mile out-and-back hike to Calloway Peak on the Boone Trail; 3.9-mile round-trip hike on the Cragway Trail; 3.2 miles out and back on the Nuwati Trail

Difficulty: Strenuous for the Boone Trail to Calloway Peak and for the Cragway circuit; moderate for the Nuwati Trail

Maps: USGS Grandfather Mountain. The best map for the hike is the Grandfather Mountain attraction trail map, downloadable from the attraction website and available free at the Grandfather Mountain entrance (south on the Parkway from Boone Fork parking area 5.2 miles to US 221 exit, right 1 mile to entrance). The state park trail map is available at trailhead registration signs. The Parkway's Tanawha Trail handout map is available at the Linn Cove Visitor Center and online from the Parkway's "Brochures" page.

Elevation gain: 2,044 feet for the climb to Calloway Peak; 1,040 feet for the Cragway circuit; 580 feet for the Nuwati Trail

Water availability: Springs cited in text; treat all water before using.

For more information: Grandfather Mountain State Park: (828) 963-9522; ncparks.gov/Visit/parks/grmo/main.php; attraction: (828) 733-4337; grandfather.com

Rough Ridge is one of the mountains' true beauty spots—and very easy to reach, to boot.

FINDING THE TRAILHEAD

The best starting point for all these hikes is the Boone Fork parking area on the Blue Ridge Parkway (GPS: 36.119889/-81.781553). An alternative, especially in winter when snow closes the Parkway, is the Asutsi Trail, which starts on US 221, 8.5 miles north of the Grandfather Mountain entrance and 1.5 miles south of the US 221/Holloway Mountain Road junction south of Blowing Rock (GPS: 36.116333/-81.777285).

THE HIKES

Looking east from Calloway Peak, the dramatic vertical drop of nearly a mile is one of the South's most noteworthy vistas. Part-time Parkway ranger Clyde Smith and a Blowing Rock Boy Scout troop built a primitive trail up this wild side of the mountain during World War II, but it had become only a memory until the Grandfather Mountain trail program referenced above reclaimed it in 1979 along with a half-century-old backpacking shelter. By the early 1980s, two new trails were added in the bowl-shaped valley beneath Calloway Peak that was once thought to be a glacial cirque like those in New England. That conclusion was based on "glacial grooves" that were later discovered to have been left by logging cables.

Starting at the Parkway's Boone Fork parking area, the connector to the Tanawha Trail leaves the lot, goes right at the first junction, then left at the next on the Tanawha Trail to cross the laminated bridge spanning the creek. The Asutsi Trail connector to US 221 branches left just over the bridge (0.4 mile to US 221) and just before the state park registration sign. At 0.4 mile, take a right on the blue circle–blazed Nuwati Trail and follow the level but rocky trail up an old logging railroad grade. A spring gushes at 0.7 mile as the trail becomes a scenic rhododendron tunnel fringed by ferns. At 1.1 miles the Cragway Trail goes left. Continuing Nuwati crosses numerous streams past campsites on the left. (Notice where a large logging cable, the cause of the "ice-carved" grooves, is held firm in the V of a tree.)

Historic Hi-Balsam Shelter has been protecting campers near Calloway Peak for three-quarters of a century.

Cross Boone Fork at 1 mile. A tent platform is off to the left before a fork. A right dead-ends at a campsite; a left rises steeply to prominent Storyteller's Rock, projecting above the valley floor at 4,500 feet, 1.6 miles from the trailhead. The 360-degree panorama encompasses the entire high-mountain valley.

The Nuwati Trail gains only about 600 feet in 1.6 miles, so it's a good beginning backpacking trip for trailside campsites and spectacular scenery. Storyteller's Rock makes a nice evening viewpoint.

The best way to hike the steep, orange circle–blazed Cragway Trail is down. Where the Nuwati Trail turns right off the Tanawha Trail (above), continue on Tanawha and at 0.6 mile go right on the white diamond–blazed Daniel Boone Scout Trail. After a gradual, switchbacking climb, the trail emerges between two rock outcroppings at 2 miles. The Daniel Boone Scout Trail continues left 0.1 mile to a group of tent platforms at about the centerpoint on the trail. To the right, Cragway descends to the Nuwati Trail. Go right, but first ascend Flat Rock View, a table-flat vantage point and perfect lunch spot.

Going right on Cragway, the trail winds along open crags, reenters woods, and emerges into a heath bald of blueberry bushes and rhododendron at Top Crag. Be careful to avoid further impact on the alpine-like Allegheny sand myrtle growing here. This view is one of the best on the mountain.

The path descends rocky crags with great views. Take a right on the Nuwati Trail (3 miles from the start), then a left on Tanawha, and the round-trip back to the Boone Fork parking area is 4 miles. If you go left first and include Storyteller's Rock before hiking out, the round-trip is 5 miles.

To reach Calloway Peak, hike the Daniel Boone Scout Trail as above and at about 2 miles pause at the middle campsite, where a side trail leads 100 yards to a spring. The Boone Trail switchbacks higher in and out of a scenic red spruce forest. At the crest of Pilot Ridge is a nice campsite on the left. Continuing, the trail enters the spruce-fir forest zone—a dark, cool evergreen area carpeted with moss and wood sorrel. After a side trip to Viaduct View, a second side trail left, at about 3.3 miles, leads to Hi-Balsam Shelter, a tiny low-lying lean-to that sleeps five (no tent camping or fires).

The Daniel Boone Scout Trail continues past a designated campsite on the left (fires permitted). At the campsite, look off in the woods to the right of the trail to see the remains of a plane that crashed in 1978. Then the trail stands on end, climbing steeply with the aid of one large ladder to Calloway Peak (5,946 feet; marked by an X), 3.6 miles from the trailhead. The panoramic view takes in the dramatic drop to the Piedmont.

The Boone Trail terminates about 0.1 mile away, across a rocky, evergreen-covered crest, at the blue diamond–blazed Grandfather Trail and Watauga (wa–TAW-ga) View, the best vantage point to the west. Backtracking, the hike is about 7.2 miles. It's virtually the same distance if you descend the Cragway Trail on the way down.

KEY POINTS

0.0   Start from the Boone Fork parking area.

0.4   Tanawha Trail junction with Nuwati Trail.

0.6   Right onto Daniel Boone Scout Trail.

2.0   Junction with Cragway Trail.

3.3   Hi-Balsam Shelter.

3.6   Calloway Peak.

7.2   Arrive back at the parking lot.

GRANDFATHER TRAIL

WHY GO?

One of the South's most rugged, spectacular, and storied trails scales ladders over cliffs to reach Calloway Peak, the mountain's highest summit.

THE RUNDOWN

General location: Off the Blue Ridge Parkway, about 20 miles west of Blowing Rock
Distance: 2 miles over the first major peak; 4.8 miles out and back to Calloway Peak
Difficulty: Strenuous

Maps: USGS Grandfather Mountain. The best map for the hike is the free trail map available from the Grandfather Mountain attraction (see below).
Elevation gain: About 840 feet from the summit parking area for the

loop of MacRae Peak; 1,800 feet to Calloway Park and back, returning on the Underwood Trail
Water availability: Spring cited in text; treat all water before using.

For more information: Grandfather Mountain State Park: (828) 963-9522 / 877-722-6762 or reserveamerica .com; ncparks.gov/Visit/parks/grmo/ main.php; attraction: (828) 733-4337; grandfather.com

FINDING THE TRAILHEAD

Start at the top of the Grandfather Mountain motor road. The historic start is opposite the summit visitor center (GPS: 36.096179 / -81.831769), but to preserve parking for motorists, park lower down in the uppermost Black Rock Trail parking lot (GPS: 36.095456 / -81.829176)—right after the "5000 feet" elevation sign. Here the Grandfather Trail Extension reaches the Grandfather Trail. If you want to start at the top and see the visitor center and Swinging Bridge (no walking is permitted on the road), take the Bridge Trail to or from the summit parking lot (0.4 mile). That trail starts across the road from the Black Rock parking area.

THE HIKES

The gold circle–blazed Black Rock Trail is a 1-mile level but rocky path across the mountain's eastern flank. It passes a formation called Arch Rock on the way to an end loop with great views of the summits above and the Parkway and Piedmont far below.

For Grandfather Trail, take the red diamond–blazed Extension spur as it rises left out of the upper parking areas (Black Rock Trail goes right) and climbs to a junction with the Grandfather Trail. Or take the Bridge Trail and leave the summit lot at the visitor center. From there, the blue diamond–blazed Grandfather Trail scrambles up a rocky pitch, turns right, and levels through spruce forests under so-called Head Bumpin' Rock. The crag-top view just beyond is growing in but it's a nice turnaround for a family stroll. Left (west) is the resort development of Sugar Mountain (with the ten-story condominium now prohibited by state law). Right (east), the land plummets to the Piedmont. MacRae Peak (5,844 feet) is the cliff-faced, evergreen-covered summit straight ahead. Peer closely at about ten o'clock to see hikers on a series of ladders that you'll climb.

Descend along cables (you'll see many), and pass the spur trail from the Black Rock parking area at 0.4 mile. (If you climb the Extension Trail, add 0.3 mile to all mileages below.) Pass a meadow to a junction at 0.5 mile, where the yellow diamond–blazed Underwood Trail goes left to the gap beyond MacRae Peak (the return route on a great loop, one of the truly spectacular short hikes in the region; 2 miles round-trip).

Stay right on the Grandfather Trail, climb more cables, then climb the first ladders, one in a fissure. A truly adventurous section of trail leads up more ladders to the clifftops above. Pause on the large ledge before the upper ladder. The visitor center is now far below.

Above that ladder, the clifftop becomes a knife-edge with a house-size boulder atop it—MacRae Peak. Climb the unnerving ladder that leans against the peak and have lunch. To the east, the Blue Ridge escarpment plummets past the Blue Ridge Parkway to the distant Carolina Piedmont. Continuing, the trail descends a steep chute with cables and a ladder to MacRae Gap, 1 mile from the visitor center. Turn back left on the Underwood Trail, 0.5 mile through crags, cliffs, mossy defiles, and evergreens reminiscent

The jagged ridge of Grandfather Mountain is a challenge, even when you can't see the Grandfather Trail's acrophobia-inducing, cliff-climbing ladders. Hiker on MacRae Peak, opposite Attic Window Peak. VISITNC.COM. PHOTO BY SAM DEAN.

of the far north. Back at the visitor center, it's an adventurous round-trip day hike of 2 miles (2.6 miles round-trip from Black Rock parking).

Remaining on the Grandfather Trail, pass through a wood sorrel–covered gap, more ladders, a boulder cave, and then straight up through the massive split in the peak. At the top of the couloir, a trail leads right to a tent platform atop the domes. To the left, the trail emerges from between rocks to a stunning western view from Attic Window Peak at 1.2 miles.

Follow the Grandfather Trail to the next gap and a side trail to Indian House Cave, a big overhang at 1.3 miles. The trail continues on an evergreen-, rhododendron-, and mountain laurel–covered knife-edge above a series of dramatic cliffs into a high, alpine-like meadow and fine campsite. Going over the next whaleback of crags, the trail winds into Calloway Gap at 1.9 miles, a traditional ridgetop campground. The orange diamond–blazed Profile Trail descends steeply left 0.3 mile to water at Shanty Spring.

Right, the Grandfather Trail climbs again, through a tiny meadow and past a campsite on the right, then through dense evergreens to the Grandfather Trail's last junction at 2.3 miles. To the left, a short spur leads to Watauga View, a west-facing ledge over Banner Elk. To the right, the white diamond–blazed Daniel Boone Scout Trail reaches Calloway Peak (5,964 feet).

Looking east from any of these peaks, you'll understand why in 1794 early botanist André Michaux thought he'd climbed "the highest mountain of all North America." The dramatic drop-off inspired him to sing the "Marseillaise" and shout "Long live

Grandfather Mountain State Park

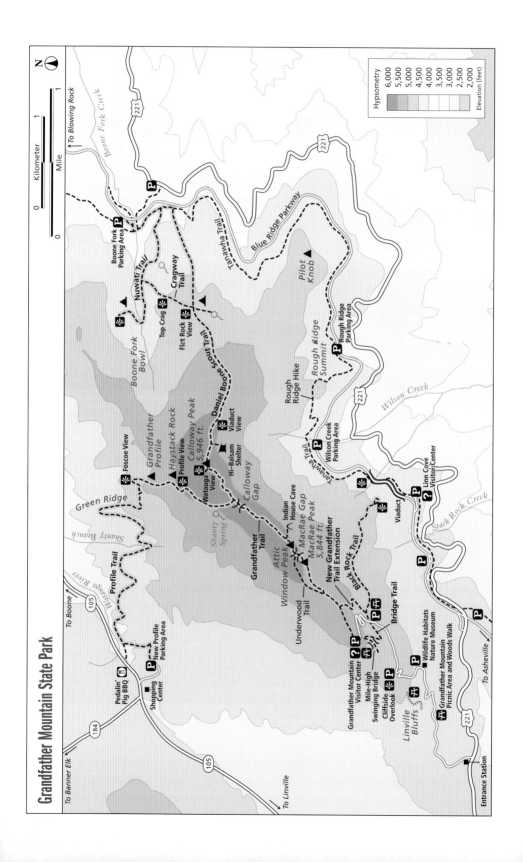

America and the Republic of France. Long live liberty, equality, and fraternity." On these rocky cliff tops you'll see the fuzzy, reddish-green leaves of Michaux's saxifrage.

KEY POINTS

0.0   Start from the parking lot across from the visitor center.

0.4   Junction with Grandfather Trail Extension.

0.5   Junction with Underwood Trail.

1.0   Junction with Underwood Trail in MacRae Gap.

1.2   Attic Window Peak.

1.3   Right turn to Indian House Cave.

1.9   Calloway Gap.

2.3   Watauga View.

2.4   Calloway Peak (2.7 miles from Black Rock trailhead). Return the way you came.

4.8   Arrive back at the visitor center (5.4 miles from Black Rock).

PROFILE TRAIL

WHY GO?

A hike up the western flank of Grandfather Mountain to Calloway Peak.

THE RUNDOWN

General location: Off the Blue Ridge Parkway, about 20 miles west of Blowing Rock
Distance: 2.8 miles round-trip to Shanty Branch; 7.2 miles round-trip to Calloway Gap, about 8 miles to Watauga View and Calloway Peak
Difficulty: Easy to moderate to Shanty Branch; strenuous to Calloway Peak
Maps: USGS Grandfather Mountain. The best map for the hike is the free trail map from the Grandfather Mountain attraction (see below).
Elevation gain: 2,130 feet
Water availability: Spring cited in text; treat all water before using.
For more information: Grandfather Mountain State Park: (828) 963-9522 / 877-722-6762 or reserveamerica.com; ncparks.gov/Visit/parks/grmo/main.php; attraction: (828) 733-4337; grandfather.com

FINDING THE TRAILHEAD

Drive 4 miles north of Linville on NC 105. Pass the junction with NC 184, and in 0.2 mile turn right on an access road that diverges east from NC 105 just north of the shopping center (GPS: 36.119285 / -81.833165). This new parking area holds 125 cars and includes a restroom facility.

THE HIKE

The Profile Trail was built in the mid- to late 1980s to replace the ancient Shanty Spring Trail, a steep and eroding trail dating from the latter half of the nineteenth century that was in the way of a proposed development (which luckily never occurred, but the Shanty Spring Trail closed nevertheless.)

The Profile Trail has dramatic views of The Profile, the multifaceted, west-facing namesake face of Grandfather Mountain. The face, or faces, is best seen north of the trailhead. (Grandview Restaurant, a few miles toward Boone, is a nice place to appreciate The Profile during a pre- or post-hike meal.)

The graded trail descends from the new parking area to the area of the trail's historic starting point, then is largely level as it wanders for its first mile along the beautiful Watauga River through a mature, New England–like forest. The trail leaves the river, climbs steeply for 0.2 mile or so, and winds into a scenic, dry drainage where you'll find the waxy evergreen-leafed ground plant Fraser's sedge, on the endangered list. (A future trail from the new parking lot will likely intersect in this area negating the descent to the river.) At about 2 miles the trail dips across Shanty Branch, the source of which is Shanty Spring, about 1.3 miles ahead. Returning to the trailhead from here makes a nice round-trip family hike of 4 miles—which is why this portion of the Profile Trail is Grandfather Mountain State Park's TRACK Trail. Pick up or download the *Uncovering Cove Forests* booklet, designed especially for this site (but useful elsewhere).

Past the stream, the trail squeezes through a fissure then winds higher in and out of the drainages above on its way around Green Ridge. Immediately below the Grandfather Profile, there's a nice view over the Watauga River Valley town of Foscoe to Mount Rogers and Whitetop, the first and second highest peaks in Virginia.

The trail switchbacks again to numerous tent sites and a grandiose campfire pit with a small seep beyond on the left. The trail ascends outstanding pathways of natural stone and switchbacks to a huge boulder with a rock-paved shelter spot. Not far beyond, the trail turns a corner to Profile View at 3.1 miles. Early mountaineers thought winter hoarfrost turned the dramatic face into a grandfather looking west.

At 3.3 miles the trail reaches Shanty Spring, where water empties from below a cliff. In his classic 1890s book *The Balsam Groves of the Grandfather Mountain*, Shepherd Dugger claimed this is "the coldest water outside of perpetual snow in the United States."

Going right at the cliff, the rocky upper Profile Trail rises through increasing evergreens to Calloway Gap, at 3.6 miles, and a junction with the Grandfather Trail amid tent platforms.

KEY POINTS

0.0 Start at the trailhead off NC 105.

2.0 Shanty Branch.

2.3 Foscoe View.

3.1 Profile View.

3.3 Shanty Spring.

3.6 Calloway Gap.

4.0 Watauga View. Left to Watauga View, right on Boone trail to Calloway Peak. Return the way you came.

8.0 Arrive back at the trailhead.

16 LINVILLE AREA

BEACON HEIGHTS

WHY GO?

This short and popular Blue Ridge Parkway leg-stretcher offers spectacular views of a nearly vertical-mile drop to the Piedmont. An option to start on the Mountains-to-Sea Trail helps hikers find solitude.

THE RUNDOWN

General location: Linville
Distance: 0.7 mile round-trip; Mountains-to-Sea Trail options: 1.1 and 4.8 miles round-trip
Difficulty: Easy; strenuous for longer Mountains-to-Sea Trail route
Maps: USGS Grandfather Mountain. The Grandfather Mountain hiking map shows the trail best and is available free at the Grandfather Mountain entrance (north 0.1 mile to US 221 exit, right 1 mile to entrance) or downloaded at the attraction website (grandfather.com).
Water availability: None

FINDING THE TRAILHEAD

The Parkway trailhead is located at milepost 305.2, 0.1 mile south of the US 221 entrance to the Parkway and 3 miles east of Linville (GPS: 36.083831 / -81.830172). To reach the lower Mountains-to-Sea Trail parking area, exit onto US 221 at milepost 305.1. At the stop sign, turn left and drive under the Parkway, immediately passing SR 1513 on the right. Continue about 0.4 mile and take the next right onto SR 1514. At about 4.2 miles from US 221, turn right onto FR 192. Park at Old House Gap at 3.5 miles (GPS: 36.064224 / -81.809058). The Mountains-to-Sea Trail enters the woods on the right. Its first white-dot blazes may not be visible from the parking area.

THE HIKE

From the trailhead (4,220 feet) walk across the state road that parallels the Parkway (SR 1513) and enter the woods where the sign says "Tanawha Trail Beacon Heights 0.2." At the next junction, the Tanawha Trail departs to the left. The Mountains-to-Sea Trail comes in from the right and goes left with the Tanawha Trail. Turn right on the Mountains-to-Sea Trail—that's also the Beacon Heights Trail to the top. Past an overhanging rain-shelter rock on the left, there's a bench on the right before the steepest, rockiest part of the trail.

The round white blazes of the Mountains-to-Sea Trail turn off right at 0.2 mile where the Beacon Heights Trail switchbacks left. (A right turn here on the MST leads to a nearby winter view; see below.) Continuing, the path reaches another bench and junction at the peak where views lie right and left. Go right to the top of a south-facing dome with great views to the Piedmont and the high peaks south along the Parkway, including Mount Mitchell. Going left, the path ascends stone steps to another dome with spectacular views of the eastern flank of Grandfather Mountain and the Pisgah National Forest's Wilson Creek drainage. Retrace your steps to the bottom (0.7 mile).

Beacon Heights is an idyllic spot to savor Grandfather Mountain's great scenery with family or friends.

KEY POINTS

0.0   Start at the trailhead parking area.

0.05 Tanawha Trail goes left.

0.2   Mountains-to-Sea Trail goes right.

0.3   Reach crest.

0.35 Summit views. Return the way you came.

0.7   Arrive back at the parking area (1.1 miles with side trail).

The longest Beacon Heights hike starts below, at Old House Gap, and rises through a forest that sees little foot traffic. Leave the secluded, leafy parking area at Old House Gap past a gate and follow an eroded, then sandy and pleasant old logging grade bordered by mountain laurel. At about 0.3 mile from the gap, go right with the Mountains-to-Sea Trail where the road grade goes left. The trail alternates between steeper and more gradual ascents as it climbs through towering hemlocks and rhododendrons to the upper drainage of Andrews Creek.

The trail reaches the top of the now-dry drainage and bears right up final switchbacks through sparser vegetation for Beacon Heights. A short, steep climb reaches a winter vista ledge on the flank of Beacon Heights (a private view for picnickers who'd rather not go any farther). Slabbing west and bisecting two boulders, the trail crests the ridge where the MST turns right on an old logging grade about 2.4 miles from Old House Gap. (To the left, the grade joins SR 1513, the dirt road you crossed from the Parkway trailhead.) Go right on the MST for a short distance to the junction mentioned above with the Beacon Heights Trail from the Parkway. A right turn there leads to the top, about 2.8 miles from Old House Gap. The round-trip is just less than 6 miles.

The private view ledge mentioned above is also a nice and easy side vista from Beacon Heights when that trail is busy. Just turn right with the MST near the top, then head left into the woods to the ledge.

FLAT ROCK SELF-GUIDING LOOP TRAIL

WHY GO?

An educational trail with plant identification signs, inspiring messages, and great views of Grandfather Mountain.

THE RUNDOWN

General location: Near Linville
Distance: 0.7-mile loop
Difficulty: Easy to moderate
Map: USGS Grandfather Mountain
Elevation gain: About 100 feet
Water availability: None

For more information: Blue Ridge Parkway, 199 Hemphill Knob Rd., Asheville 28803-8686; (828) 271-4779; (828) 298-0398 (recorded information and mailing requests); nps.gov/blri

FINDING THE TRAILHEAD

 The trail begins at Blue Ridge Parkway milepost 308.3 (GPS: 36.050937 / -81.857435), 0.4 mile south of SR 1511, a side road to the Parkway from US 221 at Linville near the classic, historic accommodations of Eseeola Lodge.

THE HIKE

Here's a rare hike—one not to miss for serious hikers and more casual Parkway motorists alike. This is a quick walk to a good view or a wonderful hour-plus stroll for a family wanting nature study or a picnic.

Not far above the parking area, where the trail loop splits, head left amid yellow jewelweed. Interpretive signs point out tree species and the shiny heart-shaped leaves of galax on the ground under the rhododendron. After passing a resting bench, step onto the quartzite outcrop of Flat Rock. The rhododendron woods quickly transition to a crag capped with gnarled pines, luxuriant moss, and lichen. Flat Rock's "bathtubs," the

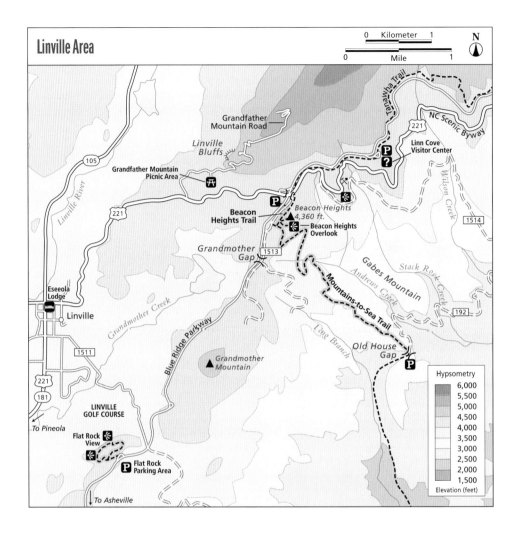

0   Kilometer   1

0   Mile   1

N

Grandfather
Mountain Road

Linville
Bluffs

Tanawha Trail

NC Scenic Byway

221

Linn Cove
Visitor Center

105

Grandfather Mountain
Picnic Area

Wilson Creek

221

Linville River

Beacon
Heights Trail

Beacon Heights
4,360 ft.

Beacon Heights
Overlook

Beacon Heights

1514

Grandmother
Gap

1513

Gabes Mountain

Stack Rock Creek

Andrews Creek

Mountains-to-Sea Trail

192

Eseeola
Lodge

Linville

Grandmother Creek

Blue Ridge Parkway

Bug Branch

Old House
Gap

1511

Grandmother
Mountain

221

181

LINVILLE
GOLF COURSE

To Pineola

Flat Rock
View

Flat Rock
Parking Area

To Asheville

Hypsometry

6,000
5,500
5,000
4,500
4,000
3,500
3,000
2,500
2,000
1,500

Elevation (feet)

interesting bowl-size basins just ahead, often contain water that eventually breaks down this solid shelf of rock.

Turn right to follow the yellow painted arrows that guide you across the breezy outcrop covered with wind-flagged evergreens. The 180-degree view includes the Linville golf course below. The Appalachian Trail crosses the far western horizon on the meadow-covered peaks of Roan, Yellow, and Hump Mountains. Walk the ledge with one of the Parkway's best views of Grandfather Mountain ahead of you. Where the trail turns right off the clifftop, step beyond to the best view of Grandfather.

The trail continues into a sheltered northern hardwood forest past more tree ID signs, including hobblebush, red maple, and striped maple. All are found both here and in New England, explaining why this forest has a northern feel at 4,000 feet. The trail passes through a ferny flat and dips right to the end of the loop, where you head left back to the parking lot. This is a good advanced Nordic ski trail easily reached from SR 1511 even when the Parkway is snowed closed.

Flat Rock is a pretty walk with the rhododendron in bloom, but Grandfather Mountain stands out even more in winter for snowshoers and advanced cross-country skiers.

KEY POINTS

0.0 Start to the left from the parking lot.

0.05 Trail splits—head left.

0.2 Trail heads onto rocky outcrop.

0.35 Trail leaves outcrop.

0.65 Trail intersects—turn left.

0.7 Arrive back at the parking area.

WHY GO?

The 5,954-acre Lost Cove and 7,350-acre Harper Creek tracts are wilderness study areas in what's often called the Wilson Creek drainage of Pisgah National Forest. Lying below Grandfather Mountain, between US 321 to the north, NC 181 to the south, and NC 90 to the east, this vast area is perhaps North Carolina's largest contiguous area of unpaved roads. Just the drive to the trailhead is one of the best mountain experiences a visitor can have. Wilson Creek was named a National Wild and Scenic River in 2000, and the highly recommended Wilson Creek Visitor Center was built in 2002 on the Brown Mountain Beach Road near Mortimer and Edgemont. Truly grand Wilson Creek Gorge offers kayakers and rafters up to Class IV rapids. Some of the state's biggest, most spectacular waterfalls hide in surrounding woods. There's also great mountain biking in this endless ripple of ridges.

There are tiny settlements, such as Gragg and Edgemont, where small cabins cluster in the woods beside rushing rivers. On the way to these hikes you'll pass Coffey's General Store in Edgemont, now closed, a remnant of when the area held bustling early-twentieth-century logging communities of thousands. Years of destructive timbering, forest fires, and a 1916 flood that followed gave impetus to the effort to establish national forests in the East. This part of Pisgah National Forest was the first. Another major flood occurred in 1940, and periodic deluges are not uncommon today.

The forest service's Mortimer Campground was a Civilian Conservation Corps (CCC) camp and is a great base of operations for hikers (April 1 through October 31; flush toilets and showers). So is nearby Betsey's Ole Time Country Store, at the junction of NC 90, Brown Mountain Beach Road, and Zigzag Lane. Owner Bruce Gray's immaculately maintained parcel contains a rental cabin, stucco tepee, campground, light food service, and more. (Find him on Facebook or call 828-758-5051.)

The surrounding area is full of little-used trails to wild destinations. Other recommended routes in the area include the 4.3-mile School-house Ridge Trail loop at Mortimer Recreation Area (with a nice waterfall just 0.2 mile from the campground and views of Grandfather Mountain from the ridge), and the Wilson Creek Trail, a 6.6-mile hike between FR 192 and FR 45 that follows one of the best trout streams in the state.

Trailheads in the area can be hard to find. Roadside camping isn't advised, nor is leaving valuables in your unattended vehicle. At the relatively low elevations of the watershed, summer days can reach into the high 80s—one reason the waterfalls are such popular spots to cool off. Not far south of Mortimer is Brown Mountain Beach, a sandy strip of Wilson Creek that attracts hundreds on hot summer weekends. In times of high water, use extreme caution. Hikers and residents have died in flash floods here. In general, trails in this area have plenty of stream crossings. Consider carrying sport sandals for water crossings.

In an area worthy of wilderness designation, hikes include short walks to clifftop views, waterfalls, and circuit hikes that are among the best in North Carolina.

THE RUNDOWN

General location: Wilson Creek watershed, just below Grandfather Mountain in the Pisgah National Forest

Distance: Out-and-back walks of 1.4 miles for the Darkside Cliffs Trail, 1 mile for the Little Lost Cove Cliffs Trail, 1.6 miles for the Hunt Fish Falls Trail, 2.4 miles to pools on the Lost Cove Trail, 2.6 miles for the Big Lost Cove Cliffs Trail; circuit hikes of 4.7 and 7.5 miles on the Lost Cove Trail

Difficulty: Easy to moderate for Darkside Cliffs Trail, Big and Little Lost Cove Cliffs Trails, and a day hike to Gragg Prong pools on the Lost Cove Trail; moderate for Hunt Fish Falls Trail; strenuous for the two Lost Cove loop hikes

Maps: USGS Grandfather Mountain. The best map is the Pisgah National Forest's *Wilson Creek National Wild and Scenic River Trail Guide*. Order online from Pisgah National Forest under "Maps and Publications" at the

USDA Forest Service website below. The Wilson Creek Visitor Center sells maps.

Elevation gains: 300 feet for Darkside Cliffs Trail; 800 feet for Little Lost Cove Cliffs Trail; 1,200 feet for Hunt Fish Falls Trail; 320 feet for the Lost Cove pools hike; 1,280 feet for Big Lost Cove Cliffs Trail; 1,600 and 2,560 feet, respectively, for the short and long Lost Cove circuit hikes.

Water availability: Water is plentiful and clean, but treat it before drinking.

For more information: Grandfather Ranger District, Pisgah National Forest, 109 Lawing Dr., Nebo 28761; (828) 652-2144; www.fs.usda.gov/nfsnc. Wilson Creek Visitor Center, 7805 Brown Mountain Beach Rd., Collettsville 28611; (828) 759-0005; open weekends Dec–Mar; daily Apr–Nov.

FINDING THE TRAILHEADS

For hikers arriving from the south and west, the best way to reach the Lost Cove/Harper Creek area is from NC 181 near the Blue Ridge Parkway. Go about 24 miles north of Morganton on NC 181 and turn right onto Mortimer Road (SR 1401). Heading south on NC 181, this is a left, 0.9 mile from the NC 181/183 junction and 2.6 miles from the NC 181/Blue Ridge Parkway junction.

Once on SR 1401, at 2.2 miles turn right at a junction (a church is on the left); in another 0.2 mile turn right on a gravel road at an intersection opposite the Long Ridge Baptist Church. After turning, you'll see an FR 464 sign on the right. At 4.3 miles the unsigned trailhead for the Big Lost Cove Cliffs Trail is on the left (GPS: 36.012080/-81.857912). At 5.3 miles, a forest service picnic and primitive camping area is located at the junction with FR 58, on the right.

Trails on the north and east side of the Lost Cove Area are reached via FR 464 east of the junction with FR 58. From that junction, the signed upper and lower trailheads for the Little Lost Cove Cliffs Trail are on the right at 0.6 mile (GPS: 36.011659/-81.844858) and 2.1 miles. (In between, at 1.6 miles, FR 464A goes left, with easy access to the middle of the Lost Cove Creek Trail.) The lower Little Lost Cove

Cliffs Trailhead is also where the signed North Harper Creek Falls Trail begins on the right. The unsigned Darkside Cliffs Trail starts on the left at 2.7 miles. The Hunt Fish Falls Trail starts on the left at about 4 miles.

For hikers arriving from the east, the best way to reach the area is via scenic back roads between Lenoir and Morganton. Both towns are reached by major highways. From Morganton take NC 181 north about 10 miles, then turn right on the Brown Mountain Beach Road (SR 1405). Go about 5 miles and turn left onto SR 1328. To reach this point from Lenoir, take NC 90 to Collettsville. Go left from NC 90 and continue south on SR 1337 just over 3 miles to a right turn onto SR 1328.

Once on SR 1328, which parallels beautiful Wilson Creek, go 4.7 miles and turn right at a T junction. Reach the SR 1328/NC 90 junction in another 4.1 miles and turn left onto NC 90. Immediately pass the Mortimer Recreation Area and take another left in 1.9 miles on the Pineola Road, which is FR 464.

From the FR 464/NC 90 junction, Lost Cove trailheads are as follows: Hunt Fish Falls Trail, 3.2 miles on the right; Darkside Cliffs Trail, 4.4 miles on the right; North Harper Creek Falls Trail and the lower trailhead for the Little Lost Cove Cliffs Trail, 5.1 miles on the left; upper trailhead for the Little Lost Cove Cliffs Trail, 6.5 miles on left. Also from this direction, the Big Lost Cove Cliffs Trail is 1 mile beyond the FR 58/FR 464 junction (8.1 miles from NC 90).

To reach the trailhead for the Lost Cove and Gragg Prong Trails from either direction, go north from the FR 464/NC 90 junction 0.2 mile to Edgemont and take the next left onto FR 981. (Coffey's General Store is just 100 yards farther on NC 90.) Bear left at the first junction (FR 451 goes right), and reach the trailhead on the left at about 4 miles.

From the north, there are routes into the area from Blowing Rock and Linville. The best is from Linville. Continue south of the US 221/NC 181 junction past the Eseeola Lodge and go left on a road marked "SR 1511." At about 1 mile cross the Blue Ridge Parkway and descend on the Roseborough Road. At about 4.5 miles go right on FR 981. The Lost Cove Trailhead is on the right in about 0.5 mile. Farther south is Edgemont and other trail accesses.

THE HIKES

Three hikes to the cliffs that clog the head of the Lost Cove valley make wonderful introductions to the area. Each is easy to moderate and offers wonderful views. Also, each is short (less than 1.5 miles), so you have time to explore nearby scenic roads.

The Big Lost Cove Cliffs Trail is a good backpacking trip for beginners. It's a short out-and-back to the top of the cliffs above Lost Cove—a high, wild area under the Blue Ridge Parkway. Vistas extend in many directions, but the prominent landmark is Grandfather Mountain. The trail departs the north side of FR 464 at an unsigned trailhead and immediately bears left, ascends steeply, and then flattens to crest and follow the broad top of Lost Cove Ridge at about 3,700 feet. The trail drops steeply for about 0.3 mile to about 3,400 feet and then runs gradually to viewpoints at about 1.3 miles. This is an easy to moderate 2.6-mile day hike that could also be a novice backpacking trip.

Not very far east down FR 464, the Little Lost Cove Cliffs Trail provides a similar hike, but between two trailheads. This view of Lost Cove is on the south side of FR 464, an old CCC-built road that bisects the Harper Creek and Lost Cove areas.

For hikers with only one vehicle, both trailheads are at virtually the same elevation, so hiking the 0.75 mile from either trailhead to the views would be equally appealing (for a 1.5-mile round-trip). From the easternmost trailhead (beside the start of the North Harper Creek Falls Trail), the road-width path climbs through an old orchard, reaches side trails north to various views of Grandfather Mountain and Lost Cove, then climbs the undulating ridge to a 3,400-foot peak with outstanding, nearly 360-degree views.

When the high flanks of Grandfather Mountain are bright with fall color, the waterfall-laced rippling ridges of the Harper Creek, Lost Cove, and Wilson Creek area far below are still green. Color down there can last into November.

Not far down FR 464, the Darkside Cliffs Trail provides a one-third-length version of the Big Lost Cove Cliffs Trail. The 0.5-mile path leaves the north side of the road from a grassy parking area. It descends to a gap and then emerges dramatically onto the top of Darkside Cliffs. The view looks down the entire length of Lost Cove, and almost straight down on Hunt Fish Falls, the next trail into Lost Cove along FR 464.

Hunt Fish Falls Trail begins at a rail-bordered parking area. In 0.8 mile the trail drops, steeply at times, from 2,400 feet to about 1,800 feet at Lost Cove Creek. This trail is often busy because it's short, only moderately strenuous, and reaches one of the area's best-known waterfalls. Hunt Fish Falls was no doubt named for two of the primary activities in the area: It's not unusual to see people fishing above the falls or in the huge pool below. Pools downstream are favorite spots to sun and swim.

You can start a loop of the Lost Cove area from Hunt Fish Falls, but the best access for a 7.5-mile loop or a 4.7-mile circuit hike is from the trailhead on FR 981 north of Edgemont. From that trailhead, start the lengthiest loop of the Lost Cove Trail by taking the trail to the right and begin a 1.1-mile climb to Timber Ridge. This is a lush, scenic walk, particularly near the top, where the trail skirts the head of a high, open drainage. Emerging on Timber Ridge, the Timber Ridge Trail descends left to the Lost Cove Creek near Gragg Prong. Go right on the Lost Cove Trail as it artfully and almost effortlessly glides among the peaks of Timber Ridge with outstanding views of Grandfather

Lost Cove Area; Harper Creek Area

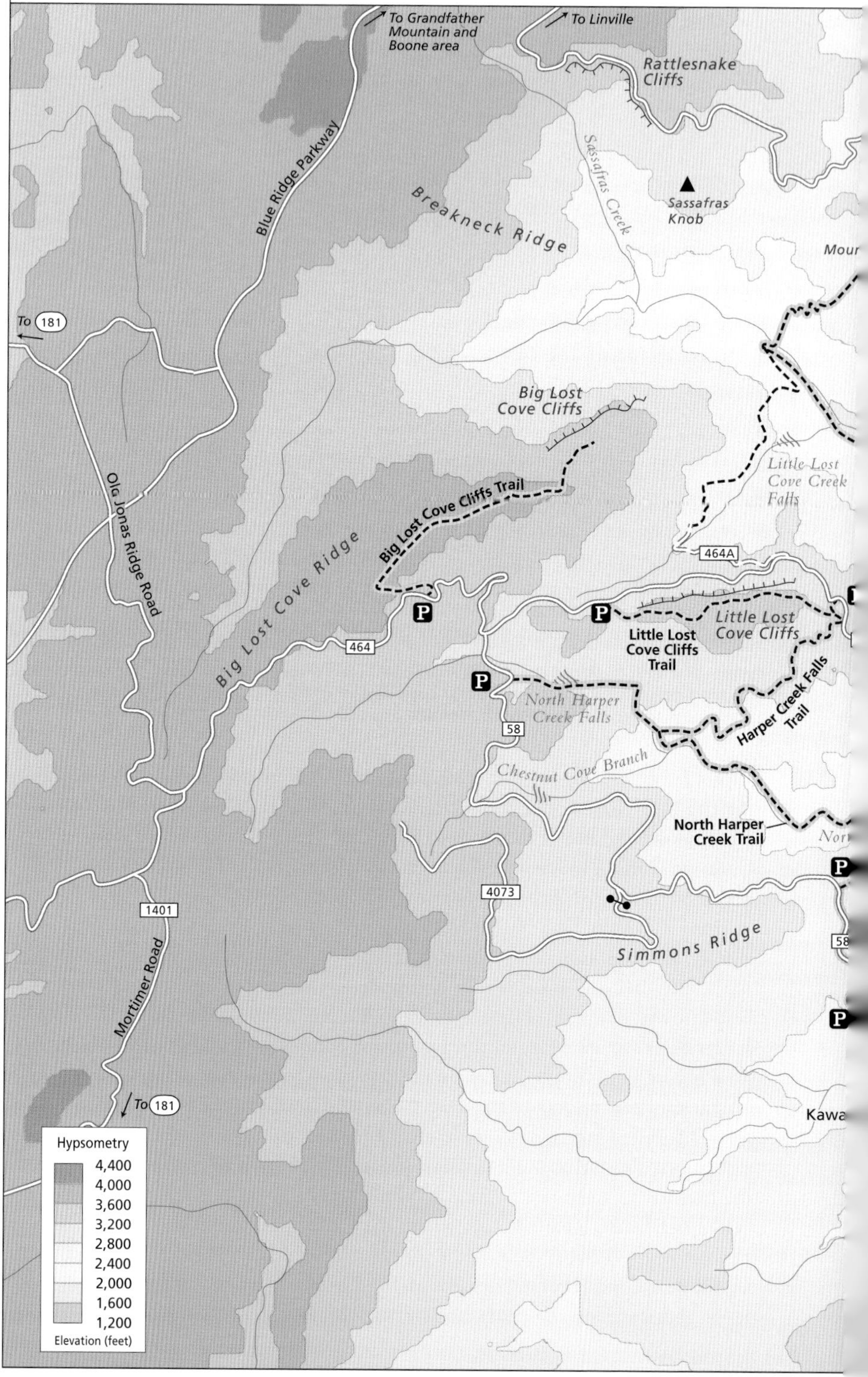

To Grandfather Mountain and Boone area

To Linville

Rattlesnake Cliffs

Blue Ridge Parkway

Sassafras Creek

Breakneck Ridge

Sassafras Knob

Mour

To (181)

Big Lost Cove Cliffs

Ola Jonas Ridge Road

Big Lost Cove Ridge

Big Lost Cove Cliffs Trail

Little Lost Cove Creek Falls

464A

P

464

P

P

Little Lost Cove Cliffs Trail

Little Lost Cove Cliffs

North Harper Creek Falls

58

Harper Creek Falls Trail

Chestnut Cove Branch

North Harper Creek Trail

Nor

P

4073

P

Simmons Ridge

58

1401

Mortimer Road

P

To (181)

Kawa

Hypsometry

	4,400
	4,000
	3,600
	3,200
	2,800
	2,400
	2,000
	1,600
	1,200

Elevation (feet)

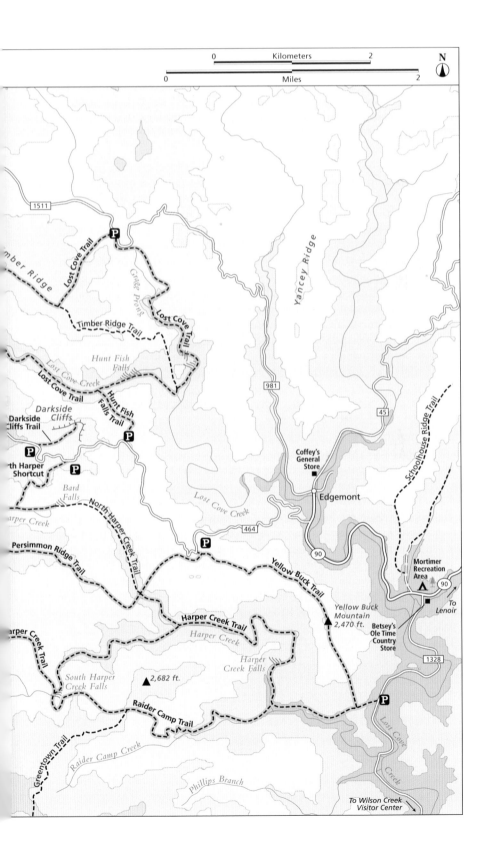

1511

Lost Cove Trail

Timber Ridge

Grade Prong

Lost Cove Trail

Yancey Ridge

Timber Ridge Trail

Hunt Fish Falls

Lost Cove Creek

Hunt Fish Falls Trail

Lost Cove Trail

981

45

Schoolhouse Ridge Trail

Darkside Cliffs

Darkside Cliffs Trail

P

P

th Harper Shortcut

P

Bard Falls

North Harper Creek Trail

Lost Cove Creek

Coffey's General Store

Edgemont

arper Creek

Persimmon Ridge Trail

P

464

90

Mortimer Recreation Area

90

To Lenoir

Yellow Buck Trail

arper Creek Trail

Harper Creek Trail

Harper Creek

Yellow Buck Mountain 2,470 ft.

Betsey's Ole Time Country Store

1328

South Harper Creek Falls

2,682 ft.

Harper Creek Falls

Raider Camp Trail

P

Greentown Trail

Raider Camp Creek

Lost Cove Creek

Phillips Branch

To Wilson Creek Visitor Center

Mountain. From Bee Mountain, at the end of Timber Ridge and about 2.1 miles from the start, the trail plummets to Lost Cove Creek.

Reaching the creek at just less than 3 miles, the trail crosses a log bridge to the southwest side. The Lost Cove Trail goes left here. To the right, the bank rises to a forest service road that is closed to traffic and is itself an easy access to this area. (It veers sharply off FR 464 between the two trailheads of the Little Lost Cove Cliffs Trail, 1.6 miles east of the FR 58/FR 464 junction.)

Here's where serious hikers have their best options for trail-less exploring. Upstream from the trail lies a third of the area's acreage. Streams split into two main drainages, offering level streamside campsites hemmed in by the crags of Big Lost Cove Cliffs and Breakneck Ridge. With one car at Big Lost Cove Cliffs Trail and the other on FR 464A, hikers could start high, follow gradual terrain from the Big Lost Cove Cliffs Trail, and dip down onto Lost Cove Creek, eventually coming out on the trail portion of FR 464A.

The trail continues down Lost Cove Creek—the rocky, boulder-strewn stream consistently wide—with nice campsites for almost 2 miles. In bright sun, the icy water gurgles between moss-covered banks. This is a prized trout-fishing location, with sandy soil on the banks and an open forest of hemlock, birch, and hardwoods.

At about 3.3 miles, Little Lost Cove Creek goes right. A short diversion here to Little Lost Cove Creek Falls is worthwhile. For the next 1.3 miles, the trail follows the stream with occasional crossings (which can be avoided; the trail eventually passes Hunt Fish Falls on the southwest side of the stream). At about 4.5 miles, the Hunt Fish Falls Trail goes right to FR 464. The Lost Cove Trail continues downstream past pools and falls and crosses Lost Cove Creek. Climbing from the creek, the Timber Ridge Trail goes left at just over 5 miles. The Lost Cove Trail skirts a parcel of private land where Lost Cove Creek meets Gragg Prong, then descends to go upstream on Gragg Prong. From here to the trailhead, the path crosses the stream several times, passing waterfalls and cascades.

At about 6 miles you approach Gragg Prong's major waterfall from below, one of the best reasons for hiking the loop in this direction. Though the climb up Gragg Prong is gradual, you've just hiked a long loop; on a hot day consider taking a dip among the cascades and pools at about 6.8 miles. One pool can only be described as a cold-water Jacuzzi. A sharp outer rim is a perfect support as you bob in a straight-walled tub 15 feet wide. Water swirls in from above and bubbles out over the lower side. As a day hike, this enticing waterfall is an easy 2.4-mile round-trip, and there are nice campsites in the area. The last 1.2 miles make a gradual return to the parking lot at about 7.5 miles.

A shorter hike, in the same direction, involves taking the Lost Cove Trail to a left turn atop Timber Ridge on the Timber Ridge Trail at 1.1 miles. At 2.3 miles leave the Timber Ridge Trail, turning left on the Gragg Prong portion of the Lost Cove Trail, and head back to the trailhead. This circuit hike is just under 5 miles.

WHY GO?

This network of streamside trails include spectacular short walks and wild circuits that are among the best waterfall hikes in western North Carolina.

THE RUNDOWN

(See map on pages 114–15.)
General location: Near Lost Cove area, Pisgah National Forest
Distance: Hikes in the area include out-and-back walks of various lengths: 1.6 miles for Upper Creek Falls loop and South Harper Creek Falls; 2.4 miles to Bard Falls; 1.5 and 3 miles to North Harper Creek Falls. Circuits of 5.6, 8, and 9 miles are also possible.
Difficulty: Moderately strenuous for all hikes, strenuous for lengthier circuits
Maps: USGS Grandfather Mountain and Chestnut Mountain. The Pisgah National Forest's *Wilson Creek National Wild and Scenic River Trail Guide* and Wilson Creek Area Map are best. Order online from Pisgah National Forest under "Maps and

Publications" at the USDA Forest Service website below. Wilson Creek Visitor Center sells maps.
Elevation gain: 960 feet to South Harper Creek Falls; 1,120 feet to Bard Falls; 350 and 1,360 feet to North Harper Creek Falls; 985, 2,440, and 1,440 feet, respectively, for the three circuits
Water availability: Water is plentiful from streams along these trails; treat before using.
For more information: Grandfather Ranger District, Pisgah National Forest, 109 Lawing Dr., Nebo 28761; (828) 652-2144; www.fs.usda.gov/nfsnc. Wilson Creek Visitor Center, 7805 Brown Mountain Beach Rd., Collettsville 28611; (828) 759-0005; open weekends only Dec–Mar; daily Apr–Nov.

FINDING THE TRAILHEAD

Trails on the north and east side of the Harper Creek area are reached via FR 464 east of the junction with FR 58 (see directions to that junction above under Lost Cove Area). From that junction, the signed upper and lower trailheads for the Little Lost Cove Cliffs Trail are on the right at 0.6 mile and 2.1 miles. (In between, at 1.6 miles, FR 464A goes left, with easy access to the middle of the Lost Cove Creek Trail.) The lower Little Lost Cove Cliffs Trailhead is also where the signed North Harper Creek Falls Trail begins on the right. The unsigned Darkside Cliffs Trail starts on the left at 2.7 miles. The signed North Harper Shortcut starts on the right at 3.4 miles, with the Hunt Fish Falls Trail on the left at about 4 miles. The signed Persimmon Ridge Trail (with immediate access to the Yellow Buck Trail) begins on the right at about 4.9 miles.

To reach the easternmost trailhead for the Harper Creek Trail, continue to a junction with NC 90 at 7.1 miles. Go right, pass Mortimer Recreation Area, and at 1.8 miles turn right onto SR 1328. The signed Harper Creek Trail starts on the right, 1.3 miles south of the junction.

For hikers arriving from the east, the best way to reach the area is via scenic back roads between Lenoir and Morganton. Both towns are reached by major highways. From Morganton take NC 181 north about 10 miles, then turn right on the Brown Mountain Beach Road (SR 1405). Go about 5 miles and turn left onto State Road 1328. To reach this point from Lenoir, take NC 90 to Collettsville. Go left from NC 90 and continue south on SR 1337 just over 3 miles to a right turn onto SR 1328.

Once on SR 1328, which parallels beautiful Wilson Creek, go 4.7 miles and turn right at a T junction. The Harper Creek Trail is on the left at 2.8 miles. Reach the SR 1328/ NC 90 junction in another 1.3 miles and turn left on NC 90. Immediately pass the Mortimer Recreation Area and take another left in 1.9 miles on the Pineola Road, which is FR 464.

From the FR 464/NC 90 junction, trailheads are as follows: Persimmon Ridge Trail (and Yellow Buck Trail), 2.2 miles on left; Hunt Fish Falls Trail, 3.2 miles on right; North Harper Shortcut, 3.7 miles on left; Darkside Cliffs Trail, 4.4 miles on right; the North Harper Creek Falls Trail and the lower trailhead for the Little Lost Cove Cliffs Trail, 5.1 miles on the left; upper trailhead for the Little Lost Cove Cliffs Trail, 6.5 miles on left. Go left on FR 58 at 7.1 miles to reach the North Harper Creek Trail, 7.4 miles on the left (GPS: 36.007128/-81.850970); the Persimmon Ridge Trail, 10.9 miles on left; and the Harper Creek Trail, 11.5 miles on the left.

Also from this direction, the Big Lost Cove Cliffs Trail is 1 mile beyond the FR 58/FR 464 junction (8.1 miles from NC 90).

To reach trails on the west side of Harper Creek area, go to the junction of FR 464 and FR 58 and head south on FR 58. From the junction, the signed start of the North Harper Creek Trail is 0.3 mile on the left. The signed start of the Persimmon Ridge Trail is on the left at 3.8 miles; the Harper Creek Trail leaves the road on stone steps on the left at 4.4 miles.

THE HIKES

The Harper Creek area is laced with trails. The main paths, the Harper Creek and North Harper Creek Trails, connect and permit hikers to tour the two main waterfall-filled drainages. Other trails link to nearby roads and create circuit hikes. With two cars, top-to-bottom hikes of these spectacular streams are very easy—but positioning the two cars can take some time. Side trails often provide quick access from adjacent roads to scenic streams. That's especially nice for those who fish, since these are excellent trout streams. I'll describe the main trails first and then recommend circuit hikes and day hikes to waterfalls.

The Harper Creek Trail, featuring Harper Creek Falls, the area's most spectacular cataract, leaves SR 1328 and climbs consistently to a junction with the Yellow Buck Trail (a return route for circuit hikers) at 0.5 mile. Continuing straight, the trail descends to nice campsites, Harper Creek, and a junction on the left with the Raider Camp Trail (also a return route for circuit hikers) at just over 1 mile. Turn right up Harper Creek; in 0.1 mile a side trail leads to views of Harper Creek Falls and a large pool below. Continuing, Harper Creek Trail reaches the North Harper Creek Falls Trail at about 3.5 miles, crossing a side stream at 4.5 miles. At just over 5 miles, the trail reaches views of South Harper Creek Falls—200 feet high and a spectacular cascade, considered the ultimate waterfall in the Grandfather Ranger District.

Just above the waterfall, the Raider Camp Trail comes in on the left. The Harper Creek Trail continues above the falls and then gradually winds away from the river, reaching FR 58 at about 6 miles. Starting here, hiking to the falls makes a moderately strenuous out-and-back day hike of less than 2 miles.

A 9-mile circuit on the south side of Harper Creek can be formed by going left at the top of the falls on the Raider Camp Trail and descending about 2.6 miles back to the Harper Creek Trail (where it's another 1 mile back to your car). To do this, take the Raider Camp Trail left across the stream, where a spur trail on the left leads to great views of the falls and Grandfather Mountain. The main trail continues, switchbacking steeply

The cataract-laced Harper Creek watershed should be a prime target for anyone excited by waterfalls.

up to a trail junction on the right with the Greentown Trail, 0.2 mile from the Harper Creek Trail. (The Greentown Trail is another nice way into this area; look for it on the Wilson Creek Area map.) Continue on the Raider Camp Trail, descending gradually then steeply dropping to Raider Camp Creek. The trail wanders past campsites through hemlocks and tulip poplars, then reaches the Phillips Branch Trail. The Raider Camp Trail then veers left, away from the creek, to cross Harper Creek and join the Harper Creek Trail, from which it's just over 1 mile back to your car. Circuit hikers could also go up the Raider Camp Trail and down Harper Creek.

Another nice circuit hike, this one about 8 miles and on the north side of Harper Creek, can be created by leaving the Harper Creek Trail where North Harper Creek branches to the right (at about 3.5 miles) on the North Harper Creek Trail. Heading north, the trail is almost level for 4 miles. Circuit hikers should turn at the junction with the Persimmon Ridge Trail, at about 0.5 mile (4 miles from SR 1328). Hikers heading back to their car at the Harper Creek Trailhead should go right (east). The trail climbs steeply for 0.2 mile, joining the Yellow Buck Trail at 0.5 mile (about 4.5 from SR 1328). From there, a left of just 0.2 mile takes you to FR 464. Circuit hikers turn right, following the old logging grade of the Yellow Buck Trail down to the Harper Creek Trail at about 7.5 miles. Back at SR 1328, you have completed an 8-mile circuit.

Above the Persimmon Ridge Trail, the North Harper Creek Trail reaches beautiful Bard Falls at about 1.3 miles. The "hole-in-the-wall" waterfall here contains an arch. The trail is an old logging railroad grade, one of many that disastrously denuded this entire area in the early 1900s. About 0.2 mile beyond the falls, the North Harper Shortcut heads right about 1 mile on a moderate and graded climb to a junction 1 mile away on FR 464. This trail permits a moderate 2.4-mile day hike to Bard Falls from FR 464.

The North Harper Creek Trail continues with stream crossings. On the left at about 3.3 miles is a waterfall where Chestnut Cove Branch joins North Harper Creek. The Harper Creek Falls Trail branches right at about 3.4 miles, another access to the creek for casual day hikers and those who want to fish. The side trail leads right about 1.3 miles to FR 464, making a nice day hike to the falls on Chestnut Cove Branch (2.8 miles round-trip) or to North Harper Creek Falls, just 0.2 mile farther on the North Harper Creek Trail. From the base of the falls, the North Harper Creek Trail climbs steeply (the only steep section of the entire trail). There are good views of the falls and surrounding area from the top. The trail levels again and ends on FR 58 at 4.5 miles. From FR 58, the falls are an easy 1.5-mile day hike with swimming possibilities.

A less-traveled circuit uses the western end of the Persimmon Ridge Trail and the Harper Creek Trail. From FR 58 (last directions above under "Finding the trailhead"), hikers can create a 5.6-mile route that descends the steeper Persimmon Ridge Trail, goes right on the North Harper Creek Trail, and right again on the Harper Creek Trail for a gradual climb back to FR 58. This hike is possible with one car because it's only a 0.6-mile walk on FR 58 between the Harper Creek and Persimmon Ridge Trailheads.

THE ACCESSIBLE WATERFALL

WHY GO?

The easiest taste of the area is the Upper Creek Trail, on NC 181 north of Morganton. The 1.5-mile loop is steep and strenuous, but take it slow and fully explore the cascades. Trails exit the parking lot in both directions. Take the trail on the left side, looking out at the view from the lot. The trail descends to the stream above the falls, crossing back and forth as you descend. Be cautious. Go right on the lower trail as it switchbacks up to the parking area (a side trail through the fence leads to informal campsites).

FINDING THE TRAILHEAD

From NC 181, the Upper Creek Trail is 0.8 mile north of the Barkhouse Picnic Area on the right (GPS: 35.960088 / -81.861013).

19 LINVILLE GORGE WILDERNESS

WHY GO?

A 12,000-acre tract of designated wilderness, Linville Gorge lies between Jonas Ridge to the east and Linville Mountain to the west. The Blue Ridge Parkway skirts the head of the gorge on the northwest, where the Parkway's Linville Falls Recreation Area provides a nice glimpse into the chasm.

Peaks on the rim of the gorge tower over Morganton and Lake James. The wild canyon, up to 2,000 feet deep in places, was first protected as a primitive area by the USDA Forest Service in 1951. It became an "instant wilderness" area with the passage of the 1964 Wilderness Act. A subsequent wilderness bill in 1984 expanded the area.

No logging has ever taken place here. Virgin forest and rugged, wild tangles of primeval density can be found in places where few people venture. Fire is an active part of the gorge ecosystem, and blazes in the past few years have blackened big parts of the wilderness. Linville Gorge is the most popular of North Carolina's wilderness areas, and only a limited number of permits are available for weekend camping between May 31 and October 31. Campers can remain in the area for only three days and two nights. Permits can be reserved in advance (for instance, June permits are available May 1) by calling the forest service office at (828) 652-2144. A limited number of first-come, first-served permits are available at the gorge's information cabin (see next page).

The gorge funnels traffic into a narrow area, concentrating trail use (the reverse of how trails at Shining Rock Wilderness funnel hikers to the crest). Those who want solitude should pursue a rugged off-trail adventure or go in late fall, winter, or spring—also the best times for bushwhacking to avoid timber rattlesnakes and copperheads, active in warmer months. If you must visit during peak season, go between Sunday and Thursday.

My trail descriptions include the forest service's assessment of how heavily each trail is used. The roughest, most strenuous, and primitive paths will be the best bet for seeing the fewest people. Several of these trails access trackless areas where the terrain invites bushwhacking. Consult the map here and the forest service's Linville Gorge Wilderness map to locate these places. Some are obvious and just off popular trails, which makes it relatively easy to find a secluded camp or lunch site. Others are large tracts just waiting for serious explorers. Except at trailheads, trails are unmarked and, in places, difficult to follow. Hikers get lost here every year. Other precautions include practicing zero-impact camping and wearing bright clothing during hunting season, late October to early January.

Hikes include a wonderful roadside view trail and a variety of others into a wilderness chasm, varying from a down-and-back trip to the bottom of the gorge to a few circuit hikes. Even if you don't venture into the gorge, the 0.2-mile trail to Wiseman's View is a worthwhile side trip that will give you a feel for the gorge and its surrounding system of forest roads.

THE RUNDOWN

General location: About 11 miles south of Linville, right off the Parkway

Distance: 0.2 mile for the Wiseman's View Overlook Trail; 1.8 miles round-trip for the Pine Gap Trail; about 3 miles for the Bynum Bluff–Pine Gap circuit; 9-mile circuit at the southern end of the gorge using the Pinch In, Conley Cove, and Rock Jock Trails

Difficulty: Easy for Wiseman's View and Pine Gap Trails; moderate for the Bynum Bluff–Pine Gap circuit; strenuous for the Linville Gorge trail circuit

Maps: USGS Linville Falls and Ashford. The best map is the USDA Forest Service map of the Linville Gorge Wilderness. www.nationalforestmapstore.com/category-s/1844.htm

Elevation gain: 520 feet for the Bynum Bluff–Pine Gap circuit

Water availability: Water is plentiful; treat for drinking.

For more information: Grandfather Ranger District, Pisgah National Forest, 109 East Lawing Dr., Nebo 28761; (828) 652-2144. Stop by the forest service Linville Gorge information cabin, 0.5 mile on the right past the Linville Falls Trail; open Apr–Oct, 9 a.m. to 5 p.m. Fri–Sun; (828) 765-7550; ncmst.org

FINDING THE TRAILHEAD

 From US 221 in the community of Linville Falls, turn on NC 183. In 0.7 mile from that junction, turn right on SR 1238, the Wiseman's View Road (also called Kistler Memorial Highway), where prominent signs direct hikers to Linville Gorge. The Linville Falls Trailhead parking is a short distance on the left (GPS: 35.950450/-81.933095); the national forest information cabin is 0.5 mile on the right (GPS: 35.945024/-81.933159).

The trails descend from the left side of SR 1238 and are listed here by their distance south of the NC 183/SR 1238 junction: Pine Gap Trail, 0.9 mile (GPS: 35.940283/-81.930159); Bynum Bluff Trail, 1.5 miles; Cabin Trail, 1.9 miles (GPS: 35.927766/-81.925359); Babel Tower Trail, 2.7 miles; Wiseman's View Trail, 3.8 miles (GPS: 35.903189/-81.907333); Conley Cove–Rock Jock Trail, 5.3 miles; Pinch In Trail, 8.2 miles.

THE HIKES

A nice prelude to a hike from the western side of the gorge is a warm-up on the Wiseman's View Trail. This easy, wheelchair-accessible 0.2-mile trail is not a long detour from the Parkway, and it will really give you the flavor of this primitive cleft in the Blue Ridge. The parking area is only 3.8 miles from the paved road. The view is spectacular, and you pass the forest service information cabin on the drive.

Unless you just hike to the river and back—which many people do to swim, fish, picnic, or camp—you'll need to have cars at two trailheads to avoid a walk along dusty SR 1238. Most hikers intent on a longer jaunt into Linville Gorge enter and exit at two different western side trails and follow the river on the Linville Gorge Trail between them. The easiest of these trails into and out of the gorge is the 0.7-mile Pine Gap Trail.

You'd be hard pressed to find a rockier ridge to run than the ramparts above the Linville River deep in the Linville Gorge. The route from Shortoff Mountain (immediate right) beyond to Table Rock and distant Hawksbill are wilderness walking at their best. PHOTO BY BILL RUSS. COURTESY OF VISITNC.COM

It drops on a rare gradual grade and descends to a junction with the Bynum Bluff Trail. A left turn leads out to a crag with spectacular views of a sharp bend in the river (avoid a right turn onto the Linville Gorge Trail on the way). Retrace your steps for a day hike of about 2 miles.

An easy circuit hike that requires just a 0.6-mile roadside walk pairs the Pine Gap Trail with the Bynum Bluff Trail. The Bynum Bluff Trail starts out gradually, reaches the point of a long promontory, then plummets down a sharp ridge to the Pine Gap Trail in 1 mile. Just beyond this junction, the Linville Gorge Trail goes right, downriver. Take in the views described above on the crag in a sharp bend in the river, or turn right for an out-and-back side trip along the river on the Linville Gorge Trail. Whichever you choose, make the easier climb out of the gorge on the Pine Gap Trail and walk the roadside for a 2.7-mile hike (if you don't go downstream).

KEY POINTS: BYNUM BLUFF–PINE GAP CIRCUIT

0.0   Start at the Bynum Bluff Trailhead.

1.0   Descend Bynum Bluff Trail to junction on left with Pine Gap Trail.

1.2   Viewpoint on river.

1.4   Right turn onto Pine Gap Trail.

2.1   SR 1238; turn left on road.

2.7   Bynum Bluff Trailhead.

Accessed from the Bynum Bluff or Pine Gap Trail, the Linville Gorge Trail descends along the west side of the river for almost 11.5 miles; the other trails that drop to join it afford other in-and-out options, many with obvious points of interest. The trail starts south around a sharp bend in the river on side-hill terrain, close under SR 1238. At just over 1 mile, the Linville Gorge Trail meets the Cabin Trail, a steep, strenuous 1-mile climb to SR 1238. On the left at the junction, a side trail juts out onto a bend in the river, reaching the peak of a 3,090-foot promontory. Continuing along the river another 0.8 mile, the trail switchbacks down, then slabs to a junction with the Babel Tower Trail at 2 miles. A side trail goes left to another summit, this one 3,035 feet, also encircled by the river. The popular Babel Tower Trail climbs a scenic ridge 1.2 miles to its trailhead on SR 1238.

From the junction, the Linville Gorge Trail switchbacks off a gap steeply down to the river. On the way to a junction with the Devils Hole Trail, on the left at 3.4 miles, there are great views of the gorge as it rises east nearly 2,000 feet to Hawksbill Mountain. The Devils Hole Trail climbs 1.5 miles to FR 210. At 3.9 miles on the Gorge Trail, the terrain flattens and there are plentiful campsites and a spring.

The trail continues under Wiseman's View and at 4.5 miles, the Spence Ridge Trail connects to the left, the most popular trail into the gorge from the east side, a comparatively gradual 1.7 miles from FR 210. Connecting with Spence Ridge Trail requires a wet crossing where the remains of a trail bridge in use between 2006 and 2013 are still visible. It was destroyed by a flood and won't be replaced.

Now the river flows directly down, the Linville Gorge Trail with it, to a junction on the right with the Conley Cove Trail at about 5.5 miles. This is a heavily used route, due largely to its lesser slope. From the junction, the Conley Cove Trail rises on a graded tread to a spring and a junction on the left with the canyon rim–running Rock Jock Trail at about 1 mile. It meets SR 1238 at 1.3 miles.

The Gorge Trail passes this junction and runs for its greatest uninterrupted length along the river, about 3.5 miles. There are plentiful places to swim and nice views across the river at popular rock climbing areas. The bulk of this section of trail flattens out.

At just more than 9 miles, the junction on the right is the Pinch In Trail, a ruggedly steep, view-packed 1.4-mile route to SR 1238. Below this trail junction, the Linville Gorge Trail gradually runs the next 2.4 miles beside the river, then fords it, to terminate. Savor the solitude and quiet at this point, then turn around and return to your vehicle along the river or the road. The true wilderness purist adventurer could concoct a wild circuit in this lower gorge area by climbing east to the Mountains-to-Sea Trail, or descending west from it.

Besides an out-and-back hike on this lesser-used portion of the lower Gorge Trail, a southern circuit exists for the experienced hiker/backpacker. Parking at the Pinch In Trailhead, descend into the gorge and hike up the canyon, exiting at the Conley Cove Trail. Go left on the Rock Jock Trail. When it exits onto SR 1238, it's only about 0.5 mile downhill south to the Pinch In Trailhead. This is a rugged 9-mile hike in either direction, exploring an area recommended by the forest service as the least-used in the gorge.

HAWKSBILL MOUNTAIN

WHY GO?

Hawksbill Mountain is a crag-capped peak on the rim of Linville Gorge Wilderness with panoramic views of summits.

THE RUNDOWN

General location: About 11 miles south of Linville, right off the Parkway
Distance: 1.4 miles round-trip. A nearby trailhead yields a longer, more gradual hike of 1.8 miles round-trip.
Difficulty: Moderate

Maps: USGS Linville Falls and Ashford. The best map is the USDA Forest Service map of the Linville Gorge Wilderness. www.nationalforest mapstore.com/category-s/1844.htm
Elevation gain: 700 feet

FINDING THE TRAILHEAD

Exit Blue Ridge Parkway at NC 181 near Pineola. Pass the NC 181/183 intersection, and 3 miles from there turn right onto Gingercake Road, SR 1264 (where a sign reads "Pisgah National Forest Table Rock Picnic Area 8.7 miles"). Measuring from there, bear left in 0.3 mile onto SR 1265 (signed "Table Rock Road"), which becomes gravel at 1.2 miles and becomes FSR 210. Pass trailheads for Sitting Bear and Devils Hole Trails at 2.7 miles. At 3.7 miles the Hawksbill Trail leaves the road on the right, with parking on the left (GPS: 35.914605/-81.878331).

THE HIKE

Hawksbill is the less-jagged summit of the prominent duo of peaks, Table Rock and Hawksbill, that dominate the skyline of Linville Gorge. It has a sloping, rocky crest and low vegetation that permits expansive views. It also offers relative privacy, at least compared with Table Rock. This hike also avoids an additional 5-mile drive on steep, winding, and dusty roads to Table Rock. Views include Table Rock itself and the cliffs and crags that make this a world-class rock climbing site.

The Hawksbill Mountain Trail enters the woods and climbs at a steady grade, then steepens. Take it slow in summer on the first 0.25 mile up the sunny side of Lettered Rock Ridge.

The path flattens, then slips off the sunny side onto a fern-bordered grade through a shady forest of rhododendron, maple, mountain laurel, and chestnut oak. The trail descends gradually, so be alert to make a sharp left at about 0.5 mile.

After the turn, the trail gradually steepens, undulating uphill through close vegetation and galax. After passing a shelter rock to the left of the trail, the path takes a hard right to the sandy soils and pines of the peak at 0.7 mile. Here, view trails fan out and trees give way to low vegetation such as Allegheny sand myrtle and sedges. Bear left on an obvious trail and wind down over prominent crags with fine views of Table Rock.

KEY POINTS

0.0   Start at the parking area.

0.5   Take a sharp left toward summit.

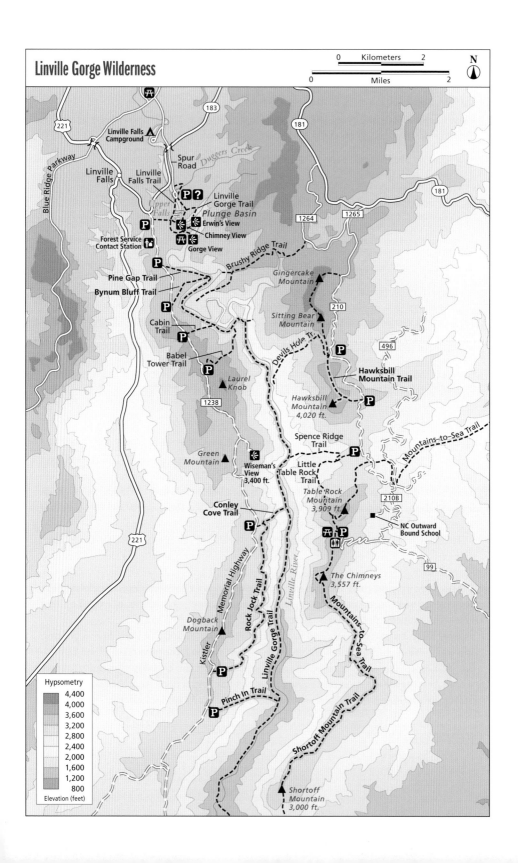

Linville Gorge Wilderness

0 Kilometers 2

0 Miles 2

N

Blue Ridge Parkway

221

183

181

Linville Falls Campground

Spur Road

Duggers Creek

Linville Falls

Linville Falls Trail

Upper Falls

P ?

Linville Gorge Trail

Plunge Basin

Erwin's View

Chimney View

Gorge View

Forest Service Contact Station

181

1264

1265

Brushy Ridge Trail

Gingercake Mountain

Pine Gap Trail

Bynum Bluff Trail

210

Sitting Bear Mountain

Cabin Trail

Devils Hole Tr.

496

P

Babel Tower Trail

Hawksbill Mountain Trail

Laurel Knob

1238

Hawksbill Mountain 4,020 ft.

P

Spence Ridge Trail

Green Mountain

Wiseman's View 3,400 ft.

Little Table Rock Trail

Mountains–to–Sea Trail

Table Rock Mountain 3,909 ft.

210B

Conley Cove Trail

P

NC Outward Bound School

Linville River

221

99

The Chimneys 3,557 ft.

Rock Jock Trail

Linville Gorge Trail

Kistler Memorial Highway

Mountains–to–Sea Trail

Dogback Mountain

P

Pinch In Trail

P

Shortoff Mountain Trail

Hypsometry

Elevation (feet)
4,400
4,000
3,600
3,200
2,800
2,400
2,000
1,600
1,200
800

Shortoff Mountain 3,000 ft.

0.7   Reach the summit. Return the way you came.

1.4   Arrive back at the parking area.

A longer, more-gradual, less-trafficked hike starts back on FR 210 at the Sitting Bear Trailhead. Ascend from the roadside parking spot to a large campsite at about 0.1 mile and go left on the obvious trail. (A right leads to Sitting Bear Rock; straight ahead, Devils Hole Trail drops 1.5 miles into Linville Gorge.) Gradually ascend the ridge to Hawksbill Mountain.

The intersection with the Hawksbill Trail is at about 0.7 mile; the summit is reached at 0.9 mile (1.8-mile round-trip).

TABLE ROCK AND SHORTOFF MOUNTAINS

WHY GO?

There are no better vistas of the rugged chasm of Linville Gorge than from its most distinctive summit, Table Rock Mountain—a craggy peak popular with rock climbers—and nearby Shortoff Mountain.

THE RUNDOWN

General location: About 11 miles south of Linville, just off the Parkway
Distance: Table Rock Mountain, 2.2 miles round-trip; Shortoff Mountain, 12.2 miles round-trip
Difficulty: Strenuous for Table Rock; more so for Shortoff Mountain
Maps: USGS Linville Falls and Ashford. The best map is the USDA

Forest Service map of the Linville Gorge Wilderness. www.national forestmapstore.com/category-s/1844.htm
Elevation gain: 609 feet for Table Rock; 1,875 feet for Shortoff Mountain

FINDING THE TRAILHEAD

Exit Blue Ridge Parkway at NC 181 near Pineola. Pass the NC 181/183 intersection, and 3 miles from there turn right onto Gingercake Road, SR 1264 where a sign reads "Pisgah National Forest Table Rock Picnic Area 8.7 miles". Measuring from there, bear left in 0.3 mile onto SR 1265 (signed "Table Rock Road"), which becomes gravel at 1.2 miles and becomes FSR 210. Pass trailheads and at 5.7 miles turn right onto FSR 210-B following sign to Table Rock Picnic Area. At 6.3 miles pass North Carolina Outward Bound School. At 7.25 miles start paved ascent to the trailhead/picnic area, reached at 8.7 miles (GPS: 35.886509 / -81.884792).

THE HIKES

The hike to Table Rock itself is far simpler than the drive to the trailhead. The Table Rock Trail parking lot is a lightly developed recreation area with tables and grills for picnicking and modern vault toilets. There's no water, and no camping is allowed. There are, however, great views; bring binoculars to watch climbers scale the cliffs.

The Table Rock Trail (combined with the Mountains-to-Sea Trail) leaves the north end of the parking area through profuse ferns and switchbacks right to the bottom of gradual steps. After a long stretch of rocky steps, the trail flattens and the footing gets easier. At about 0.3 mile the trail switchbacks right as a side trail dips left into a little gap. This is the Little Table Rock Trail, which leads to the Spence Ridge Trail.

Continuing, the white circle–blazed Mountains-to-Sea Trail goes left and the Table Rock Trail makes switchbacks to the base of the first large crag. The trail squeezes between two boulders, then switchbacks twice past a shelter rock on the right as you near the crest, where views open up to the head of the gorge, toward Linville Falls. You're at the former site of a fire tower. North, Hawksbill Mountain is the rocky, gentle peak just across the gap; Grandfather Mountain rises on the right. The tinkling of rock-climbing hardware and climber conversation drifts up from Table Rock's North Ridge route. At 1.1 miles, summit vegetation waves in the gusts so typical of a cliff-edge environment.

If you're surefooted, go south where the summit descends along a spectacular spine of rocks. Many trails wander over and among the boulders to disintegrate into climbers' paths, working their way to stomach-churning drops. Find a private crag for lunch.

To the south, just past the Table Rock parking area, is the convoluted ridge called The Chimneys. Beyond, Shortoff Mountain drops off to Lake James. Across the gorge, the prominent cliff is Wiseman's View, a recommended developed vista reached by road and a short accessible trail. Off to the right, the long crest of the Black Mountains includes Mount Mitchell.

The Shortoff Mountain Trail leaves the same parking area but heads south. It follows a gradual ridgetop, then slabs to the west of The Chimneys (3,557 feet), rejoins the ridge, then swings southeast to descend 900 feet, much of it steeply, into Chimney Gap (2,509 feet). Continuing along the Shortoff Mountain Trail (part of the Mountains-to-Sea Trail), a wet-weather spring is located 150 feet left of the trail at about 2.3 miles. The trail reaches the summit of Shortoff Mountain at about 5.2 miles (a logical turn-around for 12.2 mile round-trip). A spring is located beyond the summit in a small gap at about 5.6 miles. Paths reach clifftops where the most spectacular views in the gorge take in the deepest depths of the canyon (and reveal the impact of recent forest fires). Lake James sprawls below, a location for such memorable films as *The Last of the Mohicans* and the final scenes from *The Hunt for Red October,* where the escaped sub was supposed to be entering the coast of Maine.

20 LINVILLE FALLS RECREATION AREA

Surrounded by one of those periodic bulges in the narrow corridor of the Blue Ridge Parkway, Linville Falls is the high road's biggest waterfall (by volume of water). This oft-photographed cataract gushes 100 foaming feet into the Linville Gorge, the USDA Forest Service wilderness canyon that lies below the falls. The Parkway's easy National Recreation Trails introduce this wild chasm.

Hikes on both sides of the Linville River offer views of the falls. The routes in two separate options below start at the same small visitor center (open seasonally, offering restrooms and a bookshop) on the Linville River near Linville Falls Campground and Picnic Area.

The remoteness of the gorge kept loggers out; John D. Rockefeller donated the inspiring, virgin-forested parcel to the National Park Service in 1952. Towering hemlocks and white pines soar above rhododendron that bloom profusely in late May. This lofty forest gives way to crags and rocky viewpoints, but rock climbing is off-limits. In winter, cross-country skiers will find that these gradual trails make inspiring ski tours. When snow closes the Parkway, a forest service spur trail provides access (un-skiably steep at the top; see below).

DUGGERS CREEK LOOP, LINVILLE GORGE TRAIL, AND PLUNGE BASIN OVERLOOK TRAIL

WHY GO?
Three trails on the visitor center side of the river make the most scenic, least-visited hike to Linville Falls.

THE RUNDOWN

General location: Off the Blue Ridge Parkway, about 11 miles south of Linville

Distance: 0.5 mile for Duggers Creek Trail; 1 mile round-trip to Plunge Basin Overlook; 1.4 miles round-trip to Linville Gorge; 1.8 miles round-trip to both Plunge Basin and Linville Gorge

Difficulty: Easy for Duggers Creek Trail; moderate for Plunge Basin Overlook trail; moderate to strenuous for Linville Gorge

Maps: USGS Linville Falls. Download a Parkway handout map of Linville Falls trails at the "Brochures" link on the Blue Ridge Parkway's website (nps.gov/blri). The map is also available at the Linville Falls Visitor Center and Campground.

Water availability: Water fountain at visitor center in season

From Erwin's View, hikers can look back to spy other hikers peering down at the falls from Chimney View.

FINDING THE TRAILHEAD

Leave the Blue Ridge Parkway between mileposts 316 and 317 on the spur road to the trailhead, about 1 mile north of the US 221/Blue Ridge Parkway junction at the town of Linville Falls. The parking area is 1.5 miles from the Parkway, beyond the campground (GPS: 35.954806 / -81.927835).

THE HIKES

Just through the visitor center portico by the restrooms, go left at the junction onto the Duggers Creek Trail (the Linville Gorge Trail goes right). The path wanders 0.2 mile along beautiful Duggers Creek, past plaques with inspiring sayings, to the end of the parking lot (return to your car via the lot).

The Linville Gorge Trail goes right through inspiring hemlocks and rhododendrons. Turn right 0.3 mile from the visitor center for the easiest and best view of the falls at Plunge Basin Overlook. The path is level to a bench but then heads steeply down stone steps to a rock-walled perch above the falls (1-mile round-trip).

Back at the junction, go right; the gradual path has handrails as it skirts steep drops, descends a steep flight of steps, and turns sharply right at the bottom (the left is for the people who miss the turn). The trail follows the base of a towering cliff. When you hear river noise off to the left, keep right to the water's edge and rock-hop near the base of the thundering falls (may be too icy in winter). The emerald water may tempt you—but swimming isn't allowed.

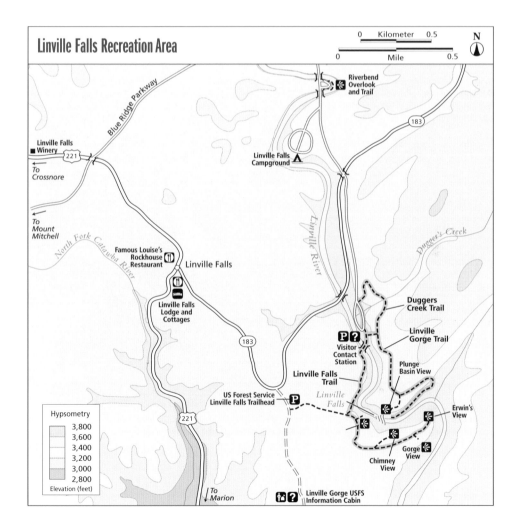

Linville Falls Recreation Area

If you linger over lunch and scan the rock-hewn amphitheater, the start of Linville Gorge, you can imagine the hemmed-in feeling William Linville and his son must have felt near here in 1766 when confronted by Native Americans—who scalped them.

The round-trip hike to here is 1.4 miles, about 1.8 miles total with Plunge Basin Overlook.

KEY POINTS

0.0   Start at the visitor center.

0.3   Plunge Basin Overlook Trail branches from Linville Gorge Trail.

0.35 Plunge Basin Overlook.

0.4   Back at junction, take trail on right to falls.

0.7   Gorge Trail reaches base of falls. Return to the visitor center.

1.4   Arrive back at the visitor center.

In winter when snow closes the Blue Ridge Parkway's National Park Service access, a nearby, easily reached US Forest Service trailhead leads to views like this.

LINVILLE FALLS TRAIL

WHY GO?
Three hikes explore virgin forest views near Linville Falls.

THE RUNDOWN

General location: Off the Blue Ridge Parkway, about 11 miles south of Linville

Distance: 1 to 2 miles round-trip

Difficulty: Easy for Upper Falls View; moderate for Chimney, Gorge, and Erwin's Views

Map: Download online map above.

FINDING THE TRAILHEAD

Directions are the same as above to the visitor center, except in winter when snow closes the Parkway. From the US 221/Parkway junction near the town of Linville Falls, go south on US 221 and turn left onto NC 183 in the community of Linville Falls. In 0.7 mile, turn right at Linville Gorge signs onto SR 1238. Even if that road is unplowed, the trailhead is just a few hundred yards ahead on the left (GPS: 35.950563/-81.933241). The path joins the Linville Falls Trail and accesses the visitor center and other trails covered in the previous option.

THE HIKE

The level, road-width Linville Falls Trail crosses the Linville River on a footbridge to more distant and more popular views of the falls. Across the bridge, parallel the river; at 0.4 mile the spur trail from SR 1238 joins on the right.

There's a side trail left to Upper Falls View, the river's first big drop, at 0.5 mile. The main trail rises through towering virgin hemlock forest, with white pine, oak, and birches, then reaches the scrubbier vegetation and drier soils on crags overlooking the gorge.

At 0.6 mile from the visitor center, another junction splits the trail at a picnic/rain shelter. Left, steep steps reach Chimney View at 0.7 mile, an oft-photographed vista of the entire falls. At the shelter, continue away from the visitor center through piney forest to the Gorge View Overlook, on the right, with an interpretive sign. The gorge appears again on the right; on the left at about 1 mile is Erwin's View, where the falls and gorge are both in sight from 3,360 feet (a 2-mile round-trip).

KEY POINTS

- 0.0   Start at the visitor center.
- 0.4   Forest service spur trail from SR 1238.
- 0.5   Side trail left to Upper Falls View.
- 0.6   Junction left to Chimney View.
- 1.0   Erwin's View. Return to visitor center.
- 2.0   Arrive back at the visitor center.

21 CRABTREE MEADOWS RECREATION AREA

WHY GO?

This is one of western North Carolina's best waterfall hikes—especially on a sunny spring day after significant rain.

THE RUNDOWN

General location: Off the Blue Ridge Parkway, about 40 miles northeast of Asheville

Distance: 2.5-mile loop, about 3.1 miles round trip with added distance from the parking area past the amphitheater

Difficulty: Strenuous

Maps: USGS Celo. Download a Parkway handout map of Crabtree Falls trails at the "Brochures" link on the Blue Ridge Parkway's website (see below), or grab one at the campground kiosk (in season).

Elevation gain: 600 feet

Water availability: Developed facilities have water May–Oct. Treat stream water.

For more information: Blue Ridge Parkway, 199 Hemphill Knob Rd., Asheville 28803-8686; (828) 271-4779; (828) 298-0398 (recorded information and mailing requests); nps.gov/blri. Reserve campsites in advance at recreation.gov. Crabtree Meadows Campground kiosk (828) 675-5444, in season.

FINDING THE TRAILHEAD

Take the northernmost entrance into the Crabtree Meadows Recreation Area (milepost 339.5) and bear left to park in the large lot beside the now-closed concession building (GPS: 35.812686, -82.143500). The Parkway has closed the trailhead near the campground kiosk to reduce congestion for campers. Hikers should take the trail past the amphitheater and turn right on the first campground road to the contact station and trailhead.

THE HIKE

Though only 253 acres, Crabtree Meadows Recreation Area, flanking Parkway milepost 339, is a small but compelling scenic enclave. There's also a campground and picnic area. A small snack bar/gift shop has been closed in recent years. Some Parkway concessions elsewhere are also struggling, so check the website for the latest.

The Crabtree Falls Loop Trail descends on a wide gravel path to the loop junction. Turn right and wind down into a shady, often wet hemlock-forested cove, where steep stone steps mark two switchbacks.

At the base of the falls, a bridge with embedded benches spans Crabtree Creek. This is one of the most picturesque falls in the Southern Appalachians—water dances down over ledges in a cascading fan of foam.

Continue across the stream and climb a sunny slope of switchbacks with great views of the falls. A bench marks the top of the climb to the crest of the cataract.

The trail then becomes intimate and easy as you wander under a hemlock forest through a tunnel of rhododendron and mountain laurel. Sunny openings in tall trees reveal mossy, grassy little bogs. It's A+ scenery as you cross a small side stream bridge and

Some hikers make the rocky traverse to the base of Crabtree Falls to revel in its cascading fan of foam.

then a bigger span at 1.3 miles, where water cascades over ledge after ledge. The trail crosses a bridge at a bog beside a bench where northern white hellebore grows in late April. At about 2.1 miles, a side trail branches right to campground Loop B (see the map to shortcut back to your car). Steer left; at the next junction you can turn right to bisect campground Loop A back to the trailhead. Or keep straight, go right at the loop junction, and return the way you started.

Crabtree Meadows Recreation Area

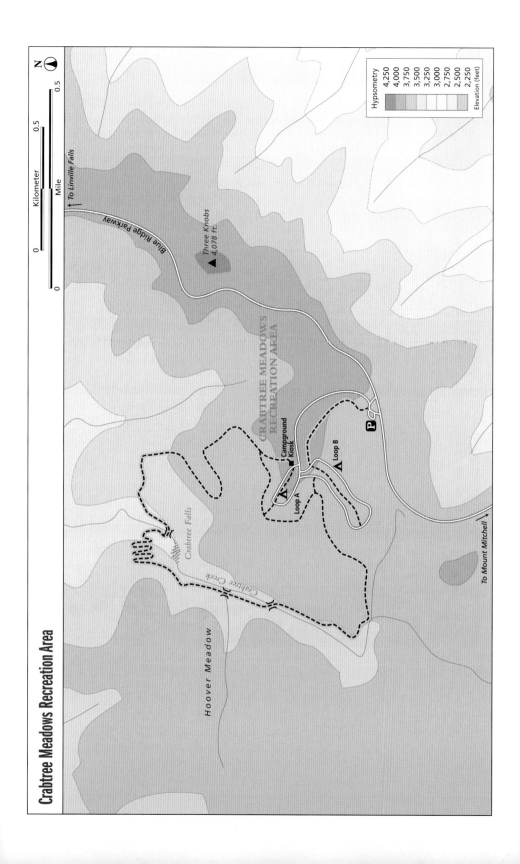

N

Kilometer

0   0.5   0.5

Mile

0

To Linville Falls

Blue Ridge Parkway

Three Knobs
4,078 ft.

CRABTREE MEADOWS
RECREATION AREA

Campground
Kiosk

Loop A

Loop B

P

Crabtree Falls

Crabtree Creek

Hoover Meadow

To Mount Mitchell

Hypsometry

4,250
4,000
3,750
3,500
3,250
3,000
2,750
2,500
2,250

Elevation (feet)

Mount Mitchell's "newish" spiraling view tower is handicapped accessible and offers great views and horizon-spotting interpretive plaques.

KEY POINTS

0.0   Park by old concession and take trail to the campground kiosk.

0.3   Trail departs former campground parking.

0.8   Descend long flight of stone steps.

01.2 Crabtree Falls.

2.4   Side trail to campground Loop B.

2.6   Side trail to campground Loop A; could go right to reach trailhead.

3.1   Arrive back at the trailhead.

Mount Mitchell is the highest peak east of the Mississippi. It's a crowning part of the Blue Ridge Parkway experience—the only motorized access to the mountain is from the Parkway, at milepost 355.3.

The nearly 2,000-acre Mount Mitchell State Park—North Carolina's first—clings to the highest peak of the Black Mountains, a serrated string of summits that juts away from the Parkway and Blue Ridge to dominate the western skyline of North Carolina. The mighty Blacks are frequently seen from the Parkway as a dark ridge crest rising above the clouds. The range includes six of the ten highest peaks in eastern North America.

Unlike that contrastingly named New England range, the White Mountains, the Blacks would have to be nearly 8,000 feet in height to reach a climate cold enough to create the treeless alpine zone found in New Hampshire at just under 5,000 feet. But the Black Mountains reign supreme, and high winds and deep snow (104 inches annually) yield a surprisingly severe climate.

The state park was established in 1915 through the efforts of then Governor Locke Craig (1913–17) and Theodore Roosevelt, among others. The park was created at a time when massive logging of the state's western mountains threatened to completely eradicate the last of the virgin forest.

Today, the park is a microcosm of the environmental factors that are destroying the world's high-elevation forests. An infestation by the balsam woolly adelgid, a pest introduced into the United States around 1900, has killed many Fraser firs. More recent studies suggest that red spruce trees have been damaged by acid rain, which inhibits a tree's ability to ingest nutrients.

Another significant factor seems to be ozone. The result is that stark tree skeletons stand tall and gray in ghostlike groves. Luckily, early 1990s changes to the Clean Air Act seem to be improving conditions in the evergreen zone. The Balsam Nature Trail is a nice introduction to this ongoing ecological issue.

The story of Mount Mitchell's crowning as the East's loftiest peak, and its naming, involves considerable controversy. Although Elisha Mitchell, a Connecticut native, is acknowledged as the first to measure the preeminent peak, that distinction was also claimed by North Carolinian Thomas Clingman, a congressman, senator, and Confederate brigadier general. In 1835 Mitchell was intrigued by the claim of early botanist André Michaux that a peak in the Black Mountains was the highest in the United States. Mitchell began measuring summits in the Black Mountains barometrically and arrived at the conclusion that one of the summits, then called Black Dome, was 6,476 feet high. As a result, the mountain was listed in an 1839 atlas as the East's highest peak.

Clingman vaulted into what was apparently already a controversy in 1855, stating that Mitchell had not measured the loftiest peak and that he had; Clingman claimed 6,941 feet for the summit. Wishing to consolidate his advantage, the elderly Mitchell returned to the mountain in 1857.

Stopping his work near the end of June, Mitchell left his party to visit the homes of former guides, including Thomas "Big Tom" Wilson. Five days later, Mitchell's son reached Wilson's cabin to learn that his father had never arrived. Wilson remembered an obscure route over the mountain that he'd shown Mitchell years before. Following that

It's easy to point out valley sights from the almost-alpine heights of the Mount Mitchell range.
PHOTO BY WORTH H. WELLER

route to the base of a 40-foot waterfall, the party found Mitchell, who had apparently stumbled in the fading light and drowned in a large pool.

Needless to say, the public immediately flocked to Mitchell's side in the debate, and a year after his burial in Asheville, he was laid to vindicated rest on "his" mountaintop. The peak officially became Mount Mitchell in 1858.

Ultimately, Mitchell's claim to the peak is enhanced by the fact that his final measurement of 6,672 feet is only 12 feet shy of the peak's true elevation—remarkable, since much later measurements were even further afield. No one in this story could complain about his place in history. Mitchell has the East's highest peak and Clingman's name adorns Clingmans Dome (6,643 feet), the Great Smokies' highest summit. And Thomas "Big Tom" Wilson has his own summit—Big Tom (6,552 feet)—1.1 miles north of Mount Mitchell on the Deep Gap Trail.

The summit is still the site of Mitchell's grave. Various view towers have marked the peak, including a medieval-appearing stone tower in 1926. In 1959 a geometrical eyesore was built, but it was mercifully replaced in 2008 with a low-profile, wheelchair-accessible tourist tower. The paved walk from the parking area to this view point is the "easiest" hike in the park.

Mount Mitchell State Park's ranger office is on the right immediately after the park entrance; next is a restaurant (open mid-May to late October). The park's small, nine-site tent campground is the East's highest (open May through October). Summit facilities include a snack bar (open June 1 through Labor Day and weekends through October) and restrooms beside the parking lot, where a noteworthy nature museum was dedicated during the summer of 2001.

In winter, motor access to the park is problematical. The Blue Ridge Parkway closes during snowfall. When the road is plowed and stable weather permits, public access is allowed from the NC 80/Blue Ridge Parkway junction. Call ahead in winter, either to the state park or the Blue Ridge Parkway, before making the drive. Backpackers must register their vehicles on trailhead forms before camping.

These are good times for trails on Mount Mitchell. In 2010 local trail enthusiast Jake Blood and like-minded hikers launched the North Carolina High Peaks Trail Association to popularize the Black Mountain range and improve its overgrown trails. The group has also become the Friends of Mount Mitchell State Park. They've upgraded trails near Black Mountain Campground, rescued the Black Mountain Crest Trail, and rerouted a section of the Mountains-to-Sea Trail. They are also orchestrating a multi-year, grant-funded rebuilding of the Mount Mitchell Trail. Check out their trail resources and group hikes at ncHighPeaks.org.

MOUNT MITCHELL TRAIL

WHY GO?
A climb through virgin forest to the summit of Mount Mitchell involves one of the great elevation changes in the East. A lower circuit makes a shorter hike.

THE RUNDOWN

General location: About 30 miles northeast of Asheville, at mile 355 of the Blue Ridge Parkway
Distance: 11.4 miles round-trip to the summit; 5.7-mile loop
Difficulty: Extremely strenuous to the summit; moderate for the lower virgin forest hike
Maps: USGS Old Fort and Mount Mitchell. The High Peaks Trail Association publishes a good map. Download the state park trail map at ncparks.gov/Visit/parks/momi/main.php. The USDA Forest Service South Toe River Trail Map is good too.
Elevation gain: 3,700 feet
For more information: Mount Mitchell State Park, 2388 State Hwy. 128, Burnsville 28714; (828) 675-4611 / 877-722-6762 or reserveamerica.com for camping reservations; e-mail: mount.mitchell@ncparks.gov. ncmst.org.

FINDING THE TRAILHEAD
Leave the Parkway at milepost 344, going west on NC 80. In 2.2 miles, turn left onto FR 472. Black Mountain Campground is on the right at just more than 3 miles (GPS: 35.751719 / -82.221163). Park in the new trailhead parking lot just outside the campground entrance.

THE HIKE
If only physically climbing a mountain earns the summit for you, this trail is your chance—nearly 4,000 vertical feet of it.

Cross the bridge into the campground, go left on the road to the group campsites, then left with the path. Your blue-blazed trail quickly turns right off of the Upper River Loop Trail (a recommended, yellow-blazed 3.7-mile streamside hike along the Toe River). You'll see white Mountains-to-Sea Trail blazes along much of this route. The trail climbs through impressive stands of hardwoods and evergreens. Stay on the Mount Mitchell Trail past the junction with the Higgins Bald Trail, on the left at 1.9 miles. The Higgins Bald Trail comes back in at 2.8 miles and climbs through virgin forest of red spruce and Fraser fir. At about 3.9 miles, join the Buncombe Horse Range Trail. Pass the Commissary Hill Primitive Camping Site; in 0.1 mile the trail turns right and makes a rocky climb toward the peak. You'll join the Balsam Nature Trail near the Mitchell summit, where a left on the paved summit trail reaches the Mount Mitchell view tower at 5.6 miles. Consider taking a right on the white-blazed Higgins Bald Trail/MST on the way down. It's only 0.3 mile farther than the Mitchell Trail and includes a nice waterfall.

The lower circuit of the Higgins Bald Trail is also a nice hike. Follow the hike as above, but turn left onto the Higgins Bald Trail at 2.8 miles. At 4.2 miles turn right onto the Mount Mitchell Trail and return to the campground for about a 6-mile hike. *Note:* Black Mountain Campground is a best-kept-secret camping spot.

KEY POINTS

0.0   Start at Black Mountain Campground.

1.5   Higgins Bald Trail goes left.

2.8   Higgins Bald Trail returns on the left.

3.9   Left on Buncombe Horse Range Trail.

4.0   Right off horse trail to climb Commissary Ridge.

5.6   Reach the summit tower.

11.4   Arrive back at the campground.

BALSAM NATURE TRAIL

WHY GO?

The Balsam Nature Trail is a self-guided interpretive trail that provides a startling introduction to acid rain deforestation.

THE RUNDOWN

General location: About 30 miles northeast of Asheville, at mile 355 of the Blue Ridge Parkway.
Distance: 0.8-mile loop
Difficulty: Easy
Maps: USGS Mount Mitchell. Download the state park trail map at ncparks.gov/Visit/parks/momi/main .php.

Elevation gain: Negligible
For more information: Mount Mitchell State Park, 2388 State Hwy. 128, Burnsville 28714; (828) 675-4611 / 877-722-6762 or reserveamerica .com for camping reservations; e-mail: mount.mitchell@ncparks.gov

FINDING THE TRAILHEAD

Take NC 128, the state park access road, from milepost 355; go all the way to the southern end of the Mount Mitchell summit parking area, near the concession/museum. Take the ascending paved Mount Mitchell Summit Tower Trail past the Old Mitchell Trail on the right, and take the next left at the Balsam Nature trail sign. The handicapped accessible path to the tower viewpoint continues up and to the right.

THE HIKE

The white triangle–blazed Balsam Nature Trail explores the highest, most Northern climate in the South. Recently improved trailside interpretive exhibits feature the ecosystem, climate, plants, and animals that live in this rarefied evergreen zone, found this far south only at elevations above 5,500 feet.

In addition to coniferous species like Fraser fir and red spruce, the most prevalent deciduous species at this elevation is mountain ash. New England plants include hobblebush and mountain wood sorrel, or oxalis, a clover-like ground covering associated with boreal forests (early June bloom). The rhododendron here blooms in late June. In addition to the yellow birch trees found on the trail, you might notice a grove of mountain paper birch, similar to the white-barked birches so often associated with New Hampshire and Vermont. The small heart-shaped leaves are the giveaway. If, as some scientists speculate, this grove is actually a separate species of birch, then only about 400 specimens exist, all within this state park. The snapdragon-like purple turtlehead grows at damp seeps along the trail. The nice view north along the Black Mountain range shows Mount Craig beyond the summit parking lot.

The Balsam Nature Trail turns left where the Mount Mitchell Trail descends Commissary Ridge to Black Mountain Campground. The trail passes a small stream, likely the highest spring in eastern America (average temperature when not frozen: 36°F), then ends at the summit parking lot.

KEY POINTS

0.0   Start at the Mount Mitchell summit parking area.

0.05 Old Mount Mitchell Trail goes right.

0.15 Tower Trail goes right.

0.6   Balsam Nature Trail turns left from Mount Mitchell Trail.

0.8   Arrive back at the parking area.

BLACK MOUNTAIN CREST TRAIL

WHY GO?

An inspiring out-and-back summit-hopping hike or backpack crosses a sparsely vegetated ridge above 6,000 feet. Views plummet 4,000 feet into adjacent valleys.

Spring brings electric colors to the crest of the Black Mountains. PHOTO BY WORTH H. WELLER

THE RUNDOWN

General location: About 30 miles northeast of Asheville, at mile 355 of the Blue Ridge Parkway

Distance: 11.3 miles one way to Bowlens Creek Trailhead. Round-trip day hikes vary: Mount Mitchell to Mount Craig, 2 miles; Mount Mitchell to Deep Gap, just under 8 miles. There's also a 6.6-mile loop of the summit.

Difficulty: Moderate to Mount Craig; strenuous for longer hikes

Maps: USGS Mount Mitchell and Celo. The High Peaks Trail Association publishes a good map.

There's also the USDA Forest Service South Toe River Trail Map. Download the state park trail map at ncparks .gov/Visit/parks/momi/main.php.

Note: The USGS quads intersect annoyingly on the trail's ridgeline location.

Elevation gain: 535 feet to Mount Craig and back

For more information: Mount Mitchell State Park, 2388 State Hwy. 128, Burnsville 28714; (828) 675-4611; e-mail: mount.mitchell@ncparks .gov. North Carolina High Peaks Trail Association: NCHighPeaks.org.

FINDING THE TRAILHEAD

Take NC 128, the state park access road, from milepost 355, and go all the way to the Mount Mitchell summit parking area. As you round the last curve into the summit parking area, the Black Mountain Crest Trail (also called the Deep Gap Trail on the way to that landmark notch) goes north on the left between log cabin picnic shelters (GPS: 35.767296 / -82.264453).

To reach the Bowlens Creek Trailhead, turn south from US 19E in Burnsville on NC 197. In 0.7 mile turn left onto Bowlens Creek Road (SR 1109). Go 2.4 miles to a hairpin curve, and take Watershed Road left a short distance to a five-car parking spot (GPS: 35.877137 / -82.284509). A sign warns of no turnaround and rough conditions ahead, so park here. The High Peaks Trail Association will likely have a new trailhead for this nationally significant hike in the next few years. If the lot is full, pass the hairpin turn and park by the small McClurd family cemetery, on the right.

THE HIKE

The first mile of the orange-triangle blazed Black Mountain Crest Trail makes a wonderful out-and-back 2-mile round-trip day hike to Mount Craig. The plaque on the peak memorializes Locke Craig, the governor who helped secure creation of this first North Carolina state park.

Pass the picnic shelters and dip down impressive stone stepped switchbacks through a spectacular spruce forest lush with ferns—the start of many miles of verdant Canadian zone hiking. At the 0.5-mile mark in the gap (about 6,330 feet), the land drops away west to Mitchell Creek and Mitchell Falls (4,400 feet), where Elisha Mitchell died. Then the trail rebounds to the open summit of Mount Craig (6,645 feet), the Blacks' second-highest peak. Looking back to the mountain you conquered by car, this view helps the peak gain in stature.

The trail dips to another gap then ascends to the summit of Big Tom (6,581 feet) at 1.2 miles. A plaque here memorializes Wilson.

The Black Mountain Crest Trail descends 0.4 mile to the Big Tom Trail, which drops east off the mountain (the return leg of the loop hike). Climb on to Balsam Cone (6,611 feet) at about 2 miles. The trail crosses Cattail Peak at 6,583 feet, then leaves the state park for national forest. Climb again briefly to Potato Hill (6,440 feet) then drop dramatically into Deep Gap at just under 4 miles. Deep Gap's shelter was torn down in 1995; now this is the site of the Deep Gap Primitive Camping Site. A spring is 300 yards down the mountain to the east.

Deep Gap, the more than 700-foot cleft visible for miles in the ridge of the Blacks, is a good turnaround point for a day hike (or backpack—it's the first place where camping is permitted as the Crest Trail makes its way north along the ridge).

KEY POINTS

0.0   Start at the Mount Mitchell summit parking area.

1.0   Reach the summit of Mount Craig.

1.6   Big Tom Trail intersects from the right.

3.9   Reach Deep Gap, a good place to turn around. Return the way you came.

7.8   Arrive back at the parking area.

The end-to-end adventure on this trail requires two cars and substantial driving. But the crest trail does continue, climbing out of Deep Gap to Winter Star Mountain (6,203 feet), where new switchbacks have tamed a dangerous rocky climb. The trail gains the lower ridge of the northern Blacks, with spectacular views. The trail goes left of the crest at about 6 miles, passing Gibbs Mountain and Horse Rock. At just more than 7 miles, the trail pitches up and slabs west of the final and most lofty of the northern Black Mountain peaks, Celo Knob (6,327 feet), at 7.5 miles. The next 4 or so miles go downhill on

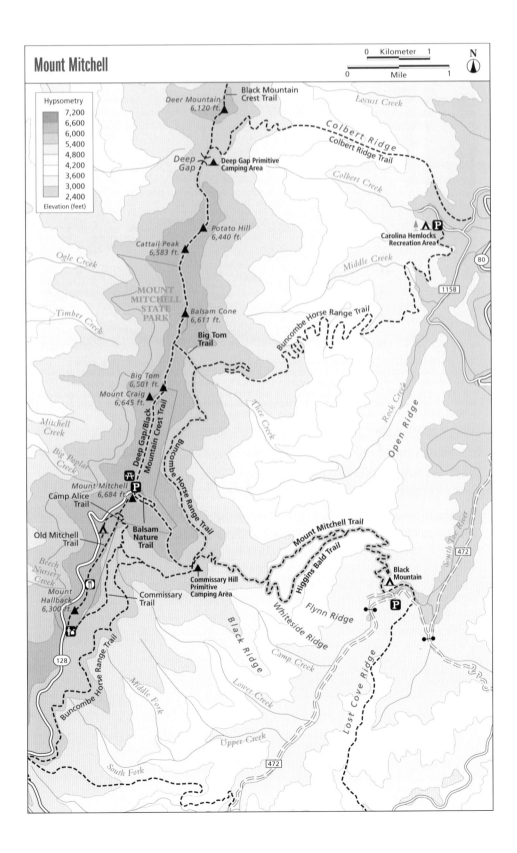

Mount Mitchell

0 Kilometer 1

0 Mile 1

N

Hypsometry

7,200
6,600
6,000
5,400
4,800
4,200
3,600
3,000
2,400

Elevation (feet)

Deer Mountain
6,120 ft.

Black Mountain
Crest Trail

Locust Creek

Colbert Ridge

Colbert Ridge Trail

Deep
Gap

Deep Gap Primitive
Camping Area

Colbert Creek

Potato Hill
6,440 ft.

Cattail Peak
6,583 ft.

Carolina Hemlocks
Recreation Area

P

80

Middle Creek

1158

Ogle Creek

MOUNT
MITCHELL
STATE
PARK

Balsam Cone
6,611 ft.

Buncombe Horse Range Trail

Timber Creek

Big Tom
Trail

Big Tom
6,501 ft.

Three Creek

Rock Creek

Open Ridge

Mount Craig
6,645 ft.

Mitchell
Creek

Deep Gap/Black Mountain Crest Trail

Big Poplar
Creek

Buncombe Horse Range Trail

Mount Mitchell
6,684 ft.

Camp Alice
Trail

P

Balsam
Nature
Trail

Mount Mitchell Trail

Old Mitchell
Trail

Higgins Bald Trail

Black
Mountain

472

Beech
Nursery
Creek

Commissary Hill
Primitive
Camping Area

P

Mount
Hallback
6,300 ft.

Commissary
Trail

Flynn Ridge

Whiteside Ridge

Lost Cove Ridge

South Toe River

Buncombe Horse Range Trail

Black Ridge

Camp Creek

128

Middle Fork

Lower Creek

Upper Creek

South Fork

472

By the time Johnson City, Tennessee, architect D. R. Beeson took this photo in 1915, Mount Mitchell was almost completely logged and Elisha Mitchell's summit monument had lost its upper obelisk and was riddled with bullet holes. Luckily, a state park would be established the following year, and over the ensuing one hundred years, North Carolina State Parks has cared for his memorial and grown to protect parks across the state. COURTESY ARCHIVES OF APPALACHIA, EAST TENNESSEE STATE UNIVERSITY, D. R. BEESON PAPERS

a switchbacking descent to the trailhead along rushing, beautiful Bowlens Creek near Burnsville at just over 11 miles.

You might try a summit circuit that uses the Big Tom Trail to return on the Black Mountain Crest Trail: Leave the summit parking area on the tower trail, then veer off left on the Balsam Nature Trail. When that trail bears left, go straight on the Mount Mitchell Trail down Commissary Ridge to the scenic and easy Buncombe Horse Range Trail, about 1.6 miles from the summit. This 15-mile, white-blazed horse trail parallels the ridge crest north to south. Go left on the old logging grade and follow the rocky but level trail north 3 miles to the Big Tom Trail. The horse trail descends right, but go left to make a steep 0.4-mile climb of about 560 vertical feet to the crest. Once on the ridge, turn left onto the Black Mountain Crest Trail at about 5 miles and prepare for a spectacular return to Mount Mitchell over Big Tom and Mount Craig for a 6.6-mile hike.

23 **CRAGGY GARDENS**

How can names like Craggy Gardens, Craggy Dome, and Craggy Pinnacle not inspire hikers? Visible from all over northwest North Carolina, these barren crests offer awesome views.

As the Blue Ridge Parkway climbs from Asheville, the sun often disappears in a Craggies-caused microclimate. Summits and clouds coalesce, lending the area the feel of much higher mountains. Be prepared for a truly peak experience.

This part of the Parkway possesses some of the high road's most dramatic scenery. You'll swear the treeless Craggies compare with Scotland. Craggy Gardens is one of the best places to savor the beauty of the seemingly alpine balds and the late-June rhododendron bloom. (For more information, see the Roan Mountain chapter.) A visitor center with new interpretive exhibits sits on the Parkway beside the start of the Craggy Gardens Trail; a nearby picnic area has restroom facilities and another trailhead.

The Mountains-to-Sea Trail passes through Craggy Gardens; not far north, near Mount Mitchell, one of the MST's best day hikes runs from Walker Knob Overlook to NC 128.

From Craggy Pinnacle, the Blue Ridge Parkway swerves north through lime green spring buds toward Balsam Gap. Evergreeen-covered Mount Mitchell and the Black Mountains rise above.

The Craggy Flats picnic shelter sits amid open meadows. It was built by the Civilian Conservation Corps.

CRAGGY PINNACLE TRAIL

WHY GO?

One of the Parkway's most inspiring 360-degree views.

THE RUNDOWN

General location: Off the Parkway, 20 miles northeast of Asheville

Distance: 1.4 miles round-trip

Difficulty: Moderate

Maps: USGS Craggy Pinnacle. Download a parkway handout map of Craggy Gardens trails at the "Brochures" link on the Blue Ridge Parkway's website (see below), or grab one at the visitor center.

Elevation gain: 252 feet

Water availability: Fountains at visitor center and picnic area May–Oct

For more information: Blue Ridge Parkway, 199 Hemphill Knob Rd., Asheville 28803-8686; (828) 271-4779; (828) 298-0398 (recorded information and mailing requests); nps.gov/blri. ncmst.org.

FINDING THE TRAILHEAD

Craggy Pinnacle Trail begins in the Craggy Dome parking area, milepost 364, north of the visitor center. A spur road leads to the parking area (GPS: 35.704180/-82.373658).

THE HIKE

At 5,892 feet, Craggy Pinnacle may be the Craggies' premier view. A veritable who's who of Southern Appalachian summits stand out on a clear day. The Mount Mitchell range dominates the northern horizon.

The path passes two resting benches on the way to a trail junction at 0.3 mile. Off to the right, a vista looks down on the visitor center. Back at the main trail, go right, to the top at 0.7 mile. Return the way you came.

CRAGGY GARDENS TRAIL AND MOUNTAINS-TO-SEA TRAIL

WHY GO?

Great views from spectacular mountaintop balds, with two shelters for picnics or if the weather threatens (as it can quickly at this elevation).

THE RUNDOWN

General location: Off the Parkway, about 20 miles northeast of Asheville
Distance: 0.8-mile round-trip from the visitor center; 1.2 miles out and back from the Craggy Gardens Picnic Area; 6.2 miles out and back via the Mountains-to-Sea Trail and another 5-mile hike on the MST from Walker Knob Overlook at Balsam Gap

Difficulty: Moderate for first two options, strenuous for the lengthy walks.
Maps: USGS Craggy Pinnacle. Download the Parkway handout map, or grab one at the visitor center.
Elevation gain: About 145 feet
Water availability: At picnic area in season

FINDING THE TRAILHEADS

Craggy Gardens Visitor Center is at milepost 364.5; the Craggy Gardens Trail begins on its south side (GPS: 35.699496/-82.380005). To reach a Craggy Gardens Picnic Area trailhead, exit the Parkway at milepost 367.6 onto unpaved Stoney Fork Road. Take the next right into the picnic area and continue to the end of the parking lot (GPS: 35.699842/-82.391144). Start the Mountains-to-Sea Trail circuit at Graybeard Mountain Overlook (GPS: 35.710849/-82.364220), milepost 363.4; and a few other hikes at Balsam Gap (GPS: 35.748428, -82.333866), milepost 359.8.

THE HIKE

From the visitor center, the trail climbs gently for 0.3 mile through a marvelously cylindrical rhododendron tunnel with benches. The trail leaves the woods in grassy Craggy Flats at a 1930s picnic shelter built by the Civilian Conservation Corps (CCC). A recently rebuilt side trail leads from the shelter left up stone steps across balds to a stone observation platform at 5,640 feet. The round-trip from the Parkway to this summit viewpoint is about 0.8 mile.

Craggy Gardens

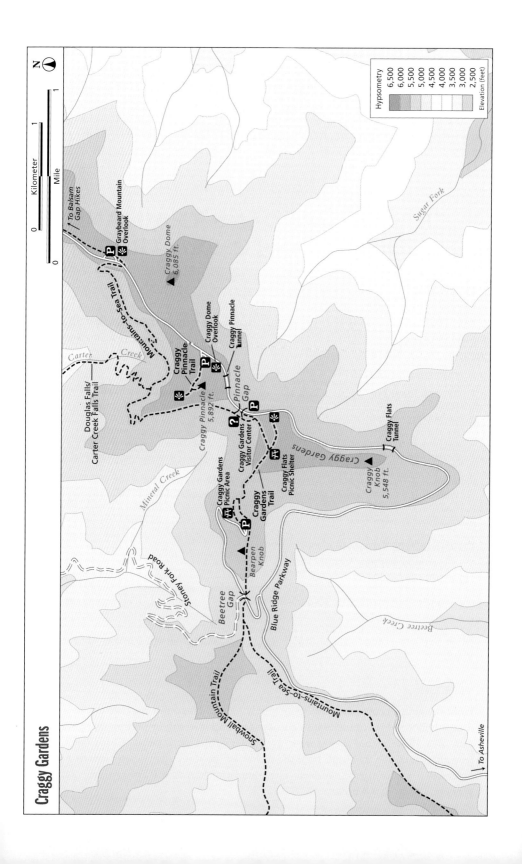

N

Kilometer
0   1

Mile
0   1

To Balsam
Gap Hikes

Graybeard Mountain
Overlook

Craggy Dome
6,085 ft.

Mountains-to-Sea Trail

Craggy Pinnacle
Overlook

Craggy Pinnacle
Tunnel

Carter   Creek

Douglas Falls/
Carter Creek Falls Trail

Craggy Pinnacle
Trail

Craggy Pinnacle
5,892 ft.

Pinnacle
Gap

Craggy Gardens
Visitor Center

Craggy Flats
Tunnel

Mineral Creek

Craggy Gardens

Craggy Gardens
Picnic Area

Craggy Flats
Picnic Shelter

Craggy Knob
5,548 ft.

Craggy Gardens
Trail

Bearpen Knob

Stoney Fork Road

Beetree
Gap

Blue Ridge Parkway

Snowball Mountain Trail

Mountains-to-Sea Trail

Beetree Creek

Sugar Fork

To Asheville

Hypsometry

6,500
6,000
5,500
5,000
4,500
4,000
3,500
3,000
2,500

Elevation (feet)

The evergreen-forested crest of Blackstock Knob is one of the Mountains-to-Sea Trail's best day hikes, seen here from Promontory Rock.

For a longer walk of just over 1 mile, start in the picnic area. The trail climbs gradually and at about 0.3 mile passes a short side trail to a gazebo shelter. The CCC picnic shelter is at about 0.5 mile. Include the summit view for a 1.2-mile round-trip.

Vistas look north from the Craggy Flats picnic shelter to Craggy Pinnacle (5,892 feet, left) and northeast to Craggy Dome (6,085 feet, right). The observation platform looks south over Craggy Knob (5,548 feet) and the Asheville watershed.

A longer walk originates north of Craggy Gardens at Parkway milepost 363.4. Take the white circle–blazed Mountains-to-Sea Trail from Graybeard Mountain Overlook south and across the road. Keep left around a ridge of Craggy Pinnacle when the Douglas Falls Trail goes right at 1.3 miles. When you arrive at the Parkway below the Craggy Gardens Visitor Center, turn on the Craggy Gardens Trail to reach the CCC shelter at Craggy Flats in about 3 miles. Include the summit for a round-trip of just more than 6 miles.

There are two more super hikes at Walker Knob Overlook in Balsam Gap just north of Craggy Gardens at Parkway milepost 359.8. From the parking area (5,317 feet), on the west side of the road, both the Big Butt Trail and Mountains-to-Sea Trail lead to superb views.

For rare close-in views of the Mitchell Range, take the Big Butt Trail left out of the parking area and follow the prominent ridge northwest. The trail eventually plummets down to NC 197, but the first 2.4 miles lead to campsites and especially great views at 1.6 miles and to Little Butt at 2.4 miles.

After Craggy Gardens, it's all downhill to Asheville, and there's no better vantage point on the Parkway's plunge than the short hike to Craggy Pinnacle and its rare plants interpretive sign.

Take the right-hand trail from Balsam Gap; the Mountains-to-Sea Trail traverses through the spectacular evergreen forests that clothe the intersection where the Black and Craggy Mountains collide. This hike runs above 6,000 feet for miles, and the trailheads are only 5 miles apart, so it's easy to spot a car on NC 128. (Go north to milepost 355.3 and go left on NC 128; the trailhead is only 0.6 mile from the Parkway on the right.) From Balsam Gap, the hike climbs across the peak of Blackstock Knob and then dips through Rainbow Gap to great views at 3.6 miles from Promontory Rock. It's a 5-mile hike to NC 128. To Promontory Rock and back from Balsam Gap is about 7 miles. The easiest hike to Promontory Rock is a 3-mile round-trip north from NC 128.

24 ASHEVILLE

Any hiker in North Carolina, especially a mountain-lover, eventually gets to hip, happenin' Asheville. More Blue Ridge Parkway visitors enter and exit the road in Asheville than at any other place.

The biggest attraction is the must-see Biltmore House and Gardens, George W. Vanderbilt's 250-room summer place that is the United States' largest home. Beyond breathtaking gardens, interiors, and artwork, the estate has hiking, mountain biking, and kayaking. The fancy Inn on Biltmore Estate and the estate's new Village Hotel, near Antler Hill Village and winery, are the perfect platforms for sampling Biltmore-raised foods, wines, hiking, biking and paddling.

Festivals are an Asheville forte, with crafts and music as a focus. August boasts the Mountain Dance and Folk Festival, the nation's oldest event focused on mountain music.

The literary heritage of the Appalachians and the increasing popularity of modern fiction about the mountains are most apparent here. Stop in at the atmospheric Malaprop's Book Store and visit Thomas Wolfe's boyhood home before you, yourself, go home again. Both Wolfe and O. Henry (William Sydney Porter) are buried in Asheville's Riverside Cemetery. You can make the short side trip to Carl Sandburg's home, Connemara, at nearby Hendersonville. From the Parkway south of Asheville, gaze out at Cold Mountain, setting of the National Book Award–winning bestseller and movie.

Literally check in to local literary heritage at the Grove Park Inn, the quintessential Appalachian hotel. The preserved historic heart of the inn, with its massive fireplace, has

If you thought the Biltmore Estate wasn't an outdoorsy destination, think again. These lands became the East's first national forest—and forestry school. A wealth of trails make America's "Downton Abbey" a great base for trail types.

a room that was frequently occupied by F. Scott Fitzgerald. It's a favorite with readers. The hotel is renowned for top-notch facilities, including a nationally significant spa. Try outdoor luxe at the USFS's Lake Powhatan Campground—just 15 minutes from Asheville. It's got hiking, biking, flush toilets, showers, and twelve amenity-packed "glamping" wall tents. Open year round. pisgahglamping.com

You can also see crafts in Asheville. The Southern Highland Handicraft Guild was born here, and the Parkway's Folk Art Center (milepost 382), just north of the city, is a showcase for the work of its members. Many, many other galleries are all over town (many on the Asheville Urban Trail). The Asheville area is a perfect base of operations for hikers.

ASHEVILLE URBAN TRAIL

The 1.7-mile Asheville Urban Trail is a nice amble through this vibrant downtown, second only to Miami Beach as the South's greatest concentration of Art Deco architecture. With thirty sculptures and exhibits, this "museum without walls" is packed with rich historical insight.

Highlights include the Grove Arcade, a classic neo-Gothic city market that reopened in 2002. The Basilica of Saint Lawrence illustrates how artisans from all over the world were lured to Asheville in the late nineteenth century by the building of the Biltmore Estate. Italian-born engineer Rafael Guastavino was struck by the mountain setting and stayed. The basilica he created has North America's largest freestanding elliptical dome. Dancers and musicians at another stop commemorate the 1927 launch of the nation's oldest mountain music event, the Mountain Dance and Folk Festival.

The Urban Trail's markers change by district; angels represent the neighborhood of *Look Homeward, Angel* author Thomas Wolfe. The book's setting—his mother's real-life boardinghouse—is here, and the Thomas Wolfe Memorial Visitor Center interprets the man who literally couldn't "go home again" after parodying his hometown's provinciality. Another exhibit treats O. Henry, and an arbor-sculpted bench honors Elizabeth Blackwell, the country's first female physician, who started her medical training while an Asheville school teacher.

The official starting point is Pack Place (GPS: 35.594719 / -82.551416), in front of the city's multifaceted, recently expanded art museum. You can download an audio tour and map of the trail by searching "Asheville Urban Trail."

NORTH CAROLINA ARBORETUM

This is a must-see facility for gardeners or anyone seriously interested in the flora of the Southern Appalachians. The 426-acre arboretum includes 36 acres of impressively landscaped gardens. From the Visitor Education Center and its impressive entrance plaza gardens, the Grand Garden Promenade leads to satellite gardens. Extensive exhibits include an internationally renowned bonsai collection. Recent improvements have been fast and furious, and passage of an education referendum promises even more.

Asheville—Downtown Urban Trail

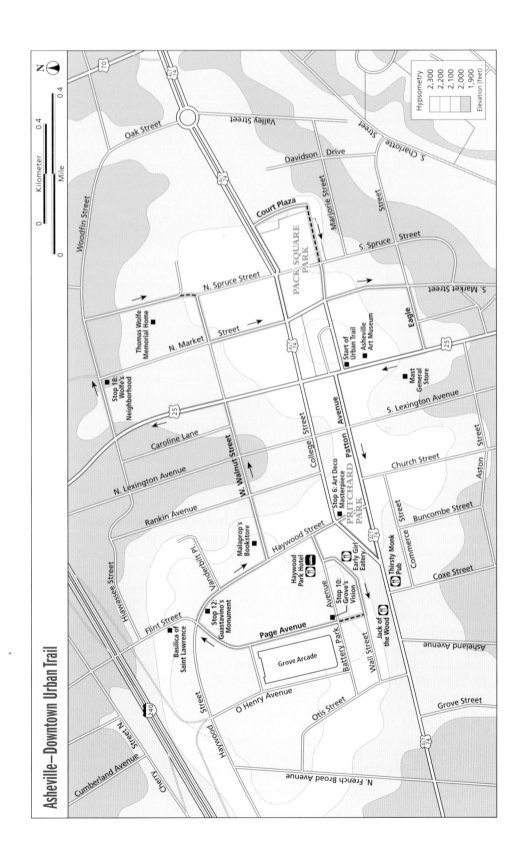

N

| Kilometer | 0 | 0.4 |
| Mile | 0 | 0.4 |

Hypsometry
Elevation (feet)
2,300
2,200
2,100
2,000
1,900

70

ALT 74

Oak Street

Woodfin Street

Valley Street

Court Plaza

Davidson Drive

PACK SQUARE PARK

Marjorie Street

S. Spruce Street

S. Charlotte Street

N. Spruce Street

S. Market Street

Thomas Wolfe Memorial Home

Street

N. Market

Start of Urban Trail
Asheville Art Museum

Eagle

Stop 18: Wolfe's Neighborhood

25

Mast General Store

25

Caroline Lane

S. Lexington Avenue

N. Lexington Avenue

College Street

Patton Avenue

Church Street

Aston Street

Rankin Avenue

W. Walnut Street

Stop 6: Art Deco Masterpiece

PRITCHARD PARK

Buncombe Street

Hiawassee Street

Vanderbilt Pl.

Malaprop's Bookstore

Haywood Street

Commerce Street

ALT 74

Coxe Street

Flint Street

Haywood Park Hotel

Early Girl Eatery

Thirsty Monk Pub

Stop 12: Guastavino's Monument

Avenue

Stop 10: Grove's Vision

Jack of the Wood

Basilica of Saint Lawrence

Page Avenue

Battery Park

Wall Street

Asheland Avenue

Street

Grove Arcade

240

O Henry Avenue

Otis Street

Grove Street

Haywood

Cherry

N. French Broad Avenue

ALT 74

Cumberland Avenue

Street N.

Whether you stay in a fancy hotel or the US Forest Service's shower-equipped Lake Powhatan Campground just 20 minutes from downtown, Asheville is all about the outdoors. From the Inn on Biltmore Estate, the city's Art-Deco buildings glow below a meadow-traversing trail.

There are miles of hiking and biking trails, a few of which continue into the adjoining Bent Creek Experimental Forest, one of the nation's earliest forest research areas. Those trails and the arboretum are increasingly popular with locals as Asheville's premier place for walking, running, and mountain biking. The Asheville Amblers Walking Club (amblers. homestead.com) recommends various hikes and leads organized arboretum walks.

The 0.7-mile Natural Garden Trail makes a nice loop if you're most interested in the Visitor Education Center and gardens. This trail is the Arboretum's interpretive TRACK Trail. Start from trailheads in the arboretum's major parking area, at the end of the Grand Garden Promenade, or adjacent to the Visitor Education Center in a garden called Plants of Promise. This foot-travel-only trail overlooks Bent Creek and the National Native Azalea Repository.

A "recreation area" trailhead is located just inside the park on the left. Hikers and mountain bikers can take the 3.4-mile gravel and natural surface road-grade loop of the Hard Times Road, Owl Ridge Trail, Rocky Cove Road, Bent Creek Road, and a connector trail back to the parking area. A short side trail explores the National Native Azalea Repository. Near the repository, Running Cedar Road connects Bent Creek Road and this longer loop with the core area. Closer to the recreation area trailhead, the Wesley Branch Trail also links the longer loop with the Natural Garden Trail and the core area. Just outside the arboretum entrance, the combined Shut-In and Mountains-to-Sea Trails leave the roadside bound for the Mount Pisgah area of the Parkway.

The latest arboretum trail map should be available at the recreation area trailhead or when you pay the parking fee. Consider joining the arboretum; members have unlimited access. For more information, contact the North Carolina Arboretum, 100 Frederick Law Olmsted Way, Asheville 28806-9315; (828) 665-2492; ncarboretum.org/plan-a-visit-or-event/trails.

FINDING THE TRAILHEAD

From Asheville take US 25 and get on the Blue Ridge Parkway at milepost 388.8, about 5 miles south of Asheville and 17 miles north of Hendersonville. Exit the Parkway at milepost 393.6 and take the first left on the ramp into the North Carolina Arboretum before NC 191. Via NC 191, the entrance is 9 miles from Asheville and 18 miles from Hendersonville (GPS: 35.501138/-82.599053).

25 CHIMNEY ROCK STATE PARK

WHY GO?

Like the bulk of Grandfather Mountain, Chimney Rock State Park is a once-privately owned commercial natural area that has become a state park. The park's historic "tourist attraction" area is operated as a concession under state management, and a fee is still charged. The core of the tourist facilities are still much as they were before state ownership (with key recent improvements to meet state guidelines). Among those changes were closure of the former boardwalk route of Skyline Trail and the entire Cliff Trail (the latter where the cliff scenes in *The Last of the Mohicans* were filmed). You can still reach Exclamation Point and in 2017 a newly rebuilt Skyline Trail opened to the top of 404-foot Hickory Nut Falls.

This has always been a travel destination that assumes you will take to the trails. In fact, the Hickory Nut Gorge location is such a natural landmark that thousands of acres of wildland had been acquired by diverse conservation groups in advance of the attraction's sale to the state in 2007.

Visitors enter Chimney Rock State Park from the picturesque village of Chimney Rock. Cross the rocky Broad River and drive through a mature forest with several nice picnic spots along the way. Be sure to stop at The Meadows, about 1,400 feet. There's an outdoor classroom, restrooms, and picnic sites, as well as The Great Woodland Adventure Trail and Discovery Den (see below).

At the top of the park road, visitors take a recently upgraded elevator through solid rock—550-million-year-old Henderson Augen gneiss. The 258-foot rise reaches the Sky Lounge deli and gift shop. From there, forty-three steps lead to awesome views atop Chimney Rock, the monolithic granite pillar that juts from the side of Chimney Rock Mountain. Lake Lure glistens in the valley, and views reach southeast to King's Mountain, 75 miles distant.

The park got its start at the turn of the twentieth century when a St. Louis physician, Lucius Morse, came to this cool, green area "seeking a more favorable climate" where he could recover from tuberculosis. He paid $5,000 in 1902 to buy 64 acres of Chimney Rock Mountain. His heirs remained stewards of the park for more than a century, eventually amassing more than 1,000 acres.

Even purist hikers should check out the park's special events calendar online—there's an impressive schedule of guided nature and bird walks led by this North Carolina Natural Heritage Area's naturalist staff (some require a fee). There are also nature photography clinics and a variety of educational programs.

Chimney Rock's steps and walkways have been modernized with state park ownership, but they still offer the craggy vistas they have since the early 20th century.

This park is the perfect place for the adventurous to try rock climbing. There's a 32-foot climbing tower, and professional instructors offer guided climbs (this requires an extra fee). The surrounding state parkland is also a climber's haven. The park's other main access point is the Rumbling Bald Climbing Access, a favorite climbing site, where a hiking trail leads to extensive bouldering opportunities.

Chimney Rock is justifiably proud that the park was featured in the 1992 film *The Last of the Mohicans*. Some of the most spectacular scenes were captured on Chimney Rock's trails. Definitely stream the movie to get yourself psyched for a visit.

Try one of these spectacular—and safe—circuit hikes through the stunningly vertical world of Hickory Nut Gorge and 404-foot Hickory Nut Falls.

THE RUNDOWN

General location: Southeast of Asheville, west of Charlotte
Distance: 1.5 miles round-trip for the Hickory Nut Falls Trail; 0.7 mile round-trip for the Exclamation Point Trail
Difficulty: Easy for the Great Woodland Adventure Trail; moderate for the Hickory Nut Falls Trail and combination of Exclamation Point and Four Seasons Trails
Maps: USGS quads Bat Cave, Lake Lure. Download a hiking map at the attraction's website (see below). The state park website also has a map (ncparks.gov/Visit/parks/chro/main.php).
Water availability: Available from developed visitor facilities
For more information: Chimney Rock Park, PO Box 39, Chimney Rock 28720; (800) 277-9611; chimneyrockpark.com. A fee is charged; annual passes are available.

FINDING THE TRAILHEAD

Chimney Rock Park is 25 miles southeast of Asheville, just east of the intersection of US 64 and US 74A in the town of Chimney Rock (GPS: 35.439747 / -82.248602).

THE HIKES

The Great Woodland Adventure Trail is an easy 0.6-mile stroll through the forest near The Meadows that's perfect for small children. Stop at Grady's Animal Discovery Den to see snakes, lizards, turtles, and other educational exhibits. "Grady" is the park's animal ambassador groundhog, the authoritative source for insightful animal information found on the trail's many handcrafted sculptures. A variety of TRACK Trail interpretive brochures are available at the trailhead kiosk for use on this and other trails in the park.

No one should miss Hickory Nut Falls Trail, a moderate 0.75-mile (1.5-mile round-trip) stroll to a vantage point at the base of one of North Carolina's most impressive waterfalls—404 feet. This nice family hike begins at the last turn below the park's uppermost parking lot. The at times graveled old road grade wanders a hardwood forest of hickory, oak, basswood, and maple. There's also a developed viewing area and a picnic table at the base of the cataract. Vistas reach across the town of Chimney Rock and up the towering rock face. After a good rain, this is a dramatic spot.

Just across the road from the Great Woodland Adventure Trail, the Four Seasons Trail is a 1.4-mile loop that rises steeply 400 feet from the elevation of The Meadows to join the Hickory Nut Falls Trail, which reaches the base of the falls. This scenic trail increases the workout for a hike to the falls (about 2.7 miles round-trip). For the most challenging hike to the summit, try the Outcroppings Trail. Head right up the staircases on Outcroppings to Chimney Rock, and you can say that you, not your car, climbed the monolith. The trail explores a garden of rock formations and viewpoints along the way.

Chimney Rock State Park

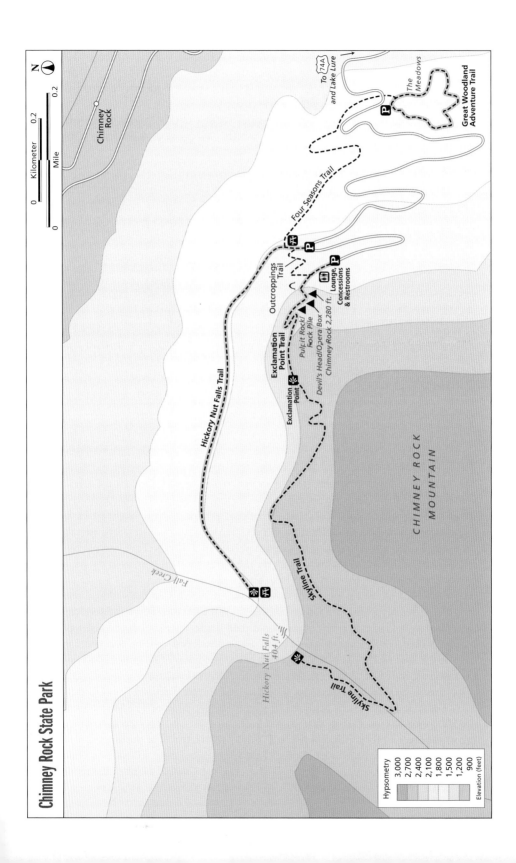

Hypsometry

	3,000
	2,700
	2,400
	2,100
	1,800
	1,500
	1,200
	900

Elevation (feet)

N

0   Kilometer   0.2

0   Mile   0.2

Chimney Rock

Fall Creek

Hickory Nut Falls Trail

Hickory Nut Falls 404 ft.

Skyline Trail

Skyline Trail

Exclamation Point Trail

Exclamation Point

Outcroppings Trail

Four Seasons Trail

Pulpit Rock/ Rock Pile

Devil's Head/Opera Box

Chimney Rock 2,280 ft.

Lounge, Concessions & Restrooms

To 74A and Lake Lure

The Meadows

Great Woodland Adventure Trail

CHIMNEY ROCK MOUNTAIN

After visiting the Sky Lounge and the Chimney, head higher on the Exclamation Point Trail, where a few noteworthy viewpoints are easy to reach. This 0.7-mile strenuous trail leaves the cliff face, enters the woods, then reemerges on the cliffs at Exclamation Point—a breezy 2,480-foot perch where Hickory Nut Gorge spreads out below. From there, take the newly constructed version of the blue-blazed Skyline Trail that leads even higher, to Peregrine Point, and beyond, where Falls Creek makes its dramatic, almost half-a-thousand foot leap off Hickory Nut Falls.

THE SOUTHWESTERN MOUNTAINS

The loftiest part of the Parkway, the section from US 74 in Asheville (milepost 384.7) to Great Smoky Mountains National Park (milepost 469.1) is the perfect hikers' route through the mountains of southwestern North Carolina. Mount Pisgah starts a section of the Parkway that soars across the highest landmasses in the East. This is where the Blue Ridge meets the jumble of mountain ranges that make up the vast heart of the Southern Appalachians. On your way to Cherokee and a memorable meeting with the massive wall of the Great Smokies, the road surveys some of eastern America's best scenery.

Despite a high and away-from-it-all experience that's second to none, off-Parkway options are close by in the Pisgah and Nantahala National Forests, including Looking Glass Rock and the Cradle of Forestry, the nation's earliest forestry school.

Classic mountain towns lie below and are at their liveliest during summer. Drop in (literally, from the Parkway) on Highlands, Cashiers, Franklin, Waynesville, Rosman, and Brevard (with its internationally known summer music festival, held June to August).

This area boasts the French Broad, Nantahala, and a raft of other rivers, and it is one of the East's best places for whitewater sports. One family-oriented trip in conjunction with the Great Smoky Mountains Railroad features a train ride up the river (which passes the location where the train wreck in the movie *The Fugitive* was filmed) and a rafting trip back down. Bryson City is a hot spot for the Nantahala Outdoor Center, known for watersports but a good stop regardless of your sport. They also offer great outdoorsy dining and lodging (noc.com).

The Forest Heritage Scenic Byway, near Mount Pisgah, passes by a number of these classic mountain towns, their inns, and restaurants. This 79-mile national forest circuit crosses the Parkway on both sides of Shining Rock Wilderness and follows US 276, NC 215, and US 64 in the vicinity of Brevard. The trip includes the Cradle of Forestry facility (see below).

The Brevard area is called the "Land of Waterfalls." The short stroll to Looking Glass Falls on US 276 is one of the roadside attractions of the Forest Heritage byway, as is the natural water slide, Sliding Rock. Many national forest campgrounds and picnic areas line the route.

Heading farther west brings you to Cherokee and the edge of the Smokies. The Oconaluftee Indian Village gives living-history insight into Cherokee culture at the time of European settlement. The Museum of the Cherokee Indian and the outdoor drama

From Asheville to Cherokee, the Blue Ridge Parkway crests at its highest point, Richland Balsam. Be sure to hike the 1.4-mile loop into the peak's spruce-fir forest.

Unto These Hills are similarly worthwhile. Don't miss the Oconaluftee River Trail for insight into Cherokee culture. Turn to the Appalachian Trail mileage log for many more day and overnight hikes in North Carolina's southwest mountains.

Don't forget a few other destinations we weren't able to get into this fourth edition of *Hiking North Carolina*. Be sure to visit the websites for the new Gorges State Park near Sapphire and DuPont State Recreational Forest. Gorges became a state park, the only one west of Asheville, in 1999. The area boasts dramatic cliffs and crags, a temperate rain forest, a section of the Foothills Trail, and a major visitor center (ncparks.gov/Visit/parks/gorg/main.php). DuPont State Recreational Forest, between Hendersonville and Brevard, is another waterfall-filled park. Landmarks include Hooker Falls and Bridal Veil Falls. Easy hikes lead to many cascades, and mountain bike trails are everywhere. Check out the park (ncforestservice.gov/Contacts/dsf.htm) and their friends group's trail descriptions (www.dupontforest.com). The USDA Forest Service Tsali Recreation Area and campground is another great mountain biking destination at Fontana Lake, near Robbinsville and Bryson City.

26 MOUNT PISGAH AREA

Mount Pisgah launches that southwestern mountain experience for hikers driving the Blue Ridge Parkway. On the way to Mount Pisgah from Asheville, it's humbling to realize that George W. Vanderbilt's Biltmore House and Gardens was just part of a 125,000-acre estate that today wraps the Parkway in the Pisgah National Forest.

Vanderbilt named this acreage Pisgah Forest after the mountain that dominates the area. Vanderbilt hired two of the United States' earliest foresters to restore and manage his lands. Following that effort, America's first school of forestry was located not far from Mount Pisgah. The aptly named Cradle of Forestry is a must-see stop for Mount Pisgah hikers.

From 5,000 feet at the Parkway's Mount Pisgah Recreation Area, the views over Pisgah National Forest are spectacular. So are the vistas from the rooms, front porches/balconies, and restaurant at Pisgah Inn. The campground is the Parkway's highest, so expect cool nights. A picnic area, camp store, laundry, and gift/craft shop round out the resources.

MOUNT PISGAH TRAIL AND PICNIC AREA CONNECTOR

WHY GO?

This heart-pumping climb accesses great views atop the conical summit of one of western North Carolina's landmark mountains.

THE RUNDOWN

General location: About 27 miles southwest of Asheville
Distance: 2.6 or 3.6 miles round-trip (from picnic area)
Difficulty: Strenuous
Maps: USGS Dunsmore Mountain and Cruso. Download a parkway handout map of Mount Pisgah trails at the "Brochures" link on the Blue Ridge Parkway's website (see below), or grab one at the campground.
Elevation gain: 726 feet

Water availability: Water fountains at developed facilities during the season; treat stream sources.
For more information: Blue Ridge Parkway, 199 Hemphill Knob Rd., Asheville 28803-8686; (828) 271-4779; (828) 298-0398 (recorded information and mailing requests); nps.gov/blri. Reserve campsites online at recreation.gov. Pisgah Inn; (828) 235-8228; pisgahinn.com. ncmst.org.

FINDING THE TRAILHEAD

South of the Parkway's Buck Spring Tunnel, turn into the Buck Spring Gap Overlook at milepost 407.7. Follow the road extension back north to the Mount Pisgah parking area atop Buck Spring Tunnel at milepost 407.6, but reached from milepost 407.7 (GPS: 35.418723/-82.747940). The trail from the picnic area leaves the northeast end of the lot at milepost 407.8 (GPS: 35.413529/-82.751283).

THE HIKE

Pass the "Strenuous Trail" warning sign at the end of the lot; the trail connector to the picnic area goes left (see below). The trail slabs the northwest side of Little Pisgah Mountain, which forces the Parkway through two nearby tunnels.

Pass a spring at 0.4 mile, and rise along the ridge crest at 0.6 mile. The trail swings left of the ridge, and a few benches appear as the trail steepens to the 1-mile mark. As you ascend the summit cone, the trail switchbacks back to the right to emerge at the observation tower (5,721 feet) for one of the Parkway's best views. The Asheville Valley and Black Mountains lie north; the crest of the Shining Rock Wilderness and the Smokies are southwest.

You can add 1 mile (0.5 mile in each direction) to the Mount Pisgah hike by starting at the picnic area parking lot and going right on the connector, which makes sense if you're planning to hike after lunch. This is one of the "transportation" paths you'll find in developed Parkway recreation areas that lead picnickers or campers between their tents or RVs and other facilities. On the way, the trail passes Buck Spring Tunnel—a rare view from the roadside rather than through the windshield.

KEY POINTS

0.0   Start at the Mount Pisgah parking area.

0.4   Pass a spring.

0.6   Ascend sharp ridge.

0.9   Trail steepens.

1.3   Summit tower. Return the way you came.

2.6   Arrive back at the parking area.

SHUT-IN TRAIL/BUCK SPRING TRAIL

Vanderbilt blazed a 17-mile trail from his estate to a hunting lodge in what is now the Mount Pisgah Recreation Area. The lodge site is on the easy-to-moderate Buck Spring Trail, which starts at milepost 408.6 near the trail map sign on the north end of the Pisgah Inn parking area (GPS: 35.403661 / -82.753269). It's a 2-mile out-and-back walk from there to the lodge site and a mere 0.2-mile round-trip from the Buck Spring Gap Overlook at milepost 407.7 (GPS: 35.415165 / -82.748505), the first parking area on the right heading out to the Mount Pisgah parking area. Climb the stone steps from the overlook and pause at an interpretive sign in a meadow. From there, walk beyond the sign to the woods and descend to the left to visit the only remaining remnant of the lodge, the old springhouse. Don't retrace your steps back up to the trail. Leave the springhouse the way you arrived but bear left across the grass along a stone wall back to the overlook.

The trail Vanderbilt took from Asheville to his hunting lodge is still in use too. The Shut-In Trail was reclaimed and is now part of the Mountains-to-Sea Trail. It runs from

From many places near Shining Rock, Looking Glass Mountain is easily seen.

the right side of the Mount Pisgah parking area (milepost 407.6) to near the North Carolina Arboretum at the French Broad Overlook (milepost 393.8). Along that route, the Shut-In Trail is nice for short out-and-back hikes. Between those trailheads it's accessible from overlooks at mileposts 396.4, 397.3, 398.3, 400.2, 401.7, 402.6, 403.6, 404.5, and 405.5.

CRADLE OF FORESTRY

FINDING THE TRAILHEAD

Go east from the Parkway at milepost 411.8 on US 276, a USDA Forest Service Forest Heritage Scenic Byway, to the Cradle of Forestry in 4 miles. It's 18 miles from Brevard (GPS: 35.349831/-82.780732).

East of the Parkway near Mount Pisgah, the 6,500-acre Cradle of Forestry is where the nation's first school of forestry grew out of George Vanderbilt's efforts to manage his land holdings. In 1889 Vanderbilt hired Gifford Pinchot, a forester and conservationist, and in 1895 he was succeeded by German forester Dr. Carl Schenck (see Schenck Forest elsewhere in this book). Budding foresters came to the estate, and in 1898 Schenck started the United States' first forestry school. A decade later, North Carolinians were among

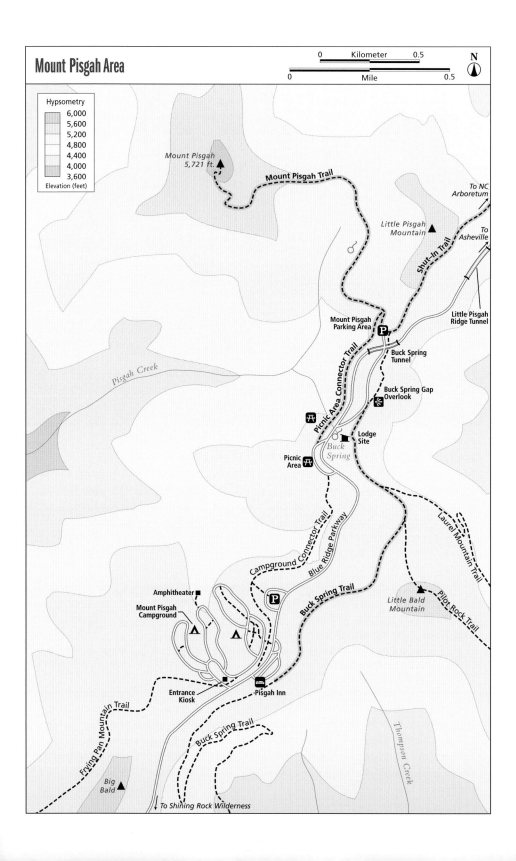

Mount Pisgah Area

Hypsometry

6,000
5,600
5,200
4,800
4,400
4,000
3,600
Elevation (feet)

Kilometer
0   0.5
0   0.5
Mile

N

Mount Pisgah
5,721 ft.

Mount Pisgah Trail

Little Pisgah
Mountain

Shut-In Trail

To NC
Arboretum

To
Asheville

Little Pisgah
Ridge Tunnel

Mount Pisgah
Parking Area

Buck Spring
Tunnel

Pisgah Creek

Buck Spring Gap
Overlook

Picnic Area Connector Trail

Lodge
Site

Buck
Spring

Picnic
Area

Campground Connector Trail

Blue Ridge Parkway

Laurel Mountain Trail

Amphitheater

Mount Pisgah
Campground

Buck Spring Trail

Little Bald
Mountain

Pilot Rock Trail

Entrance
Kiosk

Pisgah Inn

Frying Pan Mountain Trail

Buck Spring Trail

Thompson Creek

Big
Bald

To Shining Rock Wilderness

the first to see the need to protect the nation's forests from overlogging, forest fires, and erosion. The state supported the adoption of the Weeks Act in 1911, the legislation that created the East's national forests. Pinchot, Vanderbilt's first forester, became the first chief of the forest service. After Vanderbilt's death, his lands were among the earliest parcels of the Pisgah national forest, the first in eastern America.

At the "Plymouth Rock of Forestry," state-of-the-art exhibits in the Forest Discovery Center include a jostling simulator that replicates a ride on a firefighting helicopter. The entire facility is a cooperative effort between the forest service and the Cradle of Forestry Interpretive Association.

The easy, 1-mile Biltmore Campus Trail explores the early facility. Students lived and learned in the rustic assortment of mountain cabins and early buildings preserved here. The school closed in 1913, victim to a proliferation of university forestry programs. The 1.3-mile, easy Forest Festival Trail is a masterpiece of interpretation on how and why the science of forestry is practiced.

LOOKING GLASS ROCK

FINDING THE TRAILHEAD

Go east from the Parkway on US 276, past Sliding Rock and Looking Glass Falls (both great stops) to take a right onto FR 475, the Davidson River Road. The trailhead is on the right, 0.4 mile from the turn (GPS: 35.291030 / -82.776616).

The 6.2-mile, strenuous Looking Glass Rock Trail is also reached heading down US 276. The hike to 3,960 feet atop this spectacular dome of rock is probably the most popular in the entire Pisgah Ranger District. The yellow-blazed trail has been significantly hardened to withstand all the use, and it's important to stay on the trail to avoid damage to the mountain, as well as to limit impact on the peregrine falcons that are partial to its cliffs and crags. (Rock climbing is restricted on certain routes during the January–August breeding season.) The trail is steep and rugged, with switchback after switchback, but the view from the top is awesome.

27 **SHINING ROCK WILDERNESS**

Shining Rock—like the Craggy Mountains and Mount Mitchell just north of Asheville—is where the Parkway delivers some of the Southern Appalachians' most stunning scenery. The horizon peels back on an almost Western scale, and meadow-covered mountaintops march off to meet summits cloaked in evergreens and accented by milk-white crags of quartz—the area's namesake "shining rocks."

Unlike the "natural" balds of the Craggy Mountains and Roan Mountain, the meadows of the Shining Rock area were created by wildfires in the 1920s and 1940s. Few places in the South offer better views than the grasslands of the Art Loeb Trail that border the Blue Ridge Parkway. The area north and beyond the balds, the 19,000-acre evergreen-forested tract now designated as the Shining Rock Wilderness, was not as impacted by fire. In the middle of the wilderness, Shining Rock Mountain (5,940 feet) thrusts its crystal-covered crest above the trees. A more distant and appropriately named peak, Cold Mountain, rises to 6,030 feet near the northern boundary of the wilderness area. This is the isolated summit made famous in Charles Frazier's National Book Award–winning bestseller *Cold Mountain*. See map on page 176.

Backpackers, regardless of where they're headed, should try to avoid Shining Rock Gap. Just a glance at the trail map suggests why this is one of the most overused campsites in the wilderness. Regulations prohibit groups of more than ten persons, and all campfires are banned. Any backpacking plans for this area should include time to find a more-secluded site.

Aside from the scenery, part of Shining Rock's appeal is the number of circuit hikes available from surrounding valleys. This entry offers an overview of the trail network, then recommends a variety of circuits from the south, east, and west (peruse the map while reading).

Basically, Shining Rock routes center on the ridgetop Art Loeb Trail, which runs from the Parkway north across various balds and Shining Rock Mountain before turning left off the ridge, where another trail leads to Cold Mountain. This ridgetop route can be divided into roughly three sections.

The most southerly section crosses the balds of Black Balsam Knob and Tennent Mountain to Ivestor Gap. This part of the trail is flanked on both sides by gradual routes, the Ivestor Gap Trail on the west and, on the east, the Graveyard Ridge Trail and a Mountains-to-Sea Trail section. Together the side trails form a big loop around the Loeb Trail. You'll notice, though, that this southernmost section of the Ivestor Gap Trail isn't included in the recommended hikes—it is very popular with hikers and horseback riders and open to vehicles to Ivestor Gap (the wilderness boundary) during the fall hunting season.

The middle section of the Art Loeb Trail, from Ivestor Gap to Shining Rock Gap, is also flanked on the west by a less-crowded part of the Ivestor Gap Trail. Beyond Shining Rock Gap, the northernmost part of the Loeb Trail wanders alone to the valley, while the Cold Mountain Trail continues out the ridge to its summit dead end.

The drawback of the trail system is that everybody ends up on the crest. But the beauty of the layout is that the Loeb Trail and its flanking paths form wonderful summit circuits reachable by no fewer than seven access trails from nearby valleys. You'd need a calculator to count the possibilities. Wherever you roam, check the Internet first for current bear policies in the Shining Rock area. In recent years bear canisters have been required for food storage and camping has been prohibited in Graveyard Fields.

SHINING ROCK WILDERNESS CIRCUITS FROM THE EAST SIDE

WHY GO?

A variety of streamside hikes start east and rise to the crest of the Shining Rock Wilderness.

THE RUNDOWN

General location: About 35 miles southwest of Asheville
Distance: Major circuits ranging from 8.4 miles to 12.9 miles
Difficulty: Strenuous
Maps: USGS Shining Rock. The area is best covered by Pisgah National Forest's Shining Rock–Middle Prong Wilderness map. www.nationalforestmapstore.com/category-s/1844.htm

Elevation gain: 3,096 feet for shortest circuit
Water availability: Plentiful in the valleys, springs along the upper ridge crest; treat water before using.
For more information: Pisgah Ranger District, Pisgah National Forest, 1600 Pisgah Hwy., Pisgah Forest 28768; (828) 877-3265; e-mail: pisgahrd@fs.fed.us. ncmst .org.

FINDING THE TRAILHEAD

Trailheads for the Old Butt Knob, Shining Creek, and Greasy Cove–Big East Fork Trails are all located at the Big East Fork parking area on US 276, just under 3 miles north of the Parkway on the left (GPS: 35.365884 / -82.818010).

THE HIKES

A trio of trails ascends the east side of the wilderness, and they all start at the same trailhead. The more northerly two, the Old Butt Knob Trail (3.6 miles) and the Shining Creek Trail (4.1 miles), terminate in Shining Rock Gap to form the shortest circuit to the heights (8.4 miles). This hike crosses Shining Rock.

The most southerly trail, a combination of the Big East Fork Trail (3.6 miles) and Greasy Cove Trail (3 miles), makes a 6.8-mile climb to the ridge at Ivestor Gap (which includes a 0.2-mile stretch on the Graveyard Ridge Trail). Heading north from there 1.8 miles on the ridgetop Art Loeb Trail to Shining Rock Gap creates much larger loops—12.7 miles with a descent of the Shining Creek Trail and 12.9 miles going down the Old Butt Knob Trail. The level Ivestor Gap Trail also links these access trails. The winding route it takes to slab west of the Art Loeb Trail adds 0.3 mile to each hike.

To take the shortest circuit, leave the parking area on the Shining Creek Trail as it climbs away from the East Fork of the Pigeon River. At 0.7 mile, keep left in Shining Creek Gap where the Old Butt Knob Trail (your return route) goes right. The trail drops out of the gap to join Shining Creek above its confluence with the Pigeon River. From here most of the way up, the trail is within sight of the stream. Cross Daniel's Cove Creek

Shining Rock's distinctive quartzite outcrop is this wilderness area's namesake landmark.

at 2 miles and a stream rising right at 3 miles. High above, this branch starts as a trailside spring you might stop at when you pass through Beech Spring Gap on the Old Butt Knob Trail. The trail starts its steepest climb up out of the drainage and switchbacks across the headwaters of the North Prong of Shining Creek to Shining Rock Gap at 4.1 miles.

The gap is a popular camping area, and with tents and tall summer grasses, finding the Old Butt Knob Trail can be a challenge (not an issue if you climb it; see below). Turn right at Shining Rock Gap on the Old Butt Knob Trail and reach Shining Rock Mountain's crystal cap in 0.2 mile. Descend beyond to Beech Spring Gap at 4.7 miles (that spring is on the right). This next section of ridge—across Dog Loser Knob at 4.9 miles, to Spanish Oak Gap at 5.5 miles, back up to Old Butt Knob at 5.7, and even beyond, to the 6-mile mark, where the trail plummets—has gradual sections. Notice on the way down the steepest section—aptly named Chestnut Ridge—how the young American chestnuts still struggle up before falling victim to chestnut blight. There are plentiful campsites for the finding and fine views from outcrops on both sides of the trail. Then the trail drops very steeply for 1.5 miles to the Shining Creek junction at 7.7 miles. Take a left to the trailhead for an 8.4-mile circuit. If you're a baby boomer whose muscles are better on the uphill than your knees or ankles are on the way down, do this trip in reverse. (The Old Butt Knob Trail is the least-used trail on this side of the wilderness, but it's a punishing climb.)

KEY POINTS

0.0   Start from the parking area on the Shining Creek Trail.

0.7   Keep left in Shining Creek Gap where Old Butt Knob Trail goes right.

Going down Shining Creek Trail is a nice way to form the largest loop from this side. That requires a start on the Big East Fork–Greasy Cove Trail combo to the south. Start by crossing the Big East Fork highway bridge from the parking area and heading right. This old railroad grade continues for miles up the drainage amid lush streamside scenery and plentiful campsites. Cross Bennett Branch at 1.3 miles; at 3.6 miles the old railroad grade goes left up the river.

Cross and continue up Greasy Cove Trail for the steepest part of the climb. The trail veers away from the stream at 4.5 miles and climbs steeply until 5.3 miles, when the grade slackens substantially at the crest of Grassy Cove Ridge. From here much of the way to the Graveyard Ridge Trail at 6.6 miles, the trail is only steep in spots; there are possible campsites where the ridge is broadest.

Go right on the Graveyard Ridge Trail, and at 6.8 miles turn right in Ivestor Gap on the Art Loeb Trail. The path switchbacks past the peak of Grassy Cove Top, dips across a gentle gap, and heads over the next rise to a sharp drop into Flower Gap at 8 miles. The path joins an old railroad grade there and slabs east of Flower Knob past a spring on the right at 8.4 miles. Shining Rock Gap is at 8.6 miles. The descent of the Shining Creek Trail makes a 12.7-mile route (the first streamlet you encounter on the way down is from the Art Loeb Trail spring you just passed); a descent of the Old Butt Knob Trail is 12.9 miles.

BALD SUMMIT CIRCUITS ON THE ART LOEB TRAIL

WHY GO?

The Shining Rock area's most southerly summits are among the most spectacular balds in the South. The recommended circuits avoid the popular high-elevation trailheads and can be extended to include the namesake Shining Rocks in the heart of the wilderness area.

THE RUNDOWN

General location: About 35 miles southwest of Asheville

Distance: Day or overnight circuit hikes across the area's southerly bald summits of 5.2 and 8.8 miles (and a recommended out-and-back hike of only 0.8 mile). Longer circuits that include Shining Rock can be 9.1 or 12.7 miles.

Difficulty: Moderate to strenuous

FINDING THE TRAILHEAD

Park at Graveyard Fields Overlook (GPS: 35.320287/-82.846936). To reach the parking on FR 816 below Black Balsam Knob, turn right at Parkway milepost 420.2. The trailhead is 0.7 mile on the right. The Black Balsam parking area for the Ivestor Gap Trail (GPS: 35.325695/-82.882024) is another 0.5 mile beyond (but that's the Shining Rock area's busiest trailhead, and that section of the trail isn't recommended). That parking area does have modern privies.

THE HIKES

Descend from Graveyard Fields Overlook on the Parkway's loop trail, cross Yellowstone Prong, and head left. At about 0.3 mile take a right onto the Graveyard Ridge Trail. Follow this gradual logging railroad grade to a crossing of the Mountains-to-Sea Trail in a gap between Black Balsam Knob to the left and an unnamed peak to the right. These first 1.8 miles of the hike are rich with campsites, especially out of sight of the trail.

Turn left on the Mountains-to-Sea Trail as it swings north out of the gap at about 5,400 feet, rises abruptly to the 5,600-foot level, then climbs gradually past the upper edge of a large flat visible on the USDA Forest Service wilderness map. There are good campsites in this area and the remains of an old railroad camp used during logging days. The trail passes above the headwaters of Yellowstone Prong, follows an old railroad grade, and reaches FR 816 and a parking spot for the Art Loeb Trail just less than 3 miles from the start.

Take an immediate right from FR 816 onto the Loeb Trail; ascend in 0.4 mile (3.2 miles from the start) to the open vistas and waving grasses of Black Balsam Knob (6,214 feet). North, the Mount Mitchell range bulks beyond Asheville, with the High Country resort area and Grandfather Mountain beyond that. The Smokies rise dramatically to the west. This is a 360-degree panorama worthy of binoculars and a camera.

Retracing your steps from here creates a round-trip hike of about 6.5 miles from the trailhead. Even if you don't have much time, this can be a quick 0.8-mile hike from the parking area you just left on FR 816.

Follow the Art Loeb Trail north along the open ridgetop into a shrubby gap at about 5,880 feet, and then back up to eye-popping views atop Tennent Mountain (6,046 feet) about 1.2 miles from Black Balsam Knob (4.4 miles from the Parkway). The 0.7-mile descent from Tennent Mountain brings you to the Ivestor Gap Trail and a right turn on the Graveyard Ridge Trail at 5.1 miles. Continue out of the gap; the Greasy Cove–Big East Fork Trail combo heads left to US 276 at 5.3 miles. After crossing the Mountains-to-Sea Trail, you'll reach the Graveyard Fields Loop at 8.5 miles. Ascend back to the trailhead at about 8.8 miles.

KEY POINTS

0.0 Start at the Graveyard Fields Overlook.

0.3 Turn right from the Graveyard Fields Loop onto Graveyard Ridge Trail.

1.8 Turn left onto the Mountains-to-Sea Trail.

2.8 Turn right from FR 816 onto the Art Loeb Trail.

3.2 Black Balsam Knob.

4.4 Tennent Mountain.

5.1 Turn right in Ivestor Gap onto the Graveyard Ridge Trail.

8.5 Rejoin the Graveyard Fields Loop.

8.8 Arrive back at the overlook.

Keeping in mind that much of this hike is pretty gradual, if not flat, backpackers or well-conditioned walkers could extend the above circuit to include the ridgetop stretch of the Art Loeb Trail that continues north to Shining Rock Gap. From Ivestor Gap, that section of the Art Loeb Trail forms another loop with the nearly level Ivestor Gap Trail. The combination creates a big figure eight that adds another 3.9 miles to the hike, for a 12.7-mile walk from the Graveyard Fields Overlook.

If you have less time, start at the recommended spot on FR 816 and the first loop of the above circuit is about 5.2 miles (instead of 8.8 miles from the Parkway). Extend that to include Shining Rock Gap, and the hike is 9.1 miles (instead of 12.7). Either of these hikes will be 0.4 mile farther if you go to Shining Rock itself—a 0.2-mile hike out of Shining Rock Gap on the Old Butt Knob Trail.

WEST SIDE CIRCUIT AND COLD MOUNTAIN

WHY GO?

A lesser used circuit and an out-and-back option to Cold Mountain, the least-frequented part of the Shining Rock Wilderness.

THE RUNDOWN

General location: About 35 miles southwest of Asheville
Distance: 10.6 miles round-trip to Cold Mountain
Difficulty: Strenuous
Maps: USGS Shining Rock. The area is best covered by Pisgah National Forest's Shining Rock–Middle Prong Wilderness map. www.nationalforestmapstore.com/category-s/1844.htm.

Elevation gain: About 2,790 feet to Cold Mountain
Water availability: Plentiful in the valleys, springs on upper ridge crest; treat water before using.
For more information: Pisgah Ranger District, Pisgah National Forest, 1600 Pisgah Hwy., Pisgah Forest 28768; (828) 877-3265; e-mail: pisgahrd@fs.fed.us

From the Art Loeb Trail, Mount Pisgah's conical peak bisects the high evergreen ridge of the Black Mountains.

Not all Shining Rock hikes are arduous. Park on FR 816 and the balds of Black Balsam Knob are a less-than 1-mile hike to great views.

FINDING THE TRAILHEAD

The Daniel Boone Scout Camp trailhead for the Art Loeb and Little East Fork Trails is reached via NC 215. Leave the Parkway at milepost 423.2 and go 13 miles north to turn right onto Little East Fork Road (SR 1129). Go 3.8 miles to parking just beyond the Boy Scout camp's main lodge (GPS: 35.387738/-82.896297). To start the Little East Fork Trail, walk a little farther along the road, turn right across the bridge into the Scout camp, and then go left on a road that becomes the trail.

THE HIKES

There's really only one circuit from the west side of Shining Rock—a 12-mile combination of the Little East Fork and Art Loeb Trails, which start at the same trailhead. One of the area's best out-and-back hikes also starts there—the 10.6-mile hike to Cold Mountain.

The choice of which direction to hike this circuit will be arbitrary for most, as both trails gain the ridge at similar grades. Backpackers will surely decide based on where they want to camp. Starting on the Art Loeb Trail is the fastest route to the least-populated part of the wilderness—the Cold Mountain hike. It also approaches the highest terrain by climbing up the leading ridge. Taking the Little East Fork Trail descends that ridge and gets you to Shining Rock Gap sooner.

Leaving the roadside, the Art Loeb Trail switchbacks north and around a ridgeline at 1.1 miles. At 2 miles the trail crosses tumbling Sorrell Creek at the first good campsites.

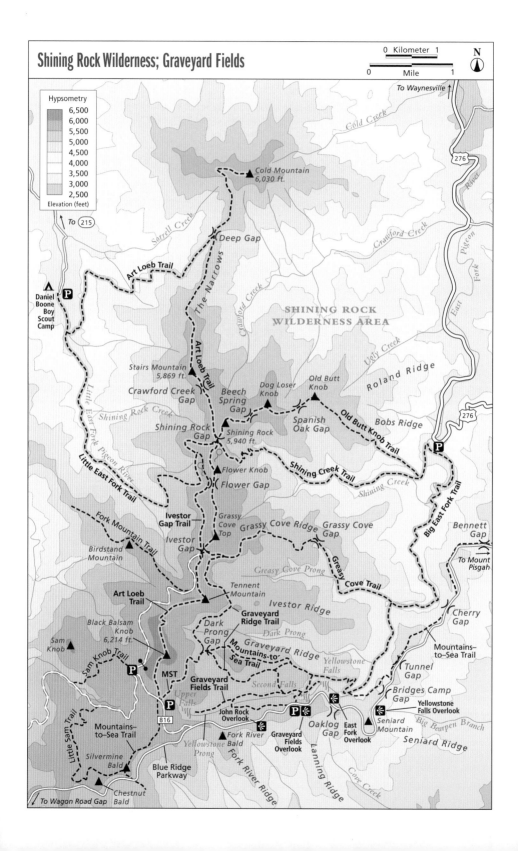

Shining Rock Wilderness; Graveyard Fields

0 Kilometer 1

0 Mile 1

N

Hypsometry

6,500
6,000
5,500
5,000
4,500
4,000
3,500
3,000
2,500

Elevation (feet)

To Waynesville ↑

Cold Creek

To 215

Cold Mountain
6,030 ft.

Crawford Creek

276

Deep Gap

Art Loeb Trail

Sorrell Creek

The Narrows

Crawford Creek

Pigeon River

East Fork

Daniel
Boone
Boy
Scout
Camp

P

SHINING ROCK
WILDERNESS AREA

Ugly Creek

Roland Ridge

Art Loeb Trail

Stairs Mountain
5,869 ft.

Crawford Creek
Gap

Beech
Spring
Gap

Dog Loser
Knob

Old Butt
Knob

Little East Fork Pigeon River

Shining Rock Creek

Shining Rock
Gap

Shining Rock
5,940 ft.

Spanish
Oak Gap

Old Butt Knob Trail

Bobs Ridge

276

P

Little East Fork Trail

Flower Knob

Flower Gap

Shining Creek Trail

Shining Creek

Big East Fork Trail

Fork Mountain Trail

Ivestor
Gap Trail

Grassy
Cove
Top

Grassy Cove Ridge

Grassy Cove
Gap

Bennett
Gap

Ivestor
Gap

Birdstand
Mountain

Greasy Cove Prong

Greasy Cove Trail

To Mount
Pisgah

Art Loeb
Trail

Tennent
Mountain

Ivestor Ridge

Cherry
Gap

Black Balsam
Knob
6,214 ft.

Graveyard
Ridge Trail

Dark
Prong
Gap

Dark Prong

Graveyard Ridge

Mountains–
to–Sea Trail

Sam
Knob

Sam Knob Trail

P

MST

Mountains-to-
Sea Trail

Yellowstone
Falls

Tunnel
Gap

Graveyard
Fields Trail

Second Falls

Bridges Camp
Gap

Yellowstone
Falls Overlook

P

Upper
Falls

816

John Rock
Overlook

Fork River
Bald

P

Graveyard
Fields
Overlook

Oaklog
Gap

East
Fork
Overlook

Seniard
Mountain

Big Bearpen Branch

Mountains–
to–Sea Trail

Yellowstone
Prong

Lanning Ridge

Seniard Ridge

Little Sam Trail

Silvermine
Bald

Blue Ridge
Parkway

Fork River Ridge

Cove Creek

To Wagon Road Gap

Chestnut
Bald

The trail continues to rise across the richly forested flank of the Shining Rock Ledge, weaving in and out of green drainages (the deepest of which is at 3.1 miles). Reach grassy Deep Gap at 3.8 miles.

Those intent on solitude should consider Cold Mountain. From the Art Loeb Trail at Deep Gap, take a left; the area's least-visited peak is just 1.5 miles north, a 5.3-mile hike from the valley. For backpackers, that plan puts Shining Rock within striking distance for day hikes.

KEY POINTS

0.0   Start at the Daniel Boone Boy Scout Camp.

2.0   Sorrell Creek campsites.

3.8   Deep Gap. (*Option*: Turn right here for the circuit hike described below.)

5.3   Cold Mountain summit. Return the way you came.

10.6   Arrive back at the Scout camp.

For the circuit, go right from Deep Gap across a rocky, knife-edge ridge called The Narrows. The ridge broadens then narrows again to Stairs Mountain (5,869 feet) at 5.9 miles. The trail enters an old railroad grade at 6.1 miles in Crawford Creek Gap and reaches Shining Rock Gap at 6.7 miles. Turn right here on the old railroad grade of the Ivestor Gap Trail; the Little East Fork Trail turns off right 0.4 mile ahead, at 7.1 miles. This old railroad grade switchbacks just below the Ivestor Gap Trail as it leaves the spruces and birches of the crest. It crosses the Little East Fork of the Pigeon River at 9.3 miles and follows the stream to emerge near the Scout camp at 12.1 miles.

28 GRAVEYARD FIELDS

GRAVEYARD FIELDS LOOP TRAIL

WHY GO?

This two-waterfall loop explores a high, alpine-like valley.

THE RUNDOWN

(See map on page 176.)
General location: About 30 miles southwest of Asheville
Distance: 2.3-mile loop, with 1.4-mile side trip option
Difficulty: Easy to moderate, with easy backpacking for beginners

Maps: USGS Shining Rock. Pisgah National Forest's Shining Rock–Middle Prong Wilderness map. www.nationalforestmapstore.com/category-s/1844.htm
Elevation gain: About 300 feet for the 2.3-mile loop; about 700 feet for the longer loop

FINDING THE TRAILHEAD

Graveyard Fields Overlook is at milepost 418.8 on the Blue Ridge Parkway, 30 miles south of US 25 in Asheville (GPS: 35.320287 / -82.846936).

THE HIKE

The big news here is that this very popular trailhead was greatly expanded and facilities significantly improved in 2014 with funding from the Blue Ridge Parkway, the USDA Forest Service, and the Blue Ridge Parkway Foundation. Solar restrooms were installed and many trail improvements went in, including sections of boardwalk and interpretive signing.

The most daunting part of the entire hike is the steep descent from the Blue Ridge Parkway. It's short, only a few tenths of a mile, but it is steep on the way back if you retrace your steps (the return described here climbs much more gradually). Otherwise, this hike is relatively easy.

The open fields here were named following a devastating 25,000-acre fire in 1925. The thousands of stumps remaining reminded some people of grave markers. The entire 50,000-acre watershed was consumed by wildfires again in the 1940s. There was a smaller fire in the late 1990s. These fires have given the Shining Rock area its largely treeless, alpine-like appearance.

This gentle stream valley makes the perfect place for a day hike, picnic, or backpacking trip, especially for beginners or those who want an easy walk to scenic camping (prohibited in recent years due to bear activity; check USFS). The area is very popular in summer and fall, though, so campers in this fragile area should observe scrupulous camping practices. Even during busy times, it is easy to find out-of-the-way sites for zero-impact camping. Key advice: Go during the week and off-season.

Leaving the edge of the Parkway overlook, the trail descends the steep paved path and then crosses Yellowstone Prong on a bridge. Go right on a side trail and down a long set of wooden steps to Second Falls (a spur of the Mountains-to-Sea Trail goes left on the

Graveyard Fields' open vistas have made it a popular day hike. The trailhead parking area was dramatically expanded in 2014.

way—more below). This lofty area—the trailhead is at 5,100 feet and the high point 5,400 feet—never gets too warm, but the pool below these falls is a great summer spot to cool off.

Retrace your steps to the bridge, about 0.5 mile, and continue. Soon the Graveyard Ridge Trail branches right up a scenic rise of open fields and forest, a nice day hike or backpack to the summits (see the Mountains-to-Sea Trail circuit described below). The Graveyard Fields Loop continues left along the stream through an open river valley. Fine campsites are just out of sight, where evergreens mingle with deciduous trees and blueberry bushes. Views reach up to the balds above.

At the 1-mile mark, the return part of the loop heads left across the stream. Hikers may continue on the right-hand trail, following a 0.7-mile side trail to the Upper Falls, a less frequently visited, more precipitous cascade with impressive views down the valley. This section of trail, a round-trip of about 1.4 miles, is steeper and rockier than the rest of the route. If you go, retrace your steps downstream and take a right turn across Yellowstone Prong at about 2.7 miles.

The return route gradually ascends through a boggy area with a high-altitude feel. You'll cross a bridge and boardwalks on the way and be back at the parking lot after a moderate to moderately strenuous hike of about 4 miles. Without the Upper Falls side trip, the loop is an easy 2.3-mile hike.

The Mountains-to-Sea Trail figures in a number of hikes at Graveyard Fields, including a side trip to Second Falls.

KEY POINTS

- 0.0 Start from the Graveyard Fields Overlook.
- 0.5 Return to bridge after side trip to Second Falls.
- 1.4 Return leg of loop goes left. Turn right for the side trail to Upper Falls (1.4 miles round-trip.)
- 2.3 Arrive back at the parking area (about 4 miles with side trail to Upper Falls).

It's a quick side trip from the Graveyard Fields Loop to see impressive Second Falls, also called Lower Falls on some trail signs.

29 GREAT SMOKY MOUNTAINS NATIONAL PARK

Great Smoky Mountains is the country's most popular national park. The distinction is due to more than the park's proximity to nearby urban areas. This United Nations–designated International Biosphere Reserve is temperate rain forest that's world-class lush. This is one of the most diverse ecosystems on Earth, with large tracts of virgin timber reminiscent of the Pacific Northwest. It's one of the largest intact natural areas in the East. A huge area of the park soars well above 6,000 feet, where cool summers and deep-snow winters prevail in the spruce-fir ecosystem of the Canadian Forest Zone. There's evidence of early settlement, and elk have been successfully reintroduced.

Any hike on the AT through the park can be crowded if you go at the wrong time, so choose carefully. Shelters and campsites can be problematical too.

Campers are required to have an overnight permit in advance that stipulates where and when they'll be camping—in essence, it's a campsite reservation system (that favors end-to-end AT hikers). The best bet is to call the Backcountry Reservation Office (8 a.m.–5 p.m.; 865-436-1297) a month in advance, or visit the park's permit website (smokiespermits.nps.gov). There is a per-person/per-night fee for trail camping permits; check the website for current rates and regulations.

Backcountry group size is limited to eight. One night of camping is permitted at a shelter (and campsite 113), three nights at a backcountry campsite. Every shelter has a small number of spaces reserved for thru-hikers, and short-distance backpackers get the rest. Campers must stay in designated sites and follow their itinerary. Do not reserve more space than needed, and call to cancel if your plans change; failure to do so excludes other campers. Besides possessing your backcountry permit, you must camp and build fires only in designated sites. No tents are permitted at shelter sites (except by thru-hikers who have no choice); call or go online to be sure of the latest policies.

When not being carried or consumed, all food must be hung at least 10 feet off the ground to avoid tempting bears. All human feces must be buried at least 6 inches deep, and all toilet use must take place at least 100 feet from campsites and water sources. Do not use soap to wash anything in a stream. Pets and mountain bikes are prohibited—except on very few trails.

You don't have to camp. The park's overnight accommodation, LeConte Lodge, is in Tennessee, but a significant part of a ridgetop hike to the lodge from Newfound Gap is actually on the state line via the Appalachian Trail. The lodge operates from late March to around Thanksgiving. It's not easy to get a reservation, but it's worth the effort to stay in the East's highest hostel. It's a premier experience, akin to the Appalachian Mountain Club "huts" of New Hampshire's White Mountains, and even the high-mountain hostels in the Alps of Europe. Hikers carry relatively light packs, with clothing, toiletries, and snacks, and the huts provide a bed and meals. Guests at LeConte Lodge stay in cabins, some of which can accommodate a few families. There's a dining building, where guests enjoy hearty meals, which can include wine, and a separate relaxation lodge with board games and more. Your best bet for reservations is to visit the lodge website and e-mail the reservation request form between August 1st and late September just before "reservations open for the year," generally October 1st for the following year. Calling after the

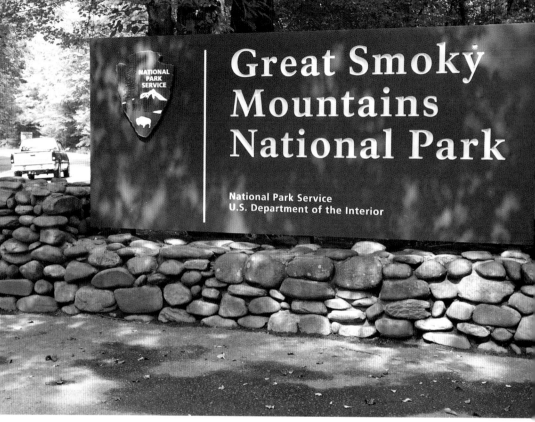

As the park service passed 100 in 2016, the Great Smokies attracted more visitors than any other national park in the United States.

reservation "opening" date is also an option. If you want to get in, you may need to take an available date. (LeConte Lodge; (865) 429-5704; lecontelodge.com; e-mail: reservations@lecontelodge.com.) Also check out the lodge blog; highonleconte.com.

The North Carolina side of the Smokies is the focus for a few adventurous motor tours that abut nice trails. The Cataloochee Valley, on the southeast side of the park, leads into a major watershed, with great streamside strolls past the preserved churches, homes, and schools of early settlers. The appeal here is possible sightings of the elk now thriving in the park.

Be sure to troll the park's website (nps.gov/grsm/index.htm) and check out the brochures available there. This park is severely challenged by its popularity. Also visit the websites of the friends groups that are helping to fund improvements: the Friends of the Great Smoky Mountains (friendsofthesmokies.org) and the Great Smoky Mountains Association (smokiesinformation.org).

CHOOSING YOUR SMOKIES HIKE

This book covers the park's trails in two places. The section below details hikes that do not involve the Appalachian Trail. These day and overnight trips lie east of the main ridge. Many great hikes that do include the AT—essentially, hikes that feature the park's loftiest elevations—are described in the chapter covering the Appalachian Trail near the beginning of this book (pages 18–25).

CALDWELL FORK

WHY GO?

Day and overnight options based around Caldwell Fork, home to some of the Smokies' most inspiring virgin forests and views from Hemphill Bald.

THE RUNDOWN

(See map on page 189.)
General location: The massive drainage lying below the Smokies' impressive Cataloochee Divide on the southeastern edge of the park
Distance: As short as you like, or a 7.4-mile circuit on the Boogerman Trail; about 10 miles for an out-and-back day hike to Hemphill Bald; two backpacking circuits of 10 and 14 miles, respectfully
Difficulty: Easy for the shortest out-and-back, strenuous for the longer hikes and circuits.
Map: Trails Illustrated *Great Smoky Mountains National Park*
Elevation gain: 1,000 feet for Boogerman Trail circuit

FINDING THE TRAILHEAD

Take exit 20 off I-40 and go west toward Maggie Valley on US 276. Take the first right onto Cove Creek Road and go 7.4 miles to a left turn, from gravel to pavement, on the road to Cataloochee. The Caldwell Fork Trail begins on the left at a small roadside pull-off just beyond the campground (GPS: 35.631386 / -83.088144).

To reach this area from the west, start at Polls Gap on the Blue Ridge Parkway's Heintooga Spur Road. Get on the Parkway 4 miles west of Maggie Valley from US 19. Drive south 2.5 miles and go right on Heintooga Spur Road. Polls Gap is 6 miles from the Parkway and 2.4 miles south of the Smokies' Balsam Mountain Campground (GPS: 35.563228 / -83.161584). Some of the destinations on the Caldwell Fork Trail can be more easily reached from Purchase Knob.

THE HIKES

The Caldwell Fork Trail bisects this huge drainage. A variety of side trails create diverse day and overnight circuit hikes. An out-and-back on the Caldwell Fork Trail itself is the first of many worthwhile walks. Nearly twenty of the Smokies' distinctive log bridges span the creek, including what may be the park's biggest, the first step away from the trailhead. The views are awesome all along the path—and from the bridges; just turn around when you want. Horse traffic is permitted, so the trail can be muddy.

A loop using the Boogerman Trail makes a 7.4-mile circuit. From the Caldwell Fork Trail, head left on the Boogerman Trail at 0.8 mile. It winds away and above the Caldwell Fork, eventually returning at 4.7 miles. Along the way, the refreshingly hiker-only path undulates through tall timber, the result of Robert "Booger" Palmer's refusal to cut the big trees on his stream-laced property. Be on the lookout for stone walls and other evidence of him. As you near Caldwell Fork Trail again, look left for the last remnants of Carson Messer's decaying cabin. Turn right to head back along the Caldwell Fork to your car.

A wealth of water is key to the Smokies' great species diversity.

KEY POINTS

- 0.0 Start at the roadside pull-off.
- 0.8 Turn left (southeast) on Boogerman Trail.
- 4.1 Turn right (north) on Caldwell Fork Trail.
- 6.6 Pass first Boogerman junction.
- 7.4 Arrive back at the pull-off.

Backpackers wanting to tackle a streamside amble along Caldwell Fork can use campsite #41, 4.8 miles from the parking area. On the way, you pass both entrances to the Boogerman Trail (on the left), the Big Fork Ridge Trail at 3.1 miles (on the right), the McKee Branch Trail at 3.2 miles (on the left; site of the Caldwell Fork community, which had a gristmill), and Hemphill Bald Trail (on the left) at 4.7 miles. Cross the last bridge over Caldwell Fork and reach campsite #41. Consider going beyond the campsite. A sign to the right soon directs you to Big Poplars, a grove of towering, centuries-old tulip poplars spared by Cataloochee resident John Caldwell. Above this point, the hardwood and hemlock forest becomes impressively mature. Backtrack for a 10-mile overnighter, or you could go past campsite #41, adding a large looping end circuit around the headwaters of Caldwell Fork.

Campsite #41, a popular horse camping site, is the perfect base camp if you catch it in the equestrian off-season. Spend two nights, and take in spectacular Hemphill Bald (described in the Purchase Knob entry).

To visit the bald from campsite #41, take the Hemphill Bald Trail to switchback up through impressive virgin forests. In 3.1 miles, at Double Gap (there's a gate into the pasture), turn right (the Cataloochee Divide Horse Trail goes left). At about 4 miles, step through a gate (private property; treat with care) into the meadow near the 5,540-foot summit of Hemphill Bald, the highest peak on this side of the park. A stone picnic table has a skyline carving with names and elevations of distant landmarks. It memorializes Tom and Judy Alexander, creators of Cataloochee Ranch. The slopes and lifts of Cataloochee Ski Area, the first ski resort in North Carolina, are just below by the ranch. Back at campsite #41, the bald is about an 8-mile round-trip. Spend a second night before backtracking to your car.

A highly recommended backpacking circuit also uses campsite #41, but from the west. It too provides access to Hemphill Bald. The Heintooga Spur Road branches from the Blue Ridge Parkway at milepost 458.2 and winds through the park with various name changes to US 441 near Cherokee. Park on the Heintooga Road at Polls Gap, 6 miles from the Parkway. The Hemphill Bald, Polls Gap, and Rough Fork Trails all meet here and create a 14-mile looping circuit with campsite #41 near the halfway mark.

For backpackers wanting the shortest, easiest second day, start on Hemphill Bald Trail to the right, where it undulates across the Cataloochee Divide (there's a spring at Maggot Spring Gap). A gate before and after Hemphill Bald (at about 4.7 miles) permits you to walk the meadow past the picnic table (an out-and-back day hike here is just under 10 miles). Head past the peak (down the meadow if you like; there's a gate below) to Double Gap, and go left down to the Caldwell Fork Trail and the campsite (at 8.5 miles—see the previous hike description). Continue up Caldwell Fork the next day, past Big Poplars, and go left on the Rough Fork Trail. It's steep out of the drainage then joins an easy railroad grade back to Polls Gap at 13.7 miles—a 5.2-mile second day.

Besides backpacking, two really special lodging options make it possible to stay right beside this terrific Smoky Mountains hiking area. Equestrian-oriented Cataloochee Ranch (800-868-1401; cataloocheeranch.com) is just below Hemphill Bald, with easy access to the bald and adjacent trails. Check out their website for a webcam view of the bald. Hearty meals and rustic cabin and lodge accommodations have made this a destination for seventy years. Not far away, and literally perched on the park boundary, The Swag Country Inn (800-7897672; theswag.com) is an upscale, nationally known destination. The Swag's 250-acre parcel includes a magical collection of cabin cottages and wonderfully private little nooks called "hideaways." From either Cataloochee or The Swag, both a cool mile high, views reach far below into cloud-filled Maggie Valley. Guests at these hostelries are also close to Purchase Knob for other great walks (see below). Serious hikers could actually hike in to stay at either of these lodges, emulating the kind of experience "hut hikers" have at LeConte Lodge. Whether you start at the Caldwell Fork Trail or at Polls Gap, either of these inns is just 6 or so trail miles away.

MOUNT STERLING/BIG CREEK/CATALOOCHEE

WHY GO?
Two day hikes and backpacking circuits take in one of the park's most accessible and stunning views from Mount Sterling, nearly 6,000 feet atop a southeastern Smokies summit. Day and circuit backpacking hikes that require no auto shuttles also explore the Big Creek and Little Cataloochee valleys that flank Mount Sterling.

THE RUNDOWN

General location: The southeastern part of Great Smoky Mountains National Park

Distance: 4 miles for the summit on the Mount Sterling Trail. An overnighter in Little Cataloochee Valley is a 16.4-mile circuit. Easy Big Creek day hikes range from 4 miles to 10.6 miles, and one- or two-night backpacks there are 10.6 and 16.8 miles, respectively.

Difficulty: Strenuous for the summit hikes; strenuous for backpacking circuits; easy to moderate for an out-and-back day hike or overnighter on Big Creek

Map: Trails Illustrated *Great Smoky Mountains National Park*

Elevation gain: 1,954 feet for the Mount Sterling Trail

FINDING THE TRAILHEADS
Park at Mount Sterling Gap (GPS: 35.700209 / -83.097517) for the primary day hike and backpack, readily reached from I-40. From North Carolina, take exit 20 off I-40 and go west toward Maggie Valley on US 276. Take the first right onto Cove Creek Road; the gap is at 15.7 miles. From Tennessee, take exit 451, Waterville. Turn left under the interstate then left again to cross the Pigeon River. Make another left, then a right, on Waterville Road. Stay on Waterville Road for 2 miles to a crossroads in the village of Mount Sterling. Go left from there 6.2 miles on Mount Sterling Road for Mount Sterling Gap.

For Big Creek area hikes, from the above junction, go straight through the intersection; the Big Creek Ranger Station is 0.2 mile ahead on the right (access here to the Appalachian Trail and Mount Cammerer via the Chestnut Branch Trail). Pass the horse use area sign and Big Creek trailhead sign to park in the lot beyond where restrooms are available (GPS: 35.751373 / -83.109649).

To start in the middle of the first Mount Sterling backpacking loop at the Pretty Hollow Gap Trailhead, pass Cataloochee Campground (see Caldwell Fork entry) and park on the right at 4.6 miles.

THE HIKES

For the shortest day hike to the 5,842-foot peak, stride away from the roadside gate on a fire road and rise through a dry-soil ecosystem. Dip through a nice gap; the Long Bunk Trail heads left at 0.5 mile (more below). The Mount Sterling Trail rises determinedly on a wonderful back-and-forth across prominent ridgelines that delineate changes in microclimate. Each new "aspect," or directional alteration of the ridgeline, is distinctive.

The first switchback crosses a ridgeline from the southeast to northeast side and keeps rising through ferns and hemlocks, then tall spruces. Nearing the upper end, the road-width trail switchbacks across to the drier southeastern side into mountain laurel and hardwoods. Soon you're high enough for a truly verdant display of lush ferns and mosses in spruce and fir forest.

The trail crests at a junction with the Mount Sterling Ridge Trail at 1.8 miles and a quiet, high-mountain feel. Go right and gradually uphill through more evergreens, and at 2 miles reach the base of the tall, rickety-seeming tower (where the Baxter Creek Trail heads away left). This fire-spotting station will look alarmingly spindly legged to the acrophobic. (Don't expect a photo from the top in this book!). It is safe though, with a truly inspiring view (even from just above the trees, thank you). This is one of the park's best perches on the massive main ridge of the Smokies. Campsite #38 lies off in the evergreens just below the tower, past hitching posts for horses. Water is available 0.25 mile down the Baxter Creek Trail on the left.

KEY POINTS

0.0   Start at the Mount Sterling Gap parking area.

0.5   Long Bunk Trail goes left.

1.8   Turn right on Mount Sterling Ridge Trail.

2.0   Reach the fire tower at the peak. Retrace your steps.

4.0   Arrive back at Mount Sterling Gap.

Two nice backpacking circuits or long day hikes also include Mount Sterling.

From the parking area above, a 15.6-mile hike lies to the south. Just above the parking area for the Mount Sterling Trail, go left down the Long Bunk Trail to reach the Little Cataloochee Trail in about 4.1 miles. Near the bottom, pass an old cemetery on the right. At the junction, go right on the road-width Little Cataloochee Trail. (Left, it's a mile to Cove Creek Road, 2.5 miles south of the Mount Sterling trailhead.) Not far on the right is a side trail to the John Jackson Hannah Cabin (father of one of the early park rangers, his grave is in the cemetery you passed on the Long Bunk Trail). There's plentiful evidence of early inhabitants, including Little Cataloochee Baptist Church (outdoor privies are nearby), the 1856 Dan Cook Place, and many walls and foundations (expect muddy conditions on this trail from horse traffic).

The trail crosses a ridge then descends to cross Little Cataloochee Creek. Beyond, it rises through the old settlement of Ola. After Davidson Gap, a rougher trail drops steeply at times down to Davidson Branch and the Pretty Hollow Gap Trail (at about 8.2 miles). Take that trail right along Palmer Creek and past the Palmer Creek Trail on the left at 9 miles. Soon your camp spot is on the right—backcountry site #39.

From even partway up Mount Sterling fire tower, there's a bird's eye view of Campsite 38.

The next morning, finish the climb to Pretty Hollow Gap, at 13.2 miles. Go right and steeply uphill. The climb moderates nearer the junction of the Mount Sterling Trail, on the right at 14.6 miles, and the peak is at 14.8 miles. From the tower, backtrack to the Mount Sterling Trail at 15 miles and back to your car at 16.4 miles (a nearly 8-mile second day, most of it downhill if you don't camp at Mount Sterling). For a three-day trip, use campsite #38 there to create a light second day of less than 5 miles.

An alternative starting point for this hike is the trailhead for the Little Cataloochee Trail, not far beyond the Little Cataloochee Ranger Station at Cataloochee Stables. That makes it an 0.8-mile walk from the trailhead to Pretty Hollow Gap Trail and the heart of the above circuit. Starting there, campsite #39 is only about 2 miles, and campsite #38 atop Mount Sterling is 7.4 miles. The second day down from Mount Sterling involves some climbing along the Little Cataloochee Trail for a 9.8-mile hike back to your car.

Starting to the north, at the Big Creek Picnic Area, there's another aggressive day hike and backpacking circuit that includes Mount Sterling, as well as a good easy day hike/ overnighter up Big Creek itself. (For the best view of these trails, refer to Appalachian Trail map 1D near the beginning of this book.)

To climb Mount Sterling from there, start at the Big Creek Picnic Area and soon cross the bridge over Big Creek. After crossing Baxter Creek, the trail follows the stream then turns to cross another creek and switchbacks up a leading ridge through inspiring virgin timber. The trail reaches Mount Sterling Ridge and climbs to the peak through an extensive, highly scenic spruce and fir forest. At 0.25 mile from the summit, there's a spring on the right. The proximity of the trailheads for the Mount Sterling and Baxter Creek Trails create another day hike or overnight option. The Baxter Creek Trail has about 4,000 feet of elevation gain, so with two cars, the easiest bet would be to start at Mount Sterling Gap, climb to the peak (perhaps camp there), and descend to the second vehicle at Big Creek for an 8.0-mile hike.

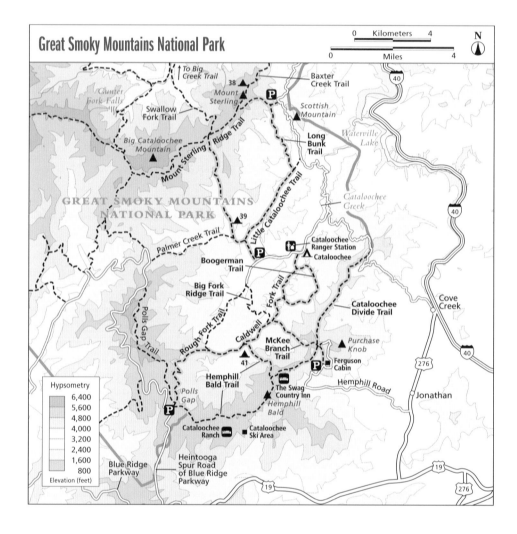

Great Smoky Mountains National Park

0   Kilometers   4

0   Miles   4

N

To Big Creek Trail

Baxter Creek Trail

40

38

Mount Sterling

P

Gunter Fork Falls

Swallow Fork Trail

Scottish Mountain

Big Cataloochee Mountain

Mount Sterling Ridge Trail

Long Bunk Trail

Waterville Lake

GREAT SMOKY MOUNTAINS NATIONAL PARK

39

Little Cataloochee Trail

Cataloochee Creek

40

Palmer Creek Trail

Boogerman Trail

P

Cataloochee Ranger Station

Cataloochee

Big Fork Ridge Trail

Fork Trail

Cataloochee Divide Trail

Cove Creek

Polls Gap Trail

Rough Fork Trail

Caldwell

McKee Branch Trail

Purchase Knob

40

41

P

Ferguson Cabin

276

Hemphill Bald Trail

Polls Gap

The Swag Country Inn

Hemphill Bald

Hemphill Road

Jonathan

P

Hypsometry

6,400
5,600
4,800
4,000
3,200
2,400
1,600
800

Elevation (feet)

Cataloochee Ranch

Cataloochee Ski Area

Blue Ridge Parkway

Heintooga Spur Road of Blue Ridge Parkway

19

19

276

The Big Creek Trail permits a variety of easy day hikes, as well as a few backpacking circuits that include Mount Sterling. Take off up the gated old logging railroad grade that rises easily its entire length along one of the park's most scenic streams. At 1.5 miles, Midnight Hole is a deep pool at the base of a ledge cascade. Mouse Creek Falls cascades spectacularly in from the left at 2 miles (an easy 4-mile round-trip day hike). There's another pool at the bridge just above. At just under 3 miles, there's a spring on the left, and the Swallow Fork Trail goes left at 5.1 miles.

Beginning backpackers should consider camping at the Lower Walnut Bottom campsite #37, at 5.2 miles (the Low Gap Trail ties in here to the Appalachian Trail; see the Mount Cammerer part of the AT entry for more). The campsite is beautiful, and it's a moderate 10.4-mile round-trip (for day hikers as well). Backpackers bound for the summit campsite of Mount Sterling, either on the first or second night, should head left on the Swallow Falls Trail (if you camped at campsite #37, add 0.2 mile to the following distances).

The trail climbs gradually, crosses a log bridge, and then steeply reaches Pretty Hollow Gap at 9.1 miles. Go left here on the Mount Sterling Ridge Trail to camp on the peak at 10.7 miles (the same route to the summit described above using the Mount Sterling Trail). Take the Baxter Creek Trail down to your car for a 16.8-mile backpacking trip.

PURCHASE KNOB

WHY GO?

This entry point to the Great Smokies offers a short easy hike to the Smokies' highest log cabin and access to Hemphill Bald and hikes in the Caldwell Fork Area. A stay at the nearby Swag Country Inn permits hikes on all these trails and a one-of-a-kind upscale national park experience.

Once the estate of Voit Gilmore and Kathryn McNeil, the 530-acre Purchase Knob tract was considered the premier piece of private property in Haywood County. Located at an altitude of 5,000 feet, in 2000 the summer home and grounds became the largest-ever private gift to Great Smoky Mountains National Park. Today, the property is the Appalachian Highlands Science Learning Center at Purchase Knob, one of many such research hubs established in national parks where school and other groups come to help scientists in residence with their research (the center is not equipped to accommodate drop in visitors). Hikers often pass by the center, including groups from The Swag, but please don't interrupt the official activities. For information on taking your school or other group to the center, call (828) 926-6251.

THE RUNDOWN

General location: On the eastern end of Maggie Valley
Distance: Between 2 and 3 miles for the Ferguson Cabin loops; about 8 miles for the circuit to Hemphill Bald; 10.4 miles for the longer circuit

Difficulty: Easy for the loop; strenuous to the bald and for the circuit
Map: Trails Illustrated *Great Smoky Mountains National Park*
Elevation gain: 1,500 feet for the hike to Hemphill Bald

FINDING THE TRAILHEAD

Leave I-40 at exit 20 and head south toward Maggie Valley on US 276. In 2.8 miles turn right onto Grindstone Road, then right again on Hemphill Road. Pass The Swag entrance road left at 7.2 miles and park discreetly 0.8 mile beyond near the gate at the Purchase Knob environmental education center (GPS: 35.574180 / -83.075237). Do not park inside the gate or block the road.

THE HIKES

Starting from the Purchase Knob gate, the best easy hike is a loop of the property that features the Ferguson Cabin. Walk up the scenic road; go left in the meadow at the trail signs to the 1870s Ferguson Cabin and explore inside. To get the most out of this hike, pick up the booklet *Log Cabins of the Smokies* when you stop at one of the park's visitor centers or online at the Great Smoky Mountains Association (smokiesstore.org). Return to your car for a 2.2 mile hike.

Or for a little loop, exit the cabin and turn right (uphill) and into the woods along the stream. At the next junction, go right on a horse trail to return to the meadow and Ferguson Cabin (about a 3.2-mile hike back at your car).

The wonderful views of Hemphill Bald can also be seen on an 8-mile round-trip hike from Purchase Knob parking. Starting the same way as above, visit the cabin and at the horse trail above, go left on a connector and at the next junction go left again on the Cataloochee Divide Trail. (McKee Branch Trail goes straight down into the park at this junction.) The divide trail is popular with horse users (most of it is wide and can be muddy). You'll pass meadows as you flank The Swag property. (Peer into the property, but please respect the privacy of the resort.) You'll pass the inn itself at about 2 miles. Just beyond, at Double Gap, a gate enters the meadow on the left and the Hemphill Bald Trail comes in from the right. Continue up on the Hemphill Bald Trail as it climbs through the forest.

At the next gate, step out into the meadow at about 4 miles and enjoy the view from a stone picnic table with a guide to distant peaks carved on top. This is private property of Cataloochee Ranch, so please be respectful. Step back into the park and return to your starting point for an 8-mile round-trip.

Much the same route as above permits a circuit hike with an overnight stay at one of the Smokies' most remote campsites—#41. At Cataloochee Divide Trail, head straight down into the park on the McKee Branch Trail. Go left on the Caldwell Fork Trail past its junction with the Hemphill Bald Trail and spend the night at campsite #41 at about 4 miles. Return up Hemphill Bald Trail and bear right in Double Gap to visit the balds. Retrace your steps, but go right on the Cataloochee Divide Trail to return past The Swag and Ferguson Cabin for an approximately 10.4-mile circuit.

OCONALUFTEE RIVER TRAIL/ MOUNTAIN FARM MUSEUM

WHY GO?

The Mountain Farm Museum may just be a stroll among historic structures, but combine it with one of the Smokies' best-kept-secret easy walks, the Oconaluftee River Trail (ORT), and you have an inspiring combination of scenery and interpretation.

The Mountain Farm Museum is a flat, 0.5-mile wander among a stunning collection of nineteenth-century backcountry farm structures that paint a vivid picture of a settler's life, complete with chickens crowing and pigs grunting. The ORT leads from the farm to Cherokee—or from Cherokee to the farm. Hiking either way offers a major dose of riverside scenery along with what may be the park's best insight into Cherokee Indian culture. A half dozen interpretive plaques on the trail movingly explain Cherokee beliefs and respect for the natural world (in English and Cherokee). The signs include

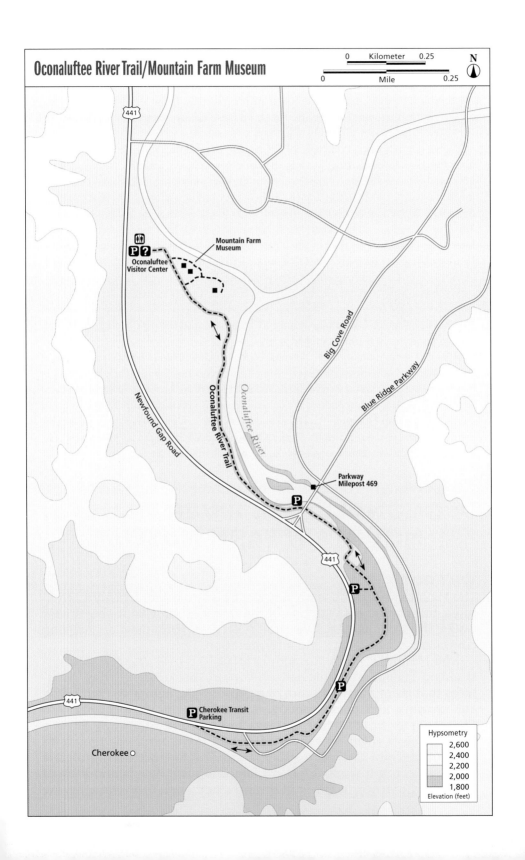

Oconaluftee River Trail/Mountain Farm Museum

Jewelweed bobbing in an August breeze demands attention along the Oconaluftee River Trail.

evocative illustrations by Cherokee artists that will make you want to visit the tribe's Qualla Arts and Crafts gallery and other cultural institutions in town. There's a bench at each sign and at other places along the path.

Higher in the park, along Newfound Gap Road, the Oconaluftee River is narrow and fast, but along the ORT, the river spreads wide and dances over ledges and around islands. The refreshingly clean smell of the water matches its emerald green color in a way that defies description. All along the river there's an open understory of grasses and ferns with many wildflowers, including bee balm and entire trail-side borders of jewelweed or touch-me-not (in late August).

One reason the ORT is a good family hike is that it's very popular with Cherokees as a place to jog or stroll with their own families. Seeing local Native Americans enjoying their ancestral homeland while you pause to read interpretive signs about Cherokee legend is a rich experience.

The ORT is one of the very few trails in the Smokies where dogs and mountain bikes are permitted. Leashed dogs are OK on the Oconaluftee River Trail, but no dogs are allowed in the Mountain Farm Museum enclosure.

FINDING THE TRAILHEAD

Park at the Oconaluftee Visitor Center (GPS: 35.513095 / -83.306514), the Cherokee Transit parking area at the edge of the park (GPS: 35.499840 / -83.303821), or at any of three pull-offs between Cherokee and the visitor center on Newfound Gap Road.

THE HIKE

Leave the visitor center's south side; the trail splits—left to the Mountain Farm Museum and right to the Oconaluftee River Trail that skirts the farm. Explore the farm buildings first, all gathered in 1950 from throughout the Smokies (signs picture many in their original locations). After you've toured the farm, exit past the Apple House near the cornfield and turn left on the ORT. The trail follows the farm's fence line then swings close to the river at the first Cherokee cultural sign.

At 0.7 mile the trail goes under the Blue Ridge Parkway bridge and side steps lead right to a roadside parking slip (the first of three recommended that permit shorter out-and-back hikes). A right turn up the rooty bank just beyond leads to the second roadside trailhead, a designated parking area on Newfound Gap road at 0.9 mile, immediately before the sign stating "Blue Ridge Parkway Next Right." At 1.2 miles from the Mountain Farm Museum a rock wall leads right to the next roadside trailhead at the park's major entrance sign (the first parking spot reached from Cherokee). The trail then crosses Big Cove Road next and reaches the sidewalks of Cherokee across from Cherokee Transit at the reservation boundary at 1.5 miles.

If you start from Cherokee, or any of the parking spots closer to the Mountain Farm Trail, you learn about Cherokee culture in a scenic, natural setting—and end your hike with the log cabins of the newcomers.

KEY POINTS

0.0   Start at the Oconaluftee Visitor Center.

0.7   Pass side steps to Blue Ridge Parkway.

1.2   Pass park entrance sign pull-off.

1.5   Reach Cherokee Transit parking. Return the way you came.

3.0   Arrive back at the visitor center.

DEEP CREEK LOOP (TOM BRANCH FALLS, INDIAN CREEK FALLS, JUNEY WHANK FALLS)

WHY GO?

This trailhead at Deep Creek Campground offers two very short waterfall walks, one the park's easiest (indeed wheelchair accessible) stroll to a spectacular waterfall, Tom Branch Falls. There's also a longer circuit hike and you can even add a tubing run or mountain bike ride along pristine Deep Creek.

THE RUNDOWN

General location: Southwestern Great Smoky Mountains National Park near Bryson City
Distance: 4.4-mile circuit with waterfall walks as short as 0.4-mile out and back and an 0.8-mile loop.
Difficulty: Easy to moderate

Maps: USGS Bryson City; Trails Illustrated *Great Smoky Mountains National Park*
Elevation gain: 600 feet for the circuit
Water availability: At National Park Service picnic area and Deep Creek Campground

FINDING THE TRAILHEAD

Take any of a number of well-signed routes north from downtown Bryson City. After passing the cluster of businesses at the park boundary, pass the Deep Creek Campground and the picnic area, both on the right. Turn left into the parking area (GPS: 35.464418/-83.434350) as you reach a bridge on the right (Galbraith Creek Road).

THE HIKE

Here's the place to film your own Mountain Dew commercial. Some "hikers" may be swimsuit-wearing, tube-toting river runners, at least on the lowest section. And mountain bikers are permitted up to the upper stream bridge on the Deep Creek Trail. This busy waterfall walk is best after rain and in off-seasons for more solitude.

Just driving in to the Deep Creek area conveys an important Smokies' impression—these summits may not tower like the Tetons, but you sense that there's a vast wildland ahead that stretches ridge after ridge beyond the park boundary. This hike takes you a ways into that forest.

The trail starts as a level road grade from a circular drop-off point for wheelchair users. Follow wide, green, pristine Deep Creek as it flows from the heart of the Smokies. Soon the sound of the stream rises to a higher pitch. As you amble up to five benches on the riverside—there's awesome Tom Branch Falls plummeting into the stream from the opposite side of Deep Creek (a 0.4-mile round-trip). The road continues along the stream past more benches and then turns right to cross a bridge. Beyond the bridge across the stream there's a great view of a favorite tubing rapid where the road climbs more steeply. At 0.7 mile the Indian Creek Trail veers right from the Deep Creek Trail at a sign

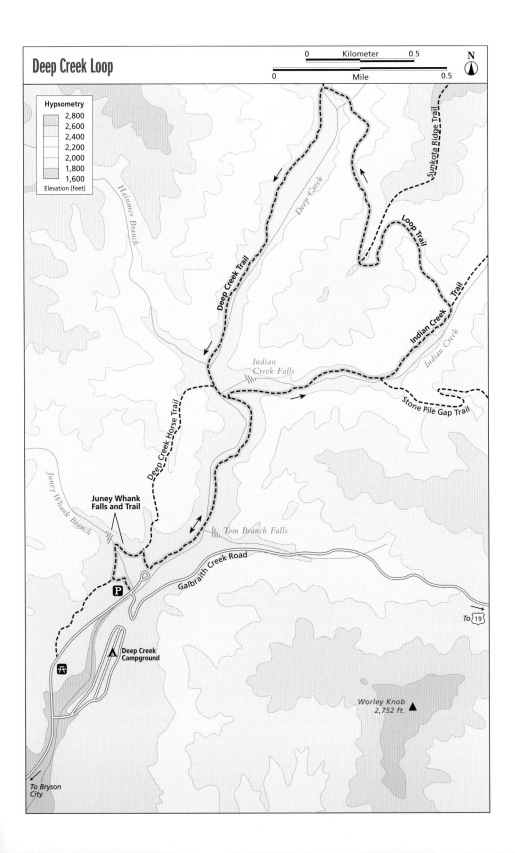

Deep Creek Loop

Hypsometry

2,800
2,600
2,400
2,200
2,000
1,800
1,600

Elevation (feet)

Kilometer
0   0.5

Mile
0   0.5

N

Sunkota Ridge Trail

Deep Creek

Deep Creek Trail

Loop Trail

Indian Creek Trail

Indian Creek

Indian
Creek Falls

Stone Pile Gap Trail

Deep Creek Horse Trail

Hammer Branch

Juney Whank
Falls and Trail

Juney Whank Branch

Tom Branch Falls

Galbraith Creek Road

P

To 19

Deep Creek
Campground

Worley Knob
2,752 ft.

To Bryson
City

prohibiting tubing above that point. (If you go left on Deep Creek Trail, the hike remains easy to the bridge mentioned below, the terminus for mountain bikers.)

Go right; in just a few hundred feet, a side trail descends left to scenic Indian Creek Falls (a 1.4-mile round-trip from the parking area). Continuing on the Indian Creek Trail across another bridge, you pass Stone Pile Gap Trail as it drops right at 1.5 miles. Beyond, the road grade trail rises with the river above rhododendron–lined streambanks into a drier forest. Turn left on the Loop Trail at 1.5 miles. After a level stretch, it rises steeply up to Sunkota Ridge at 2.3 miles. If anything, the trail drops more steeply off the other side. As you pass a massive white oak, the sound of Deep Creek comes from below. The trail levels and rejoins the Deep Creek Trail at a T junction at 2.5 miles. Right, the easy old logging railroad appears trail-like on its way higher past campsite #60 (a good beginner backpack). Left, the gravel road crosses a bridge (the upper limit of mountain bike access). The pool below must be 15 feet deep.

The trail drops steeply at only one point on its way to another bridge and back to the Indian Creek Trail junction at 3.5 miles. From there it's another 0.7 mile back to your car for a 4.2-mile circuit. From the trailhead on the Deep Creek Trail to the pool by the bridge, it's 3.4 miles out and back.

If you don't have enough time for this longest hike, try the Juney Whank Falls Trail, an easy 0.8-mile loop that's great for kids. Take the wide road grade up and left from the parking lot to a junction with the Deep Creek Horse Trail. Turn right up the wood steps, and shortly turn right again at the "Falls" sign. The trail dips down nice rock steps and crosses a scenic bridge below the falls with an embedded bench. There's a perfect rock seat at the base of the falls where you could almost picture a romantic poet perched there pondering. Near the falls, "This is not a trail" signs are actually embedded in some bootleg paths that might mislead the inexperienced. The hike leaves the falls on the bridal trail then turns right and dips to the Deep Creek Trail for another right back to your car.

Camp at Deep Creek Campground (especially sites #30 and up) and you won't need to cope with a busy parking area. Just step up onto Galbraith Creek Road and go left across the bridge. For more easy hikes in the entire park, see the author's *Best Easy Day Hikes Great Smoky Mountains National Park.*

KEY POINTS

0.0   Start at the trailhead.

0.2   Tom Branch Falls (0.4-mile round-trip).

0.7   Right on Indian Creek Trail; side trail in a few hundred feet to Indian Creek Falls.

1.5   Left on the Loop Trail.

2.5   Turn left, back on the Deep Creek Trail.

3.5   Pass Indian Creek Trail.

4.2   Arrive back at the trailhead.

30 JOYCE KILMER MEMORIAL FOREST

WHY GO?

The Joyce Kilmer Memorial Forest is a 3,800-acre tract now combined with the Slickrock Wilderness to form a wild and wildly popular area in the extreme southwestern mountains of North Carolina, not far from the Tennessee state line.

An easy figure-eight circuit comprises two trails through the mightily impressive forest of poplar, hemlock, oak, and beech, substantial portions of which are virgin. In all likelihood, there are trees here that were growing when Columbus landed in the New World. And many were flourishing before Europeans disturbed the comings and goings of the Cherokee Indians. Age estimates for the biggest of the trees range from 300 to 500 years. Many trees top 100 feet and are up to 20 feet around at the base.

The hike described here includes a memorial to poet Joyce Kilmer, author of the poem "Trees." The forest is massive, inspiring, and crowded on summer and fall weekends. Plan accordingly if you wish to use the potential silence of the tall trees for quiet contemplation.

A National Recreation Trail explores one of the most stunning parcels of virgin hardwood forest left in the Southern Appalachians.

THE RUNDOWN

General location: Near Robbinsville
Distance: 1 mile for the Joyce Kilmer Trail loop; 2 miles for the Poplar Cove Loop
Difficulty: Easy
Maps: USGS Santeetlah Creek. The preferred hiking map for this area is the Joyce Kilmer–Slickrock and Citico Creek Wilderness Map, available from the USDA Forest Service. www.national

forestmapstore.com/category-s/1844.htm
Elevation gain: 440 feet
Water availability: Water in season at the trailhead at the Joyce Kilmer Picnic Area
For more information: Cheoah Ranger District, Nantahala National Forest, 1070 Massey Branch Rd., Robbinsville 28771; (828) 479-6431; e-mail: cheoahrd@fs.fed.us

FINDING THE TRAILHEAD

The trailhead is about 15 miles northwest of Robbinsville. Leave Robbinsville going north and stay on US 129. After about 8.9 miles, go left on SR 1134 at the "Joyce Kilmer Mem. Forest" signs. The junction is well marked. Follow signs at the next junction to reach the parking area in 6.5 miles from US 129. The trail starts behind the visitor shelter, just off the parking area (GPS: 35.359002 / -83.928516).

THE HIKE

The Joyce Kilmer Trail leaves the parking area and climbs gradually along Little Santeetlah Creek. It crosses the stream and swings back to join the Poplar Cove Trail at a

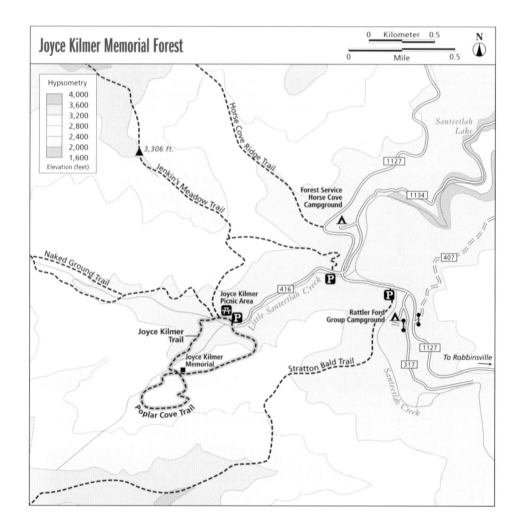

Joyce Kilmer Memorial Forest

Hypsometry
Elevation (feet)
- 4,000
- 3,600
- 3,200
- 2,800
- 2,400
- 2,000
- 1,600

0 Kilometer 0.5

0 Mile 0.5

N

▲ 3,306 ft.

Santeetlah Lake

Horse Cove Ridge Trail

Jenkin's Meadow Trail

Forest Service Horse Cove Campground

1127

1134

Naked Ground Trail

407

Joyce Kilmer Picnic Area

416

Little Santeetlah Creek

Joyce Kilmer Trail

Rattler Ford Group Campground

Joyce Kilmer Memorial

Stratton Bald Trail

1127

317

To Robbinsville →

Poplar Cove Trail

Santeetlah Creek

---

plaque memorializing poet and journalist Joyce Kilmer, who died during World War I combat in France and was buried there in 1918. Returning on the trail from here creates a 1-mile loop hike.

Take a right to enter the upper loop on the Poplar Cove Trail, which ventures through hardwood forest and plentiful yellow poplars, some truly huge. The deep soils of the fertile valley are well watered by the ridges above. The result is an internationally known grove of giant trees. The trail reaches its high point then gradually descends back to the Kilmer memorial. Take a right and the lower loop back to the parking lot to complete a 2-mile circuit.

HIGHLANDS AREA

BARTRAM TRAIL

WHY GO?

The Bartram Trail was the dream of Walter G. McKelvey of Brevard, North Carolina, a retired landscape architect. McKelvey spent the early 1970s acquiring government approval and planning a route, but he died just before the meeting he'd planned to charter the North Carolina Bartram Trail Society. Countless volunteers have contributed to his effort to build this trail honoring early botanist William Bartram, whom the Indians called *Puc Puggy*, a Muskogean name meaning "the flower hunter."

Bartram was a Philadelphia-born naturalist and explorer whose trips expanded the world's awareness of Cherokee culture and the profuse flora and fauna of the Southern Appalachians. Sparked by his fascination with "primitive, unmodified nature," Bartram wandered southwestern North Carolina from 1773 to 1777 and published *The Travels of William Bartram* in 1791 (still in print and highly recommended). The book was immensely popular, especially in Europe, where it was praised by writers such as Thomas Carlyle and Samuel Coleridge. Indeed, he and his botanist father, John, were close acquaintances of Benjamin Franklin, who was instrumental in popularizing their

Pristine Whiterock Gap is one of many inviting swales and summits on the Bartram Trail.

discoveries in Europe. William Bartram named a new tree species he discovered in Georgia for Franklin.

Today, the 115-mile, yellow-blazed Bartram Trail is now complete with seven sections and about 78 miles of hiking in North Carolina. The 11.5 miles of the trail from Wallace Branch to Wayah Bald, at 5,342 feet the trail's high point, were designated as a National Recreation Trail (NRT) in 1985 and make a strenuous and spectacular backpacking trip. The Georgia section of the Bartram Trail is also an NRT (see *Hiking Georgia*, FalconGuides).

This section of trail is perhaps the Bartram Trail's best part. An outstanding ridge walk, perfect for backpacking or day hiking, the graded trail traverses a rarely visited ridge and spectacular summits.

THE RUNDOWN

General location: North of Highlands
Distance: 8.5 miles one way, with shorter out-and-back day hikes from either end
Difficulty: Moderate to moderately strenuous from Jones Gap; strenuous from Buckeye Creek
Maps: USGS Scaly Mountain. The best map of the trail is a pamphlet published by the North Carolina Bartram Trail Society (they also sell a guidebook; see below).

Water availability: Stephens Creek Spring, the only reliable water source, is just off-trail, 1.3 miles north from Jones Gap.
Best season: Year-round
For more information: The North Carolina Bartram Trail Society, ncbartramtrail.org; e-mail: info@ncbartramtrail.org. Nantahala Ranger District, Nantahala National Forest, 90 Sloan Rd., Franklin 28734; (828) 524-6441; e-mail: nantahalard@fs.fed.us.

FINDING THE TRAILHEADS

To reach the Jones Gap Trailhead from Highlands, go west on US 64/NC 28 from downtown Highlands. At 4.5 miles, turn left onto SR 1620, Turtle Pond Road. After 1.1 miles, turn right onto SR 1678, Dendy Orchard Road. At 1.4 miles, at the top of a hill, turn left at a sign onto FR 4522 (narrow but well-maintained), which reaches the trailhead in 2 miles. The trail leaves the parking area to the right (GPS: 35.075964 / -83.287995). (From Franklin, at the US 64/441 junction, go south on US 64/NC 28 for 12.8 miles to Turtle Pond Road.)

To reach the Buckeye Creek Trailhead from Dillard, Georgia, the junction of US 441 and GA 246, take US 441 north for 5.2 miles and turn right onto SR 1636 (Tessentee Road). In 3.8 miles, turn left onto SR 1640 (Buckeye Branch Road). Go 0.6 mile, park on the right at a trailhead sign, and follow the logging road past the gate.

THE HIKE

This hike combines easy access, masterful design, gradual grade, and backcountry character. Section 2 of the Bartram Trail is a well-kept secret in the Highlands Ranger District of Nantahala National Forest. On this less-visited trail, hikers can enjoy relative solitude. Another plus for the area: pristine scenery. The forests on this hike are mature and inspiring, and there are spectacular rocky summits. You'd want to hike here even if no trail existed.

The best and easiest hike for scenery involves going northwest from Jones Gap (4,360 feet); the greatest climb to the ridge occurs on the hike north from the Buckeye

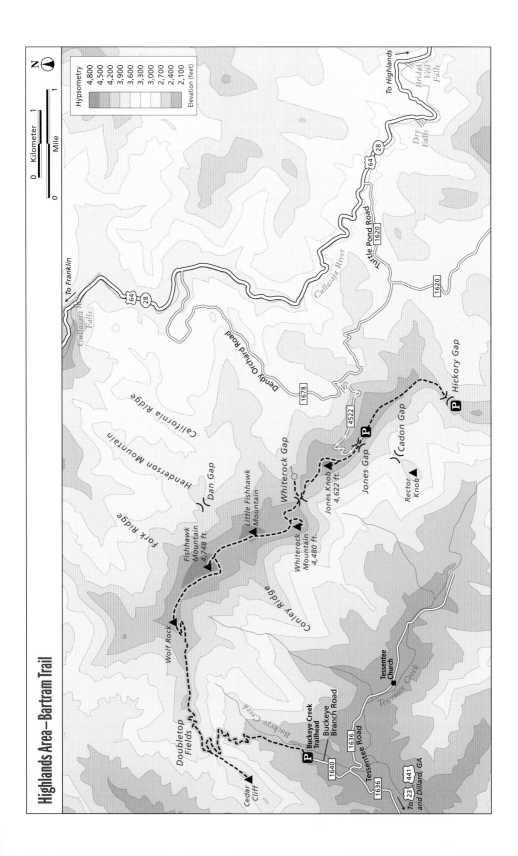

Highlands Area – Bartram Trail

Hypsometry

	4,800
	4,500
	4,200
	3,900
	3,600
	3,300
	3,000
	2,700
	2,400
	2,100

Elevation (feet)

N

0   Kilometer   1

0   Mile   1

To Franklin

Cullasaja Falls

64   28

64   28

To Highlands

Bridal Veil Falls

Dry Falls

Cullasaja River

Turtle Pond Road

1620

1620

Dendy Orchard Road

1678

Henderson Mountain

California Ridge

Fork Ridge

Dan Gap

Fishhawk Mountain
4,748 ft.

Little Fishhawk Mountain

Whiterock Gap

Whiterock Mountain
4,480 ft.

4522

Jones Gap   P

Jones Knob
4,622 ft.

Cadon Gap

Rector Knob

Hickory Gap   P

Conley Ridge

Wolf Rock

Doubletop Fields

Cedar Cliff

Buckeye Creek

Buckeye Creek Trailhead   P

1640

Buckeye Branch Road

1636

Tessentee Road

1636

Tessentee Church

Tessentee Creek

23   441

To Dillard, GA and Dillard, GA

Creek Trailhead (2,400 feet). The stiffer climb from Buckeye Creek is graded and less frequented.

From the Jones Gap Trailhead, the yellow-blazed path enters a wildlife plot, then the woods. A blue-blazed trail goes left in 0.3 mile to a western view from Jones Knob (4,622 feet), a nice 0.8-mile round-trip day hike. Go right on the Bartram Trail as it slabs east of Jones Knob through a fern-covered forest. On the descent north there's impressive rhododendron forest and a moss-covered ledge. The trail descends into Whiterock Gap; just as it turns down, a view from a pristine dome is on the left beyond the trees.

There's a campsite in Whiterock Gap at 1.3 miles, where a sign directs you right to Stephens Creek Spring (about 800 feet off-trail). The trail gradually slabs up the eastern side of Whiterock Mountain to a junction, at about 2 miles, with another blue-blazed side trail to the summit (4,480 feet). The 0.3-mile climb to the peak makes a neat passage between rocks to expansive views north along the ridge from a dome. This is a *great* day hike, at about 4.6 miles round-trip.

The trail continues north on a sharp ridge through mature white oak forest to Little Fishhawk Mountain at 3 miles. The trail dips off the summit on a ridgeline bearing left and skirts the cone of Fishhawk Mountain (4,748 feet), the highest summit on the ridge. A steep blue-blazed trail goes right to the peak, where a plaque commemorates Bartram's travels.

Beyond Fishhawk the trail descends the ridge west to a memorable view at Wolf Rock at 3.9 miles. For the next 2 miles, the trail descends gradually to Doubletop Fields at 5.5 miles. Here's a surprise: An old, wheelless Macon County school bus sits by the trail, obviously the last vehicle to wander up here on a now-overgrown road.

Descending through wildly wind-gnarled trees, the path switchbacks to a viewpoint on a crag and then exits through open forest to the final gap on the ridge, just before Cedar Cliff. This high, breezy site is a fine campsite (perfect for backpackers starting at the Buckeye Creek Trailhead, 3 miles and 1,000 feet below). A sharp left at the gap descends through a boulder-strewn forest with plentiful ferns, then switchbacks to join an overgrown logging grade at about 7 miles. The old grade passes a recovering clear-cut and goes right to continue into the woods on the grassy logging grade to the gate above audible Buckeye Creek at about 8.5 miles.

WHITESIDE MOUNTAIN NATIONAL RECREATION TRAIL

WHY GO?
A spectacularly scenic loop trail with views from some of eastern America's highest cliffs.

THE RUNDOWN

General location: Between the towns of Highlands and Cashiers

Distance: 2 miles round-trip

Difficulty: Moderately easy to moderate

Map: USGS Highlands

Whiteside Mountain's gut-wrenching vertical face is a treat for climbers and hikers too. It rivals the face of Cannon Mountain in New Hampshire's Franconia Notch.

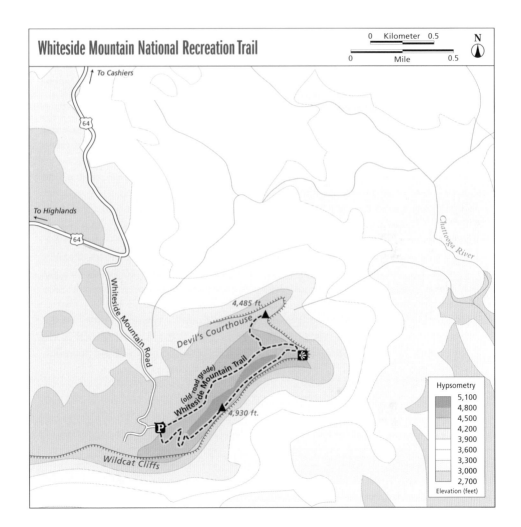

Whiteside Mountain National Recreation Trail

Water availability: There is no drinkable water at the trailhead or on the trail.
For more information: Nantahala Ranger District, Nantahala National Forest, 90 Sloan Rd., Franklin 28734; (828) 524-6441; e-mail: nantahalard@fs.fed.us

FINDING THE TRAILHEAD

From Cashiers, take US 64 west about 4.7 miles and turn left onto Whiteside Mountain Road (marked by a forest service sign). In 1 mile turn left into a parking area (fee) with a vault toilet (GPS: 35.080701/-83.143820).

THE HIKE

This spectacular scenic loop offers a colorful display of wildflowers in early spring and boasts views from some of the East's highest cliffs, which tower 400 to 750 feet along the southeastern side of the 4,930-foot summit. Only Cannon Mountain in New Hampshire's White Mountains compares.

From the trailhead, located near the kiosk in the parking area, follow the trail into the woods to where the loop begins. The summit was once a private tourist attraction where buses ferried visitors to the top along the wide, now-forested old road, which veers to the left at the intersection (right is your return route). As the gradual climb rounds the ridge, a grand vista of dome-faced peaks opens to the south, east, and north. Looking east, the Chattooga River breaks out of the higher mountains and flows into a deep, broad valley more than 2,000 feet below.

Continuing on, enter the woods along the cliffs beside stretches of railing and dramatic views of precipitous domes. (Take care not to bushwhack off to the left; the vegetation abruptly gives way to thin air.) The clifftop trail passes several viewpoints and crests along the summit. Tread lightly around the fragile vegetation that clings in these areas, including Allegheny sand myrtle, luxuriant ferns, and many varieties of sedge and trillium. Look for bluets and violets, flame azalea and *rhododendron vaseyi*, the rare pinkshell azalea.

Completing the loop, the trail descends then switchbacks more steeply down steps before emerging onto the old road for a left turn toward the parking lot for a 2-mile hike. Those seeking a more strenuous hike can follow the loop in reverse.

The best views of the cliffs from below can be had from the Chattooga Valley, on the gravel Whiteside Cove Road (SR 1107) between Highlands and Cashiers. Easiest access is south from Cashiers on NC 107, with a right turn onto the road just past the High Hampton Inn—a great base of operations (www.highhamptonresort.com).

PIEDMONT

32 PILOT MOUNTAIN STATE PARK

WHY GO?

New Hampshire's Mount Monadnock may have the gall to claim the name, but Pilot Mountain is the definitive monadnock in this state or any other. Pilot is an outlier of the Sauratown Mountains that includes Hanging Rock State Park.

This mountain has undisputed sentinel status. The Saura Indians called it Jomeokee, which means "great guide" or "pilot." Later settlers also used it as a beacon for navigation. Today, as always, Pilot Mountain is visible from all over northwestern North Carolina (including the Blue Ridge Parkway). The surrounding area is well worth a visit. Park visitors can drive to the summit area beside Little Pinnacle but hikers can't actually reach the peak of Pilot Mountain called Big Pinnacle (2,420 feet). This quartzite plug has been so resistant to erosion that it is surrounded by an uninterrupted rampart of cliffs. At one time, prior to its 1968 establishment as North Carolina's fourteenth state park, the peak was a commercial tourist attraction and hikers could climb stairs and ladders to the top. That ended to preserve nesting sites for the many ravens and raptors that soar around the cliffs (subject of one of many fascinating interpretive panels around the upper parking lot). Nevertheless, there are excellent viewpoints on Little Pinnacle, a perfect perch from which to watch the September and October hawk migration, and the Jomeokee trail encircles the base of the Big Pinnacle cliffs. Other paths provide diverse options and the park also permits rock climbing on summit crags, all reasons why the park can be so crowded on weekends that's it's difficult to reach the upper trailheads. Luckily there are a few great hikes to the peak from lower down.

Below the mountain, The Bean Shoals acreage on the Yadkin River enlarges the park to almost 4,000 acres. The area encompasses two of the most scenic miles of the Yadkin and part of a 165-mile canoe trail. Trails afford good views of the river (and nice fishing spots).

There are forty-two tent and RV campsites just inside the entrance of the park and a few reservation-only paddle access campsites in the park's river section. Picnic areas are adjacent to the summit parking area and near Horne Creek on the north side of the Yadkin River.

Various hikes wind through this western Piedmont state park dominated by a dramatic, rock-crowned summit. One primarily equestrian route winds for 6.6 miles through a wooded corridor between the peak and a nearby river parcel on the Yadkin River.

THE RUNDOWN

General location: Pilot Mountain State Park, 22 miles northwest of Winston-Salem

Distance: 0.3-mile out-and-back for the the park's TRACK Trail; about 0.8-mile lollipop loop for the Jomeokee Trail around Pilot Mountain; about 2 miles for Ledge Spring Loop around the summit; 6.6 miles for the park's premier hike, a climb to the Ledge Spring summit circuit on the Grindstone Trail. The park's new Mountain Trail is a 4.3-mile loop. The Corridor Trail is 6.6 miles one way between the park units. In the river unit, Bean Shoals is 1 mile and the Ivy Bluff Trail is a 1.3-mile round-trip.

Difficulty: Easy for the TRACK, Bean Shoals Canal, and Ivy Bluff trails; moderate for the Jomeokee Trail; moderately strenuous for the newly reconfigured Mountain Trail, Corridor Trail and Ledge Spring Loop; strenuous for the Grindstone/Ledge Spring Loop circuit.

Maps: USGS Pinnacle and Siloam. Download the state park trail map at ncparks.gov/Visit/parks/pimo/main.php.

Elevation gain: 1,100 for the Grindstone Trail and Ledge Spring Loop circuit starting at the park office, 400 for the Mountain Trail hike; under 200 for the Jomeokee, Bean Shoals and Ivy Bluff trails

Water availability: Water is available at trailhead restrooms during the warmer months at both the campground and the summit. No water is available at the backcountry campsites (water from the river must be treated).

For more information: Pilot Mountain State Park, 1792 Pilot Knob Park Rd., Pinnacle 27043; (336) 325-2355/ 877-722-6762 or reserveamerica.com for camping reservations. Horne Creek Farm Visitor Center; (336) 325-2298. For more on the Sauratown Trail, go to sauratowntrails.org.

FINDING THE TRAILHEADS

Take US 52 north of Business I-40 in Winston-Salem for 22 miles and exit at Pilot Mountain State Park. Go left at the stop sign, then left into the state park. From the north take the same exit and follow the signs, then turn right into the park. To reach the Yadkin River section of the park, exit US 52 at the Pinnacle exit, immediately south of the Pilot Mountain State Park exit. The 10-mile route is well signed.

Corridor Trail parking is available on the north end, near Pilot Mountain State Park proper, by exiting the park entrance and going right to a stop sign. Turn right on the Old Winston Highway, cross a railroad track and make a right on old US 52. Go about 0.25 mile and turn right onto Surry Line Road. Go 1.7 miles to a left onto Culler Road where a big parking area is on the right (GPS: 36.328108/-80.463055).

To reach parking for the Corridor Trail on the south end at Bean Shoals Canal Access, exit US 52 at the Pinnacle exit and follow the signs to Horne Creek Farm. Continue beyond that for 0.4 mile, where you pass the park entrance on the left; in another 0.2 mile, park on the left (GPS: 36.267445/-80.495563). For the Bean Shoals Trail, enter the park instead of passing it; stay right and park near the river (GPS: 36.259020/-80.495361).

Find the Ivy Bluff parking area south of the river from SR 1545/NC 67, in the town of East Bend. From Main Street (SR 1545), go north on Fairground Road. In 0.5 mile bear right onto Shady Grove Church Road. At 1 mile turn right onto Shoals Road and into the park at 3 miles (GPS: 36.253161/-80.508732).

THE HIKES

The two most scenic walks from the summit parking lot lead to the little and big pinnacles of Pilot Mountain. There's also a short nature walk, the park's TRACK Trail.

The summit parking area seems to cling to its perch atop Pilot Mountain State Park. The peak offers mesmerizing views of another mountainous state park, Hanging Rock, just across a gap in the Sauratown Mountains. PHOTO BY MITCH STOVER

There's a good viewpoint beside the parking lot but hike to Little Pinnacle by going right of the restrooms. The paved path offers access to fenced viewpoints overlooking the gap between the crags and Big Pinnacle. Use caution. One of the fatalities that have occurred here happened when a hiker climbed over the railing and grabbed a clifftop tree limb—which broke.

The first right leads to a nice wheelchair accessible view toward Winston-Salem's distant skyline. The second right leads up a rocky path to a spectacular vista of the rock-ringed summit of Pilot Mountain. The Sauratown Mountains continue east, including the summits of Hanging Rock State Park. On clear days, rolling flatlands stretch out dramatically 1,400 feet below.

The TRACK Trail and Jomeokee trailheads are nearby behind the restroom. Head back from Little Pinnacle and go right. To circle the summit of Big Pinnacle, turn right on the Jomeokee Trail along the north side of Little Pinnacle and dip through the gap you were just looking over. The trail is wide and impressively surfaced with 1,000 tons of quarried stone slabs installed in 2004. You'll pass the Ledge Spring Trail on the right. Jomeokee Trail continues out of the gap, splits into a loop, and circles the summit past rocky nooks perfect for hikers to have lunch. There is no path to the summit, and rock climbing isn't permitted here. The total hike, out and back, is 0.8 mile.

Back at the trailhead a right turn takes you back toward the parking lot past the TRACK Trail, a gradual 0.3-mile out-and-back through the summit forest to a good view. Pick up the *Fire on the Mountain* brochure on this TRACK Trail to understand fire's role in parks like Pilot Mountain. Controlled burns—fires set by park managers—are

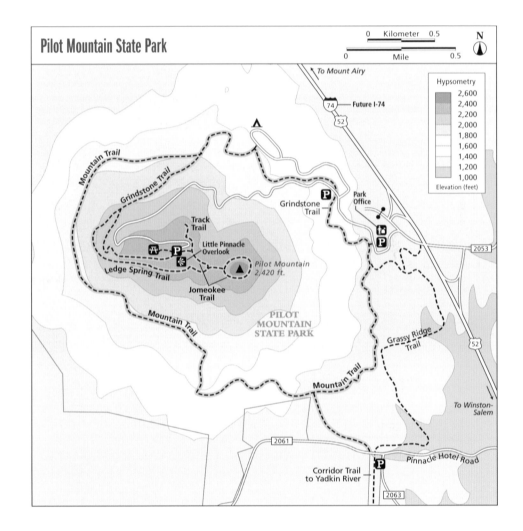

Pilot Mountain State Park

used regularly here to enhance species diversity and reduce the accumulation of combustible fuels that might actually destroy the forest. Fire is such a natural part of the ecosystem that Pitch pine and Table Mountain pine, seen all over this summit, actually require the heat of a fire to open their cones and release seeds. Read the parking area interpretive signs for more.

The 2.2-mile Ledge Spring Loop, a longer, more rugged way to loop Pilot Mountain's summit area, is another enjoyable hike from the upper parking lot. Marked with yellow and blue circles, the Ledge Spring Loop combines Ledge Spring and the upper Grindstone Trail. Leave the southwestern corner of the summit parking area (don't be funneled down right into the picnic area). The trail passes a rock climber registration board and wanders along a fence with gates used by climbers who scale cliffs that lie off to the left. At 0.8 mile, where the blue circles of the Grindstone Trail go right to the park office, turn left on yellow-circle blazed Ledge Spring Trail. The next 1.1 miles follows the base of cliffs where popular rock climbs have names like Pool Hall, Foreign Trade Zone,

Pilot Mountain State Park–River Section

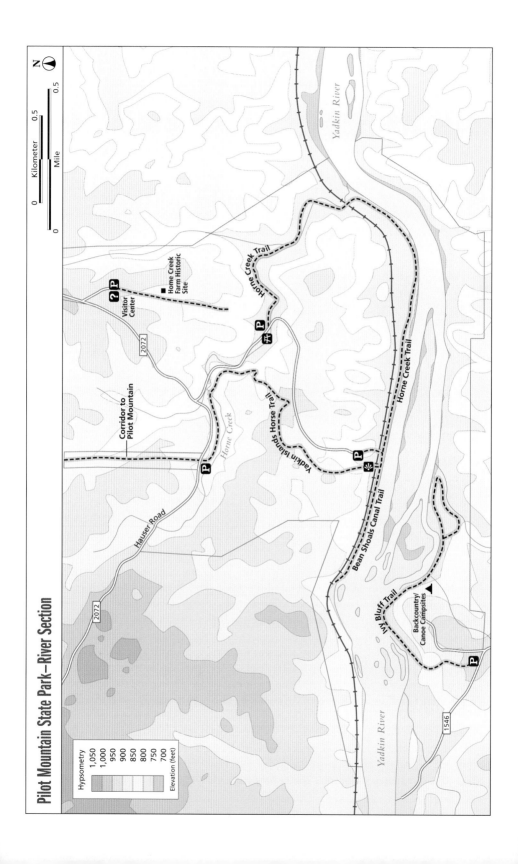

Hypsometry

1,050
1,000
950
900
850
800
750
700

Elevation (feet)

N

0   Kilometer   0.5

0   Mile   0.5

Visitor Center

Home Creek Farm Historic Site

2072

Corridor to Pilot Mountain

Hauser Road

2072

Horne Creek

Horne Creek Trail

Yadkin Islands Horse Trail

Horne Creek Trail

Bean Shoals Canal Trail

Ivy Bluff Trail

Backcountry/Canoe Campsites

1546

Yadkin River

Yadkin River

Three Bears and Big Gully. Turn left when you hit Jomeokee and it's just over two miles round-trip to the parking lot. (Circle Jomeokee to add 0.5 mile.)

The Grindstone Trail is a good starting point lower in the park if you want the strenuous way up Pilot Mountain. From the park office at the bottom of the park road, the trail follows blue circles past an overflow parking area and skirts the campground as it gains 500 feet in elevation in 2.2 miles of beautiful open forest. Stay left where the new Mountain Trail veers right (more below). At the junction with the Ledge Spring Trail, go right and make the summit loop described above. Retrace your way back down the mountain on Grindstone for a strenuous 6.6-mile hike (just more than 7 miles including the Jomeokee loop).

In late 2015, the red circle–blazed Mountain Trail was turned into a loop around the entire peak of Pilot Mountain. The trail drops from Ledge Spring Trail and circles much of the mountain at roughly 1,500 feet, returning back to Grindstone at the park office. The 4.3-mile Mountain Trail loop really showcases the scenic woods that drape Pilot Mountain's mid-slopes. Best of all a side trail now links the Mountain Trail to the Pinnacle Ridge Road trailhead. This access point outside the park is uncrowded and permits hikers to make the summit loop of the Mountain and Grindstone trails without driving up the park's summit road.

The white circle–blazed Corridor Trail, most popular with horseback riders, runs from the upland portion of Pilot Mountain State Park (accessed by the equestrian Grassy Ridge Trail) to parking at the entrance to the park's Bean Shoals Access. There are views back to Pilot Mountain along the way. From that lower parking area, the white triangle–blazed Yadkin Islands Horse Trail is a 1.5-mile out and back ride to a bluff near the railroad tracks above the Yadkin. Horses are no longer permitted to cross the tracks to the river but hikers will enjoy a few river bank trails. From a nearby main trailhead on the north side of the river, an access path crosses the tracks. To the right, the Bean Shoals Canal Trail is an out-and-back walk of about 1 mile where the stone walls of the uncompleted nineteenth-century Bean Shoals Canal (1820–25) are visible, built so bateaux could circumvent the rapids of Bean Shoals. Go left across the railroad tracks and the Horne Creek Trail follows the river, then turns north following Horne Creek to end in 2.5 miles at the picnic area you passed on the way to the trailhead. Spot another car or hike out and back for a 5-miler. On the south side of the river, reached from the town of East Bend, the 1.3-mile, red circle–blazed Ivy Bluff Trail passes the park's two large backcountry campsites to terminate in a loop beside two big islands in the river. The sites are intended as riverside canoe/kayak camps but backpackers are welcome—just don't assume these are overflow sites for the park's car campground. If you don't float in, only backpackers will find it convenient to camp here (privy available, treat water from the river).

Another good option for park visitors is a short side trip to Horne Creek Living Historical Farm, a North Carolina Historic Site that preserves an 1880s agricultural lifestyle (https://historicsites.nc.gov/all-sites/horne-creek-farm). An easy, self-guided, 0.4 mile out and back interpretive walk explores the early twentieth-century farm of Thomas Hauser's family. At any given time you'll find costumed interpreters demonstrating primitive farming technology. The tasks vary by season and include corn shucking, sheepshearing, and plowing with draft animals, as well as events like ice-cream socials. The state park and Horne Creek Living Historical Farm aren't far apart but they have different hours of operation, so be sure to explore the farm from its own visitor center.

Easily accessible from Piedmont cities, Hanging Rock State Park is an eyeful for flatland-weary hikers. The small collection of summits cluster together, forming a high bowl around a pristine lake. The peaks of Hanging Rock, Moore's Knob, and Cook's Wall jut up to 2,500 feet, highest of the Sauratown Mountains. From the rural area around the park, at 800 feet in elevation, the summits soar remarkably. The rocky cliffs have made this a regionally significant rock climbing hot spot that got its start in the 1950s. Below the peaks, the park contains an amazing number of waterfalls (most with relatively recent trail improvements). The park's easy Upper Cascades Falls Trail and accessible Rock Garden Trail are now an interpretive TRACK Trail—the perfect place to enjoy the program's *Waterfall Wonders* brochure.

The summits may not be high enough to offer too much respite from the heat of a Piedmont summer, but vegetation like mountain laurel, rhododendron, galax, oak, fern, and hemlock clothes the slopes and drainages. You'll notice small lizards on the trail during summer hikes, and you might see salamanders streamside.

Just getting to the park brings scenic rewards. You'll see ancient log cabins in the area, and the quaint town of Danbury, the Stokes County seat, has a beautiful century-old courthouse that anchors a National Historic District.

In the 1920s a Florida developer had planned to build a mountain resort on 3,000 acres of what is now Hanging Rock State Park. The financing failed, and local interests directed the land into state ownership in the mid-1930s. Then the Civilian Conservation Corps (CCC) stepped in. Hanging Rock is a monument to the CCC. The park's roads, trails, 12-acre lake, and a stone bathhouse, now on the National Register of Historic Places, were all built in seven years by CCC Camp 3422. Be sure to see the CCC exhibit and video in the visitor center.

Hanging Rock has group camping and developed sites for tents and self-contained RVs, six vacation cabins, and two picnic areas. Fishing for plentiful bass and bream is permitted in the clear, cold lake (state license required), and rowboats and canoes are available for rent in summer. A designated swimming beach has snack service and changing facilities. The Mountains-to-Sea Trail has been routed through the park.

COOK'S AND MOORE'S
WALL TRAILS

WHY GO?
Two loop hikes north of Winston-Salem offer spectacular views from rocky cliffs that are popular with rock climbers and an adjoining interpretive trail.

THE RUNDOWN

General location: Hanging Rock State Park

Distance: Cook's Wall Trail, 4.6 miles round-trip, with shorter view hikes of 1.2, 1.6, and 2.8 miles; Moore's Wall Trail, 4.3 miles round-trip; Chestnut Oak Nature Trail, 0.7-mile loop

Difficulty: Moderate for nearby views; moderately strenuous for Cook's Wall and Moore's Wall; strenuous for a combination of the two. Moderate for the nature trail.

Maps: USGS Hanging Rock. Download the park's map at ncparks. gov/Visit/parks/haro/main.php.

Elevation gain: Approximately 680 feet for Cook's Wall; 879 feet for Moore's Wall

Water availability: The park is open year-round, and water is available at a variety of facilities, primarily picnic areas, restrooms, a concession stand, campgrounds, and, in winter, at the park office. Streams are crossed on both hikes (treat this water before drinking).

For more information: Hanging Rock State Park, 1790 Hanging Rock Park Rd., Danbury 27016-7417; (336) 593-8480 / 877-722-6762 or reserveamerica.com for camping reservations.

FINDING THE TRAILHEADS

From Winston-Salem and I-40, the fastest route to the park follows US 52 North, taking a right at exit 118 onto NC 65 into Rural Hall, then a left onto NC 66. About 0.5 mile beyond the tiny burg of Gap, go right onto SR 1001 to the park entrance.

The Cook's Wall and Moore's Wall Trails both begin in the most distant lakeshore parking area after you enter the park. Just stay straight at the junctions, passing a major junction with a left to the visitor center/picnic area and a right to the campground. Leave the parking area at the corner closest to the lake on the wide path leading to the bathhouse and beach (GPS: 36.390655/-80.266939).

THE HIKES

The Cook's Wall Trail is probably the least-traveled of the park's main trails—a great choice for a busy summer or fall weekend. The hike dead-ends at Cook's Wall, for a 4.6-mile out-and-back hike. If you'd rather shorten the walk, you can omit Cook's Wall itself; there are great views at Wolf Rock and House Rock, both accessible on a 3-mile loop. The shortest hike on this trail is an out-and-back walk to a view at Wolf Gap, about 1.6 miles.

From the parking area, take the road-width trail and make a sharp left. Do not go up the stone steps of the bathhouse but head up the trail steps even farther left. A sign points to the right along the fence line parallel to the building and the lakeshore. Take this busy trail with the knowledge you'll soon be on more solitary terrain.

Make the first left onto the Chestnut Oak Nature Trail. You can pick up the guidebook to the twenty-four numbered posts at a box on the interpretive path or get one at the visitor center. The easy 0.7-mile loop from the parking area isn't particularly steep, but the footing is irregular and rocky.

Take the first left off the nature trail and follow the blue triangle blazes up the scenic, graded Wolf Rock Trail as it climbs through galax and mountain laurel, all reminiscent of higher North Carolina mountains. At the ridgetop trail junction in Wolf Gap (about 0.6 mile from the parking area), the white diamond–blazed Cook's Wall Trail goes right; left, the Wolf Rock Trail leads to a junction with the Hanging Rock Trail.

Indian Creek's cascades cool off many a summer hiker at this mountain range in the Piedmont.

Viewpoints are close. Wolf Rock is 0.2 mile to the left (a 1.6-mile round-trip), but for the shortest hike to a view, go right here to a rock outcrop on the immediate left for a 1.2-mile round-trip. Continuing along the ridge, the blue square–blazed Magnolia Springs Trail drops right to the Moore's Wall Trail at about 1.1 miles (your return route).

The Cook's Wall Trail climbs gradually, then more steeply, up to House Rock at about 1.4 miles. This flat-topped cliff is a spectacular spot with a perch and south-facing view of Winston-Salem and Greensboro on clear days. Hanging Rock is off to the left. Retrace from here for a 2.8-mile hike

Continuing, the trail climbs very steeply another 0.8 mile through rhododendron and mountain laurel to 2,400-foot Cook's Wall. Ravens often soar overhead. To the west the graceful wave of the Sauratown Mountains crest toward the plug of Pilot Mountain. To the northwest the rippled wall of the Blue Ridge juts up, surprisingly close, on its march into Virginia. Moore's Wall rises to the north. This is the place to picnic, 2.2 miles from your start.

Retrace your steps for a 4.4-mile round-trip. Or create a circuit: Go left on the Magnolia Springs Trail; its meandering 0.4-mile descent ends at a few small bridges over a stream and a junction with the red-blazed Moore's Wall Trail at about 3.7 miles. Here the most energetic hikers might go left and hike the Moore's Wall loop for a serious, almost 8-mile day hike.

To return to the parking lot more quickly, go right, cross a zigzagging boardwalk, and take a right at the next junction where the return loop of the Moore's Wall Trail comes in on the left at about 4.3 miles. You'll cross a boardwalk over the lake's boggy inlet. Side trails might make this confusing: Just stay right—avoid the Lake Path, on the north shore of the lake, in favor of the south shore, following the stretch of the Chestnut Oak Nature Trail you missed earlier. This lakeside walk on the nature trail is beautiful in fall. Back at the bathhouse, the entire hike is 4.6 miles.

The scenery of the Moore's Wall Loop Trail makes it the park's most-traveled major trail, but it is about 4.3 strenuous miles, so unless it's peak autumn color, the trail shouldn't be too crowded. Begin as for the Cook's Wall Trail, but keep right at the Chestnut Oak Nature Trail along the lake, pass the second nature trail link left, and cross the boardwalk that bridges the feeder stream. Take the next left and pass a junction with Magnolia Springs Trail at about 0.9 mile. Stay right, on the trail marked by red circles (Moore's Wall).

The trail climbs gradually through streamside hardwoods before branching right at about 1.5 miles where the Tory's Den Trail starts (also the blue circle–blazed longest route to Tory's Den and Falls; see below). From that junction, the trail climbs 300 steep feet, making a major leftward switchback to the main ridge of Moore's Wall. Then it's a ridge ramble to the peak. The popular rock climbing site, with cliffs up to 400 feet high, lies off to the left. The ridge levels off across Moore's Knob, the highest peak in the Sauratown Mountains (2,580 feet). An old North Carolina Forest Service fire tower, at about 2.9 miles, provides great views. (Climber access is below, just past Tory Den Falls with a right turn on Hooker Farm Road.)

The descent from the tower to the campground passes Balanced Rock and a formation called Indian Face and then plummets to Cascade Creek. After a climb from the creek, turn left behind the park's amphitheater and, keeping right, reach the campground road at 4.2 miles. Follow the red dots on the road to the sign near site 39 directing hikers back toward the lake. At the junction with the Moore's Wall Trail, go left past the lake to the parking lot for a truly mountainous 4.3-miler.

HANGING ROCK

WHY GO?
This popular and spectacular hike climbs the rock-capped vantage point of Hanging Rock. Other trails reach scenic waterfalls, and a few short paths are accessible to wheelchairs.

THE RUNDOWN
General location: Hanging Rock State Park
Distance: 2.6 miles round-trip for the Hanging Rock Trail. Round-trip hikes to Hidden Falls and Window Falls can range from 0.8 mile to about 1.2 miles.
Difficulty: Easy to moderately strenuous for waterfall trails; moderately strenuous for Hanging Rock Trail

Maps: USGS Hanging Rock. Download the park's map at ncparks. gov/Visit/parks/haro/main.php.
Elevation gain: About 590 feet for Hanging Rock; about 300 feet to Window Falls
Water availability: The park is open year-round, and water is available at a variety of facilities, primarily at picnic areas, restrooms, a concession stand, campgrounds, and, in winter, at the park office.

FINDING THE TRAILHEADS

Hanging Rock Trail begins in the visitor center/picnic area parking lot, the second road to the left after entering the park (GPS: 36.395072 / -80.265104). The trail starts on the right, about halfway down the lot. Continue to the end of the parking lot for the Window Falls and Hidden Falls Trails and historic picnic shelters.

THE HIKES
The orange circle–blazed Hanging Rock Trail is very popular in summer and on weekends. For privacy, the best time to hike here is in spring and winter and on weekdays.

From the visitor center lot, the road–width paved trail descends to a swale before crossing a stream and beginning its climb to Hanging Rock. The trail climbs steeply and changes to a gravel/earthen surface. There are benches at intervals, and the Wolf Rock Trail at 0.5 mile (a mountain path with a backcountry feel) branches off to the right before the steepest climb.

The Hanging Rock Trail gains a height of land, where there's a resting bench, then turns right and follows a ridgetop to the base of the prominent crag aptly named Hanging Rock. This is a nice place to rest. From here the trail bears right and steepens, climbing over steps and roots to a left turn onto the summit ridge. Viewpoints lie off to the right as you walk toward the craggy prow of Hanging Rock (2,132 feet), itself a fine vista. Views stretch north across farmland and swing west to south where Moore's Knob and Cook's Wall appear, encircling the park's high lake, just out of sight. Rock climbing and rappelling are prohibited here. Retrace your steps.

The red square–blazed Indian Creek Trail starts at the end of the visitor center parking area by the water fountain and descends in 3.6 miles to a parking area for the Dan River Canoe Trail (best done with two cars). The park is proud of this path—it protects an entire watershed from headwaters to its drainage into the Dan.

Weeks after autumn color has vanished in the mountains, Hanging Rock State Park's viewpoints offer a not-so-instant replay.

The upper portion is most popular for relatively easy access to three waterfalls. Hike through the picnic area past the restrooms and classic CCC-built picnic shelters and down an intensively developed gravel trail. Go right at the elaborately landscaped junction to see Hidden Falls at 0.4-mile, an 0.8-mile round-trip.

Continue down more steeply into a scenic gorge. Descending a stunning flight of stone steps (built in 2001), turn right to a viewpoint where you can see a flake of rock with a hole in it. That's the window. Some hikers skirt the viewpoint railings and descend to peer through the window—which reveals the small cascade of Window Falls. That's discouraged, but use extreme care if you do so—this area is the slippery top of a much bigger waterfall just below! Round trip is 1.2 miles. Trail steps lead down to that second set of falls, which drop straight off a clifftop. Some hikers strip to bathing suits here and climb behind the curtain of falling water. Again—use care.

For an accessible TRACK Trail interpretive hike to a waterfall, take the Upper Cascades Trail at the west corner of the visitor center parking lot. This gradual trail crosses the park road, where a paved spur leads left to the formation called Rock Garden. Right, it winds into the gorge of Cascade Creek to an observation deck at the falls. The round-trip hike is 0.6 mile. Be sure to take the *Waterfall Wonders* brochure with you.

Other parking areas offer waterfall walks. Find the Lower Cascades Trail by taking a left outside the park entrance, then an immediate left onto Hall Road. The trailhead is on the right (GPS: 36.414749 / -80.264865). An easy amble leads through locust fencing to the edge of the gorge where amazing boardwalks and then stone steps descend into a Hudson River School–style grotto at the base of the falls. Here's a pool worthy of a dip. Round-trip is 0.8 mile.

Hanging Rock State Park

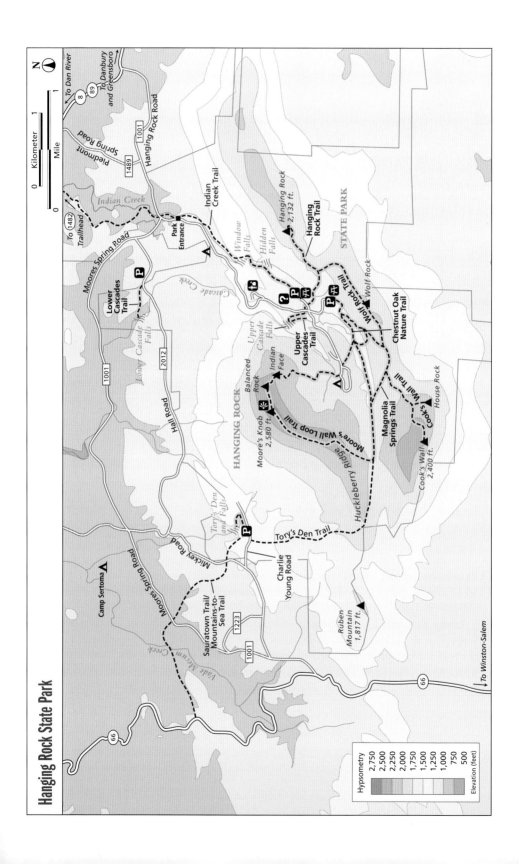

The mountainous state parks northwest of Winston-Salem and Greensboro are a tribute to the scenery of the Sauratown Mountains. VISITNC.COM

Tory's Den Trail is 2.7 miles to the falls from the Moore's Wall Loop Trail, but it's only a 0.4-mile round-trip from its own parking area. Pass the Lower Cascades parking area (see above) and make the next left onto Mickey Road. Again take the next left, onto Charlie Young Road; the trailhead is on the left (GPS: 36.401734 / -80.299794). Not far beyond, a right on Hooker Farm Road leads to Moore's Wall climber parking.

Leave the lot (this is a horse trail too) and enjoy a view of the falls before descending on a hiker-only trail to Tory's Den. It's been said this cave is where Tories held the daughter of a local patriot during the American Revolution.

From the parking area the horse/hiker trail heads west. Just before it crosses the road on its climb to the Moore's Wall Loop Trail, the Mountains-to-Sea Trail departs/arrives from the west on its way 7.4 miles through the park (as the Tory's Den and other trails).

BETHABARA PARK

WHY GO?

Woodsy trails and colonial roads make Bethabara Park a nationally significant place to go history hiking. The first Moravian settlement in North Carolina (1753) was one of the earliest backcountry Carolina communities. Bethabara's religious focus makes it one of the best-documented colonial villages in the country. North Carolina state archaeologist Stanley South's work at the site in the 1960s helped pioneer "the study of historic archaeology in the United States." Since then, the Moravian Church has reclaimed the location of the early village, restored many colonial buildings, and aggressively expanded the surrounding nature park from 30 acres in 1970 to its present 183 acres. They've even bought and removed apartment buildings (bravo!). That fits with this community's unusual early respect for the environment. Christian Reuter of 1750s Bethabara was the first "forest ranger" in North Carolina, and he had to say yes before trees could be cut. His plant inventories have been used to reintroduce trees now missing from the site.

Bethabara is a wildlife preserve and a nature study area, but your first stop should be the Bethabara Visitor Center's engaging exhibits and costumed interpreters. The gift shop's spicy, wafer-thin Moravian cookies are the perfect period trail snack. The facility is a highly recommended resource for school groups. Just outside, the 1788 Gemeinhaus church is the only such eighteenth-century German structure left in the country. Other historical landmarks include the only French and Indian War fort reconstructed on its original site. British prisoners were housed here after the Battle of Kings Mountain, and Cornwallis's army chased Nathanael Greene over adjacent roads on the way to the Battle of Guilford Courthouse.

Bethabara visitors shouldn't miss nearby Salem. Settled after Bethabara, Salem became the biggest Moravian town and a founding part of the present-day city of Winston-Salem. Today, the restored Old Salem National Historic District is North Carolina's version of Colonial Williamsburg. Pair both these Moravian historic sites and you have a destination worth an entire weekend.

THE RUNDOWN

General location: Northern Winston-Salem

Distance: A walk around the historic village, a loop of the arboretum, or an out-and-back to God's Acre are all about 0.6 mile. Walks around a boardwalk wetland are about 2.5 miles and 1.2 miles round-trip.

Difficulty: Easy to moderate
Maps: USGS Rural Hall. Download trail maps from the park website (see below). Maps are also available at all times in a rack outside the visitor center.
Elevation gain: Negligible

Water availability: The visitor center has an outside water fountain by the fort in warm seasons.
For more information: Bethabara Park, 2147 Bethabara Rd., Winston-Salem 27106; (336) 924-8191; bethabarapark.org

FINDING THE TRAILHEAD

Take Silas Creek Parkway north from Business I-40 in west Winston. Bear left on Silas Creek Parkway Extension just before Wake Forest University. Turn left at the light onto University Parkway just beyond a car dealership. Turn left again at the traffic light onto Bethabara Park Boulevard. From there, cross a railroad track at 1 mile and turn left onto Bethania Station Road. Shortly come to a three-way stop; go left onto Bethabara Road. Make an immediate left and park behind the visitor center opposite the log palisade of the fort (GPS: 36.155940 / -80.297218).

THE HIKES

Any visitor to this park will check out the restored buildings (tours are available April to December) and loop the 0.6-mile Colonial Arboretum behind the visitor center, but hikers wanting a real trail experience will find plenty of additional paths. Besides the main trails that explore forested heights, streamsides, and wetlands, there are a wealth of side trails the park's literature calls "spurs." They may not be well marked or pruned, but if you bring a bushwhacker's sense of adventure and keep your eyes on the park's free maps, it's easy to get a good dose of woodsy wandering.

Walk southeast down Bethabara Road from the visitor center to see an 1812 log house, the 1803 Buttner House (the oldest distillery structure in the country), and the Potter's House (1782); then swing back past the Gemeinhaus church into the fort. Just beyond the stockade, a reconstructed 1753 village has log structures, excavated foundations, and gardens. This stroll is about 0.6 mile.

Forest loops above the village are among the best hikes. Go straight out the bottom end of the fort and left on the paved greenway trail. Turn right over the creek on a bridge and two streamside trails link back to the greenway, permitting a loop. As the road-width trail rises through mature forest, turn right at the first junction and the Springhouse Trail follows Monarcas Creek back to the greenway. At the second junction, the Monarcas Creek trail goes left to follow, then cross, the creek, forming a loop back to the greenway closer to the Gemeinhaus church.

At the second junction mentioned above, bear right up the slope on the God's Acre Trail. Christian Reuter's early surveys praised the rich forest here, and in 1761 botanist John Bartram pronounced this area "a great treasure-house." At the next junction, the God's Acre Loop goes left and right—a nice 0.5-mile circuit around the wooded knob with the God's Acre graveyard perched on its crest. Keep straight past the loop and the trail passes a bench beside God's Acre's ancient grave stones. Retrace your steps and this hike is about 0.6 mile round-trip. Or cross the cemetery and exit to the south to again hit God's Acre Loop, first on the left, then the right, each returning to the God's Acre Trail you hiked from the fort. Combine the village and the God's Acre loop for a 1.1-mile hike. There's also a Spring Flower Trail that forms another loop between the

Woodsy paths explore Bethabara's Piedmont preserve, a place botanist John Bartram pronounced a "great treasure-house."

creek below and God's Acre. For the above hikes, and other loops near the visitor center, including what the park calls its "Woodland Loop," grab either Bethabara's "Overview East Side" or "Woodland Loop" trail map.

The park's longest hikes require taking the paved greenway west from the fort and across Old Town Drive, where a large lake and wetland flank Reynolda Road. Pick up the park's "Overview West Side" or "Mill Creek Loop" map for this area; it's easy to hike as much as 3 miles. Across Old Town Drive (with its small parking area), pass a power-line swath and keep right on the greenway when the Mill Creek Trail goes left (your return route). This inspiring section of centuries-old wagon road once led to a gristmill on nearby Mill Creek. Pause at the old millstone beside the trail and read the interpretive sign. When the greenway swerves left, continue on the North Wetland Trail along Bethabara Park Boulevard. Near its end at a private school, loop back past a picnic shelter and take the boardwalk out into the lake. Even with cars pulsing by on Reynolda Road, this ecologically significant site has great wildlife watching and birding (126 species have been recorded). The park's *Marsh Boardwalk Trail* brochure is a handy introduction.

Backtrack on the North Wetland Trail, but turn right away from the roadside on the Marsh Boardwalk Trail through the wetland. At the South Wetland Trail, turn right along Mill Creek and then right again on a side trail to another boardwalk at the water's edge. (This and the other observation point across the lake used to be connected until a flood damaged the linking span.) Backtrack to the South Wetland Trail, but stay straight across Mill Creek on a bridge and go left on the greenway. At the next junction, take the greenway trail left back across Mill Creek then turn right on the Mill Trace Trail (where the old mill's foundation lines the creek bank). The Mill Trace Trail eventually runs into the paved greenway, where a right takes you back to the visitor center. Prolong the woodsy walk by turning right before the greenway onto the Mill Creek Trail, which reenters the paved trail closer to Old Town Drive. This "Mill Creek Loop" is about 2.5 miles.

To make a quicker visit to the boardwalks, park beside the supermarket at Reynolda Commons Shopping Center on Reynolda Road (GPS: 36.155940 / –80.297218). Take the sidewalk southeast along Reynolda Road and across the bridge; turn right and head down steps to a paved trail beneath the span. Exiting from under Reynolda Road, take the first trail left across a bridge to the boardwalk viewpoint (then head back for a quick nature walk).Or reverse the hike above. Leave the boardwalk and go left on South Wetland Trail, left again on the Marsh Boardwalk Trail, and left again to the second boardwalk on the North Wetland Trail, and then retrace your steps.

SALEM LAKE AND SALEM CREEK TRAILS

WHY GO?

Nearly 1,500 acres of wooded land encloses Salem Lake, a scenic 365-acre water impoundment for the city of Winston-Salem. The multiple-use recreational area was built in 1919, and the 7-mile path that loops the lake was partially built by the Civilian Conservation Corps (CCC) in the 1930s. Since then, the city and the local Friends of Salem Lake group have expanded and formalized the network.

Fishing is a primary activity, and Salem Lake is stocked with bass, crappie, white perch, bream, catfish, and carp. There's a fishing pier, but no angling is allowed from the shore. The marina's Fishing Station shop sells bait and tackle and refreshments and rents johnboats and kayaks in season. There's no swimming, but paddleboards are permitted.

The Salem Creek Trail that starts at the lake was the first of Winston-Salem's greenway paths (1985). The route creates wonderful opportunities for residents to walk or bike between neighborhoods, recreation sites, and shopping areas. These trails are also enjoyable because the water coursing beside the path in Salem Creek flows from Salem Lake and is nicely unpolluted and inviting.

Both the unpaved, level path around scenic Salem Lake and the paved greenway trail along the creek are popular with hikers and bicyclists.

THE RUNDOWN

General location: Eastern Winston-Salem

Distance: A 7-mile lake loop on the Salem Lake Trail, designated the first-ever cycling TRACK Trail in 2015, can be extended to 9.6 miles from a nearby greenway trailhead for the Salem Creek Trail. That 4.5-mile greenway has numerous out-and-back possibilities for hikes of many lengths, including the 3.2-mile round-trip to Salem Lake from Reynolds Park Road and a 2-mile out-and-back walk from Marketplace Mall.

Difficulty: Easy, in part barrier-free

Map: A trail map is viewable online at the Winston-Salem Recreation and Parks Department website (see below).

Elevation gain: Negligible on the greenway and lakeshore trails. There are only two ups and downs of less than 20 vertical feet on the lakeshore, but the trail steeply rises and falls about 50 feet as it passes below the dam (walk your bike).

Water availability: In season water fountains are available at both trailheads and year-round at the marine.

For more information: Winston-Salem Recreation and Parks Department; cityofws.org. Hikers should stop in at the marina's Fishing Station shop for a trail map and information; report minor accidents to that number first: (336) 650-7677.

FINDING THE TRAILHEAD

To reach the Salem Lake Trail and the two easternmost trailheads for the Salem Creek Trail, take US 52 north from Bypass I-40, or south from Business I-40, and exit on Stadium Drive. After exiting, turn left then immediately right at the stoplight onto Martin Luther King Jr. Drive. Turn left onto Reynolds Park Road 0.4 mile from the stoplight. Measuring from that turn, pass the Reynolds Park Road greenway parking area on the left at 0.7 mile. Pass the Reynolds Park Golf Course, and at 1.8 miles turn left onto Salem Lake Road; the Salem Lake Trail parking lot is 0.5 mile on the right, before the gate at the marina (GPS: 36.092963/-80.192344). To join the Salem Creek Trail from the Salem Lake Trail parking area, take a paved connector that leads west from the lake parking area, across the gated entrance to the marina.

To reach Marketplace Mall, the western end of the Salem Creek Trail, exit I-40 at Peters Creek Parkway (exit 192). Turn left to the next light, the junction with Silas Creek Parkway. Measuring from there, go straight on Peters Creek Parkway 0.3 mile and turn right into Marketplace Mall on Hutton Street. Turn left immediately inside the mall parking area, and follow the perimeter lane around to the left back corner of the lot at the greenway signs (GPS: 36.072420/-80.253958).

THE HIKES

The Salem Lake Trail starts in a parking lot by a picnic area that occupies a promontory near the Salem Lake Dam. While bikers and hikers prepare for the trail, picnickers and sightseers use benches and picnic tables that overlook the lake, marina, and playground. The trail is a recently resurfaced single-lane road about 10 feet wide that leaves the lot to the east beside a signboard. Except for 0.5 mile of paved trail near the dam, the tread is packed gravel, so mountain bikes or hikes are most appropriate. Staying close to the banks, with frequent views, the trail passes periodic metal mileage markers, an occasional bench, and shoreline rocks suitable for rests and picnics (but fishing from the banks isn't allowed). On this TRACK Trail, you'll also find nine stations where interpretive plaques explain lake ecology and teach bicycling skills.

Even a rain shower can't dampen a hiker's enthusiasm for the wildlife viewing opportunities all along the shoreline of Salem Lake. PHOTO BY MICHAEL HICKS.

The trail traces the shape of the lake and crosses a bridge at about 1.1 miles where a side stream tumbles over scenic ledges and rocks and often attracts picnickers. At about 1.3 miles the trail climbs its steepest ascent and then descends around a promontory and enters the longer, narrower part of the lake.

The trail continues to follow shallow coves through tall deciduous forest and then turns into a large cove at 2.6 miles. It crosses this arm of the lake on a reinforced treadway that separates the open cove on the left from a marshy area on the right. This spot often resounds with frog sounds in warm weather. At about 3.6 miles the path exits at a gate and parking onto Linville Road (about 0.4 mile south of exit 10 on Business I-40 via Linville Road). Go left on the roadside, then left again where the trail reenters the woods at a gate and resumes its loop of the lake.

From the parking spot on Linville Road, the northern side of the lake is one of the best choices for interesting out-and-back hikes. Coves are smaller, and the trail winds in and out of dense pine-populated woods. Informal biker side trails occasionally lead up through the woods and down to the next leg of the trail. At about 5 miles, the picnic area, trailhead, and marina become visible on the opposite shore.

The trail rounds the point of another promontory at 6 miles and swings right, crossing a bridge that spans a northern arm of the lake, where views include a railroad bridge near Business I-40.

Winston–Salem—Salem Lake and Salem Creek Trails

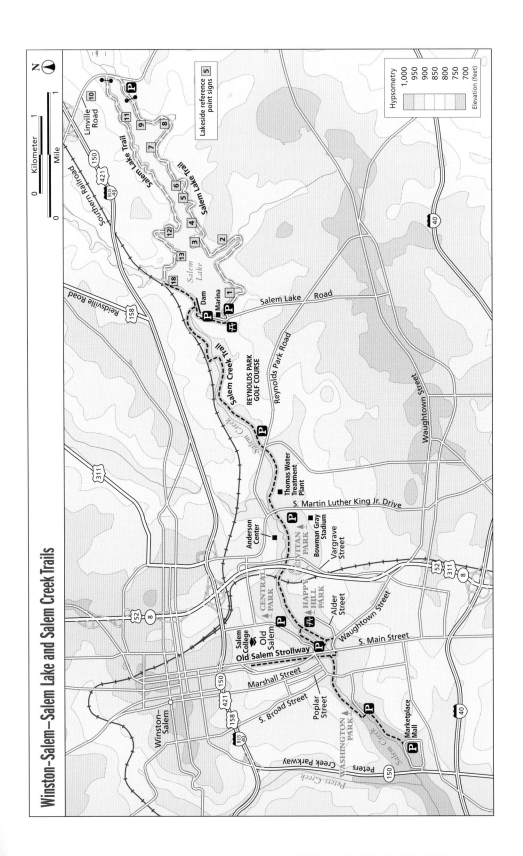

Hypsometry

	Elevation (feet)
	1,000
	950
	900
	850
	800
	750
	700

Lakeside reference point signs [5]

Reentering the woods at about 6.2 miles, the trail becomes paved, rises over a hill, and steeply drops to a T junction below the dam at 6.5 miles. To the right, the paved Salem Creek Trail follows Salem Creek 4.5 miles, with numerous trailheads along the way. The closest, 1.3 miles west at Reynolds Park Road, is an alternate starting point that turns the Salem Lake Trail into a 9.6-mile loop.

Going left at the greenway trail junction, the Salem Lake Trail immediately dips across a low-water bridge below the dam. (**Note:** If this crossing is flooded, you will have hiked almost 7 miles and be blocked from reaching your car! Check the water level in advance at the Fishing Station. Attempt to cross at low water only.) Beyond the bridge, the trail climbs steeply and crests a hill above the fenced marina, then descends to a stop sign at the marina gate before reentering the trailhead parking area at 6.9 miles.

The Salem Creek Trail is a paved path between Marketplace Mall and the Salem Lake Trail that passes occasional picnic tables and resting benches. The most enjoyable section of the trail lies between Reynolds Park Road and Salem Lake. From the Salem Lake Trail parking area, head west around the marina and down across the bridge to a junction with the Salem Creek Trail (which goes right and steeply uphill) at about 0.4 mile.

Going left, follow the Salem Creek Trail 1.3 miles to a short, uphill side path left to a parking area, picnic shelter, and playground on Reynolds Park Road. Start here for a recommended hike that permits a loop of the lake. Leave this Reynolds Park Road trailhead east toward the lake; the wooded trail passes the green expanse of Reynolds Park Golf Course, crosses a weir, wanders through a scenic little gorge, and gradually parallels railroad tracks high on the north side of the creek. The nicest finish for a hike in this direction is to go left on the Salem Lake Trail for about 0.3 mile to the bridge and views near the northern arm of the lake. That's about a 1.6-mile (3.2-mile round-trip) hike from Reynolds Park Road.

Heading west from the Reynolds Park Road trailhead, the trail goes under Reynolds Park Road and keeps its secluded woods character. Eventually the holding ponds of the Thomas Water Treatment Plant appear on the left. The trailside vegetation recedes to open fields where the trail goes under Martin Luther King Jr. Drive, just south of Reynolds Park Road and Winston-Salem State University, and not far north of Bowman Gray Stadium (about 0.5 mile from the Reynolds Park Road trailhead). The path enters the Civitan Park section of the greenway, one of the nicer portions of the trail. It wanders past baseball diamonds and passes a pedestrian bridge on the right with access to Winston-Salem State University. Then comes Vargrave Street, and the trail goes under US 52 and a railway trestle about 0.9 mile from Reynolds Park Road.

Passing a neighborhood on the left, a side trail crosses a bridge to Central Park while the main trail skirts Happy Hill Park and its pool. At a cluster of trail access points just beyond, turn right and another bridge leads into Central Park to trailhead parking on East Salem Avenue at about 0.9 mile from Vargrave Street (1.8 miles from the Reynolds Park Road trailhead). Go left, and an access leads to Waughtown Street where a right turn continues the greenway by crossing South Main Street. From this Central Park trailhead on East Salem Avenue, an out-and-back hike east toward Salem Lake is a 3.6-mile round-trip to the Reynolds Park Road trailhead. A hike from here all the way to the bridge turnaround point north of Salem Lake is 3.8 miles one way.

West of South Main Street, the trail crosses a neat pedestrian bridge and connects north to the Strollway, a 1.2-mile lightly paved urban rail-trail that leads to Old Salem (a restored colonial village—and a perfect complement to hikes in Bethabara Park).

Lake Brandt sprawls below this guy hanging out on the Nat Greene Trail near Greensboro, one of the best urban hikes in the state. VISITNC.COM

Continuing west, the trail crosses South Broad Street, passes a trailhead in Washington Park and reaches its terminus at Marketplace Mall in 1 mile. Starting there, it's a nice hike away from the mall as the trail rises and dips along the right bank of Salem Creek. Entering Washington Park, the trail reaches a major parking area where it crosses a bridge to the "left" side of Salem Creek at about 0.5 mile. (That Washington Park trailhead access road is a short distance south of where the greenway crosses South Broad Street.) Across the bridge, ball fields and a dog park flank the trail. Fitness tasks continue a short distance, then the path enters the woods along the stream emerging at the bridge on South Broad. This pleasant hike is 1 mile from the mall trailhead and just under 0.5 mile from the Washington Park trail bridge, round-trips of 2 miles and 1 mile respectively.

35 GREENSBORO

GREENSBORO WATERSHED TRAILS

WHY GO?

Greensboro's Lake Brandt watershed is unique in a state where many reservoirs are subdivision sites for million-dollar McMansions. At least for now, there's a relative lack of development and a growing network of wonderful trails, even newly preserved land, such as the Richardson-Taylor tract, where the new, volunteer-built Bill Craft Trail is a premier day hike.

The 785-acre lake, named for Mayor Leon Brandt (1907–08), was built in 1925 as a drinking-water reservoir for the city and expanded in 1958. The 750-foot buffer around it protects a portion of the city's 40 miles of hiking trails. This is a world-class natural space just minutes from the city.

Lake Brandt's isolated coves are outstanding in fall, when the shoreline forests blaze with color. Winter, so often mild in the Piedmont, is a wonderful time to watch seasonal migrations of waterfowl on pearl-gray days. You might see people fishing too.

On the way from Greensboro, before hiking these trails, consider sampling the Greensboro Science Center, a growing nature museum, planetarium, and zoo of regional significance (greensboroscience. org; 336-288-3769).

THE RUNDOWN

General location: North of Greensboro, in the watershed at Lake Brandt and Bur-Mil Park
Distance: Out-and-back hikes of many lengths are possible in the Lake Brandt area. A lake-looping circuit is about 10 miles (on the Nat Greene, Owl's Roost, and Piedmont Trail, and a small portion of the Atlantic & Yadkin Greenway). Adjacent Bur-Mil Park has 4.5 miles of trails, arranged in 0.8- and 2-mile loops. The Bill Craft Trail is 3.5 miles one way.
Difficulty: Easy except for the lengthiest circuit hikes

Maps: USGS Lake Brandt. Download a trail map at the Greensboro Parks and Recreation website (greensboro-nc.gov/index.aspx?page=1359).
Elevation gain: Negligible
Water availability: At the Lake Brandt Marina Nat Greene trailhead, a main-office water fountain is available Apr–Oct (and in winter when employees are present). At Bur-Mil Park, water and restrooms are available daily year-round at the clubhouse.
For more information: Greensboro Parks and Recreation; (336) 373-3816; greensboro-nc.gov.

FINDING THE TRAILHEADS

Access Lake Brandt trails via US 220 (Battleground Avenue) in north Greensboro. To reach the trailheads for the Nat Greene and Piedmont Trails, turn right from US 220 onto New Garden Road at signs marking the Guilford Courthouse National Military Park. Take the next left onto Old Battleground Road. Measuring from that junction, turn right at 0.5 mile onto Lake Brandt Road, left at 1.75 miles onto Lake Brandt Road/Lawndale Drive, and left at 2.9 miles into the Lake Brandt Marina for the Nat Greene Trail (GPS: 36.166661/-79.837887). For informal Nat Greene access on weekends, make the last left into Wharton School near the marina and park in the first parking area. Walk to the right of the building. For the Piedmont Trail, go another 0.3 mile beyond the marina to parking on left beyond the dam spillway (GPS: 36.174263/-79.838326).

The other trailhead for Nat Greene is located on Old Battleground Road. Follow the directions to Lake Brandt Marina, but pass Lake Brandt Road. The trail starts on the right side of Old Battleground Road 0.5 mile beyond that turn at a small trailhead and signboard at the Bicentennial Greenway bridge (GPS: 36.142378/-79.855945).

To reach the main northern trailhead for the Atlantic & Yadkin Greenway and access to the northerly Owl's Roost Trail, drive north on US 220. Pass Strawberry Road (SR 2321) about 3.7 miles north of New Garden Road and in 0.1 mile turn right into a new greenway trailhead (GPS: 36.177642, -79.882297).

To reach Bur-Mil Park, and access to the Atlantic & Yadkin Greenway, Bur-Mil Park's Big Loop, Little Loop and the Owl's Roost Trail, drive north on US 220 from New Garden Road to a right onto Owl's Roost Road, at 2.5 miles, and make the next left into the park. The main trailhead for the Bur-Mil Park Big Loop Trail is the second parking area on the left past the driving range (GPS: 36.166929/-79.870172). To reach the lakeshore trailheads, bear right to pass the clubhouse and down the road to lakeshore parking areas just past the Wildlife Education Center near a pond.

For the Richardson Taylor tract, head north from the Lake Brandt Marina 1.5 miles and turn right onto Plainfield Road for 2.1 miles to a parking area on the left (GPS: 36.179793/-79.805757). To spot a car at the northern trailhead, leave the Plainfield Road trailhead and go east 0.9 mile to North Church Street. Turn left and in 0.5 mile turn left again onto Spencer-Dixon Road. In 1.7 miles turn left onto Simpson-Calhoun Road into the multi-school campus of the Northern Guilford High School and Middle School. The road dead-ends at the trailhead in 0.5 mile (GPS: 36.201572/-79.808358).

THE HIKES

The three trails that flank Lake Brandt are among the best of the expanding network of paths to, from, and around Greensboro's watershed lakes. They permit wonderful out-and-back walks from various trailheads. The trails link into an expansive circuit hike that loops the lake.

Named for Gen. Nathanael Greene (see Guilford Courthouse National Military Park), the Nat Greene Trail is a state historic trail that leads west from the Lake Brandt Marina to Old Battleground Road in 3.2 miles. If the marina is closed, park at the gate; a trail winds down to the main trailhead. The main, hiker-only path enters a tall pine and deciduous forest with an open understory of running cedar. In summer the lake shimmers through the vegetation, especially in the evening, when the sun casts a golden light. This is a great kids' walk. (The rousing Wild Turkey Trail mountain bike/multiuse path starts nearby and parallels Nat Greene.)

Near the start, an interpretive trail with plant identification signs and an "outdoor classroom" goes left to the Jesse Wharton Elementary School.

The main trail splits just past a bridge, the right fork closer to the lakeshore, where freshwater mussels lie on the sandy bottom. The trails merge, round a cove, and cross a larger stream at 1.5 miles. Undulating through mature pine and deciduous woods, Nat Greene intersects the Atlantic & Yadkin Greenway (hereafter A&Y Greenway), a paved railroad grade, at 2.5 miles. (It goes left to the Guilford Courthouse National Military Park, right to Bur-Mil Park and beyond.) Just to the right, there's a bench and landscaped rest area by what I call the Nat Greene Trail Bridge over the southern arm of the lake. The Nat Greene Trail crosses the greenway, first going left and then veering right off the pavement along the shoreline, eventually following a long boardwalk through a marshy stream before exiting the woods beside Old Battleground Road and the Bicentennial Greenway Bridge at about 3.2 miles.

To loop the lake, turn right on the A&Y Greenway, cross the bridge, then go right again on the Owl's Roost Trail into the lake's most isolated area. The main, backcountry-like Owl's Roost Trail sticks close to the shore, but a newer network

Early to mid-November is a magical time on Lake Brandt. Color is bright, and waning fall light ramps up the golden glow.

of more interior multiuse paths has been developed that explores this peninsula that park personnel call The Horseshoe. That includes the mountain bike only Shady Side Trail. When Owl's Roost reaches the A&Y Greenway, head north past Bur-Mil Park across the next lake bridge and turn right on the Piedmont Trail (see details below). In just under three miles the trail reaches Lake Brandt Road where a short, 0.2-mile walk south past the lake's dam returns you to the Nat Greene trailhead at the marina.

Besides the option of looping the entire lake on Nat Greene, Owl's Roost, and Piedmont Trails, this part of the lake offers nice out-and-back hikes from trailheads north of the lake. From Strawberry Road or Bur-Mil Park, the A&Y Greenway leads south toward the Nat Greene Trail Bridge (3.5 miles from Strawberry Road one way). The railroad-grade trail leaves Strawberry Road south, and in a few tenths of a mile, the Piedmont Trail leaves left to run the north shore of the lake. Stay with the kudzu-lined greenway and cross the 300-foot bridge over the northern arm of the lake (an out-and-back hike to here is a great kids' walk). Across that bridge in Bur-Mil Park, the Big Loop Trail branches right (see below). Stay with the greenway and steps lead right to Bur-Mil Park's pond #1 and a parking area (about 0.5 mile from Strawberry Road, another good starting point). Just past the pond, bear left off the greenway with wooded Owl's Roost Trail as it follows the lakeshore then drops to cross a stream. Around a cove and past some homes, the trail rises and falls with views back to Bur-Mil and crosses a stream at about the 1-mile mark. At 2.6 miles, a nice view to the marina (the start of Nat Greene Trail) opens down the lake. This is a good picnic/turnaround spot for a round-trip hike of just more than 5 miles from Strawberry Road or 4 miles from Bur-Mil Park pond.

The trail continues below steep slopes along the south side of the promontory, passing more fire roads leading right. Mountain bikes are permitted on this trail, and the roads provide faster connections. Along the lake, the beautiful pine and deciduous forest is heavy with isolation and quiet. This area is about 3.5 miles from Strawberry Road, about 3 miles from Bur-Mil Park (a 7- or 6-mile round-trip, respectively). Not far beyond,

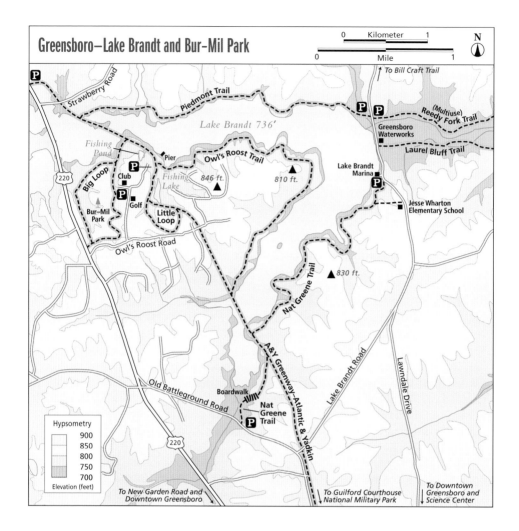

0   Kilometer   1

0   Mile   1

N

To Bill Craft Trail

Strawberry Road

Piedmont Trail

Lake Brandt 736'

(Multiuse)
Reedy Fork Trail

Greensboro
Waterworks

Laurel Bluff Trail

Fishing
Pond

Pier

Owl's Roost Trail

Lake Brandt
Marina

220

Big Loop

Club

Fishing
Lake

846 ft.

810 ft.

Bur–Mil
Park

Golf

Little
Loop

Jesse Wharton
Elementary School

Owl's Roost Road

Nat Greene Trail

830 ft.

A&Y Greenway-Atlantic & Yadkin

Lake Brandt Road

Lawndale Drive

Old Battleground Road

Boardwalk

Nat
Greene
Trail

Hypsometry

900
850
800
750
700

Elevation (feet)

220

To New Garden Road and
Downtown Greensboro

To Guilford Courthouse
National Military Park

To Downtown
Greensboro and
Science Center

emerge onto the paved A&Y Greenway. Turn right and return to either northern trail-head for a nice long lakeshore loop.

The northernmost leg of the lakeshore circuit, the hiker-only Piedmont Trail, can be hiked from the west starting from Bur-Mil Park or the new greenway parking area near Strawberry Road, or from the east via the trailhead just north of Lake Brandt Marina. From Strawberry Road area, turn left (south) from the A&Y Greenway on the Piedmont Trail at about 0.3 mile, toward Lake Brandt Road, 2.8 miles away. (From Bur-Mil Park pond, go north, cross the greenway bridge, and in 0.3 mile turn right.)

On its way along the shore, the Piedmont Trail passes a broad, boggy area; crosses three streams; and at about the 1.5-mile mark traverses a boardwalk. The trail undulates to nice lakeside views and great lunch spots (easy to reach from Lake Brandt Road). Through scattered cedars, the trail joins an old grade to Lake Brandt Road.

Linking all of these trails together, in either direction, creates one of North Carolina's best urban nature walks, about 10 miles. Parts of this hike have been designated as the Mountains-to-Sea Trail.

Just across the road from the Piedmont Trail, the Reedy Fork Trail runs 3.5 miles along a creek, then the shore of Lake Townsend, to parking on Plainfield Road. A bit south, opposite Lake Brandt Marina, just across the nearby dam, the Laurel Bluff Trail also leaves the roadside and follows Lake Townsend 3.3 miles to a trailhead on North Church Street. Both are nice out-and-backs or two-car hikes.

Back within Bur-Mil Park, there are two basic hikes. To hike the 2.2-mile loop around the western portion of the park, a level trail popular with runners and mountain bikers, start at the driving range. The trail swerves around soccer fields and goes west to parallel Owl's Roost Road toward US 220. Go to the right with the trail as it turns north.

The trail follows a stream drainage north, then heads east along the shore of Lake Brandt. A right turn brings you back to the trailhead parking area. The park's Little Loop leaves the A&Y Greenway south of the Wildlife Center and winds around pond #2 to the right of the greenway.

A burgeoning batch of new trails are being built in the area. A new gem in the water-shed trail system is a 2013 extension of the Mountains-to-Sea Trail north from Plainfield Road through the 450-acre Richardson-Taylor tract. There's a nice 1-mile loop from this parking area (where a trailhead stone memorializes Bill Craft, namesake of this trail section). From the loop, the main trail runs 3.5 miles north along a wetland past a wildlife-viewing platform where great blue heron nests are visible in the trees. The trail crosses the lush head of the wetland to climb past a power line, then through wooded upper slopes past another wetland and viewing platform. There's a stream bridge before the trailhead at the Northern Guilford High and Middle School campus (with easy student access to this wonderful trail). Spot two cars and this is a surprisingly scenic urban hike.

THE LATHAM PARK AND LAKE DANIEL GREENWAYS

WHY GO?
Latham Park was given to the city of Greensboro in 1924 by cot-ton merchant, industrialist, and civic mover-and-shaker J. E. Latham (1866–1946). Adjacent Lake Daniel Park, a similar urban green spot, is connected by a short stretch of sidewalk. Together they buffer Buf-falo Creek from nearby neighborhoods and provide an interesting case study in evolving urban stream management.

During the 1930s and 1940s, this stream through a deforested urban floodplain was "channelized" to quickly usher floodwaters out of town. Floods and erosion continued, but in 1993 the philosophy changed.

The path of the stream was permitted to meander in the chan-nels; then rocks were scientifically placed to further affect flow, alter-ing the accumulation of sediment and creating fish-friendly pools. Forest is reclaiming the area, with trees growing on the banks as well as on adjacent fields. The result is enhanced scenery and vastly improved habitat for wildlife. The growing shade makes it cooler for people and fish; decreasing water temperatures and rising oxygen levels are boosting fish populations. Keep an eye out for interpretive signs, especially at the Lake Daniel Park tennis courts where a portion of the greenway path is an interpretive TRACK Trail. These two interconnected greenway trails make a nice city stroll (and a great bike ride).

The best news from Greensboro is the city's downtown greenway, a major project that will connect to the greenway covered here and loop the entire downtown with links to other greenways, including all the way to Guilford Courthouse National Military Park, Lake Brandt, and beyond. Check the website: downtowngreenway.org.

THE RUNDOWN

General location: Downtown Greensboro
Distance: 3.5 miles one way; 1.2 for Latham Park Trail, 1.9 miles for Lake Daniel Trail, with a 0.4-mile connector
Difficulty: Easy
Maps: USGS Lake Brandt. Maps are available at the city parks and recreation website (greensboro-nc .gov/index.aspx?page=1359).

Elevation gain: Negligible
Water availability: Water fountain in season at Lake Daniel tennis court restrooms/playground and at Latham Park Tennis Center
For more information: Greensboro Parks & Recreation Trails Division; (336) 545-5961; www.greensboro-nc .gov

FINDING THE TRAILHEAD

Plentiful streetside parking is available along the trail route and at the two tennis facilities, including at the start of the Lake Daniel Park TRACK Trail on Mimosa Drive (GPS: 36.078176, -79.809934). Good starting points also include Friendly Shopping Center, for a short walk to the western terminus on Friendly Avenue.

THE HIKE

This open and wooded terrain along Buffalo Creek near downtown Greensboro is at times downright scenic. An end-to-end walk and back would net a 7-mile hike, but this trail may be best done in sections. Choose based on this section-by-section overview.

To start at Friendly Center, the trail's western terminus, park at the south end of the shopping center at the corner of Friendly Avenue and Green Valley Road. Cross Green Valley, take the sidewalk under Wendover Avenue, and then go left. The first section, from Friendly to Elam Avenue, is open and undulating opposite Wesley Long Hospital. It descends at the end, crosses a bridge, and takes a right across Elam. To create a loop back to Friendly Center, go left at Elam and follow the sidewalk on Benjamin Parkway over Wendover to a left on Green Valley past the O. Henry Hotel and back to your car. This boutique business hotel was named for the pen name of native son and short-story author William Sydney Porter. This and adjacent greenway sections are memorable exercise escapes for guests of the O. Henry and the nearby Proximity Hotel, one of the country's greenest businesses (ohenryhotel.com/proximityhotel.com).

Greensboro—Latham Park and Lake Daniel Greenways

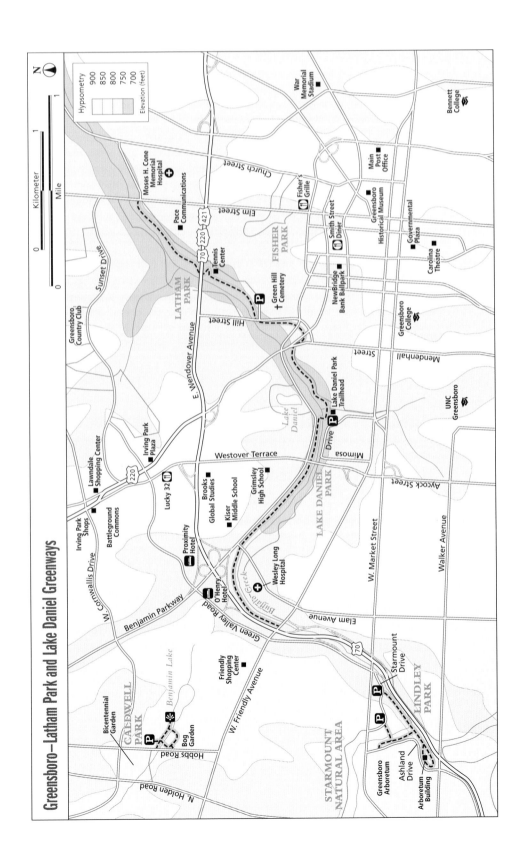

N

Hypsometry

	900
	850
	800
	750
	700

Elevation (feet)

Kilometer

Mile

LATHAM PARK

FISHER PARK

LAKE DANIEL PARK

CALDWELL PARK

STARMOUNT NATURAL AREA

LINDLEY PARK

Greensboro Country Club

Sunset Drive

Moses H. Cone Memorial Hospital

Pace Communications

Tennis Center

E. Wendover Avenue

Hill Street

Green Hill Cemetery

Lake Daniel Park Trailhead

Mimosa Drive

Westover Terrace

Brooks Global Studies

Kiser Middle School

Grimsley High School

Lucky 32

Irving Park Plaza

Lawndale Shopping Center

Irving Park Shops

Battleground Commons

W. Cornwallis Drive

Proximity Hotel

O'Henry Hotel

Benjamin Parkway

Green Valley Road

Wesley Long Hospital

Buffalo Creek

Elam Avenue

W. Market Street

Avcock Street

Mendenhall Street

Greensboro College

UNC Greensboro

Walker Avenue

Benjamin Lake

Friendly Shopping Center

W. Friendly Avenue

Hobbs Road

N. Holden Road

Bicentennial Garden

Bog Garden

Greensboro Arboretum

Arboretum Building

Ashland Drive

Starmount Drive

Lake Daniel

Church Street

Elm Street

Smith Street Diner

Fisher's Grille

NewBridge Bank Ballpark

Greensboro Historical Museum

Governmental Plaza

Carolina Theatre

Main Post Office

War Memorial Stadium

Bennett College

70 220 421

220

70

The next stretch to Westover Terrace is flat and open along the creek, with trees lining the path along Benjamin Parkway. Near Westover Terrace, exercise stations appear where the greenway goes under the road.

Beyond Westover Terrace, the greenway runs the open roadside and shows the best evidence of rapid streamside reforestation. It crosses a bridge over Buffalo Creek with access to Lake Daniel Park, start of the TRACK Trail (brochures aptly feature "The Need for Trees," birds, bugs). There are tennis courts, picnic tables, restrooms, and play equipment in this recently upgraded area. There's another bridge past the tennis courts, and then the trail crosses a traffic circle on Lake Drive and passes a basketball court.

The greenway hits the sidewalk on Mendenhall Street, where the TRACK Trail ends, a 1-mile round-trip. Crossing Smith Street and Battleground Avenue, the greenway reappears to parallel and then cross Hill Street to Latham Park. Passing the awesome Latham Skate Park, basketball courts, ball fields, and the Latham Park Tennis Center, the trail veers past corner convenience stores and takes an underpass beneath Wendover Avenue (watch for speedy bike traffic and slippery surfaces).

The final section of the greenway passes a monument to Latham, exercise stations, and a table and benches. It crosses Cridland Road, passes more exercise stations and benches, and then reaches its eastern terminus on Elm Street across from Moses H. Cone Memorial Hospital. (There's streetside parking just up the street beside the hospital's wooded grounds.)

GREENSBORO GARDENS— ARBORETUM, BOG GARDEN, AND TANGER FAMILY BICENTENNIAL GARDEN

WHY GO?

These three parks are in close proximity. Greensboro Arboretum has paved garden paths, ornamental shrub displays, and a woodland trail with plants reminiscent of the mountains. The Bog Garden explores a surprising, secluded wetland. And the Bicentennial Garden has Greensboro's showiest flower display.

THE RUNDOWN

General location: Near Wendover Avenue in western Greensboro
Distance: Arboretum, 1.7 miles of trails; loops of the Bog Garden and Bicentennial Garden are 0.7 mile and 0.8 mile
Difficulty: Easy, except for stone steps on the Bog Garden's bluff-top trail. All three parks are accessible in part by wheelchair.
Maps: Download a map of each of these gardens at the Greensboro Beautiful website (see below). Ask a Bicentennial Garden employee at the office for the excellent Bog Garden plant brochure (consider returning it for the next user).

Elevation gain: Negligible
Water availability: The Arboretum and Bicentennial Garden have water fountains and restrooms in season.

For more information: Greensboro Beautiful is instrumental in these parks, and their website has a lot of information; (336) 373-2199; greensborobeautiful.org

FINDING THE TRAILHEAD

 For the arboretum, exit Wendover Avenue at Market Street. From the south, turn left onto Market, then immediately left again as if to go back onto Wendover southbound. Then turn immediately right onto one-way Starmount Drive. From the north, exit onto Market to the light and go straight as if to reenter Wendover. Turn right onto Starmount Drive.

Best parking is on the left at the first lot, close to Wendover Avenue (GPS: 36.073190 / -79.836853). Closest parking for the Woodland Trail is to pass through Starmount, go left on Market, then left again on Ashland Drive. Park on the right by the apartments beside the Arboretum Overlook (GPS: 36.071607 / -79.839667). Pick up the trail brochure at the office, 0.2 mile beyond.

For the Bog Garden and Bicentennial Garden, go west from Wendover on West Market Street. Turn right not far beyond on Holden Road. Go north, taking the eighth right turn onto West Cornwallis Drive. Take the next right onto Hobbs Road. The first right is the main Bicentennial Garden lot (GPS: 36.092911 / -79.841348). The next left on Starmount Farms permits immediate roadside parking for the Bog Garden (GPS: 36.091553 / -79.840221).

THE HIKES

These three garden parks were originally developed by citizen members of Greensboro Beautiful. They are now operated by a partnership between the organization and the city Parks and Recreation Department. Please consider supporting Greensboro Beautiful's holiday wreath and decoration sale in November. It features North Carolina Fraser fir and helps fund the group's efforts.

The 17-acre Greensboro Arboretum opened in 1991 along the floodplain of North Buffalo Creek beside Wendover Avenue. From my preferred parking area above, a paved path leads away and branches into a Y. The unpaved Woodland Trail closes the top of the Y to make a nice circuit of just over 1 mile.

Head out along the trail past an increasing number of streamside pergolas and gardens of flowering shrubs. Go right at the split onto the right side of the Y; the garden's R. R. Allen Family Butterfly Garden and Fountain is on the left, with nice niches of calm. Pass a bridge that goes right to more parking and restrooms by the ball fields. Bear left past a playground and up to Ashland Drive to go left along the road to the Blanche S. Benjamin Arboretum Overlook. The viewpoint takes in the fountain below.

At the overlook, step into the woods. The singletrack Woodland Trail goes farthest left along the edge of the bluff overlooking the other branch of the streamside paved path. The much wider Shade and Shrub Trail keeps more right, along Ashland Drive.

This is no huge tract of forest, but plant diversity hints at a mountain woodland. Among the trees and plants you'll see at the trail's twenty-eight numbered stations are tulip poplar, shagbark hickory, black oak, eastern hemlock, dogwood, redbud, black locust, pawpaw, wild grape, black cohosh, jack-in-the-pulpit, false Solomon's seal, trillium, Christmas fern, and much more.

The Bog Garden's boardwalk meander near Friendly Shopping Center is an almost subtropical experience.

The Woodland and Shrub Trails join at an outdoor classroom. Beyond that, the now single path passes many plantings and empties down to the paved path that makes up the leftward side of the Y. A restroom and indoor classroom are on the right (with parking beyond on Ashland Drive), with a display of dwarf conifers. Take the side trail that branches left through a winter garden and vine collection. These pergolas are the garden's main display areas (one a wedding spot). There are bridges back and forth and pocket garden spots. Loop back to the main paved path and head right to the apex of the Y, then right again to your car.

The Bog Garden Trail is a refreshingly natural spot, perfect for birding and wildlife observation. Extensive boardwalks explore the lakeside wetland, and an earthen trail climbs to a forested knoll. The total walk, much of it wheelchair accessible, is about 0.8 mile.

Enter from Starmount Farms at the kiosk and dip away from traffic sounds into an instant Eden for animals and birds. Squirrels scamper and birds of all sorts flit about (112 recorded species). Benches abound (there's even a tree seat). Go left and a bridge crosses the creek starting the larger loop of a two-loop trail system.

The lower loop encircles a clean creek, explores the wetland shore of Benjamin Lake, and leads out to another entrance on Hobbs Road. The trail often follows boardwalks with observation decks. Bald cypress trees send up knees near the lake, and yellow flag iris and other lush plants create an almost subtropical scene for a Piedmont city. A side loop climbs an adjacent wooded bluff using stone steps to reach a small loop beside Northline Avenue (another entrance point). The side trail rejoins the main loop near a waterfall feature called the Dr. Joe Christian Serenity Falls, named for the physician who spearheaded the project with diverse participation from local sponsors after the Benjamin family donated the the 21-acre property in 1988.

The Bicentennial Garden in adjacent Caldwell Park was dedicated in 1976 and includes paved paths, benches, and extensive displays of flowering bulbs. The garden includes the site of the historic David Caldwell Log College, an early backcountry school. Paths total about 0.8 mile.

GUILFORD COURTHOUSE NATIONAL MILITARY PARK

WHY GO?

Woods-walkers will prefer the trails around nearby Lake Brandt, but Guilford Courthouse National Military Park is a jewel. It's the site of the pivotal Revolutionary War battle of Guilford Courthouse on March 15, 1781, and the story of the American general, Nathanael Greene, who gave his name to Greensboro (mysteriously minus the "e"). Don't miss the impressive visitor center and museum, film, historic dioramas, artifacts, outdoor musket firings on weekends, and an annual weekend-long reenactment on the battle's anniversary.

A 2.5-mile one-way paved road—one lane of which is a designated bike path—loops through the park. The road has eight designated stops; new roadside interpretive signing is extremely well done. The road is gated daily at 5 p.m. and turned over to cyclists, joggers, and walkers, an easy amble that is especially nice on summer evenings (pets must be on-leash, and in-line skating is not permitted). Paved paths branch from the road, creating loops, and a stretch of colonial road bisects the park. There are connections to other adjacent parks too.

The park's forests are mature and impressive. An almost-manicured understory of evergreens and ornamental trees sprouts below towering pines and hardwoods, where evening sidelight pierces the shade. Bridges span streams that run through the undulating terrain where forest gives way to hilly meadows. Heights of land overlook tight valleys, the perfect place to stage a battle. Add the early-morning curl of mist in swales below silent cannons, and Guilford Courthouse National Military Park is a moving setting.

Twenty-eight monuments crop up, some in remote locations (the visitor center sells a guide to the memorials, as well as the indispensable overview of the war in the South, *The Road to Guilford Courthouse*, by John Buchanan). Monuments range from grave markers and

Snowfall is rare in Greensboro but insight into history is not at Guilford Courthouse National Military Park. Stellar interpretive signing tells a moving Revolutionary tale not far from Cornwallis Drive.

obelisks to a massive equestrian statue of General Greene. The park's excellent interpretive signing provides a memorable account of a battle the British barely won. Cornwallis's forces were so pummeled by the daring Greene that Cornwallis retreated to the coast, virtually abandoning the South to the Revolutionary Army and laying the groundwork for his defeat at Yorktown just seven months later.

Don't miss the City of Greensboro's adjacent Tannenbaum Historic Park, opened in 1988. Only a block or so away, at the corner of Battleground Avenue and New Garden Road, the park is centered on the exhibit-filled Colonial Heritage Center and the Hoskins House, a restored home that was built on that site in 1778 and used as a residence during the battle. A relocated barn dates from 1820, and a blacksmith shed is the site of living-history programs. In March Tannenbaum hosts an annual re-creation of the battle. Hundreds of uniformed participants stirringly reenact the fight during a three-day encampment, where the public can wander among tents and campfires.

This is a fine urban hiking destination with paved and graveled forest paths, including a colonial road used in the battle.

THE RUNDOWN

General location: Greensboro
Distance: The roadside bike lane, often used by walkers, is a 2.5-mile loop. Other hikes range from loops of 0.3 and 0.5 mile to a 2-mile out-and-back hike on the park's wooded paths. Recent paths add to the options.
Difficulty: Easy and partly barrier-free
Maps: USGS Lake Brandt. Download a map at the park's website (see below).

Elevation gain: Negligible
Water availability: Water is available throughout the year at the visitor center. There is a water fountain at a satellite restroom facility open spring through fall.
For more information: Guilford Courthouse National Military Park, 2332 New Garden Rd., Greensboro 27410; (336) 288-1776; nps.gov/guco

Greensboro's city-circling Downtown Greenway is unique. Best of all, it links to great urban walkways like Latham Park and Lake Daniel greenways and seems likely to soon carry pedestrians all the way to Guilford Courthouse National Military Park and Lake Brandt.
PHOTO BY TED PATRICK, COURTESY GREENSBORO DOWNTOWN GREENWAY

FINDING THE TRAILHEAD

 The park is located between Old Battleground Road and Lawndale Drive in northwestern Greensboro, 0.5 mile off Battleground Avenue (US 220) on New Garden Road (GPS: 36.130813/-79.846518).

THE HIKES

The easiest stroll involves crossing the parking lot from the visitor center and taking the paved path that departs in the same direction as the start of the loop road. Cross the bike path at the first junction to loop left along the location of the American First Line past the second stop on the road tour, called the "Fragmented Attack." Old-style timber fences stand in the woods, and squirrels chatter everywhere. The hike loops back to the visitor center in about 0.2 mile.

Another easy walk, and one that nicely extends the one above, leaves the visitor center parking lot at its farthest point from the building (about where the walk above ends) and heads across Old Battleground Road for a counterclockwise loop. Cross the A&Y Greenway and continue on the paved path paralleling the loop road. At the third stop on the loop road, the location of the American Second Line titled "Sustained Firefight," the path leaves the road left (stay left at the next junction) through the woods to the Greene monument, with its stirring, archaic wording. Pass the monument and go left onto the old colonial road to the greenway that parallels Old Battleground Road; cross there or at the nearby corner crosswalk back near the visitor center to another group of monuments

Greensboro—Guilford Courthouse National Military Park

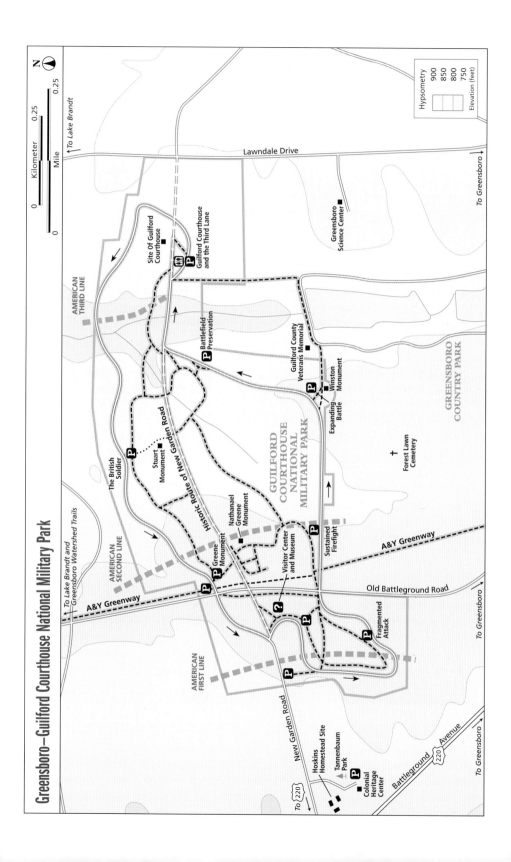

under tall trees. One honors the local Quaker women who tended the wounded of both sides. A left just beyond these monuments leads to the visitor center. The two connected loops total about 0.6 mile.

To create the lengthiest walk from the visitor center, take the walk described above, but as you leave the roadside near stop 3 bound for the Greene monument, turn right onto the first trail through the woods, a trail that creates the park's longest trail loop. Wander through woods to the next junction by open meadows. Left and right is a small inner loop around this valley where, until recently, historians believed the decisive Third Line battle action took place involving Greene's Continental troops. Go right, cross a bridge, and rise to a roadside obelisk, the Cavalry Monument, and exhibits at a roadside stop called "Battlefield Preservation." Continue back into the woods on the small inner loop, but take the next right through the woods. Go right again and stay on the gravel of colonial New Garden Road. Keep left along a short stretch of the paved road, then go back onto the gravel road past a trail that goes left back into the woods. Just beyond are roadside restrooms and a water fountain. A sign here describes the backcountry courthouse of old (road stop 6, "Guilford Courthouse and the Third Line"). Retrace your steps, but go right on the trail you passed into the woods. The cannons you encounter sit on what researchers now believe was the Third Line, where the decisive action happened. From the skirmish line below this high point, Cornwallis ordered grapeshot fired into his own ranks to turn the tide of battle against the Americans, who seemed to be winning.

Continue, turning right over the next bridge and returning to the meadows and the small inner loop. Go right, past the Regular's Monument. In the field below beside the colonial road, the small obelisk and interpretive sign of the Stuart Monument tells the stirring story of a British officer's death, an incident noted in the name of the nearby roadside stopping point, The British Soldier. Continue right, through the woods, and turn right again, off the small inner loop to roadside stop 8, the Greene Monument. Cross the street back to the visitor center for an approximately 2-mile walk.

You might also park at stop 3 or 8 on the road, walk to the area of the Greene monument, and follow the tree-lined thoroughfare of the old colonial road. When the road reaches the bluff overlooking the meadow, turn and circle the opposing bluffs of the small inner loop. Heading back on the colonial road after the loop is a walk of 0.8 mile.

A paved parking lot on Old Battleground Road (across from the visitor center and visible from the Greene monument) is a favored parking area when the park's loop road is gated and the visitor center is off-limits. This is also a major trailhead for the A&Y Greenway, which leads north to many miles of lakeshore hiking near Lake Brandt (see that entry).

The park's longest walk is the 2.5-mile paved bike path. To add an interesting side trip to that hike, follow the path away from the loop road at the Winston Monument, loop tour stop 4, Expanding Battle, site of the last shots fired by American riflemen. Follow this into adjacent Greensboro Country Park, go left around the northern part of the lake, and then go left again past the zoological exhibit area of the Greensboro Science Center to reenter the military park near stop 6 on the loop tour road.

Hikers who combine parts of the tour road with the trails can greatly expand the shorter strolls into satisfying walks. A glance at the map will make these options obvious.

WHY GO?

High Point Lake was built in the early 1920s to serve as a water supply for the city of High Point. The Piedmont Environmental Center (PEC) was started on 376 acres of city lakeshore in 1972, and the Bicentennial Greenway (commemorating the ratification of the US Constitution) became possible in 1989 when the citizens of Guilford County approved a $1.5 million bond issue. Gibson Park, just north of the PEC parcels and the major trailhead for the Bicentennial Greenway, started with a 1990 purchase of 200 acres by Guilford County. From the Piedmont Center Office Park, the Bicentennial Greenway will be extended past the airport to Guilford Courthouse National Military Park in northern Greensboro, where the greenway is growing toward High Point.

These trails near High Point Lake are good, close-to-home places to enjoy nature. Sections of the trails wander through quiet pine forests carpeted with running cedar. Other stretches at times explore towering deciduous woods. The trails provide nice views of the lake's isolated coves, especially in fall. Winter brings seasonal migrations of waterfowl. The area boasts more than thirty species of mushrooms.

Before hiking these and other area trails, sample the resources of the PEC, a great place to learn. The PEC has some exhibits, including a 70 × 40-foot outdoor map of North Carolina that visitors walk across on their way to the trailhead. The PEC is not a museum but a program-driven institution that offers educational classes and field trips. Hiking boots are not necessary on these developed trails. A pair of sturdy running shoes will do.

Offering extensive hiking in a lakeshore natural area, PEC trails connect with the paved Bicentennial Greenway.

THE RUNDOWN

General location: High Point, one city in the Piedmont Triad that also includes Greensboro and Winston-Salem

Distance: The PEC's elaborate trail networks total 11 miles and permit hikes of many lengths, including looping circuit walks that combine with the 6.5-mile Bicentennial Greenway. On PEC land, the Bill Faver Lakeshore Loop is about 1.8 miles and can be 2.2. The greenway/Deep River Trail circuit is about 4.6 miles. Gibson Park's Twin Ponds Trail and Black Powder Trail make a few loops possible in the 1 mile range, and just south of those ponds, a newish circuit called the Long Rifle Loop is just more than a mile. An out-and-back greenway walk to the park's wildlife observation deck is about 1.4 miles.

Difficulty: Easy, except for the lengthiest circuit hikes

Maps: USGS Guilford and High Point East. Download the area's trail maps at the PEC and Gibson Park websites (see below).

Elevation gain: Negligible

Water availability: Water and restrooms are available at trailheads year-round at the PEC and Gibson

Park and during the warmer seasons at Jamestown Park golf course picnic area, just across East Fork Road (SR 1545) from the greenway trailhead.
For more information: Piedmont Environmental Center, 1220 Penny Rd., High Point 27265; (336) 883-8531; https://www.highpointnc.gov/Facilities/Facility/Details/Piedmont-Environmental-Center-18; open 9 a.m. to 5 p.m. Mon–Fri; Gibson Park, 5207 West Wendover Avenue, High Point, NC 27265, (336) 641-2040.

FINDING THE TRAILHEADS

Access to trails at the Piedmont Environmental Center and Bicentennial Greenway is easiest from West Wendover Avenue and I-40 in Greensboro. From I-40 exit 214, take Wendover Avenue west 3.6 miles to a left into Gibson Park, where the Twin Ponds Trail starts on the right at 0.5 mile and the greenway access is at 0.55 mile (GPS: 36.029237 / -79.944314). To reach the PEC, continue south on Wendover past Gibson Park; go left on Penny Road (SR 1536) at 4.4 miles and reset your odometer. To reach Jamestown Park go left at 0.8 mile onto East Fork Road (SR 1545). In a short distance, turn right into the park and immediately right into picnic area parking. To reach the PEC, continue south on Penny Road and turn left into the parking area at 2.1 miles (GPS: 36.004284 / -79.954332).

THE HIKES

Piedmont Environmental Center trails focus on two lakeshore parcels. The southern parcel that surrounds the center is 151 acres between Penny Road, the lake, and Jamestown Park's golf course. The tract contains about 4 miles of trails bounded by the lake on the east and about 1.5 miles of the Bicentennial Greenway on the north and west.

The longest trail walk, a 1.8-mile loop, follows the white-blazed Bill Faver Lakeshore Trail from the south end of the PEC parking lot. The trail enters the woods and descends over boardwalk bridges to lake level, where the trail goes left along the shore around the first cove. Go right at the junction just beyond, and follow the lakeshore. Make a right to include the Raccoon Run Trail, a blue-blazed, 0.4-mile side trail that loops onto a promontory jutting out into the lake that makes a loop of the Faver Trail 2.2 miles.

Follow the Raccoon Run loop around the peninsula and go right again on the Bill Faver Lakeshore Trail. Keep right again along the shore when the Dogwood Trail goes left (and creates the second-longest loop back to the center). Remains of an old homesite are visible, and a wildlife-viewing blind also sits near the lake. The trail winds away from the lake, parallels the greenway (a short trail to the right links them), then veers left to return past the PEC's Wildflower Trail to the trailhead.

Shorter loops are possible. The Wildflower Trail is only 0.4 mile, and even toddlers can navigate the tiny circuit created by the Bill Faver and green-blazed Chickadee Trails. Kids would also enjoy a circuit of the Bill Faver and yellow-blazed Fiddlehead Trails; just take the first left past the cove and return to the center.

The northern parcel of PEC property contains the most backcountry hiking. A 1.5-mile section of the Bicentennial Greenway flanks the western side of this 225-acre tract bordered on the east by the lake.

The red/white-blazed Deep River Trail and orange/green-blazed Hollis Rogers Pine Woods Trail (opened in summer 1995) are the attractions here. From the picnic parking area at Jamestown Park, the greenway and Deep River Trail form a major circuit of about 4.5 miles; a few other circuits are also possible.

In High Point, wetlands near the Deep River become prime wildlife-viewing opportunities at Piedmont Environmental Center.

To hike the biggest loop, leave the Jamestown Park picnic area, walk to the park entrance on East Fork Road, and cross the street. Turn right on the paved greenway and parallel East Fork Road for about 0.4 mile through beautiful forest. Where the greenway crosses East Fork Road, the Deep River Trail goes left into the woods. (There isn't much room on the roadside here, but a few cars could probably use this trailhead to create a Deep River/Rogers Pine Woods Trail circuit with no greenway walking to mar an otherwise backwoodsy hike.)

From this point, the Deep River Trail goes north, winding away from the lake into a deep cove, crossing a bridge, and doing the same thing again. Just across the second bridge, the Hollis Rogers Pine Woods Trail goes left. The Deep River Trail goes right but stays away from the lakeshore and climbs to a high point with chunks of white quartz in the trail. The second leg of the Pine Woods Trail comes in on the left. Between these two trailheads, the Pine Woods Trail explores a towering loblolly pine forest that is periodically burned. From Jamestown Park, or East Fork Road, this Pine Woods/Deep River Trail circuit is a short day hike.

The Deep River Trail continues north along the lake, staying high on hardwood-covered bluffs. The trail crosses a bridge, leads deep into a cove, then crosses a double bridge over a rocky, fern-bordered creek. As the trail approaches the head of the lake, the bluffs give way to flat lakeshore and the trail crosses swaths of cleared forest at a power line and gas pipeline. The trail swings away from the lake into a final cove, passes an extensive growth of running cedar, crosses a muddy area, and ascends wooden steps onto Sunnyvale Road and the greenway. To the right, the greenway immediately takes a left to the Gibson Park observation deck, 0.5 mile away, and Gibson Park trailhead, 1.2 miles. To the left, the greenway goes 0.8 mile back to the Jamestown Park picnic area.

If you'd like more woods walking, cross the road, descend wooden steps, and again take the Deep River Trail. Follow plentiful blaze posts north along bluffs that rise above the creek. The trail descends to creek level, crosses a bridge, then briefly and steeply climbs into and across the pipeline swath and Sunnyvale Road. The trail reenters the woods and joins the greenway again. To the right, the greenway shortly arrives at Jamestown Park.

The Bicentennial Greenway is a pleasant walk. North of Gibson Park, it is a typical urban paved trail, but between the PEC and Gibson Park, the greenway is often bordered by scenic forest. It also undulates, which makes it one of the more interesting greenways in the state. Indeed, it is a pleasant out-and-back walk from any of its most worthwhile trailheads: the PEC or Jamestown and Gibson Parks.

One of the nicest stretches is south from Jamestown Park. At first the paved greenway parallels the road through tall trees. After it crosses East Fork Road, the path's surface becomes gravel, grass, and pine needles. It follows the fence line at Jamestown Park golf

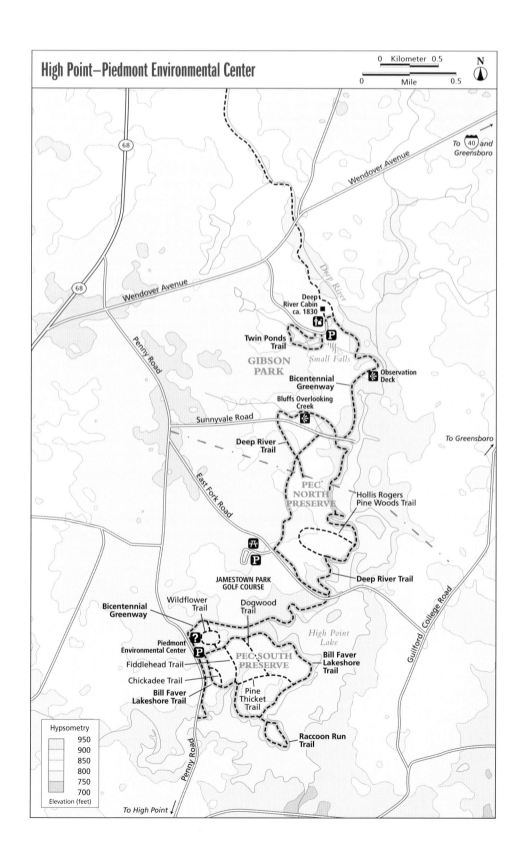

High Point–Piedmont Environmental Center

0   Kilometer   0.5

0   Mile   0.5

N

To 40 and Greensboro

Wendover Avenue

68

68

Wendover Avenue

Penny Road

Deep River

Deep River Cabin ca. 1830

Twin Ponds Trail

P

GIBSON PARK

Small Falls

Observation Deck

Bicentennial Greenway

Bluffs Overlooking Creek

Sunnyvale Road

Deep River Trail

East Fork Road

PEC NORTH PRESERVE

Hollis Rogers Pine Woods Trail

To Greensboro

A

P

JAMESTOWN PARK GOLF COURSE

Deep River Trail

Guilford College Road

Wildflower Trail

Dogwood Trail

Bicentennial Greenway

High Point Lake

Piedmont Environmental Center

?

P

Fiddlehead Trail

PEC SOUTH PRESERVE

Bill Faver Lakeshore Trail

Chickadee Trail

Bill Faver Lakeshore Trail

Pine Thicket Trail

Penny Road

Raccoon Run Trail

Hypsometry

950
900
850
800
750
700

Elevation (feet)

To High Point

course, but the trees are tall, and the lakeside stroll is enjoyable. The second and bigger set of steps (which include a novel ramp for bikes) is a nice turnaround point.

Immediately south from Gibson Park, the greenway is less wooded and a little sunnier (and hotter in summer). The wildlife observation deck makes a good destination, 0.7 mile south of Gibson Park. A boardwalk viewpoint reaches into the cattail-covered wetland where High Point Lake becomes the Deep River again. In morning and evening, there is excellent birding here.

In Gibson Park, the Twin Ponds Trail and Black Powder Trail permit a mile or ramble that encircles two grassy ponds in a wooded area known for profuse blackberries in summer. The path passes the ranger residence. From the park's main parking area, just past the Twin Ponds Trail, a connector reaches the greenway. A right leads to the observation deck described above, but a number of new trails also permit loops between the Twin Ponds Trail and the Deep River Trail and greenway south of the observation deck (see the park's online map).

A side trail to the left arrives at one of the few pre–Civil War cabins left in the area. Just a stroll from the parking lot, the Deep River Cabin was built between 1800 and 1830 in a sizable community of people who lived on the shores of Deep River before the Civil War. The community dwindled in the late 1800s with the waning of its primary industries, including the manufacture of the Jamestown long rifle, many of which were used in the Civil War.

37 ENO RIVER AREA

WHY GO?

The rippling Eno River winds for 33 miles from its headwaters in Orange County to Falls Lake in Wake County. Two state parcels offer access. One, Eno River State Park, focuses on the river; the other, Occoneechee Mountain State Natural Area, preserves an adjacent summit.

Eno River State Park's 3,867 acres protect 13.5 scenic miles of the river. This park is a real gem. Saved by citizen action from being dammed, more and more of the Eno is being preserved to tell a story of natural and human history in the Piedmont. More acreage is being protected along the river in this area, and more trail mileage will be added too. The Mountains-to-Sea Trail now runs through the park with the extension of the Laurel Bluffs Trail. A major summer fundraiser, the Eno River Association's Festival for the Eno, celebrates the river, and the future bodes well for this being one of the state's premier urban preservation success stories.

The historic town of Hillsborough amply illustrates that. Hillsborough lies between Occoneechee State Natural Area and Eno River State Park and its aggressive development of riverside parks and the 2-mile Riverwalk greenway (part of the Mountains-to-Sea Trail / MST) demonstrates the potential for preservation along this scenic stream. The MST is gradually linking adjacent state lands to many "trail towns" like Hillsborough where urban amenities, dining, lodging and history complement a hike across the state or just a weekend escape. Historic sites are plentiful (don't miss Ayrmont) and the town makes a hip base of operations for all the surrounding parks.

All of this exciting trail activity is happening where the Eno's rapids cross the fall line dropping from the Piedmont to the coastal plain—one reason the rich history of the area and the river includes an early Indian trading path and many gristmills. The Eno alternates between wide, slow-moving sections and sprightly whitewater, making it popular for kayaking and canoeing from Hillsborough through the park to Falls Lake. The Eno's fall-line location and cleanliness account for its diverse aquatic life. It contains ten species of freshwater mussels, five of which are on the endangered species list and all of which are a favorite food of muskrats. The sixty-one species of fish found in the Eno represent a quarter of those recorded in the state and include largemouth bass, bluegill, and catfish. The river is also home to the Neuse River waterdog, a rare aquatic salamander.

Eno River State Park's 28 miles of blazed trails usually follow the river and its rocky bluffs, passing through forests of sycamore, river birch, ash, and musclewood. But the trails also wander away from the river up rocky hills of nearly 1,000 feet that sustain vegetation remarkably similar to the mountains. Prevalent plant species here are mountain laurel, rhododendron, pine, hickory, and oak. The park's

From many places on the trails of Occoneechee State Park, impressive cliffs remind hikers of the mountains. PHOTO BY BILL RUSS. COURTESY VISITNC.COM

Many of the park's trails gain added interest by sticking to the banks of this sprightly Piedmont river.

noteworthy natural resources make it the perfect place to learn about nature. Curriculum-based environmental education can be arranged; contact the park.

The Eno is important for its human history. Early on, Eno and Shakori Indians built dams to trap fish in the rapids. After European settlement, more than thirty grist-, flour-, and sawmills dotted the river starting in the 1700s. A post–Civil War revival in 1880 brought a mill every few miles. The modern industrial era dawned with the Eno Cotton Mill in 1896. The sites of Few's Mill (1758–1908) and Holden's or Cole Mill (1811–1908) are in the western parcel of the park. Hikers can still encounter nineteenth-century ruins. The well-preserved site of Guess Mill, with a dam, millrace, and chimney, is visible on the Laurel Bluffs Trail. You'll get goose bumps when you realize that 150 years ago, these wagon roads were the I-40 of their time, linking farms with mills and coastal residents with the backcountry. The Piper-Cox House, a late nineteenth-century home beside the Buckquarter Creek and Holden's Mill Trailhead near park headquarters, is occasionally open for tours (call the park for tour schedule).

The park is great for novice backpackers. In the Few's Ford parcel five numbered sites branch off the Fanny's Ford Trail 1 mile from the parking area. Each site has a tent pad, and there's a pit toilet nearby.

No fires are permitted; there is no water at the sites, but a water fountain is available at the day hiker trailhead. A group walk-in camping site is about 0.25 mile from the trailhead. There's another backcountry campground at the Cole Mill tract. A camping fee and permit are required that can be reserved on the park's website, but campers must physically stop in to supply details and pick up a "camper" card to display on their vehicle.

At nearby Occoneechee Mountain State Natural Area, a 190-acre tract west of Eno River State Park, trails take you to the highest point in Orange County. The summit of Occoneechee Mountain is 867 feet, which earns it vegetation akin to mountain sites. The rich chestnut oak forest on the relatively undisturbed summit ridges represents the easternmost range of plants such as Catawba rhododendron and the mountain laurel–galax community, a plant pairing often seen much higher up. Groundhogs and wild turkeys are also among the park's mountain-appropriate residents. Hiking and fishing in two ponds are the big attractions.

The park is also special because it's the easternmost occurrence of the brown elfin butterfly, restricted to the higher, cooler range of mountains to the west. A noteworthy population remains at Occoneechee, flitting through the trees 350 feet above the winding Eno.

Many hikes explore the Eno River's environ as it tumbles over fall-line ledges and into deep pools. Other trails reach Occoneechee summit.

THE RUNDOWN

General location: Eno River State Park, northwest of Durham

Distance: 0.5-mile loop for Eno Trace TRACK Trail; 2.8 miles for the Fanny's Ford Trail; 3.8 miles for Cox Mountain Trail; 1.5 miles for the Buckquarter Creek Trail; 4.1 for the Buckquarter Creek/Holden's Mill Trail circuit; 8 miles for a new section of the Mountains-to-Sea/Laurel Bluffs Trail, about 3 miles for the Bobbitt Hole/Cole Mill Trail circuit; 1.3 miles for the Pea Creek Trail; 3.1 miles for Pea Creek/Dunnagan Trail circuit; 1.5 miles for the Pump Station Trail; up to 6.5 miles for a circuit of the Laurel Bluffs and Pump Station Trails. The Occoneechee Mountain Loop Trail is 2.2 miles.

Difficulty: Easy for Eno Trace and Fanny's Ford Trails; moderate for everything else except moderately strenuous for the Cox Mountain Trail

Maps: USGS Durham NW and Hillsborough. Download the state park map for Eno at ncparks.gov/Visit/parks/enri/main.php, and for Occoneechee at ncparks.gov/Visit/parks/ocmo/main.php.

Elevation gain: Negligible on most trails; about 620 feet on Cox Mountain Trail

Water availability: The Eno is clean, but hikers should treat it before using or get water from park facilities. There are water fountains beside the picnic area at the main Few's Ford trailhead in the Cole Mill parking area.

For more information: Eno River State Park, 6101 Cole Mill Rd., Durham 27705-9275; (919) 383-1686; e-mail: eno.river@ncparks.gov. Occoneechee Mountain State Natural Area, 625 Virginia Cates Rd. (same mailing and e-mail address as Eno); (919) 383-1686. For more history visit tradingpath.org. or ncmst.org.

FINDING THE TRAILHEADS

The park is located northwest of Durham and reached from exit 170 on I-85. Going west, exit onto US 70 and turn right in 0.1 mile onto Pleasant Green Road (SR 1567). If coming east, exit and turn left onto US 70 West. Go back under the interstate 0.7 mile to a right onto SR 1567. Go 2.2 miles to a left turn onto Cole Mill Road (SR 1569). The park entrance to the Few's Ford parcel of the park is on the right in 0.8 mile, and the park headquarters is at 1 mile. The first turn to the right beyond the headquarters leads to the trailhead for the Buckquarter Creek and Holden's Mill Trails (GPS: 36.078066/-79.007095). Beyond that turn, the road ends after 0.2 mile in a parking area that serves the Fanny's Ford, Cox Mountain, and Eno Trace Trails (GPS: 36.073821/-79.006248). Campers heading to walk-in campsites should use camper parking on the left.

To reach the park's Cole Mill and Pump Station parcels, at Cole Mill Road, turn right from Pleasant Green Road (instead of left to the park office). Go 1.15 miles and turn right into the trailhead parking area for the Cole Mill, Bobbitt's Hole, Pea Creek, and Dunnagan Trails (GPS: 36.056452/-78.979450). There are restrooms and picnic tables.

To reach the trailhead for the Pump Station Trail, go beyond the Cole Mill parking area and take the next left onto Rivermont Road. Just past the bridge over Nancy Rhodes Creek, about 0.5 mile, park on the left side of the road by the park signs (GPS: 36.058556/-78.965681).

To reach the Cabe Lands Trailhead, take exit 170 off I-85 going east, pass the first Eno Park sign, and in a few miles, go left at the second light onto Sparger Road. Cross I-85 and take the first left on Howe Street to parking on the right (GPS: 36.039831/-78.990364). To take the Mountains-to-Sea Trail through Cabe Lands, spot cars at Pleasant Green Access, close to US 70 on Pleasant Green Road (GPS: 36.047270/-79.011466), and beyond the Pump Station Trail access at an Eno River Association trailhead on Guess Road (GPS: 36.072312/-78.933693).

To reach Occoneechee Mountain State Natural Area, leave I-85 at exit 164 just south of Hillsborough. Go north on Churton Street and left at the light onto Mayo Street. Make a left onto Orange Grove Road. In about 0.5 mile, turn right onto Virginia Cates Road and into the natural area, past the ponds to the parking lot and restrooms (GPS: 36.060518/-79.117222).

WESTERN ENO RIVER STATE PARK

THE HIKES

The Eno Trace Trail is a red dot–blazed, self-guided nature trail and the park's interpretive TRACK Trail. Follow the Cox Mountain Trail from the main parking area; Eno Trace goes left. The trail is level on the river but has a steep descent at the start. The 0.5-mile loop passes benches and exhibits about trees and the river habitat, here on display beside a pretty green stream. This is a nice spring wildflower hike.

Continuing past an intersection with the Eno Trace Trail, the blue dot–blazed main Cox Mountain Trail descends, passes an access trail on the right (from a separate parking area for campers), and reaches the wood-and-cable suspension bridge across the Eno at about 0.2 mile. Take the bridge across the river and go 60 yards to a major trail junction. There, a left leads to a wilderness shelter and a group campsite (off to the right). A right at the junction leads to the Cox Mountain and Fanny's Ford Trails.

Early residents along the Eno followed roads that crossed the river at fords like this one.

Take a right on the blue dot–blazed, old road grade of the Cox Mountain Trail. Pass the first left of the Cox Mountain Trail; then an old grade bears right (the route where the Fanny's Ford loop of the trail returns). Stay left and pass the second trail to the left, the other side of the Cox Mountain loop. The purple dots of the Fanny's Ford Trail turn east and follow the river back to rejoin the Cox Mountain Trail. Near that junction on the way back, you'll pass Few's Ford. Part of this trail was the old Hillsborough Coach Road, a turnpike back when bridges were rare and roads forded rivers at these shallow shoals.

There are five campsites in the end-loop area, a loop of about 1 mile; the total round-trip is about 2.8 miles.

Following the same route over the suspension bridge, make the second left onto the Cox Mountain Trail along the river; the first trail immediately climbs steeply to the park's highest summit, Cox Mountain. The second trail wanders the old coach road by the river; it goes under a power line and along the bank where mature trees form a canopy over the water. Look for streamside evidence of the Holden's Mill dam. The trail leaves the river along a stream, climbing into a hardwood forest. A small dip separates the two crests of Cox Mountain, both about 680 feet. Again pass under the power line and steeply descend through a pine forest. A bench is located about halfway down, useful for those who go up this side of the trail. At the junction, go right and back across the suspension bridge for a 3.8-mile hike.

Probably the best hike in western Eno, for solitude and scenery, is a circuit of the Buckquarter Creek and Holden's Mill Trails. The red dot–blazed Buckquarter Creek Trail is 1.5 miles, but a combination of the loops creates a 4.1-mile hike with no backtracking. Switch sides of the loop in the middle to alternate upland and riverside scenery. There is evidence of beaver activity on the riverbank portions of both trails. Two ancient log cabins lie on the higher Buckquarter Creek Trail.

From the Piper-Cox Museum parking area, the first past park headquarters, walk down to the river and go east along the bank. The Buckquarter Creek Trail immediately splits. The right fork, the upland part of the loop, where there are wintertime views from the ridge, explores once-cleared land that was a farm a half-century ago; a cabin lurks off the trail to the right, another lies off-trail not far beyond. The river side of the loop rises on stone steps over an outcrop with good views of the river's most impressive rapid. Both parts of the path rejoin near the river at a bridge over the canal-like side stream of Buckquarter Creek. Return here for a 1.5-mile hike.

Cross the bridge to another trail split, this time for the yellow dot–blazed Holden's Mill Trail, two loops totaling about 2.6 miles. The forest floor here is open except for Christmas fern. With the river gurgling on one side, birds call from the tall pines and hardwoods towering overhead. Farther along, big outcrops and rocky crags line the river, creating a scene reminiscent of the mountains. Both branches of the trail pass beneath the same power line visible across the river on the Cox Mountain Trail. The trails again join at a tiny side stream amid an inspiring forest, and the shorter end loop of the Holden's Mill Trail branches out.

This loop explores the remains of Holden's Mill, actually looping below and then above the still-visible stone wall. Not far from the end of the loop, on the upland side, an old road branches north. A side trip here leads past an old tobacco barn on the right, a startling two-story log cabin on the left, and an old collapsed hunting lodge on the right. Though not shown on the park map, this old road is visible on the USGS topographic quad.

A newer, more northerly loop, with ruins from early residences, adds even more appeal to this side of the river. The Ridge Trail, marked with blue U's, leaves the Buckquarter Creek Trail on the upland section near the creek. This is another historic road—the old Ridge Road to Roxboro. Stay left when the Knight Trail goes right and the trail crosses Buckquarter Creek on stones or by wading. Just beyond, as the trail turns right, ruins hide off the trail to the left. Stay left (past the junction with the Shakori Trail). The Ridge Trail climbs more than 200 feet on the way to a gate at the park boundary, along the way passing a group campsite.

Eno River Area

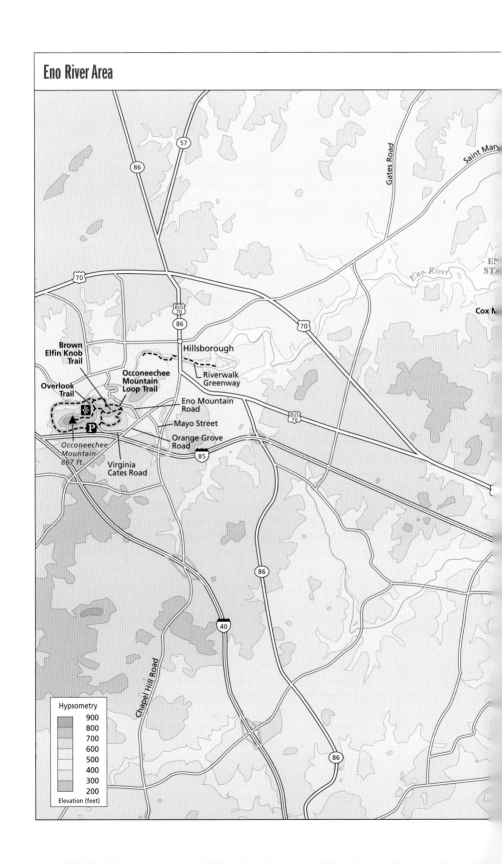

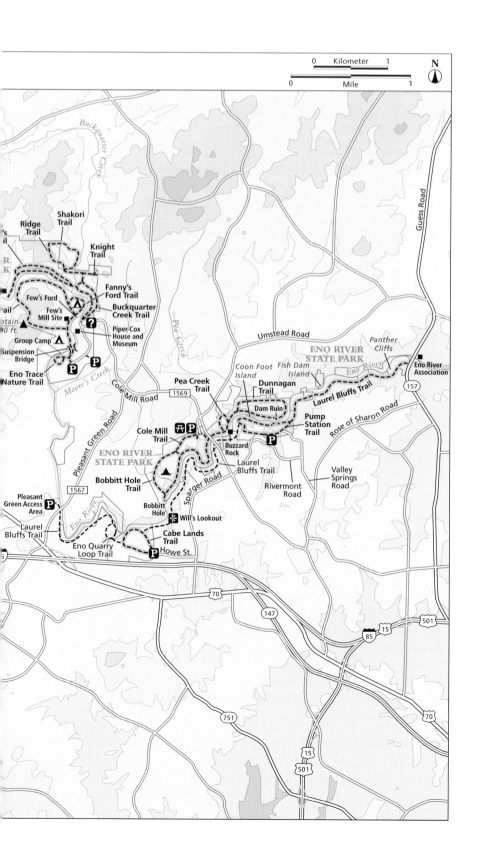

Kilometer

Mile

N

Buckquarter Creek

Shakori Trail

Ridge Trail

Knight Trail

Fanny's Ford Trail

Few's Ford

Few's Mill Site

Buckquarter Creek Trail

Piper-Cox House and Museum

Group Camp

Suspension Bridge

Eno Trace Nature Trail

Moore's Creek

Cole Mill Road

Pleasant Green Road

Pea Creek

1569

Umstead Road

ENO RIVER STATE PARK

Panther Cliffs

Coon Foot Island

Fish Dam Island

Eno River

Eno River Association

157

Pea Creek Trail

Dunnagan Trail

Laurel Bluffs Trail

Dam Ruin

Pump Station Trail

Rose of Sharon Road

Guess Road

Cole Mill Trail

Buzzard Rock

Laurel Bluffs Trail

Valley Springs Road

ENO RIVER STATE PARK

Bobbitt Hole Trail

1567

Sparger Road

Rivermont Road

Pleasant Green Access Area

Eno River

Bobbitt Hole

Will's Lookout

Laurel Bluffs Trail

Cabe Lands Trail

Eno Quarry Loop Trail

Howe St.

70

147

751

85 15

501

15

501

70

The alert hiker will spot evidence of early settlers beside many trails along the Eno.

Near that northwestern point, go right on the second junction of the yellow U–blazed Shakori Trail and descend back to Buckquarter Creek (keep your eyes open for the chimneys of another nineteenth-century home). Stay right on the Ridge Trail when the Knight Trail goes left (it reaches the Piedmont Trail—both go to nearby neighborhoods). This northern loop, added to the Buckquarter Creek Trail, creates a 3.8-miler. Check out tradingpath.org for more on the area's old roads and residences.

The southernmost trails on the western side of the state park are located in the Cabe Lands tract. The main Cabe Lands loop trail leaves the lot toward the Eno in a rocky area known as Cabe's Gorge. The red-blazed path splits into a loop and passes the site of Cabe Mill, where the millrace and other evidence are still visible. This loop is 1.2 miles, but you can add 0.8 mile to the hike, for a 2-mile round-trip, by also going west on the blue dot–blazed Eno Quarry Trail and circling the scenic 4-acre pond.

There's a new section of the Mountains-to-Sea Trail here, an extension of the park's Laurel Bluffs Trail, that's worth considering. Its yellow dot blazes run along the south side of the river linking the Cabe Lands' trails west to the Pleasant Green access and east to and past the red dot-blazed Pump Station Trail to Guess Road (park at the Eno River Association). Spot cars at those access points and this quiet section of trail is an 8-mile hike that also evidences the MST's white dots. To start, take the MST under Pleasant

Green Road. End by walking up to the roadside at Guess Road. Walk left across the bridge and cross Guess Road to the association headquarters; or at a break in the guard-rail, take an informal path left and descend to the MST. Go left under the bridge and immediately go left up the yard to the Eno Association parking (or stay on MST, then go left on Eagle Trail back to their parking area). Support the Eno River Association and their successful annual Festival for the Eno at enoriver.org.

On this hike, the trail passes Bobbitt Hole, a longtime swimming hole nearly 20 feet deep and one of the park's most scenic spots. You could also camp on this hike, but you have to wade the river near Bobbitt Hole to use the park's Piper Creek campsites. There are, after all, many fords of this often-shallow river. After crossing the fourth footbridge on the section, take an informal trail left to a mill site and a rocky ford spot just before Bobbitt Hole. Plan this hike in low water, and be sure to have your camping permit.

Continuing on, the MST passes Cole Mill Road, winds up from the Eno, skirting cliffs and rocky bluffs. Fish Dam Island precedes a hard right in the river. Gebel Rock and Panther Cliffs are highlights before Guess Road. Along the way, the trail passes a hunting lodge chimney and foundation and follows the millrace at the obvious ruins of the Guess Mill Dam.

EASTERN ENO RIVER STATE PARK

THE HIKES

Other good hikes are located in the eastern Cole Mill and Pump Station parcels of the park. From the central picnic area trailhead on Cole Mill Road, the Cole Mill and Bobbitt Hole Trails form a figure-eight walk of about 2.6 miles on the north side of the river (across from the MST).

Leaving the parking lot at the water fountain, turn right on the Cole Mill Trail (blazed with yellow dots) and go under a power line. The return end of the trail, with access to the Pea Creek Trail, leaves the corner of the parking area closest to the river. The quickest way to reach Bobbitt Hole—a deep pool at a major turn in the river—is to turn left on the connector between the two trail loops, passing under a power line to go right on the Bobbitt Hole Trail (blazed with red dots). The trail follows the river through the park's typical riparian forest and crosses a bridge over Piper Creek (namesake of the park's backcountry campsite) and reaches Bobbitt Hole. The main trail goes right to complete the loop, but a dead-end spur goes left to the end of the pool. Fewer people swim at Bobbitt Hole since the park ended vehicular access. The bottom is unchecked, so use caution if you're tempted. Backtrack from there, continue on the loop, and go under a power line.

The trail rises from the river to its high point in a mature forest of oak, hickory, and beech. Cross another creek, on stepping-stones. At the junction with the connector between the Bobbitt Hole and Cole Mill Trails, go left on the leg of the trail you came in on to return quickly to the parking area for a 2.5-mile hike. If you go right, Cole Mill Trail follows a long bend in the river, creating a figure eight of about 3 miles.

Many of Eno River State Park's trails are the historic roads of yesteryear.

That leg of the Cole Mill Trail returns to the end of the parking lot closest to the river. Just below that parking lot, the Pea Creek Trail branches from the Cole Mill Trail and goes northeast under the bridge that carries Cole Mill Road over the Eno River. Heading downstream, the 1.3-mile Pea Creek Trail and the 1.8-mile Dunnagan Trail form a 3.1-mile figure eight that is flatter and easier than the circuit formed by the Bobbitt Hole and Cole Mill Trails.

The Pea Creek Trail (blazed with blue dots) passes under a power line. After the trail splits, the right branch follows the river past Buzzard Rock. It heads inland along scenic Pea Creek, a rocky stream that is particularly nice after rainfall. The trail reaches a bridge on the right that links it to red dot–blazed Dunnagan Trail. Above the bridge, the Pea Creek Trail continues to follow the creek, then turns left to rejoin itself on the way back to the parking area (a 1.3-mile hike).

If you take the red dot–blazed Dunnagan Trail, continue straight after crossing the bridge. The trail splits, ascends, and follows a ridge. A cemetery and old homesites with ruined chimneys are ridgetop points of interest. Near the eastern end of the trail, as you descend to the river, notice Durham's first city water plant, in use from 1887 to 1927, on the other bank. Views of the old ruin are actually better from here than from the Pump Station Trail on the other side. The trail follows the river back to the bridge.

The Pump Station Trail is the springtime choice for wildflowers. The eastern end of the 1.5-mile, red dot–blazed loop trail passes the ruins of the old drinking water treatment plant. The middle of the riverside leg of the trail passes an impressive, but breached, stone dam that once impounded water for the pump station.

Take alternate sides of the Pump Station loop and go out and back on Laurel Bluffs to create a 6.5-mile hike along a memorable stretch of the Eno.

OCCONEECHEE MOUNTAIN STATE NATURAL AREA

THE HIKES

The main hike here is the 2.2-mile, red circle–blazed Occoneechee Mountain Loop Trail. The hike is a rocky ramble around the highest peak in Orange County, with some pretty convoluted terrain and super scenery at spots like Panther's Den. Take in the higher elevations on a loop of the Overlook and Brown Elfin Knob Trails.

Leave the parking area on a graveled grade and turn right near the ranger residence for the basic hike here, a 2.2 mile loop of the red circle–blazed Occoneechee Mountain Loop Trail that undulates all around the perimeter of the park. The orange circle–marked Chestnut Oak Trail and the blue circles of the Brown Elfin Knob Trail cross the crest of a side summit (767 feet). The Overlook Trail reaches a fence enclosed side view at an impressive outcrop. Hikers can spot the river far below and peer out at the countryside past russet colored cliffs. You can also bisect the loop on Chestnut Oak Trail to the wooded peak and towers of Occoneechee Mountain (867 feet), about 350 feet above the river.

38 DUKE FOREST

In the 1920s, Duke Forest was formed from farms and woods to buffer the developing campus of Duke University. Clarence F. Korstian led the establishment of the university's School of Forestry in 1938, and today the tracts are an invaluable laboratory for students and scientists.

Since the last edition of this book, public use of road-like "fire trails" and informal paths in this urban tract has exploded. The forestry and research focus continues, but recreation has elbowed its way into the mix. The 2004 designation of Significant Natural Heritage Areas (SNHAs) in the forest—unique areas recognized by the North Carolina Natural Heritage Program—has prompted new restrictions on timbering activities and sparked new trail construction and heightened trail maintenance and management. An earnest scientific mission explains why "none of the (original) trails were intentionally developed and designed to withstand long-term use," but luckily, recent construction of sustainably designed trails is accommodating science, public access, and protection of the environment. As these new paths take hold, hikers should avoid using the remains of old trails or hiking off-trail. And consider volunteering or donating to help the forest facilitate recreation.

The forest is open only from dawn to dusk. Managers ask that mountain bikers stay strictly on the area's road-width fire trails, many built by the Civilian Conservation Corps (CCC). Bushwhacking, cross-country hiking, or geocaching are prohibited to protect research plots throughout the forest. Enter only at the designated public access points, and do not block gates with vehicles. Dogs must be on-leash. Developed picnic facilities can be rented and are the only locations where open fires are permitted. Please read and heed the forest rules that are prominently posted at all access gates. In recent years, vehicle break-ins have been a problem at this urban forest. Best bet: Leave nothing of value in your ride.

DURHAM AND KORSTIAN DIVISIONS

WHY GO?

Duke University owns a handful of woodland tracts totaling more than 7,000 acres. Research and education are the focus, but public foot travel is permitted on fire roads and recently improved trails.

THE RUNDOWN

General location: Duke University, southwest of Durham

Distance: Hikes range from about 1 mile for an out-and-back walk to Laurel Hill Bluffs and a loop of the Shepherd Nature Trail to 2.9 miles for the Al Buehler Cross-Country Trail and about 5 miles for a circuit of the Concrete Bridge and Wooden Bridge Road Fire Trails.

Difficulty: Easy for Laurel Hill Bluffs and the Shepherd Nature Trail; moderate for longer walks
Maps: USGS Northwest Durham, Hillsborough, and Chapel Hill. The best map of Duke Forest can be purchased from the website below (recent changes are shown on the site's downloadable maps).

Elevation gain: Negligible, with a few ups and downs on Korstian Division trails
Water availability: No designated water sources in Duke Forest, so bring your own.
For more information: Office of Duke Forest, Duke University; (919) 613-8013; dukeforest.duke.edu. Closures due to logging and other activities are listed on the site.

FINDING THE TRAILHEADS

To reach the Durham Division of Duke Forest and the trailhead for the Al Buehler Cross-Country Trail from the east, take exit 175 from I-85 and go south on US 15/501. Take the NC 751 exit (exit 107) and go left on NC 751. In 0.4 mile turn right into the gravel parking lot (GPS: 35.997017 / -78.951417).

To reach other trailheads in this tract go right (west) on NC 751; all but one trailhead are on the left. From the traffic light at the US 15/501 exit, go 0.6 mile to gate 3 (GPS: 36.007057 / -78.966038), 1.3 miles to gates 7 (GPS: 36.012039 / -78.973940) and C (latter, on the right), 2 miles to gate 11 (GPS: 36.019899 / -78.984445), and 2.5 miles to gate 12 (GPS: 36.025337 / -78.989393). The T junction with US 70 is at 3 miles; go left there to I-85 at 4.2 miles.

From the west leave I-40 at the NC 751/University exit (exit 170) and turn right onto NC 751 at 1.2 miles. All but one trailhead are on the right. From I-85, gate 12 is at 1.7 miles, gate 11 is at 2.2 miles, gates 7 and C are at 2.9 miles (the latter on the left), and gate 3 is at 3.6 miles. A right turn onto Erwin Road (SR 1306) at 4.1 miles from I-85 takes you to the Korstian Division.

To reach the Korstian Division of Duke Forest and the Bluffs Trail, follow the directions above for the Durham Division. After exiting US 15/501 go right on NC 751, then immediately left on Erwin Road (SR 1306). Go south past Mount Sinai Road (SR 1718) at 1.7 miles, pass gate 27 and New Hope Creek at about 2.4 miles, and take the next right on Whitfield Road (SR 1731) at 3.1 miles. The start of the Bluffs hike, gate 26, is on the right 0.7 mile after the turn to Whitfield Road (GPS: 35.977836 / -79.016466). Gate 25 is reached at 1 mile (GPS: 35.977958 / -79.022605), and gate 24 is located at 1.5 miles (GPS: 35.977471 / -79.030423).

THE HIKES

At 2,400 acres, Duke Forest's Durham Division is the largest of the forest tracts. Just across NC 751 south of the main Duke University campus, the Al Buehler Cross-Country Trail is a favorite hike/jog honoring the university's legendary track coach. Going west from the gravel parking area on the south side of NC 751, the 2.9-mile, gravel loop trail roughly follows Brownings Branch, then Sandy Creek, in a triangle around the Duke University golf course that passes emergency phones. Add on the 0.6-mile fitness loop in the northeast corner of the trail to make the hike about 3.5 miles. In 2019 the fitness loop was completely renovated with 20 new fitness stations.

The bulk of the Durham Division acreage lies west of there, between NC 15/501 and NC 751's intersection with US 70. Three nice hikes are possible in this area. Going west from the Al Buehler Cross-Country Trail on NC 751, you'll pass forest access gates 3 through 13 and lettered gates on both sides of the road. Picnic shelters are accessible to renters via gates F and C (where the Shepherd Nature Trail is located).

Duke Forest is particularly popular when the hot Piedmont summer turns to fall.
COURTESY OF DUKE FOREST

Between gates 3 and 7, hikers have a 1.5-mile semicircular hike with two cars or a 3-mile out-and-back walk from either trailhead. Hitting the trail from gate 3, one of the forest's oldest stands lies off on the left opposite a once similar-aged stand on the right that's been harvested. Pass Pine Thicket Fire Trail on the left, and cross Mud Creek on a scenic wooden bridge. The trail turns from south to north and crosses a creek. Where the next fire trail heads right to gate 6, bear left to gate 7.

Directly across the road from gate 7, gate C accesses the Shepherd Nature Trail, one of the forest's outstanding resources. In 2017, the trail's treadway and facilities were greatly improved and the path's worn and outdated interpretive signs were replaced with state-of-the-art displays. This is one of the Piedmont's most insightful interpretive hikes. Topics include the forest's ecology, management, and history of human use. The trail goes left into the woods from the fire trail where a picnic shelter lies beyond. The 0.8-mile loop wanders up and down across small streams through mixed pine and hardwoods. Check the website; the trail's interpretive signs can be studied online. School and other groups are encouraged to register online before their visit and consider renting the picnic shelter by the trailhead.

Farther west, Couch Mountain (640 feet), the tract's highest prominence, has two trailheads. Starting on the fire trail at the first gate (11), pass two other fire trails that branch left. Go left on the third fire trail; to reach the end loop on the summit, keep straight where a trail soon goes left (the Couch Mountain Fire Trail that starts at gate 20).

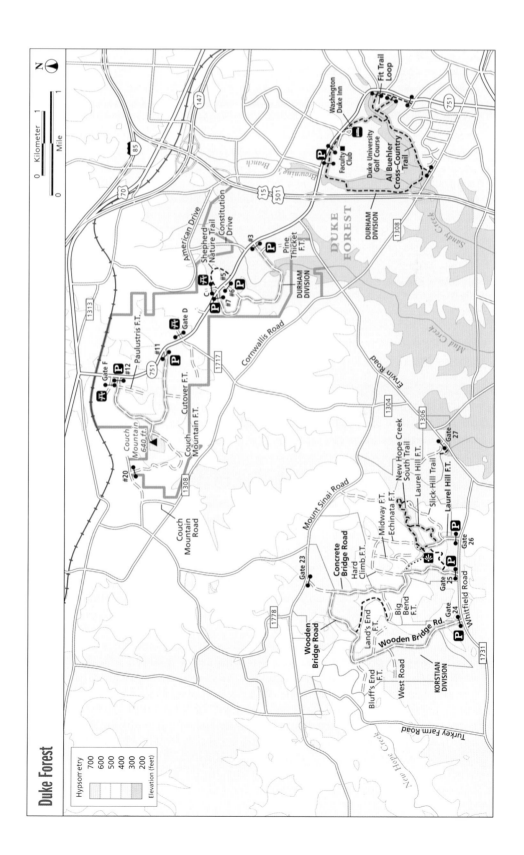

Duke Forest

N

0 Kilometer 1

0 Mile 1

Hypsometry

700
600
500
400
300
200

Elevation (feet)

Fit Trail Loop

Washington Duke Inn

Duke University Golf Course

Faculty Club

Al Buehler Cross–Country Trail

751

DUKE FOREST

DURHAM DIVISION

1308

Sandy Creek

Mud Creek

Browning's Branch

85

70

147

15
501

American Drive

Shepherd Nature Trail

Constitution Drive

Pine Thicket F.T.

#3

#5

#6

#7

Gate D

DURHAM DIVISION

P

P

P

P

Cornwallis Road

1313

Paulustris F.T.

#11

Gate F

#12

Gate F

751

Cutover F.T.

Couch Mountain F.T.

1717

Couch Mountain 640 ft.

#20

1308

Couch Mountain Road

Erwin Road

1304

1306

Gate 27

Laurel Hill F.T.

Slick Hill Trail

New Hope Creek South Trail

Laurel Hill F.T.

Midway F.T.

Echinata F.T.

Gate 26

Mount Sinai Road

Gate 23

Concrete Bridge Road

Hard Climb F.T.

Big Bend F.T.

Gate 25

Gate 24

Whitfield Road

1731

Wooden Bridge Road

Land's End F.T.

Wooden Bridge Rd.

Bluff's End F.T.

West Road

KORSTIAN DIVISION

1778

Turkey Farm Road

New Hope Creek

Retrace your steps and go left on the main fire trail. It turns sharply right along a power line to gate 12 on NC 751, approximately a 2.5-mile hike.

The 2,000-acre Korstian Division is Duke Forest's scenic gem. Two loop hikes from gate 26 to Laurel Hill Bluffs are the most scenic walks in the forest. On the north-facing outcrop above New Hope Creek, Catawba rhododendron and mountain laurel bloom far from their normal mountain habitat. This area has seen major trail improvement in recent years—please stay on the new paths to heal environmental impact.

Leave gate 26 on Laurel Hill Fire Trail and stay left when the Slick Hill Fire Trail and then Laurel Hill Trail bear right. The fire trail ends where trails branch left and right. Left, a connector goes to Concrete Bridge Road and gate 26 (another starting point); turn right on the gradual new Rhodo Bluff Trail. Take a left on the Rhodo Bluff Spur across boardwalks to rocky crags above the creek (please stay on the trail). Retrace your steps from here for an out-and-back walk of just more than 1 mile.

From the bluffs, two trails connect down to the stream to create loops with the trails you passed on the way in (the Slick Hill Fire and Laurel Hill Trails). Take either the newly improved Creek Connector or the High & Dry Trail to where the New Hope Creek South Trail wanders downstream on one of the forest's most attractive walks. A rapid about 200 yards east of the bluffs is a popular spot to cool off in summer. The Laurel Hill Trail soon leads right to the Laurel Hill Fire Trail you came in on, creating a loop of about 1.3 miles back at gate 26.

Continuing on New Hope Creek, there's a scenic island in the stream just past a streamlet on the right. Near more rock outcroppings overlooking New Hope Creek, the now streamside trail makes a short end loop. Going right, the Slick Hill Trail departs uphill to Slick Hill Fire Trail, the first trail you passed near gate 26. This biggest loop is a 2-mile hike back at your car.

Gate 25 is about 0.3 mile west of gate 26, and that offers other options, the most exciting being a way to expand the biggest loop from gate 25. Leaving gate 25 on the Concrete Bridge Road, hike in to New Hope Creek (passing the gate 26 connector on the way, your return route). At the creek, turn right along an unimproved part of New Hope Creek South Trail that floods in high water. Climb up the Creek Connector to visit the bluffs and then continue around either of the loops described above. Back above the creek on Laurel Hill Fire Trail, turn west onto the gate 25 connector back to your car—a long woodsy walk of 3 miles.

Also from gate 25, the Concrete Bridge Road makes a nice hike to gate 24. The fire trail crosses New Hope Creek and veers left where Hard Climb Fire Trail branches right to a variety of side routes. Go left and continue on Concrete Bridge Road, passing Big Bend Fire Trail as it heads left to the river. Turn left onto Wooden Bridge Road (straight ahead the Concrete Bridge Road reaches gate 23 on Mount Sinai Road).

Follow Wooden Bridge Road by going left at the next T intersection. Now heading south on Wooden Bridge Road, the trail turns sharply northwest and crosses New Hope Creek on a wooden bridge. Across the creek the trail passes under a power line, turns sharply south again, and passes the Bluff's End Fire Trail on the right. Continuing, the trail again goes under the power line past Land's End Fire Trail on the left, West Road on the right, and makes its way to gate 24 at about 4 miles. Taking the trail from gate 25 out as far as the second bridge makes an out-and-back hike of about 5 miles. Or go left at that bridge on a streamside path back to Big Bend Fire Trail for a woodsier loop of similar length.

39 WILLIAM B. UMSTEAD STATE PARK

Despite Raleigh-Durham International Airport and I-40 literally hugging the boundary of William B. Umstead State Park, the 5,579 acres in the park's two main tracts (Reedy Creek, emphasized here, and Crabtree Creek) have real appeal for hikers.

The bulk of the park was acquired in 1934 under a Resettlement Administration program that turned exhausted farmland into recreation areas. The Civilian Conservation Corps (CCC) went to work; the park debuted in 1937 and was deeded to the state in 1943 for $1. In 1950, during the dark days of Jim Crow, a second parcel was added to create a separate park for African Americans. The larger park was named for conservation-minded former governor William B. Umstead in 1955. The two parks merged in 1966 when segregation ended. The park's visitor center, built in 2001 in the Crabtree Creek part of the park, where the most developed facilities are located, does a great job of interpreting park history, including the ongoing evidence of the CCC and the many gristmills once found in this part of the Piedmont.

With state park stewardship, the area is now reverting to towering deciduous forest like it was prior to 1774, when a land grant opened the area to settlement. An isolated 50-acre tract, the Piedmont Beech Natural Area, recalls that forest with an impressive stand of virgin trees more than 300 years old.

The park has 22 miles of hiking-only trails and 13 miles of "MUTs"—not dogs, but "multiuse trails" for horseback riding, mountain biking, and foot traffic (labeled "MUT" on the map). Three lakes allow fishing; rowboats and canoes are available in Big Lake, the park's largest at 55 acres (no private boats allowed). Public swimming is permitted only in one lake for renters of the park's extensive cabin camps, which are available for youth groups and nonprofits. The park also has a tent campground with showers, open March 15 to December 1, and a twenty-five-person, 1930s accommodation called Maple Hill Lodge. Two primitive group camping areas are open year-round. No backpack camping is permitted.

When considering hikes or even mountain bike rides in Umstead, keep in mind that this park's multiple loops of road-width MUTs seamlessly connect to adjacent urban trail systems. The Reedy Creek MUT links south to greenway trails across I-40 in Cary's extensive trail network, forty years old in 2019. That gives hikers and bikers great pedestrian access to Umstead from Cary (get the town's trail map on this page: https://www.townofcary.org/recreation-enjoyment/parks-greenways-environment/greenways). That same connectivity reaches to Raleigh's greenway network, from the Cedar Ridge MUT in the east, and the Reedy Creek MUT in Umstead's southeast corner (to the NC Museum of Art, see Reedy Creek Trail in entry 41). In that latter area, Umstead's out-and-back hiking path the Loblolly Trail also leaves the park and connects to and beyond Schenck Forest (see entry 40).

COMPANY MILL CIRCUITS

WHY GO?
A variety of hikes in a state park on the fall line.

THE RUNDOWN

General location: Reedy Creek section, William B. Umstead State Park, west of Raleigh

Distance: Two looping nature walks, 0.7 mile on the Inspiration Trail; two longer circuit hikes of approximately 5 and 5.9 miles on parts of the Company Mill Trail; a circuit of Company Mill and Sycamore Trail of 9 miles; a short interpretive TRACK Trail of 0.6 mile

Difficulty: Easy for the shortest stroll; moderate to moderately strenuous for the longest circuits

Maps: USGS Cary, Raleigh West, Bayleaf, and East Durham. Download a trail map at the park's website (see below).

Elevation gain: Undulating terrain, without sustained elevation changes

Water availability: The picnic area where Reedy Creek trails start has restrooms and water year-round; the park's visitor center is open 9 to 5 p.m. daily year-round. Treat stream water before using.

For more information: William B. Umstead State Park, 8801 Glenwood Ave., Raleigh 27617; (919) 571-4170; ncparks.gov/Visit/parks/stmo/directions.php; e-mail: william .umstead@ncparks.gov

FINDING THE TRAILHEAD

The Reedy Creek area trails begin near I-40. Heading east on I-40, take exit 287, the Cary-Harrison Avenue exit. Go left at the stoplight onto Harrison Avenue, which leads immediately into the park. After entering the state park, take a left into the parking area where trails leave the end of the lot on both sides (GPS: 35.836265/-78.759381). Just across I-40 from the park, the upscale Umstead Hotel and Spa is a great base of operations for exploring the park. It's within walking distance, and guests can reserve free mountain bikes; theumstead.com.

To reach the Crabtree Creek Section, leave I-540 north of Raleigh at either exit 7 or 7B. Take Glenwood Avenue/US 70 northwest and make a left onto Umstead Parkway. Turn left into the visitor center for the Sal's Branch Trailhead (GPS: 35.880706/-78.758268). For the Oak Rock Interpretive TRACK Trail, stay right beyond the visitor center to the first part of the last long parking area on the left (GPS: 35.874266/-78.760785). For the Sycamore and Potts Branch Trails, pass that left and park near the end of the last parking area (GPS: 35.871570/-78.760885).

THE HIKES

The easy Inspiration Trail is an aptly named loop through a large forest in a designated natural area of virgin beech forest along Crabtree Creek. Leave the left end of the lot on the orange square–blazed Company Mill Trail. Go left on the Inspiration Trail loop, marked with blue diamonds. There are benches for quiet contemplation. Back at the parking lot, it's a 0.7-mile round-trip.

The Company Mill Trail, just less than 6 miles, is the longest loop on this side of the park. Beyond the Inspiration Trail, the Company Mill Trail descends and crosses a metal bridge over lazy, 15-foot-wide Crabtree Creek.

Cross the bridge to a T junction; go right, and in 100 feet notice a pile of boulders on the opposite side of the stream. These rocks indicate the ruins of a dam and gristmill,

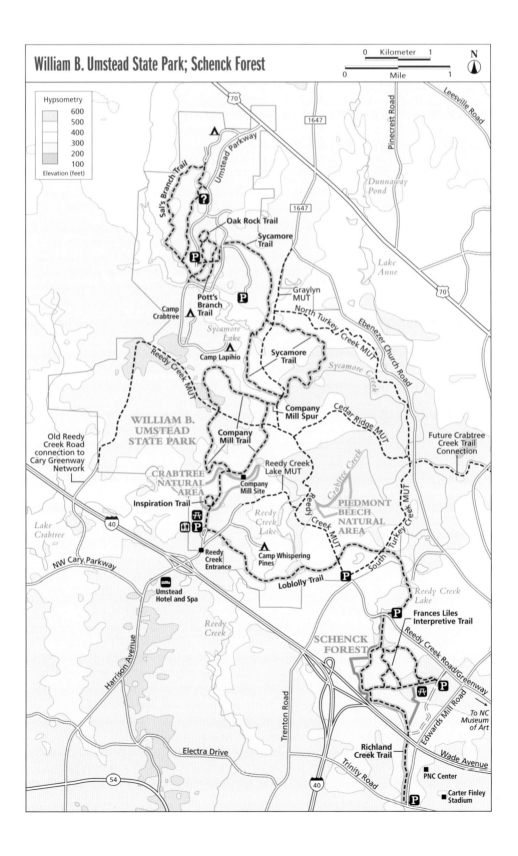

William B. Umstead State Park; Schenck Forest

0   Kilometer   1
0   Mile   1

N

Hypsometry
600
500
400
300
200
100
Elevation (feet)

Leesville Road

70

1647

Pinecrest Road

Dunnaway Pond

1647

Lake Anne

70

Umstead Parkway

Sal's Branch Trail

Oak Rock Trail

Sycamore Trail

P

Pott's Branch Trail

P

Graylyn MUT

North Turkey Creek MUT

Ebenezer Church Road

Camp Crabtree

Sycamore Lake

Camp Lapihio

Sycamore Trail

Sycamore Creek

Cedar Ridge MUT

Reedy Creek MUT

WILLIAM B. UMSTEAD STATE PARK

Company Mill Spur

Company Mill Trail

Old Reedy Creek Road connection to Cary Greenway Network

CRABTREE NATURAL AREA

Inspiration Trail

Company Mill Site

Reedy Creek Lake MUT

Crabtree Creek

Future Crabtree Creek Trail Connection

PIEDMONT BEECH NATURAL AREA

Lake Crabtree

40

Reedy Creek Lake

Reedy Creek MUT

South Turkey Creek MUT

NW Cary Parkway

Reedy Creek Entrance

Camp Whispering Pines

Loblolly Trail

P

Reedy Creek Lake

Umstead Hotel and Spa

Reedy Creek

P

Frances Liles Interpretive Trail

Reedy Creek Road/Greenway

Harrison Avenue

SCHENCK FOREST

P

To NC Museum of Art

Edwards Mill Road

Trenton Road

Electra Drive

Richland Creek Trail

Wade Avenue

54

40

Trinity Road

PNC Center

P

Carter Finley Stadium

an early economic focal point of the Raleigh area, in use as early as 1810. Farmers used flatboats or wagons to haul grains and produce here for sale and processing. The community gathered for dances and for swimming and boating in the pond behind the dam.

Nearby, one of the mill's grindstones is displayed beside the trail. It had been assumed that the millstones, possibly manufactured in France, had washed away or been stolen, but in the winter of 1993–94 a park historian exploring the riverbed found the stone standing upright against the bank 200 feet below the dam. National Guard helicopters lifted it out of the stream. The round-trip to this nice turnaround point is about 2 miles.

Continuing east, not far from the dam, an old eighteenth-century stage road bears left and uphill, where some ruins are visible. The main trail follows a side ravine and rises to the Reedy Creek MUT, a centuries-old route between Raleigh and Durham. A left on this 0.7-mile link bisects the Company Mill Trail loop across a height of land that separates the park's two stream drainages. The Reedy Creek MUT continues west past the Company Mill Trail, to the Old Reedy Creek Road park access, another starting point that's also connected to Cary's greenway trails. Dropping off the ridge to a junction at 2.3 miles, the 0.2-mile Company Mill Spur goes right, a link to the Graylyn MUT that connects to the Sycamore Trail, an adjacent loop hike from the other side of the park (more below). Going left, the trail passes the George Linn Mill site, in use in 1870 but now difficult to identify. The trail climbs gently along a stream, passing lush ferns, then climbs the ridge to the Reedy Creek MUT, about 1 mile from the last junction and 3.3 miles from the parking area. Company Mill Trail descends to Crabtree Creek at 4.4 miles and then crosses a small stream to the loop junction at about 4.9 miles. Back at the parking area, the hike is 5.9 miles. If you bisect the Company Mill Trail using the Reedy Creek MUT, the loop is a bit more than 5 miles.

For a really nice long day hike, head right on the Company Mill Spur at 2.3 miles, then left on the Graylyn MUT over a rustic old bridge, and turn right on the blue triangle–blazed Sycamore Trail. Wander the drainage above Sycamore Creek, then turn away left at 3.6 miles to follow a side stream. Leaving the stream, the trail crosses the Graylyn MUT then reaches the Sycamore Trail loop junction at 4.4 miles. Go left on Sycamore Trail and switchback down along Sycamore Creek not far below Sycamore Lake. Go right again at 5.3 miles on the Graylyn MUT, then right again on Company Mill Spur to end on that loop (see above). That total hike is just more than 9 miles and includes the scenic heart of the Sycamore Trail, the park's longest single trail at 7.2 miles when hiked from its start near shelter number one reached from the Crabtree Creek entrance.

Also from the Reedy Creek parking area, the park's Loblolly Trail runs 2.7 miles to the park boundary (and beyond to Schenck Forest). It's a nice out-and-back walk, but a return on the Reedy Creek MUT can turn it into a loop (see the map).

The Crabtree Creek part of the park has other trails worth considering. From the visitor center the orange circle–marked Sal's Branch Trail forms a nearly 3-mile loop, part of it a lakeside walk above Big Lake. From the most distant parking area beyond the visitor center, three other loops circle to the east from the same parking area. At the first part of the parking area, the 0.6-mile, white square–marked Oak Rock Interpretive Trail is the park's TRACK Trail. The trees here are big (take *The Need for Trees* brochure). There's evidence of the early CCC construction at Umstead, and a side trail reaches inspiring Oak Rock, a big oak growing out of a jumble of boulders.

Farther down the lot, the orange diamond–blazed Pott's Branch Trail makes a 1.3-mile loop. That loop is bisected by the Sycamore Trail as it leads 2.1 miles to where its own loop splits (the section already mentioned in the longer Company Mill hike above).

40 SCHENCK FOREST

WHY GO?

Like Duke Forest near Durham, Schenck Forest is a university research tract. Just southeast of Umstead State Park, the woodsy 245 acres serve North Carolina State University's Department of Forestry. It was established in 1936 with the planting of 80 acres of loblolly pine on exhausted fields by the Depression-era Works Progress Administration. The forest has an easy loop hike called the Frances Liles Interpretive Trail. The lengthy Richland Creek Trail also passes through the forest, connecting to William B. Umstead State Park's Loblolly Trail to the west and PNC Arena and North Carolina State University's Carter Finley Stadium to the east. The forest's main parking area on Reedy Creek Road is close to the paved Reedy Creek Greenway, which also links west to the state park's multiuse trails (and Loblolly Trail) and runs east to the North Carolina Museum of Art and downtown Raleigh. That makes it easy to ride your bike to hikes at Schenck Forest and Umstead State Park. No dogs, bikes, horses, hunting, or geocaching are permitted in the forest—and do not block gates.

THE RUNDOWN

(See map on page 271.)
General location: William B. Umstead State Park, Raleigh
Distance: 6 miles one way on Richland Creek Trail/Loblolly Trail; 1.2 miles round trip for the Frances Liles trail. When linked with the Liles trail, Richland Creek and Loblolly Trail circuit hikes are about 5 miles round-trip from PNC Arena and 10 miles round-trip from Umstead State Park's Reedy Creek starting point.
Difficulty: Moderately strenuous for the 6-mile end-to-end hike and out-and-back circuits. The Frances Liles Trail and related loops are easy.
Maps: USGS Cary and Raleigh West. Download trail maps at the parks' website (see below).

Elevation gain: Minimal, except for undulating terrain in Umstead State Park
Water availability: Water is available year-round in the picnic area near the Umstead State Park trailhead and during summer at the Schenck Forest picnic area.
For more information: William B. Umstead State Park; ncparks.gov/Visit/parks/wium/main.php. Schenck Forest; (919) 515-2883; Schenck Forest: sites.google.com/a/ncsu.edu/ncsudof-forests/home/carlalwinschenckmemorialforest#TOC-Map; e-mail: naturalresources@ncsu.edu

FINDING THE TRAILHEADS

To reach the Loblolly Trail's northern trailhead in William B. Umstead State Park, head east on I-40, taking exit 287, the Cary–Harrison Avenue exit. Go left at the stoplight onto Harrison Avenue, which leads immediately into the park. After entering the state park, take a left into the parking area where the trail leaves the end of the lot on the right.

To reach the southern terminus at PNC Arena, take Wade Avenue exit (289 from I-40) then exit at Edwards Mill Road. Go south and turn left into the

Center at 0.5 mile. Make an immediate left into the trailhead parking area (GPS: 35.800918/-78.725417).

To reach the Schenck Forest's Frances Liles Interpretive Trail, also take the Wade Avenue and Edwards Mill Road exits, but go north 0.8 mile and turn left onto greenway-flanked Reedy Creek Road. Go another 0.2 mile and turn left into the trailhead. Park under the trees by the gate, but don't block it (GPS: 35.815865/-78.723339). Park here and spot another car at Umstead State Park or PNC Arena to hike the upper or lower sections of the trail. From Schenck, one option is to walk the roadside greenway for 1.3 miles to the park's Trenton Road gate at the Trenton Road/Reedy Creek Park Road junction. From there, the shortest route to the state park's Loblolly Trail parking area is to go left on the Reedy Creek MUT, then left again on the Loblolly Trail.

THE HIKES

From parking near the PNC Arena, take the paved white-blazed Richland Creek Trail along a chain-link fence to a grassy sewer line right-of-way. A lighted pedestrian tunnel goes under Edwards Mill Road at 0.3 mile. At about 0.6 mile, a longer lighted tunnel goes under Wade Avenue. This portion of the trail may not be well-maintained and may confound even experienced hikers.

North of Wade Avenue, the white-blazed trail passes through Schenck Forest. Follow the streambank left, with meadows off to the right. At about 1.2 miles a road-width earth-surfaced grade goes right (and leads to the forest's formal parking area, creating a big loop—see the map and below). The sounds of Wade Avenue accompany the path along scenic Richland Creek. Throughout the area, signs note types of trees and describe forestry practices. The loblolly pine, the trail's namesake when it enters Umstead State Park, is everywhere. Near the upper end of Reedy Creek Lake, the path enters a forested wetland where beavers have gnawed river birch, red maple, and sweet gum. Deer and wood ducks are often visible.

At about 2 miles, as you near the lake, the trail intersects the Frances Liles Interpretive Trail (more below). Beyond, Richland Creek Trail rises higher above the lake to Reedy Creek Road, which spans the lake at just more than 2 miles.

Cross Reedy Creek Road and the greenway through a break in the guardrail. Right, the scenic paved greenway leads to the NC Museum of Art, left to Umstead State Park. Across the road, the trail dips into a damp forest around a cove then rises to drier ground. Side paths lead to lakeshore views and fishing spots. Pass a subdivision near the dam, part of a tide of development in the area. Follow the path past privacy fences to the base of the dam and go right. Cross a gate and follow a grassy old grade as it turns left back into rising woods.

At just more than 3 miles in the middle of the woods, a signpost marks the meeting with Umstead State Park's Loblolly Trail, which leads onward 2.7 miles to the main trailhead at the Reedy Creek entrance to the park.

Just beyond the post, the blue square–blazed Loblolly Trail crosses the red circle–blazed South Turkey Creek MUT that loops through the park (left, it's not far to the park's Trenton Road gate—see "Finding the trailhead"). The path crosses a stream near a small woodland lake just less than 4 miles from PNC Arena. A few tenths farther, Loblolly crosses the Reedy Creek MUT. (A left on this MUT back to the Trenton Road gate permits a loop back to Schenck Forest via the roadside greenway trail.)

The final section of the Loblolly Trail passes into the more developed part of Umstead State Park through open, fern-filled forest, undulating over ridges and three stream

Schenck Forest's Frances Liles Interpretive Trail can be a short loop or part of a longer hike.

crossings, the lattermost being Reedy Creek. The Loblolly Trail crosses the park maintenance road (about 5.7 miles from PNC Arena) to end at the Reedy Creek parking area,
about 4 miles from the greenway crossing on Reedy Creek Road, just less than 6 miles
from PNC Arena.

Even without the Loblolly Trail, Schenck Forest's Frances Liles Interpretive Trail is
an ideal destination—but again many hikers find this and other trails in the forest to be
ambiguously marked. The trail opened in the early 1980s. Past the gate, the log-lined trail
starts with a right turn off the forest road and leads through tall loblollies toward meadows akin to the pine savannas of the coastal Croatan National Forest. A left at the first
junction leads to a picnic shelter area (also reached with a short walk down the gated road
from the trailhead). Plaques at the well-appointed, grassy picnic spot honor Carl Alwin
Schenck (1868–1955), founder and director of the Biltmore Forest School, birthplace of
forestry in America. His ashes were scattered here.

Go right at that first junction and again at a second to descend into a mixed pine and
deciduous forest where signs identify trees and explain forestry practices. The trees reach
impressive proportions where the open understory is covered in Christmas ferns. Wind
down a scenic stream drainage over bridges. At the next junction, a right shortly reaches
the Richland Creek Trail and an old hydrological stream flow station (at about 0.5 mile).

The simplest hike is to go left at the junction just above the Richland Creek Trail.
The path becomes a forest road past interpretive signs. Where the road turns right, bear
left on the path through a scenic pine grove. You eventually reach a T junction at a

You can be minutes from traffic and still feel like you're in a forest along Raleigh's miles of greenway paths.

more-trafficked forest road. Left, the road leads directly to the picnic area and gate by your car, for a 1.2-mile hike. To the right, this forest road intersects the Richland Creek Trail (see the map) at the edge of Schenck Forest near the trail tunnel. With connections like that, the Richland Creek Trail, Liles Trail, and other forest roads make Schenck a wonderful parcel to explore on its own. For out-and-back day hikes, start on the Richland Creek Trail from the PNC Arena and loop the Liles Trail for a 5-mile round-trip circuit. From Umstead State Park, the circuit is about 10 miles round-trip. Either way, Schenck's picnic area makes for a good mid-hike lunch spot.

41 RALEIGH

WHY GO?

These are exciting times in Raleigh. With about 40 new miles of trail added in five years, the city and its greenway-loving residents are putting the finishing touches on a more than 100 mile system of greenways that's not just the largest urban trail network in the state. Raleigh aspires higher, to double the trail system in 30 years. The city's world-class trail system connects neighborhoods to significant natural, cultural, and commercial attractions forming an alternative transportation system for pedestrians. On top of that, new city parks linked by the trails are being designed to provide a wide range of complementary activities. Now more than ever, Raleigh can be called "the park with a city in it."

While budget cutting has hobbled trail initiatives elsewhere, Raleigh is making trails a priority. City ordinances require developers to grant greenway easements in undeveloped areas targeted by the greenway master plan. And Raleigh residents consistently support greenway and park bond referendums. It's no wonder this progressive state capital excites trail enthusiasts.

Most Raleigh greenways are paved urban paths, but many portions are downright scenic and even natural-surfaced. One section of trail dispenses orange vests for use during bow hunting season! The city's 27-mile Neuse River Trail and a 60-mile path along Falls Lake are enticing parts of North Carolina's Mountains-to-Sea Trail. The Reedy Creek Greenway links other paths in downtown and reaches all the way to Umstead State Park via the North Carolina Museum of Art campus by traversing the longest pedestrian bridge in the state. Expect expansion to continue. In the next few years, the Crabtree Creek Trail will also reach Umstead State Park, spanning all of Wake County with a greenway.

THE RUNDOWN

(See map on page 283.)
General location: Raleigh
Difficulty: Easy to moderate
Distance: Greenway system hikes range from short to lengthy. See the individual hikes below.
Maps: USGS Raleigh East for Buckeye Trail; Raleigh West for Lake Johnson, Shelley Lake (Bent Creek and Sawmill Trails), and Lake Lynn. To appreciate the options and locate trailheads, download a copy of the city's Capital Area Greenway System map on this page: raleighnc.gov/parks/content/

PRecDesignDevelop/Articles/Capital AreaGreenwayTrailSystem.html.
Elevation gain: Negligible, with gradual grades
Water availability: Many greenways have warm-weather water fountains on premises or at adjacent public parks. But it's better to bring your own.
For more information: Raleigh Parks, Recreation and Cultural Resources, PO Box 590, Raleigh 27602; (919) 996-3285; e-mail: parkplan@raleigh nc.gov; mountainstoseatrail.org/

In rural areas around the state capital, the Mountains-to-Sea Trail passes through pastoral Piedmont scenes.

CRABTREE CREEK TRAIL

FINDING THE TRAILHEAD

This hike starts at the east side of Raleigh Boulevard at its intersection with Crabtree Boulevard, just southeast of Capital Boulevard. Parking is available on Crabtree Boulevard just 0.1 mile west of its junction with Raleigh Boulevard where the trail leaves the roadside (GPS: 35.803670 / -78.610492). From the same parking area, there's also nice lakeside wildlife viewing from a greenway boardwalk west of Raleigh Boulevard.

THE HIKE

This paved section of the Crabtree Creek Trail in southeast Raleigh (once called the Buckeye Trail) is one of Raleigh's earliest greenways and leads to some of the most unusual scenery in the system. From Raleigh Boulevard, the wooded trail heads east along the floodplain. At about 1.4 miles it leaves the creek to parallel Crabtree Boulevard past a playground and recreation fields. Back in the woods, the most interesting section of the trail passes through rich forest containing the namesake buckeye, as well as river birch and pine. There are good views of the creek and surrounding forest atop creekside bluffs. An out-and-back hike from the trailhead to here is about a 4-mile round-trip. From the bluffs, it's about 0.5 mile east to Milburnie Road (greenway parking at 2901 Milburnie Rd.). A round-trip hike there and back is about 5 miles. From Milburnie Road, the newest section of the Crabtree Creek Greenway turns left to rejoin the creek on its way another 4.1 miles to Anderson Point Park on the Neuse River.

To visit a wetland wildlife-viewing area west of Raleigh Boulevard on the greenway, walk southeast toward the hike above, but turn left across Crabtree Boulevard and go north on Raleigh Boulevard. Cross the Crabtree Creek Bridge and turn left on the greenway across a lengthy boardwalk over marshy wetlands and open water to a gazebo viewing shelter. Turn around for an 0.8-mile round-trip hike or continue to where the boardwalk meets the soil tread.

LAKE JOHNSON TRAIL

FINDING THE TRAILHEAD

The Lake Johnson Trail, in southwest Raleigh, lies adjacent to I-40/440 and is reached via exit 295. Exiting there, go north on Gorman Street and turn left onto Avent Ferry Road. The main trailhead parking area is beside the lake at the Water Front Program Center, 4601 Avent Ferry Rd. (GPS: 35.762834 / -78.714302), but the best trailhead may be near Athens Drive High School stadium. To start there take a right from Avent Ferry Road onto Athens Drive before reaching the Water Front Program Center parking area. Turn left just after the high school on Jaguar Park Drive toward the Lake Johnson pool. Stay right into the large stadium parking area, where a trail connects to the lake's northwest end (GPS: 35.769983 / -78.717746).

THE HIKE

The Lake Johnson Trail loops this scenic 150-acre lake with paved and unpaved wooded trails. The lake is also popular for boating (many kinds of craft available for rent) and fishing (not allowed from lakeshore). Avent Ferry Road and a separate pedestrian bridge (the latter not shown on our map) split the lake, permitting small loops on each end or a larger circle of the entire lakeshore. Going east from the Waterfront Program Center trailhead, the paved path winds along the lakeshore in mature forest, then turns with the lakeshore and crosses the dam and spillway at about 0.8 mile. A left before the dam, and after, leads to another parking area on Lake Dam Drive (GPS: 35.763073 / -78.703826) where the Walnut Creek Trail heads downstream 15 miles to the Neuse River. Across the dam, keep right where the Walnut Creek link goes left. The main trail parallels the shore; at about 1.1 miles, a woodsier path turns right along the lakeshore. Take that if you want to hike beside the water (more below). Ascend a ridge to a trail split—go either way; the trails meet after looping a knob. At their junction, close to 2 miles into the hike, the trail descends south then turns west through stands of bigleaf magnolia.

Turn right at a junction on a paved side trail that splits into an end loop with access to a lakeshore viewpoint. The woodsy path along the lakeshore also passes this view. Take the paved loop back to the main path and the greenway and woods trail join again by the nearby South Lake parking area on Avent Ferry Road (GPS: 35.758998 / -78.716955). To return to your car, cross the 700 feet of boardwalk bridge that reaches the program center side of the lake. The total hike is about 3.5 miles on the paved trail, a little shorter on the lakeshore trail with the more natural experience.

To loop the western side of the lake, go under Avent Ferry Road to an unpaved woods path along the southern lakeshore. (You could just hike this side of the lake by crossing the boardwalk from the program center boathouse and then Avent Ferry Road.) At the

Raleigh's lakeshore greenway trails offer a wealth of wildlife viewing opportunities. This Great Blue Heron is chilling in Lake Lynn.

head of the lake, about 1.1 miles from the road, a 380-foot boardwalk crosses Walnut Creek. Just beyond the boardwalk, a paved trail goes left 0.2 mile to the parking area near the high school stadium and an unpaved path branches right along the northern side of the lake. It's about 0.9 mile back to the program center at Avent Ferry Road for a little more than 2-mile hike. The loop of the entire lake is just over 5.5 miles via the paved trail on the eastern side of the lake, about 4.4 miles if you take the woods trail instead.

LAKE LYNN

FINDING THE TRAILHEAD

The Lake Lynn Trail, in northwest Raleigh, starts at the main parking area below the dam off Lynn Road between Leesville Road and Ray Road (GPS: 35.872514/-78.697738). The less-urban Lake Lynn Park Trailhead (GPS: 35.887417/ -78.698030) is located at 7921 Ray Rd., 1.4 miles north of Lynn Road; make a left into the park.

THE HIKE

Lake Lynn is a jewel in Raleigh's greenway crown, looped by a section of the Hare Snipe Creek Trail greenway. Unlike more circular lakes in the system, Lake Lynn is narrow; its shore hike offers a wealth of coves, albeit with residences not far away. The paved trail provides a particularly natural experience near the marshy head of the lake, where 0.5 mile of boardwalks skirt away from the banks and wander over the water to enclose coves and create a unique lakeshore hike.

The 2.2-mile hike starts from the parking area below the dam on Lynn Road; another recommended trailhead is located near the marshy upper end of the lake where the greenway leaves the loop to reach the Lake Lynn Community Center in Lake Lynn Park. Leaving the main parking area on Lynn Road, take the feeder path to the greenway loop and go right (east) across the dam. The trail swings north past the first of many residential developments and crosses a boardwalk bridge over a cove. The next boardwalk bridges a wooded cove between two other urban lakeshore developments. By the time you finish this hike, you'll think you're wandering through a remarkably woodsy resort condo complex.

The trail leaves the city growth as it enters Lake Lynn Park near the head of the lake. It swings across wetlands on a lengthy and impressive boardwalk, at times over water, other times over marshland. The first section of boardwalk holds a trail junction. Left, the boardwalk continues the lakeshore loop; straight, it reaches land and joins a paved path to the parking area at the community center, about 0.4 mile (which makes the lake loop 3 miles for hikers starting there).

Go left across Hare Snipe Creek and the boardwalk reaches another junction, where a right turn dead-ends where the boardwalk used to reach a nearby neighborhood. Go left and cross a long stretch of water. Again on the lakeshore, a paved side trail leads right to a neighborhood. Continuing, the trail crosses a long boardwalk not far from shore that then encloses a cove. Just beyond that point, the trail leaves the park, passes other developments, and crosses two more boardwalks before rounding a point back to the trailhead.

SHELLEY LAKE/SERTOMA PARK

WHY GO?

The loop trail around Shelley Lake, in north-central Raleigh, is 2.1 miles, with 4.3- and 5.3-mile circuits of the lake available from separate greenway starting points (which without looping the lake are hikes of 2.2 and 3.2 miles).

FINDING THE TRAILHEAD

The parking area below the Shelley Lake Dam (GPS: 35.856399/-78.662214) and the lot at Sertoma Arts Center (GPS: 35.857780/-78.666188) are both on West Millbrook Road between Creedmoor and Six Forks Roads. Reach the Bent Creek Drive start by taking Six Forks Road 1.5 miles north from West Millbrook Road near the lake to a left on Longstreet Drive. Drive 0.2 mile; the trail leaves from the junction of Longstreet and Bent Creek Drives (GPS: 35.874149/-78.647431). To start on Sawmill Road, follow the directions above but pass Longstreet Drive; 2 miles from West Millbrook Road, go left on Sawmill Road. The trail begins on the left, just past Brandywood Court (GPS: 35.881685 / -78.652942).

THE HIKE

The paved Mine Creek Greenway Trail includes a 2.2-mile loop of 53-acre Shelley Lake and radiates away from the lake in a number of directions. The northernmost of those corridors splits, permitting lake loops to start as far as 1.6 miles away (creating a 5.3-mile hike; see below). To start at the main trailhead, park at the Sertoma Arts Center, with picnic tables, ball courts, and a kids' playground. From there the access trail dips through a cultivated corridor of birch trees past fitness stations to the lakeshore trail junction at 0.1 mile. Take the paved trail left (north) and an offset bridge that has decks for fishing leads over a small arm of the lake. An observation point on the other side provides a panoramic view. A return from there is a short, scenic walk of about 0.3 mile.

Back below the arts center, take a right to go south on the trail and skirt the lake past another view spot, boathouse, and restrooms with an emergency phone. The path turns around the end of the lake, and a side trail goes right to parking on West Millbrook Road at about 0.3 mile. The main trail crosses the top of the dam past sports fields where connections also branch right to the parking area. In that direction, the southern branch of Mine Creek Trail veers left under West Millbrook Road.

Bearing left past the dam, away from Millbrook Road parking, continue north on Mine Creek Trail through fields east of the lake and into woods. The paved Snelling Branch Trail departs right and runs 0.8 mile to Optimist Park; parking is just off Northclift Drive (GPS: 35.864351 / -78.648043). A short distance beyond, the main trail crosses Bent Creek to where the Mine Creek Trail goes right, away from the lake, at about 1.3 miles (a nice starting point; see below). Turn left there to follow the lake loop west through tall trees past a paved side trail on the right to Lakeway Drive at about 1.7 miles. Past the observation point and bridge, and back at the trailhead, it's a round-trip of about 2.1 miles.

To make this hike longer—and woodsier—start at one of two distant trailheads reached on the northerly branches of the Mine Creek Trail. From the junction of Longstreet and Bent Creek Drives, the East Fork Mine Creek Trail reaches the Shelley Lake Trail in 1.1 miles (a 4.3-mile round-trip around the lake). Starting at Longstreet and Bent Creek Drives, the trail leads through impressive forest and then crosses Mine Creek where an unpaved portion of the main Mine Creek Trail branches to the right at about 0.4 mile on its way to Sawmill Road (another starting point; read on). Head south along the creek through an arching canopy of river birches; the trail goes under the Lynn Road bridge, passes more river birch, and goes under North Hills Drive to join the loop of Shelley Lake.

The best way to lengthen and "naturalize" the Shelley Lake loop is to start on Sawmill Drive. This 0.9-mile unpaved part of Mine Creek greenway (formerly the Sawmill Trail) leaves the south side of Sawmill Road and crosses numerous bridges as it follows Mine Creek. You'll notice sections of mature forest and rock outcroppings in the creek. The trail intersects the paved trail where the East Fork Mine Creek Trail comes in on the left at 0.9 mile. Going right on that trail, you join the Shelley Lake loop at 1.6 miles for a round-trip circuit hike of 5.3 miles.

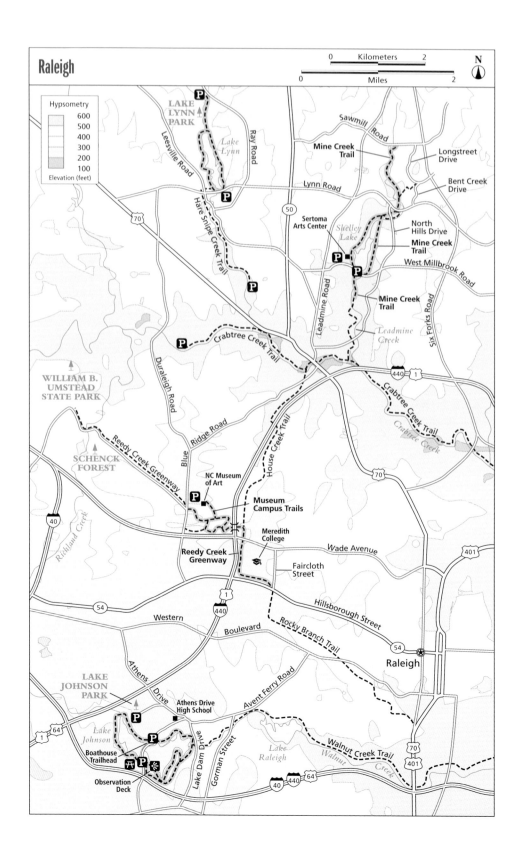

Raleigh

Kilometers
0   2

Miles
0   2

N

Hypsometry
600
500
400
300
200
100
Elevation (feet)

LAKE LYNN PARK

Leesville Road

Lake Lynn

Ray Road

Sawmill Road

Mine Creek Trail

Longstreet Drive

Bent Creek Drive

Lynn Road

50

Hare Snipe Creek Trail

70

Sertoma Arts Center

Shelley Lake

Mine Creek Trail

North Hills Drive

Leadmine Road

West Millbrook Road

Mine Creek Trail

Six Forks Road

Leadmine Creek

Crabtree Creek Trail

Duraleigh Road

440 1

Crabtree Creek Trail

Crabtree Creek

WILLIAM B. UMSTEAD STATE PARK

Blue Ridge Road

House Creek Trail

70

SCHENCK FOREST

Reedy Creek Greenway

NC Museum of Art

Museum Campus Trails

40

Richland Creek

Meredith College

Reedy Creek Greenway

Wade Avenue

401

Faircloth Street

Hillsborough Street

54

1

440

Western

Boulevard

Rocky Branch Trail

54

Raleigh

Athens Drive

LAKE JOHNSON PARK

Athens Drive High School

Avent Ferry Road

Lake Dam Drive

Gorman Street

Lake Raleigh

Walnut Creek Trail

70

Lake Johnson

Boathouse Trailhead

Observation Deck

1 64

Walnut Creek

40 440 64

401

The Mine Creek Trail south of West Millbrook Road, once called the Ironwood Trail, is itself a scenic, 1.6-mile out-and-back amble along the creek. The trail leaves the parking area below the dam, goes under West Millbrook and Shelley Roads, then crosses stream bridges on its way to North Hills Drive. (Along the way, paths leave left then right to nearby North Hills Drive and the Stannard Trail.)

REEDY CREEK TRAIL

WHY GO?
This greenway is 4.9 miles one way, but shorter walks wander through the North Carolina Museum of Art's 164-acre campus, the nation's largest "art museum park."

FINDING THE TRAILHEAD
 The greenway makes a nice walk from Meredith College at the corner of Hillsborough and Faircloth Streets (GPS: 35.793721/-78.684546). The North Carolina Museum of Art makes another good trailhead, with parking just north of Wade Avenue on Blue Ridge Road (GPS: 35.809221/-78.705322).

THE HIKE
The Reedy Creek Trail turns west from the House Creek Trail greenway at Meredith College to cross I-440 on its way past the North Carolina Museum of Art all the way to Umstead State Park. This is the perfect greenway to ride your bike to the museum or start a hike or tour of Umstead's awesome network of trails.

From the corner of Faircloth and Hillsborough Streets (with shopping center parking and eateries), the greenway passes through the open scenery and recreation fields of the Meredith College campus, giving students there and at nearby North Carolina State a direct route west to recreation.

The trail leaves the campus under Wade Avenue and soars over I-440 on a 660-foot, triple-arched span, the state's longest pedestrian span. The path dips then climbs, passing enticing side trails as it curves through the evolving offerings of the North Carolina Museum of Art's expansive grounds. Artwork is everywhere, including artist-designed bike racks and benches. Art installations grab the eye. The obelisk *Crossroads/Trickster I* marks the start of one trail. The Reedy Creek Trail now continues directly through the grounds and beyond but it passes right beneath the massive billboard-like sculpture *Wind Machine* before reaching the museum's parking areas on Blue Ridge Road.

From there, the greenway follows Reedy Creek Road where lanes are separated by a "traffic calming" median of simulated fieldstone intended to insulate greenway users from traffic. The pleasant parkway passes Schenck Forest's parking area on the left, the Richland Creek Trail at Reedy Creek Lake, and terminates at Trenton Road, the start of Umstead State Park's network of hiking/biking loops.

All this makes the museum a hiking destination. Management has aggressive plans to re-create the composition of native species found when European settlers first arrived in its forest and fields. Make a day of out of touring this wonderful institution and walking

Thomas Sayre's artwork *Gyre* is part of the hiking experience on the paths of the North Carolina Museum of Art. COURTESY NORTH CAROLINA MUSEUM OF ART

the many unpaved trails that wander off the greenway and the museum's main trail, the 1-mile Blue Loop that circles near the museum's two buildings. The Blue Loop has its own artsy attractions, including the big ellipses of a work called *Gyre*. One trail follows the creek along scenic bluffs and crosses an arched, laminated bridge to rise through a beautiful tallgrass prairie setting. A little loop in the woods hides one of the neater art installations, *Cloud Chamber for the Trees and Sky*, an oversize camera obscura structure that inverts an image of the sky inside.

Major changes to the museum's grounds are underway, so check the website for the latest trail configuration (https://ncartmuseum.org/visit/the_park).

42 SOUTH MOUNTAINS STATE PARK

WHY GO?

South Mountains State Park is in the largest and loftiest of the mountain ranges that lie east of the Blue Ridge.

The range sprawls across 100,000 acres in three counties, with 18,000 acres in the park (just 7,500 acres in the Jacob Creek watershed is open to the public). Luckily, substantial now-unused backcountry seems likely to see trail development. Until then, the existing parcel is amply laced with 47 miles of well-marked trail for hiking, horseback riding, and mountain biking. The park's 17-mile mountain-bike loop is a rare state park opportunity.

Like many similar North Carolina state parks, these tracts were identified by National Park Service inventories of Civilian Conservation Corps (CCC) areas in the 1930s. Another of those was Hanging Rock State Park, with a highly recommended visitor center exhibit on the CCC. In the South Mountains, that period started in the 1930s when Camp Dryer was built at Enola. The CCC built a fire tower on Benn Knob, one of the park's highest points (2,894 feet), but it was removed in the early 1990s; there's now no view from the park's southern border.

Don't expect just singletrack paths—the roads built by the CCC are still in play as trails. These old woods roads (some are actually paved) explain why the park is a "multiuse" destination for horseback riders and mountain bikers. The result is a complex mix of trail symbols on the park map that makes it a bit challenging to plan a quiet woodsy walk without horse poop and mountain bike swoop—but it's possible. Some singletrack trails are designated "hiking only."

The early history of the area reflects the size of the South Mountains. Park literature says the range actually served as a barrier between the Cherokee and Catawba Indians. Gold was discovered in 1828 but dwindled by the early 1900s. It's speculated that flakes of mica in mud used to seal log cabins inspired the name of the park's Shinny Creek (pronounced "shiny").

For hikers, topography is the coolest thing about South Mountains State Park. Unlike some isolated summit parks where it's up and down to the peak, the South Mountains are a real range. Once you climb the 800 or so vertical feet—not insubstantial—from less than 1,400 feet at the trailhead to 2,200-plus feet and above, you're atop a system of ridgelines where the walking is much easier and the elevations rise to 3,000 feet.

The experience is akin to hiking farther west in North Carolina's mountains. There are rich, moist drainages—where one of the state's best waterfalls shoots over an 80-foot drop—drier, hotter intermediate slopes, and broad uplands where lush pine and hardwood forests are straight out of the Southern Appalachians. It's not far from Charlotte, which invites crowds, but the upper elevations evade much of that visitation. There are backcountry campsites at elevation, and lofty drainages that invite bushwhacking into truly quiet enclaves (campers must use designated sites). In 2006 a 7,500-square-foot visitor center debuted at South Mountains, with 1,200 square feet of exhibit space.

This big mountain range in the Piedmont offers a variety of backpacking loops, a significant waterfall, and perhaps the state's best wheelchair-accessible streamside nature trail.

THE RUNDOWN

General location: South of Morganton

Distance: 0.6 mile for the Hemlock Nature Trail loop; round-trips of 1.9 miles to Jacob Fork Overlook, 4 miles to Chestnut Knob Overlook, 2 or 2.5 miles to High Shoals Falls; longer day hikes or backpacking loops in the 7- to 9-mile range

Difficulty: Easy for the Hemlock Nature Trail; moderately strenuous to the falls; strenuous for most other hikes

Maps: USGS Benn Knob, Casar, and South Morganton. Download the trail map from the state park's website (see below).

Elevation gain: Negligible for Hemlock Nature Trail; 920 feet to Jacob Fork Overlook; 480 feet for High Shoals Falls

Water availability: Filter stream water sources before using.

For more information: South Mountains State Park, 3001 South Mountain Park Ave., Connelly Springs 28612; (828) 433-4772; ncparks.gov/ Visit/parks/somo/main.php; e-mail: south.mountains@ncparks.gov

FINDING THE TRAILHEAD

Leave I-40 at exit 105 and go south on NC 18. In 11 miles turn right onto Sugarloaf Road (SR 1913) at the park sign (others follow). In 4.2 miles go left on Old NC 18. Turn right in 2.7 miles onto Ward's Gap Road (SR 1901). After 1.4 miles on SR 1901, bear right into the state park on South Mountain Park Avenue (SR 1904). The Jacob Fork parking area is 3.4 miles from the turn onto SR 1904 (GPS: 35.602439 / -81.629118).

THE HIKES

The basic hike here is an out-and-back walk (2 miles) or loop (2.5 miles) of the blue circle–blazed High Shoals Falls Loop Trail. At the lower end of the lot, enter the paved trail into the picnic area (the far left trail is the nature trail). Pass a nice exhibit (including a raised-relief map) and go left on a gravel road just beyond. After a restroom the white diamond–blazed Chestnut Knob Trail goes right. Stay straight, pass a junction left where the nature trail enters, and cross a bridge over Shinny Creek.

Pass picnic tables and exhibits and stay straight where the orange hexagon–blazed Headquarters Trail goes right (this is abbreviated "HQ Trail" on the map). The loop splits at the next junction; go left along the rocky stream and you can't miss Hugo Rock, exposed by its namesake hurricane in 1989. Cross the stream and a side trail leads right to the falls' view platform above a deep pool (at 1 mile, 2 miles if you hike back). Continue

High Shoals Falls, the centerpiece of South Mountains State Park, is the park's most popular day hike.

on the main trail up a massive flight of wood steps to a view at the top of the falls. Cross a bridge where a homestead and mill stood in the 1800s. The road–width trail leaves the stream through hemlocks and keeps right at two signed road junctions. The white square–blazed Upper Falls Trail coincides with the loop between these intersections. At the second junction where Upper Falls Trail goes left, go right on the loop and dip steeply down through scenic evergreens. Passing a gate to deter horses and bikes, the trail plummets to the loop junction. Head left, the way you came in.

Near the bottom, bear right and take in the Hemlock Nature Trail. Or start with it. The trail has many sponsors, and the result is the best streamside nature trail in the state. It's unpaved, but wide and smooth and packed with multilayered eco-insights. There are streamside pullouts with exhibits (a raised-relief plaque of animal tracks, water snakes) and big, impressive dioramas (a trout stream ecosystem). The nature trail loop is 0.6 mile.

The next best short day hike is to views at the Jacob Fork River Gorge Overlook and on Chestnut Knob (2,199 feet). Take the first right past the picnic area on the white diamond–blazed Chestnut Knob Trail. It climbs through one major switchback from lush hemlocks into dry, piney woods. Higher up, it winds with more switchbacks to a junction after gaining 450 feet of elevation. Go right a hundred yards to a bench at Jacob Fork River Gorge Overlook. High Shoals Falls is visible straight across in the cleft on the opposite ridge. A round-trip from here is about 1.9 miles.

Heading up, the terrain eases. You've gained that higher part of the park where this trail and others gently undulate on ridges and wind through flats that may tempt you off-trail. A last switchback left takes you up toward the crest of Chestnut Knob and a flight of wood steps. At the junction, Chestnut Knob is to the right; go left and, despite the climb back up, descend to the rocky perch of Chestnut Knob Overlook (about 2 miles/4 miles round-trip). I encountered a 14-year-old hiker here from Wrightsville Beach who called it "the most beautiful view you've ever seen." The highest part of the park spreads out all around.

This trail starts one of the park's best longer day hikes or backpacking trips for the physically fit. Refer to the map as these circuits are described. It starts steep, but the Sawtooth Trail campsites are not far from Chestnut Knob. Back at the intersection above the overlook—all mileages now include visiting Chestnut Knob Overlook, so subtract 0.4 mile round-trip if you don't—continue a few tenths of a mile to a junction with the blue hexagon–blazed horse/hiker Sawtooth Trail at 2.4 miles. (Campers would go right and then take the first spur left to reach the campsites at 2.9 miles; add that 1 mile out-and-back to the mileages below if you're camping. A trail beyond the campsite leads downhill to a stream for water.)

From the junction with the Sawtooth Trail, at 2.4 miles, the hike continues along a ridgetop for 1.1 miles to a left on the orange square–blazed Horseridge Trail (3.5 miles if you don't camp). It glances by a peak at 2,262 feet and then goes left at 4.3 miles on the red square–blazed hiker-only Possum Trail. This gradually descending ridge walk intersects the blue diamond–blazed Shinny Trail at 5.7 miles. Go left to the Shinny Creek campsites and the orange hexagon–blazed Headquarters Trail at about 6.1 miles. (Backpackers staying here will have a 4.2-mile second day, a 7.1-mile total hike at this point.) A left on orange hexagon–blazed Headquarters Trail continues the moderate descent to the High Shoals Falls Loop Trail at about 6.8 miles and the Jacob Fork parking area at about 7.3 miles (8.3 miles for campers).

An alternate energetic overnighter involves Chestnut Knob. Leave the upper side of the Jacob Fork parking area on the hiker-only Little River Trail and go left at the first junction—still the blue triangle–blazed Little River Trail, but now for both horses and hikers and easier than the climb up Chestnut Knob Trail. Keep left on Little River Trail at about 1.2 miles (the orange circle–blazed Turkey Ridge Trail goes right), then left again at 2.1 miles. At the next junction, go left at 2.5 miles on the blue hexagon–blazed

The upper elevation trails at South Mountain are a popular destination for backpackers who appreciate not having to drive all the way to the mountains.

Sawtooth Trail; the campsite connector is a right turn at 3.4 miles (campsites at 3.7 miles). Finish the loop over Chestnut Knob, going down the steepest stretch of the white diamond–blazed Chestnut Knob Trail for a hike of about 6.6 miles if you include Chestnut Knob Overlook. If you don't camp, this 6-mile day hike is a more gradual route to both Chestnut Knob and Jacob Fork River Gorge Overlooks. This alternative also easily plugs into the longer loop above that descends the Possum Trail for a 9.1-mile loop (with the Shinny Creek campsites as a second night after 4.2 miles between sites and an easy third-day hike-out of 1.2 miles).

For the easiest overnighters, consider hiking the very first backpacking circuit above (Chestnut Knob, Sawtooth, Horseridge, Possum, etc.) in reverse. It is much more gradual than either of the loops described above that start at Chestnut Knob. Following the bottom of the High Shoals Falls Loop Trail, take a right on the Headquarters Trail. The Shinny Creek campsites are only 1.2 miles in this direction—fine for beginners or those with a late start.

Heading this way also offers another, easier multiday overnighter or long day hike of roughly 7 miles on trails to the south. Starting on High Shoals Falls Loop Trail, go up the

South Mountains State Park

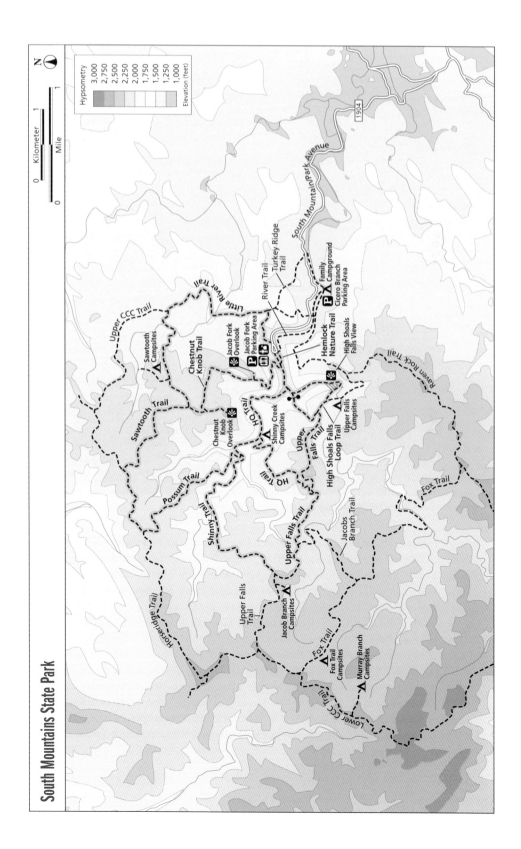

Hypsometry

Elevation (feet)
- 3,000
- 2,750
- 2,500
- 2,250
- 2,000
- 1,750
- 1,500
- 1,250
- 1,000

Kilometer

Mile

N

Upper CCC Trail

Little River Trail

Sawtooth Campsites

Chestnut Knob Trail

Jacob Fork Overlook

Jacob Fork Parking Area

River Trail

Turkey Ridge Trail

South Mountain/Park Avenue

1904

Family Campground

Cicero Branch Parking Area

Hemlock Nature Trail

High Shoals Falls View

Sawtooth Trail

Chestnut Knob Overlook

HQ Trail

Shinny Creek Campsites

Upper Falls Trail

High Shoals Falls Loop Trail

Upper Falls Campsites

Raven Rock Trail

Possum Trail

Shinny Trail

HQ Trail

Upper Falls Trail

Jacobs Branch Trail

Fox Trail

Horseridge Trail

Upper Falls Trail

Jacob Branch Campsites

Fox Trail Campsites

Murray Branch Campsites

Fox Trail

Lower CCC Trail

From Chestnut Knob Overlook, High Shoals Falls hides in the cleft across the valley.

orange hexagon–blazed Headquarters Trail to the Shinny Creek campsites at 1.2 miles. Continue right on the blue diamond–blazed Shinny Trail, which reaches the Upper Falls Trail at about 3.8 miles. Campers make a right here on white square–blazed Upper Falls Trail and then left to the Jacob Branch campsites in 0.3 mile for night two at about 4.1 miles. (Deduct that 0.6-mile campsite side trip if you're day hiking.)

From Jacob Branch campsites, descend the Upper Falls Trail. Night-three camp is at Upper Falls campsites at about 6.7 miles (2.6 miles from the Jacob Branch site). Head down past High Shoals Falls Loop Trail for about an 8.1-mile circuit, just 7 miles if you don't camp. (**Note:** To avoid the crowd on High Shoals Loop, leave camp on the Upper Falls Trail and go left on the white circle–blazed Raven Rock Trail, then left on the red triangle–marked River Trail to the Main Jacob Fork parking area at about 9.4 miles.) The River Trail is the park's easy TRACK Trail. It's formal starting point is the interpretive brochure kiosk at the Cicero Branch parking area near the family camp ground. The circuits above utilize hiker-only trails as much as possible.

43 UWHARRIE NATIONAL FOREST

WHY GO?

Whoever first thought of acquiring federal land in this part of North Carolina had a great idea. Close to increasing millions of people, the Uwharrie National Forest is an attractive "best kept secret" where state-designated Scenic Byways meander through the remnants of North America's oldest mountain range.

The state's smallest and only Piedmont national forest sprawls for 51,000 acres over rolling ridges between the Pee Dee River and Badin Lake and the towns of Asheboro and Troy. This long-inhabited but sparsely developed area exhibits aboriginal settlement as early as 12,000 years ago, making it the East's most archaeologically significant national forest. Town Creek Indian Mound State Historic Site is nearby, as is Pisgah Covered Bridge, one of the state's oldest. The North Carolina Zoological Park is another local attraction.

Uwharrie National Forest began with federal land acquisitions in the early 1930s. In 1961 President Kennedy declared the 43,000-acre reserve a national forest. In the early 1980s the Reagan administration proposed selling 42,000 acres of Uwharrie. The second Bush administration proposed the same in 2006. Luckily, community outcry quashed both schemes. The 5,025-acre Birkhead Mountains Wilderness was designated in 1984 and is the only legislated wilderness in the Carolina Piedmont.

The northerly Uwharrie Mountains are in the national forest; the more southerly Uwharries are across the river in Morrow Mountain State Park. They rise only modestly from stream valleys at 450 or so feet to rounded summits and rocky, boulder-dappled ridges. The highest in the northern Uwharries is 970-foot Cedar Rock Mountain on the edge of the Birkhead Mountains Wilderness. If you walk these ridges in winter and early spring, the Uwharries feel like higher mountains. Beyond the fringe of leafless trees, the horizon peels back to distant blue ridgelines.

European agricultural settlement started in the 1760s. Birkhead Mountains' namesake John Birkhead, born in 1858, accumulated 3,000 acres by 1900 and tilled the land with tenant farmers. His plantation, now covered in maturing hardwoods, makes up the bulk of the wilderness. Chimneys, rock walls—and QR coded interpretive posts linked to a cell phone audio tour (more below)—inspire hikers to ponder the past as they hike the Uwharrie Trail.

Over the years, the forest service has expanded Uwharrie's acreage, enhanced public access, and greatly improved facilities. There are major campgrounds and miles of trails for hiking, horseback riding, mountain biking and OHV (off-highway vehicle) use on Badin Lake and elsewhere, plus primitive camps and picnic areas.

In warmer months, ticks and venomous snakes are common, so winter is probably the best time to hike. Second best may be late fall (autumn color is nice into November) and early spring. Remember—you and your pet should wear blaze orange during hunting seasons.

Wonderful, woodsy circuit hikes are possible in Uwharrie National Forest, some of substantial length. Uwharrie and Dutchman's Creek Trails form a figure eight that, when linked with forest roads used by mountain bikers, can create hikes of many lengths. There's also an interpretive walk beside the ranger station on the Densons Creek Trail.

THE RUNDOWN

General location: The central Piedmont, between Troy and Asheboro

Distance: The Uwharrie National Recreation Trail is 21.5 miles. The Uwharrie–Dutchman's Creek figure eight is 20.5 miles from the south and 22.1 miles from Yates Place camp on the north. The southern half of the Uwharrie–Dutchman's Creek circuit is 12.4 miles; the northern circuit is 9.7 miles. The Birkhead Mountains Wilderness circuit can be 7 or 10 miles. Densons Creek Trail has hikes of 1.0 and 2.2 miles; the Badin Lake Trail offers 2.5- and 6.7-mile lakeshore loops.

Difficulty: Easy for the Densons Creek Trail; moderate for the Badin Lake Trail; moderate to moderately strenuous for the Birkhead Mountains Wilderness circuit; moderately strenuous for both Uwharrie–Dutchman's Creek circuits

Maps: USGS Eleazer and Farmer for the Birkhead Mountains Wilderness; USGS Troy, Morrow Mountain, and Lovejoy for the Uwharrie Trail. The USDA Forest Service's Birkhead Mountains Wilderness map and topos are for sale at the Troy ranger station.

Elevation gain: Negligible for Baden Lake Trail and Densons Creek Trail; about 740 feet for the Birkhead Mountains Wilderness circuit; 1,344 feet for the southern hike of Uwharrie–Dutchman's Creek circuit; 1,100 feet for the northern hike

Water availability: Water near the headwaters of streams in the Birkhead wilderness is relatively clean, but it should be treated before drinking. The Uwharrie Ranger Station has a water fountain at the Densons Creek Trailhead.

For more information: Uwharrie National Forest, 789 NC-24, Troy 27371 (NC 24-27 now bypasses Troy; coming from the north, take the Biscoe Road exit for the ranger station); (910) 576-6391; e-mail: uwharrie@fs.fed.us. Download the national forest's *Recreation Guide*, brochures, and maps at www.fs .usda.gov/nfsnc (click through to the Uwharrie for a list of links to literature).

DENSONS CREEK NATURE TRAIL

FINDING THE TRAILHEAD

This trail starts behind the Uwharrie Ranger Station, about 1.8 miles east of the NC 24/27 and NC 134 junction in Troy (GPS: 35.361581/-79.863141).

THE HIKE

The Densons Creek Nature Trail, built behind the Uwharrie Ranger Station in 1974 by the Youth Conservation Corps, is one of the forest's most worthwhile trails. The white-blazed path has designated stops keyed to an interpretive brochure available in the office.

The trail starts between a split millstone. The route is a two-loop trail. The shorter loop, a 1-mile circle, is closer to the trailhead. The longer, 2.2-mile loop goes left at the first junction; the short loop goes right. The long loop wanders out to Densons Creek and back, with each side of the loop crossing SR 1324 on the way.

The path at times explores half-century-old pine and hardwood forest noted for patches of running cedar and diverse wildlife; quiet morning or evening rests on the trail benches may be rewarded with animal sightings. The trail leads past a pre-1935 sawmill site and an old homestead used before 1910. Sizable Densons Creek is visible from a clifftop.

The Uwharrie's Birkhead Mountain tract is the only designated wilderness in the Piedmont.

The trail also connects to the 0.5-mile, fourteen-station, Uwharrie Fitness Trail. To start at that trailhead, leave the ranger station toward Troy and turn immediately right onto Page Street. The trail starts on the right just past the forest's maintenance center.

BADIN LAKE TRAIL

FINDING THE TRAILHEAD

Take NC 109 from Troy about 10 miles and turn left onto Mullinix Road (SR 1154). Turn right at a T junction onto FR 544. After 2 miles, turn left onto FR 597 and go 0.6 mile to a right onto FR 597B. Pass the Arrowhead Campground entrance, and start the trail by the Cove Boat Ramp (GPS: 35.438956 / -80.074228).

THE HIKE

Another favorite, but easier, hike, the white-blazed Badin Lake Trail is a 6.7-mile loop that starts near Arrowhead Campground (downloadable map on the forest's website under "Publications"; click "Badin Lake Recreation Area"). Go north from the trailhead and wander the lakeshore. The first right north of the campground starts the smaller, 2.5-mile loop back to your starting point. Heading north, pass Badin Lake Campground; the trail swings east around a major point before leaving the shoreline to rise through hardwood forest. Cross the road to Badin Lake Campground and return past Arrowhead Campground.

UWHARRIE AND DUTCHMAN'S CREEK TRAILS

FINDING THE TRAILHEAD

The southernmost trailhead for the Uwharrie and Dutchman's Creek Trails (and the Wood Run system of mountain bike trails) is on the right side of NC 24/27, 10 miles west of the NC 134/24/27 junction in Troy (GPS: 35.310261/-80.043527). From downtown Charlotte, the trailhead is on the left about 51 miles via US 74 then NC 24/27 (2.4 miles from the start of the Pee Dee River/Lake Tillery Bridge).

The northern trailhead for the Uwharrie–Dutchman's Creek circuit is near the Yates Place primitive campground on SR 1146. Just west of the NC 24/27 trailhead described above, 1.1 miles from the Pee Dee River/Lake Tillery Bridge, turn north from NC 24/27 on River Road (SR 1150). Measuring from there, turn right on the unpaved Dusty Level Road (SR 1146) at 5.9 miles. The Uwharrie Trail crosses the road at 8.2 miles, and the Yates Place Trailhead is on the right at 8.5 miles (GPS: 35.365005/-79.988814).

To reach Yates Place from Troy, go west from the junction of NC 24/27 and NC 134 to turn right onto NC 109 at 0.5 mile. At 5.4 miles turn left onto Correll Road (SR 1147). At 7.3 miles turn right onto unpaved SR 1146. Yates Place is on the left at 7.9 miles; the Uwharrie Trail crossing is at 8.2 miles.

To reach the Uwharrie Trail's next parking area to the north, take NC 109 from Troy as above but pass SR 1147; the trailhead is 0.9 mile beyond on the right side of NC 109 (GPS: 35.398595/-79.981642).

For an even more northerly Uwharrie trailhead, from Troy take NC 109 but pass the above trailhead. Just beyond, in Uwharrie, turn right onto the Ophir Road (SR 1303). Just past Ophir, turn right onto Flint Hill Road (SR 1306) and go 1.8 miles to the Jumping Off Rock Trailhead on the right, just past Barnes Creek (GPS: 35.480222/-79.951513).

THE HIKES

The Uwharrie Trail is the area's icon of long-distance hiking. This National Recreation Trail is the most formal 21.5-mile section, which runs south to north from NC 24/27 to SR 1306. Forty white-blazed miles of the once 53-mile path are hikeable today, and partners such as the Three Rivers Land Trust and the national forest are working hard to buy enough land to reopen its entire length. The original route was blazed between 1972 and 1975 by an Asheboro Boy Scout troop. Troop leader and trail pioneer Joe Moffitt (who passed away in early 2015) built the trail and founded the Uwharrie Trail Club to maintain it. To appreciate the citizen-sparked trail effort and learn about local history, take your smartphone on this hike. Eagle Scout Chris Moncrief had the idea to erect QR-coded signs along the route to present cell phone audio programs about the trail and area, many based on Moffitt's book, *An Afternoon Hike into the Past: Roving in the Uwharrie Mountains.* Some of the twenty-four posts may be out of cell phone range, and the Birkhead Mountains Wilderness prohibits such signs, so download the program before hiking at threeriverslandtrust.org/ut-audio-tour/.

Four primitive camps are accessible by side trails and have pit toilets but no drinking water. Other campsites are plentiful along the trail, again, many constructed by Joe Moffitt and the Scouts who built the trail.

Perhaps the most accessible portion of the Uwharrie Trail is the section covered here—the 9.6 miles between the southernmost terminus on NC 24/27 and SR 1146 at

The village of Uwharrie sits amid rolling hills and distant views.

Yates Place camp. Here the trail plays tag with the yellow-blazed, 11.7-mile Dutchman's Creek Trail, built specifically to create a figure-eight circuit for day hiking or backpacking. Streams, lush creekside vegetation, and areas of mature forest are big attractions. Also, many forest roads, now designated as the Wood Run mountain bike trail system, wind through the area and are open to hiking and permit experienced hikers to create custom circuits of many lengths.

On NC 24/27 at a major trailhead, the Uwharrie Trail heads left of the signboard and the gated, gravel road called the Wood Run Road starts to the right; the Dutchman's Creek Trail enters the woods to the right of that. Wood Run is the heart of an adjacent system of primarily mountain biking routes that can be used by hikers; I suggest some possible connections below. Significant improvements to those biking trails and even roads have made them more attractive to hikers. This description covers each loop as a separate day hike from trailheads on the south and north, then discusses the lengthiest figure-eight loop.

From this southern terminus of the Uwharrie Trail, the lower half of the Uwharrie–Dutchman's Creek loop is a 12.4-mile circuit.

The Uwharrie Trail leaves NC 24/27 and ducks under a power line at 0.3 mile. The trail descends along Wood Run Creek and crosses it at 1 mile, then climbs and crosses the Keyauwee mountain bike trail (which branches west of the Wood Run Trail) at 2 miles, where a yellow-blazed spur leads 0.4 mile right to Wood Run Camp (a large camping field with no facilities). There's a junction here with Wood Run Road, 1.7 miles on that road from the parking area. This first section of the Uwharrie Trail and Wood Run form a nice 4.1-mile circuit—a good beginner backpacking trip, partially on a wooded road with a designated campsite in the middle.

Continuing, the Uwharrie Trail branches left down Upper Wood Run Creek. It leaves the creek in a side drainage and climbs steeply north over the summit of Dennis Mountain (732 feet) at 3.7 miles. Off to the west, you can see Morrow Mountain in winter.

Dropping off the northern ridge of Dennis Mountain, the trail again crosses Keyauwee at 4 miles and swings down to the lowest elevation and most significant stream of the hike (about 380 feet on Island Creek) at about 4.5 miles. Crossing then following Island Creek up the next drainage, the path crosses Wood Run Road. From here, Wood Run goes to the right to the parking lot.

Go straight; at the next junction, where the Uwharrie Trail continues on, turn right onto the Dutchman's Creek Trail at about 6.7 miles. The Dutchman's Creek Trail crosses Wood Run Trail twice in the next 0.5 mile on either side of a dip into and out of the headwaters of Island Creek. At the second junction with Wood Run Trail, a right returns the flagging hiker to the parking lot in about 3 miles, compared with another 5 miles on the Dutchman's Creek Trail. That shortcut reduces the circuit to less than 10 miles.

Taking the Dutchman's Creek Trail instead, hikers climb steeply for 0.5 mile, cross the Supertree mountain bike trail, gain a ridgetop at 700 feet, and stay there for 1 mile or so. Then the trail dips to a drainage and climbs, again crossing Supertree, to the high point of this hike, an unnamed peak at 768 feet. The trail swings south, crossing a stream at just more than 9 miles, then turns north and west along the forest service boundary. Finally heading south, the trail hits the parking lot at about 12.4 miles.

The 9.7-mile northern half of the figure eight starts on SR 1146 at Yates Place primitive campground. From there reach the trail on a short spur from the west side of the campground and descend along the north slope of a knob for about 0.4 mile to a junction. Right, the Uwharrie Trail crosses SR 1146 in 0.1 mile (no parking). Go left on the Uwharrie Trail for another 0.5 mile to a junction with the Dutchman's Creek Trail, on the right at about 1 mile. Left, the Uwharrie Trail continues gradually south through the heads of three drainages before dipping to the upper end of Dutchman's Creek at about 2.5 miles.

Climbing away from the creek, the trail crosses two gated forest roads to a junction with the Dutchman's Creek Trail at about 3.8 miles.

Turn right on the Dutchman's Creek Trail and descend north to Island Creek and the low point of this hike (about 420 feet). The drop into and climb out of this steep notch, the portal where Little Island Creek breaks out of the higher Uwharries, is one of the more dramatic elevation changes. The path crosses this scenic stream and then climbs the rocky rise of the flanking peak and over the 700-foot summit at about 5.5 miles. The trail dips off the ridge passing below a sliver of private land to a junction with FR 518 at 6 miles. FR 518 goes left about 0.75 mile to SR 1150, creating a rarely used access to this part of the trail. (To reach it, go west 1 mile from the NC 24/27 Uwharrie Trail parking area; turn right on SR 1150 and go just more than 4 miles to the roadside start of FR 518.)

Passing FR 518, the trail climbs into a gap between an unnamed summit and 820-foot Lick Mountain. The trail leaves the gap and rises steeply to run the summit ridge of Lick Mountain. Dipping steeply to Dutchman's Creek, the trail rises through a towering hardwood forest, continues upstream, and then veers left, climbing to the Uwharrie Trail at about 8.8 miles. Go left, and in 0.5 mile turn right (ahead the Uwharrie Trail crosses SR 1146 in 0.1 mile) on the spur to arrive at Yates Place campground at about 9.7 miles.

Both the northern and southern circuits of the Dutchman's Creek and Uwharrie Trails make great separate circuits for overnight backpackers. The entire figure-eight circuit is a wonderful three-day trip—easily the Piedmont's best backpacking trip.

Beyond this figure-eight hike, another nice stretch of the Uwharrie Trail runs north between NC 109 and SR 1306. Park on SR 1306 to choose between two short day hikes. Just east of the Jumping Off Rock Trailhead, a short hike reaches the aptly named rocks high above Barnes Creek. Just south of the parking area, the trail climbs a not-insignificant 500 vertical feet to Dark Mountain, one of the Uwharries' most rugged summits. There are great wintertime views here, and QR-code post 15 tells some haunting tales.

BIRKHEAD MOUNTAINS WILDERNESS

WHY GO?

The main circuit of the Birkhead Mountains Wilderness is 7 miles using the Birkhead Mountain, Hannah's Creek, and Robbins Branch Trails from the Robbins Branch Trailhead. From the recommended Thornburg Farm access, that loop is 10 miles. From Tot Hill, it's 9.7 miles.

FINDING THE TRAILHEADS

The Birkhead Mountains Wilderness circuit is best started at trailheads on Lassiter Mill Road (SR 1107), most easily reached via NC 49 southwest of Asheboro. From US 220 in Asheboro, take the US 64/NC 49 exit; follow NC 49 toward Charlotte 7.4 miles to a left turn onto Mechanic Road (SR 1170). Coming from Charlotte on NC 49, this is a right turn at about 70 miles. Measuring from NC 49, turn right from the stop sign at 0.6 mile onto Lassiter Mill Road (SR 1107). The roadside Thornburg Trailhead is on the left at 2.4 miles (GPS: 35.620953/-79.945652). For the Robbins Branch Trailhead, stay south on SR 1107 (bear left at next junction with SR 1174) and turn left at 5 miles onto unpaved FR 6532 (GPS: 35.590157/-79.948517). This more isolated trailhead is 0.6 mile off the main road. To the north, the Tot Hill Farm Road trailhead is on SR 1142 (GPS: 35.636628/-79.904697). SR 1142 makes a semicircle between two junctions on NC 49 just north of Mechanic Road toward Asheboro.

THE HIKE

The Birkhead Mountain Trail itself runs 5.9 miles north to south through the wilderness, but its southernmost trailhead on SR 1114 abuts private land—an ongoing roadblock to fully connecting the Uwharrie Trail that enthusiasts hope will be remedied.

Best access points are the well-marked, well-maintained parking areas reached from SR 1107 on the western side of the wilderness and the Tot Hill Farm Trailhead on SR 1163.

Robbins Branch is the area's busiest trail, so from that trailhead, leave the parking lot on a level path and go right on the Hannah's Creek Trail at 0.4 mile. The Uwharrie

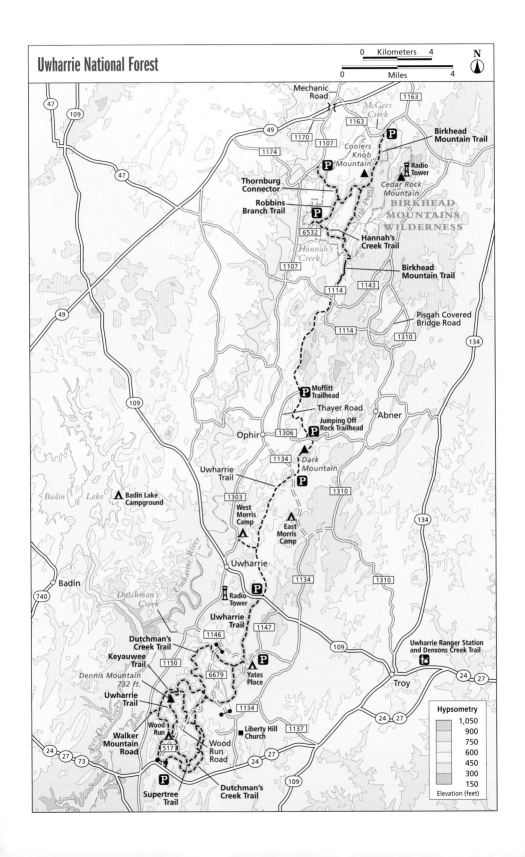

Uwharrie National Forest

Kilometers 0 — 4

Miles 0 — 4

N

Mechanic Road

McGees Creek

1163

1163

1170

49

1107

1174

Birkhead Mountain Trail

P

Coolers Knob Mountain

Radio Tower

Thornburg Connector

Cedar Rock Mountain

Robbins Branch Trail

P

BIRKHEAD MOUNTAINS WILDERNESS

6532

Hannah's Creek Trail

Hannah's Creek

1107

Birkhead Mountain Trail

1114

1143

Pisgah Covered Bridge Road

1114

1310

134

P Moffitt Trailhead

Thayer Road

Abner

Jumping Off Rock Trailhead

Ophir

1306

P

1134

Dark Mountain

Uwharrie Trail

P

1303

1310

134

Badin Lake

Badin Lake Campground

West Morris Camp

East Morris Camp

Uwharrie

P

1134

1310

Badin

Dutchman's Creek

Radio Tower

Uwharrie Trail

1146

1147

Uwharrie Ranger Station and Densons Creek Trail

Dutchman's Creek Trail

Keyauwee Trail

1150

109

1134

24 27

Troy

24 27

Dennis Mountain 732 ft.

Uwharrie Trail

6679

Yates Place

P

Walker Mountain Road

Wood Run

1134

Liberty Hill Church

1137

24 27 73

517

Wood Run Road

24 27

109

P

Supertree Trail

Dutchman's Creek Trail

Hypsometry

	Elevation (feet)
	1,050
	900
	750
	600
	450
	300
	150

47 109

47

49

109

Trail's QR-coded posts were not permitted in the wilderness, but download stops 1–6 for use in the Birkhead. In this area, audio spot 6 urges you to explore the nearby Cooper's homeplace and cemetery, with the grave of a Revolutionary War soldier and a ghost story. The trail dips through tall oak and holly before crossing Robbins Branch at about 1 mile to parallel Hannah's Creek. The path crosses a drainage, passes the remains of an old house, and finally climbs to a junction with the Birkhead Mountain Trail at about 1.8 miles.

To the right, the trail descends to private land. Backpackers could take a 0.5-mile side trip in this direction to camp on the North Prong of Hannah's Creek near the wilderness boundary.

Go left from the Hannah's Creek Trail onto the Birkhead Mountain Trail (at about 1.8 miles) and start a climb of about 600 feet over the next few miles. This ascending ridge runs north past various Scout-built campsites. In this area hikers may notice the remains of John Birkhead's early plantation and a fallen chimney at the homesite and graveyard of Christopher "Kit" Bingham and wife, Dolly Bingham. (Audio program QR code number 3 describes the Bingham place.) Farther along the ridge, at about 3.8 miles, the Robbins Branch Trail comes in from the left.

North of this junction, the Birkhead Mountain Trail runs 2.7 miles to SR 1142, the Tot Hill Farm Road. On that stretch of trail, there are nice ridgetop campsites on Coolers Knob Mountain and a vista east to Cedar Rock Mountain at about 5.3 miles, about 1.6 miles north of the Robbins Branch Trail junction.

Looping left on the Robbins Branch Trail at 3.8 miles, the path dips into the headwaters of Robbins Branch and follows the stream to a final crossing at about 5 miles. The path passes evidence of early farming, then turns left where the Thornburg connector trail goes right. The trail crests along a scenic, rock-punctuated ridgetop scattered with quartz crystals. It gradually descends, passing a grassy area and campsite, to the Hannah's Creek Trail junction at 6.6 miles and returns to the parking area at about 7 miles.

Starting at the Thornburg access point lengthens the loop by 3 miles and permits you to check out the 1855 Lewis Thornburg house, the lower floor of which was a Civil War–era post office. The Thornburg approach rises along an old road grade and then a gradual ridge to join the Robbins Branch Trail.

If you're not in the mood for company, this wilderness and the Uwharries in general are particularly appropriate for trail-less travel, especially in winter (but avoid hunting season). Coolers Knob Mountain east of the Birkhead loop is a good trailless area to target for a solitude-filled side trip. There's also the Camp Three Trail, a path that heads east at a trail sign you'll see north of the Robbins Branch Trail (on the left as you're hiking south from the Tot Hill trailhead). The yellow-blazed trail dips across the North Prong of Hannah's Creek to open hardwood forest at the old Boy Scout Camp Three. Heading south then west the trail passes a rock formation and ties back into the Birkhead Mountain Trail. State game land newly rescued from development just east of the wilderness also provides access to this Camp Three Trail area. From High Pine Church Road (GPS: 35.597477 / -79.886261), a grassy road grade once intended to access a subdivision leads to the edge of the wilderness. Formal trails aren't planned in this hunting access tract but with good map and compass/GPS skills it's easy to reach the wilderness boundary and navigate the big hardwood forest beyond where frequent flats make attractive campsites.

Recent energetic volunteer trail building and land acquisition by the Three Rivers Land Trust have resulted in the Uwharrie Trail being reopened between the Birkhead

Quartz is scattered along the ridgetop path of the Robbins Branch Trail.

Mountains Wilderness and the southernmost sections of the Uwharrie Trail. The new Joe Moffitt Trailhead, located on Thayer Road (GPS: 35.50735300 / -79.95279288), accesses this section and honors the trail's founder. Nevertheless, a roadside walk is still needed to link this section to the Birkhead Mountains Wilderness and permit a hike of the entire trail. Luckily, the land trust and dedicated volunteers appear poised to eventually save the entire 40-mile route of this historic trail for the public. Keep tabs on these efforts at threeriverslandtrust.org.

44 MORROW MOUNTAIN STATE PARK

WHY GO?

Morrow Mountain State Park is a wooded, hilly area where more than 15 miles of hiking trails wander over and between modest mountains. That means these forested summits offer a pretty good shot at solitude.

The 4,742-acre park occupies the southern Uwharrie Mountains, a range that mostly lies north of Lake Tillery in the Uwharrie National Forest and on adjacent private land in Stanly, Montgomery, and Randolph Counties. The park has a 106-unit campground for tents and RVs, with restrooms and showers, two picnic areas, a museum, a boat ramp, rental canoes, kayaks, stand up paddleboards, six cabins (spring through fall), a swimming pool, and the Kron House, the restored home of a physician who served the isolated area in the mid-1800s. The park opened in 1939, and many facilities, including the stone poolside bathhouse, were built by the Civilian Conservation Corps (CCC).

These ancient Uwharrie Mountains aren't high. Morrow Mountain, the highest peak in the state park, is only 936 feet. A motor road reaches the mountaintop picnic area and views of Lake Tillery, formed by the Yadkin, Uwharrie, and Pee Dee Rivers. Hikers can walk to this crest but may prefer trails to the park's three other highest peaks: Sugarloaf, Hattaway, and Fall Mountains. A spur from the Sugarloaf Mountain Trail leads to four backcountry campsites with a pit toilet (no water). A camping permit is required, and a fee is charged.

You may notice downed timber in the park, the result of Hurricanes Hugo in 1989 and Fran in 1996 and a destructive ice- and snow-storm in 2000.

Part of the appeal of this park for serious hikers is that few of the trails are graded, flat paths. Instead, the hikes described below are largely blazed routes through little-disturbed woods. Side-hill sections tend to have roots, rocks, and leafy cover that make them uneven, giving a nice primitive atmosphere for hikers who want to feel like they are in the mountains—without the long drive. Switchbacks ease elevation gains, but there are some steeper sections.

Despite being close to Charlotte, and receiving 350,000 visitors a year, relatively few backpackers camp here; the trails, particularly those farthest from Morrow Mountain, are often deserted. That's especially true off-season, when the panorama is a pleasant view of rolling ridges and the lake seen through bare oaks and scattered pines. The park also has 16 miles of popular red-, white-, or blue-blazed bridle trails, mostly forest roads, in three loops, which also may be used for hiking (hurricane damage in 2018 is still requiring reconstruction of some horse trails at press time).

Hike in a moderately mountainous state park where a road reaches the crest of Morrow Mountain and terrain is reminiscent of the Blue Ridge.

THE RUNDOWN

General location: Northeast of Charlotte on the shore of Lake Tillery
Distance: 0.8-mile loop for the Three Rivers Nature Trail. Other loops include 2 miles for the Hattaway Mountain Trail; 2.8 miles for the Sugarloaf Mountain Trail; 4.1 miles for the Fall Mountain Trail ; and an out and back of 5.2 miles for a hike to and around the Morrow Mountain summit from the museum parking lot trailhead.
Difficulty: Easy for the Three Rivers Nature Trail; moderate for Fall and Morrow Mountains; strenuous for Hattaway and Sugarloaf Mountains

Maps: USGS Badin and Morrow Mountain. Download the trail map from the park's website (see below).
Elevation gain: About 800 feet for Hattaway Mountain Trail; 820 feet for Fall Mountain Trail; 640 feet for the Sugarloaf Mountain Trail
Water availability: Available in-season from trailhead restrooms and other visitor facilities
For more information: Morrow Mountain State Park, 49104 Morrow Mountain Rd., Albemarle 28001; (704) 982-4402; ncparks.gov/Visit/parks/momo/main.php

FINDING THE TRAILHEAD

The park is about 40 miles, or a 1-hour drive, east of Charlotte on NC 24/27. Turn right from NC 24/27 onto the Morrow Mountain Road (SR 1798). Measuring from the park entrance, Sugarloaf Mountain Trail parking is on the right at 0.6 mile (GPS: 35.365522/-80.092077). For Hattaway Mountain Trail, go left at 0.8 mile (right leads to Morrow Mountain) and take a left for parking at 1.3 miles (GPS: 35.377241/-80.072415). To reach the Fall Mountain and Three Rivers Trailhead, go right at 1.3 miles; keep right at the next two lefts to reach the boat ramp parking on the left at about 1.6 miles (GPS: 35.381375/-80.062497).

THE HIKES

The Hattaway Mountain Trail is a 2-mile hike that starts gradually at the pool bathhouse and soon reaches a split. Go right for the easier ascent. The orange square–blazed path runs flatly around the north side of Hattaway Mountain, gradually entering and then paralleling a stream drainage within sound of the water. You may notice a bridle trail across the stream. The mountain laurel–lined path turns from west to east on a steep, rocky climb to the park's third-highest summit. The trail gains a western knob and then follows a ridge to a rocky traverse of the main peak (about 800 feet). After a steep drop to the loop junction, go right to the parking lot.

Another option from the parking area is the easy 0.6-mile, blue diamond–blazed Quarry Trail loop. This is Morrow's TRACK Trail, a kid-friendly path with educational interpretive brochures at the trailhead. The trail was named for a small quarry on the hike that the CCC used for stone to build picnic shelters and a barbecue pit on the path, and the park's bathhouse. There's a restroom on the trail (open late March through November).

The 4.1-mile Fall Mountain Trail can begin near the boathouse, on the northeastern end of the boat ramp parking area, or, along with the Three Rivers Trail, at the southwestern corner of the lot. The latter route is the least steep. Leave the parking area on

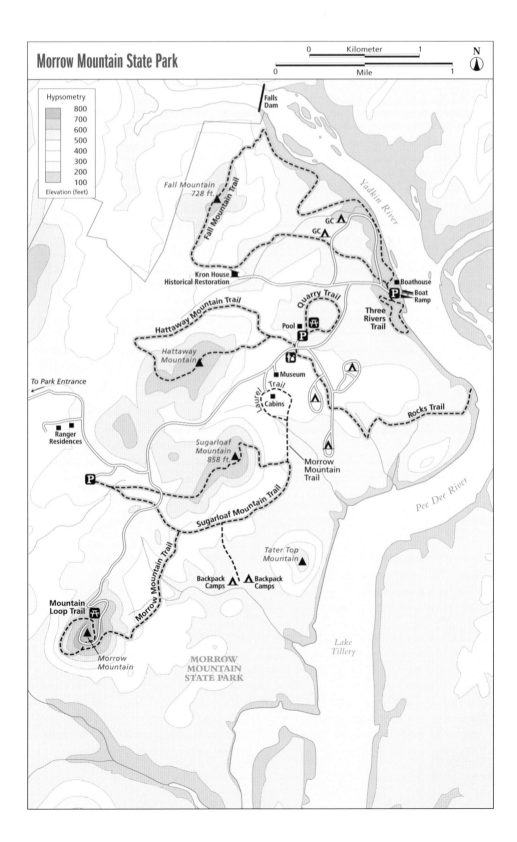

Morrow Mountain State Park

Hypsometry

800
700
600
500
400
300
200
100

Elevation (feet)

0   Kilometer   1

0   Mile   1

N

Falls Dam

Yadkin River

Fall Mountain Trail

Fall Mountain 728 ft.

GC

GC

Kron House Historical Restoration

Quarry Trail

Boathouse

Boat Ramp

Three Rivers Trail

Hattaway Mountain Trail

Pool

Museum

Hattaway Mountain

Laurel Trail

Cabins

Rocks Trail

To Park Entrance

Ranger Residences

Sugarloaf Mountain 858 ft.

Morrow Mountain Trail

Sugarloaf Mountain Trail

Pee Dee River

Tater Top Mountain

Backpack Camps

Backpack Camps

Mountain Loop Trail

Morrow Mountain Trail

Morrow Mountain

MORROW MOUNTAIN STATE PARK

Lake Tillery

the orange triangle–blazed trail and pass a junction on the left with the Three Rivers Trail. You'll cross two road-width access paths to group campsites, then descend and cross a stream. At just more than 1 mile, pass the Kron House and steeply ascend the southern end of Fall Mountain. The trail turns north across the 700-plus-foot summit. The northern end of the mountain is extremely rugged, and many crags and outcrops have views of Falls Dam and the Yadkin River. At the base of the mountain, the trail navigates crags along the shore before veering away and then back to the lake. Cross a stream and parallel the group camp access path to the boathouse.

The Three Rivers Trail is a pleasant add-on to this hike. The easy, blue hexagon–blazed nature loop is 0.8 mile total. Go left from the Fall Mountain Trail just out of the parking lot, and cross the boat ramp road. The self-guiding trail explores a marshy area and offers wildlife-viewing opportunities. The trail's high point affords good views of the rivers that come together here to form Lake Tillery.

The Sugarloaf Mountain Trail leaves the bridle trail parking area just inside the park and enters a flat, rocky pine forest. It splits and crosses a stream in more deciduous woods. Take the left fork through this scenic area, and cross the motor road that leads right to Morrow Mountain. The orange diamond–blazed trail then climbs up the northwestern slope of Sugarloaf, the park's second-highest peak. On this next stretch of trail, it's easy to trace the geology of this typical volcanic monadnock, or isolated summit, so prevalent in central North Carolina. The trail ascends a leading ridge over volcanic slate and then snakes over volcanic ash tuff on the side of the mountain. The final conical cap, at 858 feet, is composed of volcanic flint, or rhyolite. The trail then winds steeply down the eastern side of the mountain.

Where the descent slackens, the Morrow Mountain Trail comes in on the left from the museum (where it runs concurrently with the Laurel Trail loop around the cabin area). The Sugarloaf Mountain Trail (and the Morrow Mountain Trail; they also run concurrently here) now bear right and start a level traverse around the mountain. A junction leads left to backcountry campsites isolated in a stream drainage between the Morrow Mountain Road and Lake Tillery. The blue triangle–blazed Morrow Mountain Trail branches left to Morrow Mountain's summit leaving the Sugarloaf Mountain Trail. The Sugarloaf Mountain Trail rises and then crosses the road and passes the split of the loop to the trailhead at just less than 3 miles.

This parking area also starts a nice hike to Morrow Mountain. Just take the right fork on the way out on the Sugarloaf hike and go right up to and around the summit and back for a little more than 3-mile hike. The scenic, red square–blazed 0.8-mile summit loop hike is separately named the Mountain Loop Trail. This easy upper loop is also accessible from the mountaintop parking and picnic area. If you start at the museum and take the entire Morrow Mountain Trail from the cabin area to the summit and back, it's about 5.2 miles.

Another hike, the blue square–blazed Rocks Trail, starts just past the museum on the right at the park office. It reaches a dead end at the water's edge with good views and solitude. Parallel the campground road through the camping area. Go left across the road (the trail right goes to the amphitheater). Go left again on the horse trail. Follow the horse trail and then turn right from it with the blue blazes along the flank of a rise to the left. The trail dips to the water at about 1.3 miles, for a round-trip of 2.6 miles.

45 CHARLOTTE

The Mecklenburg County Parks and Recreation Department boasts a diverse system of trails, with just more than 50 miles of greenways and nature preserves with singletrack trails. Local parks help protect regional resources, such as a piece of the Piedmont Prairie at McDowell Nature Preserve. The effort has just reclaimed a major urban stream corridor in downtown, the heart of a greenway expected to be 19 miles long and reach all the way to the South Carolina state line. Charlotte greenway construction hasn't kept up with projections in recent years but a significant growth spurt for the city's urban trail network is underway.

MCALPINE CREEK AND JAMES BOYCE PARKS

WHY GO?
A streamside greenway and adjoining forest park make up miles of hiking on paved paths and woods trails. James Boyce Park offers the woodsiest walks.

THE RUNDOWN

General location: Lansdowne area of Charlotte
Distance: Hikes range from short to 3 or 4 miles
Difficulty: Easy to moderate, with some portions barrier-free
Maps: USGS Charlotte East and Mint Hill. Download maps at the Mecklenburg County Parks and Recreation website (see below).
Elevation gain: Negligible
Water availability: Water is available year-round at the McAlpine Greenway's main trailhead, during the warmer months at the Boyce Park trailhead.
For more information: Mecklenburg County Parks and Recreation Department, 5841 Brookshire Blvd., Charlotte 28216; (980) 314-1000; https://www.mecknc.gov/ParkandRec/Greenways/OpenGreenways/Pages/default.aspx. McAlpine Greenway Park Office; (704) 552-8213.

FINDING THE TRAILHEADS
McAlpine Creek Park's main entrance is at 8711 Monroe Rd. (GPS: 35.150873/-80.743635). To reach Boyce Park, take Monroe Road south from McAlpine Creek Park and go right onto Sardis Road North to another right on Sardis Road. On Sardis, the third street to the left is Old Bell Road, another greenway trailhead (GPS: 35.136184/-80.767286). Continuing on Sardis, take a right on Boyce Road; immediately beyond the Charlotte Preparatory School, turn right into the park (GPS: 35.144781/-80.766803).

Besides being a linear paved path, McAlpine Creek's possibilities include a few looping forest walks.

THE HIKES

McAlpine Creek Park was the first of Mecklenburg County's greenway parks in 1979. A paved streamside trail stretches from Sardis Road north to Independence Boulevard (and beyond), encompassing streambanks and forests along McAlpine and Irwin Creeks. The main path is buffered from neighborhoods (many with greenway access) by marshes, meadows, and hardwood forests, some explored by unpaved trails that wander away from the stream. A few of these climb to James Boyce Park, the best access for hikers who want loop walks with some change in elevation.

James Boyce Park's 73 acres close to Sardis Road were a city park before the 1992 merger with the county. The park contains baseball fields, a playground, picnic shelter, and restrooms.

The McAlpine Creek Park office is located at the Monroe Road entrance, along with a 3-acre lake, a wooded, 3-mile cross-country jogging course, sports fields, and picnic facilities. Together, the parks boast creekside hardwood and mixed pine forests, including some of the largest cottonwoods in the state. This natural area also has a diverse assortment of migrating waterfowl and seasonal birds.

The basic hike is the out-and-back greenway walk along McAlpine Creek, about 2 miles from the Old Bell Road parking area east to the park office (a 4-mile round-trip). The best hikes connect that greenway with woods paths north of the creek to form loops. Start at Boyce Park and the easiest woodsy walk descends from the park's main parking area down to what is called the Nature Trail, a forest path along the creek below the heights of Boyce Park. For a short nature hike from the map sign at the Boyce Park parking lot, head across the ball fields where another sign marks a trail entrance into the woods. Dipping from the ball-field elevation to the wooded floodplain of McAlpine Creek, the earth-surfaced trail drops through pleasant pines and leafy hardwoods and then splits. Take either of the two lefts (right, the trail heads to the greenway). When the level trail reaches a paved trail to the left, take that uphill back up to the ball fields just across from the parking area for a nice leg-stretcher.

The best bet for an hour-long walk is to make a loop from Boyce Park by combining the Nature Trail and the McAlpine Greenway. Enter the woods as before, but go right across a stream bridge with a bench through big beeches and oaks to reach Weir 4, a low-water bridge on McAlpine Creek. (**Caution:** If the water is high, don't cross; head back and take the Nature Trail.) Cross the weir and go left on the McAlpine Greenway Trail.

After 1 mile on the greenway (1.2 miles from the trailhead), take a left across Weir 3 on a paved neighborhood access trail. To the immediate right, the primitive Cottonwood Trail heads east along the creek, a less-used extension of the Nature Trail. Bear left where paved side trails go right to Pineburr Road and then Tara Street and you're back on the unpaved Nature Trail about 1.3 miles from the start. The next 0.5 mile to Boyce Park is a pleasant walk through tunnel-like vegetation and tall trees. Pass the Sardis Swim and Racquet Club and bear right on the paved trail through piney woods that climbs back up to Boyce Park. There are other trails in this area, but they all arrive back at or near Boyce Park's parking area and restrooms. Total distance is about 2 miles. To lengthen the hike, stay straight on the Nature Trail and ascend to Boyce Park the way you started for a 2.4-mile hike. Parking at the Old Bell Road trailhead avoids the climb to Boyce Park, for a hike that's also 2.4 miles.

The less-frequented, primitive Cottonwood Trail passes through an impressive forest that rangers say may contain the largest cottonwood in the state. Hikers from either of the above trailheads can easily lengthen the circuit hikes just described by adding the Cottonwood Trail and the section of the McAlpine Greenway Trail that parallels it across the creek.

To just hike the Cottonwood Trail, leave the parking area at the park headquarters, follow the paved path to Weir 2 and go right. At about 0.2 mile, you'll pass under a railroad bridge and Monroe Road, emerging on the longest stretch of the McAlpine Greenway Trail (note the side trail dropping down from Monroe Road on the left).

Go right across Weir 3 at 0.9 mile and immediately go right onto the Cottonwood Trail. This is a wonderful wooded walk through towering cottonwoods with glimpses across the wide creek to the greenway trail. After about 0.7 mile (1.6 miles from the start), the trail emerges onto Monroe Road, where hikers should walk to the right over the bridge that spans the greenway. Once over, take that side trail onto the greenway trail and go under the bridge for a return to the parking area (about 2 miles).

Adding the Cottonwood Trail loop onto the loop formed by the Nature and McAlpine Greenway Trails from Boyce Park adds about 1.5 miles to those hikes, creating walks of about 3.5 and 3.9 miles. Omitting Boyce Park, the big Nature Trail–Cottonwood Trail loop is about 4 miles from either the Monroe Road or Old Bell Road entrances.

LITTLE SUGAR CREEK GREENWAY AND FREEDOM PARK

WHY GO?
A heart-of-downtown greenway along a restored urban creek offers miles of outdoor exercise and adjacent dining and drinking options.

THE RUNDOWN

General location: Downtown Charlotte, or "Uptown," as they say here

Distance: A 3.7-mile stretch of greenway for short walks; almost 8 miles out and back

Difficulty: Easy to moderate, with most portions barrier-free

Maps: USGS Charlotte East and Mint Hill quads. Download maps at the Mecklenburg County Parks and Recreation website (see right).

Elevation gain: Negligible

Water availability: Water is available during the warmer months at many fountains and year-round at adjacent eateries.

For more information: Mecklenburg County Parks and Recreation Department, 5841 Brookshire Blvd., Charlotte 28216; (980) 314-1000; https://www.mecknc.gov/Parkand Rec/Greenways/OpenGreenways/ Pages/default.aspx. McAlpine Greenway Park Office; (704) 552-8213.

FINDING THE TRAILHEADS
There's a small but very convenient public lot in Elizabeth Park at the corner of East 4th Street and North Kings Drive (GPS: 35.217159 / -80.833213). There's also parking across the street at Thompson Park, 1129 East 3rd St. (GPS: 35.215857 / -80.833442). There's also free public parking in the same area at the Target store at 900 Metropolitan Ave. (GPS: 35.213911 / -80.835066). Freedom Park, on the other end of the greenway, has plentiful parking off of 1900 East Blvd. (GPS: 35.196328 / -80.838752).

THE HIKES
The section of the Little Sugar Creek Greenway between Freedom Park at Princeton Avenue and East 7th Street beside Central Piedmont Community College is nothing

short of a real achievement for Charlotte. An underground urban creek has been freed and its banks landscaped with vegetation and plazas. It's a showplace outdoor experience with skyscrapers towering above and restaurants and shopping all around. The hikes here follow a straightforward paved path that courses beside Little Sugar Creek. Through Freedom Park north to Carolina's Medical Center, the way is tree-covered and leafy. But from East Morehead Street to East 7th Street, the trail is more an urban promenade, passing under road bridges, with gradual ramping exits to landscaped public spaces. As the landscaping matures and the amenities in this corridor build out, Charlotte's "uptown" greenway will become a truly distinctive place to hike and bike in an urban setting where a great meal doesn't require a backpack.

MCDOWELL NATURE PRESERVE

WHY GO?

McDowell Nature Preserve is a 1,100-acre Mecklenburg County park on Lake Wylie (a weekend and holiday entrance fee is charged March through October). Ninety percent of the park is undeveloped, and the woods and water locations make for good wildlife viewing and birding (facilitated by a 7 a.m. opening and closing at dark). There are woodsy and watery walks, with a full assortment of park amenities. The neatest asset is a full-spectrum campground with six 9 × 12 "rent-a-tents." Don't feel like digging out the gear? Just grab a sleeping bag—your four-person wall tent with cots awaits. (County residents get a discount; call 704-583-1284 for details.) The campground has drive-in RV and tent sites as well as primitive tent sites and a cabin.

The park's nature center includes exhibits on park ecology, a classroom, restrooms, and a gift shop (open seven days, 9 a.m. to 5 p.m., Sunday 1 to 5 p.m.). There are plentiful picnicking options, canoe and paddleboat rentals, a playground, etc.

This lakeshore county natural area offers trails that explore streamsides, the banks of Lake Wylie, and even a prairie.

THE RUNDOWN

General location: 18 miles southwest of Charlotte
Distance: Hikes range from about 1 to 3 miles.
Difficulty: Easy to moderate, with one barrier-free trail
Maps: USGS Lake Wylie. Download a color trail map brochure at the website below.
Elevation gain: Negligible

Water availability: Available year-round at park facilities
For more information: McDowell Nature Preserve, 15222 York Rd., Charlotte 28278; (704) 588-5224; https://www.mecknc.gov/ParkandRec/StewardshipServices/NatureCenters/Pages/McDowell.aspx.

FINDING THE TRAILHEADS

Go south on I-77 from Charlotte and take exit 90. Go right for 2 miles and then left on NC 49 (York Road). The park is 4 miles on the right. Park at the nature center (GPS: 35.100712 / -81.019880) or beyond, at the end of the road past the picnic pavilion.

THE HIKES

From the McDowell Nature Center, the Shady Hollow and Cove Trails make a nice circuit hike. Leave the nature center parking to the northwest and follow the yellow circle blazes down through Shady Hollow, a good place to spot wildflowers. Stay right to a picnic area as you near the lake, about 0.6 mile. Walk the spur to the main road and go right; at 0.8 mile the blue square–marked Cove Trail leaves the road left. It weaves along the lakeshore offering plentiful opportunities to see birds and wildlife. Take your lunch—picnic tables hide in nooks along this path. Cross to the picnic pavilion parking area and walk the road to your car (1.6-mile hike), or emerge at the end loop parking for the red triangle–blazed, wide and paved Four Seasons Trail. Take that, and go right before a bridge to the nature center, following the yellow squares of the Pine Hollow Trail (about 1.8 miles).

From the end loop parking lot, the fully accessible Four Seasons Trail makes a 0.5-mile loop along a creek with benches and a ramp to the stream. This hike also starts the park's nicest woods ramble—a circuit of the Creekside and Cedar Ridge Trails. Most people hike between the nature center and the lake, so this is the least-traveled trail in the park. Wildlife-spotting can be good.

Leave Four Seasons Trail on the yellow square–marked Pine Hollow Trail and then go left with the blue circle blazes of the Creekside Trail loop. The trail visits a field, as well as upland and bottomland streamside habitats. Kick off on the red square–blazed Cedar Ridge Trail through big forest and it returns to the Creekside Trail. The round-trip is about 2.2 miles. You can lengthen this circuit a bit from the nature center by taking one leg of the yellow square–blazed Pine Hollow Trail (or include that entire loop, which mingles with the Sierra Trail—about 3.1 miles).

For a short loop closer to the nature center, take the park's TRACK Trail, which includes the above trails. The 1.2-mile route leaves the brochure kiosk at the nature center and goes left on Pine Hollow Trail, right on the Four Seasons Trail, and then crosses a bridge. Take the right side of the red-marked loop closest to the stream; then turn right with the yellow squares of Pine Hollow Trail across a few bridges. Return to the nature center on Pine Hollow, or veer left and follow the green circle–blazed Sierra Trail back to Pine Hollow and the start of the hike. Brochures about birds, lichens, and bugs accompany this hike. There's also a bilingual *folleto* (brochure), *Nature's Hide & Seek* (*El Juego del Escondite en la Naturaleza*), in English and Español that can be downloaded to use here or elsewhere: kidsinparks.com/sites/default/files/brochure/download/Hide Seek_Bilingual_1_0.pdf.

The final hike of note in the park is the Chestnut Trail. Leave the nature center on the Sierra Trail loop and take the orange square–blazed Oak Hill Trail across the park road toward the lake. Go left or right at the junction of the red circle–blazed Chestnut Trail as it explores a stream valley and a tall forest of shagbark hickory and tulip poplar (1.4 miles round-trip). You can also start this trail at the trailhead parking just inside the start of the campground loop (first left into the park). That hike is about 1.2 miles.

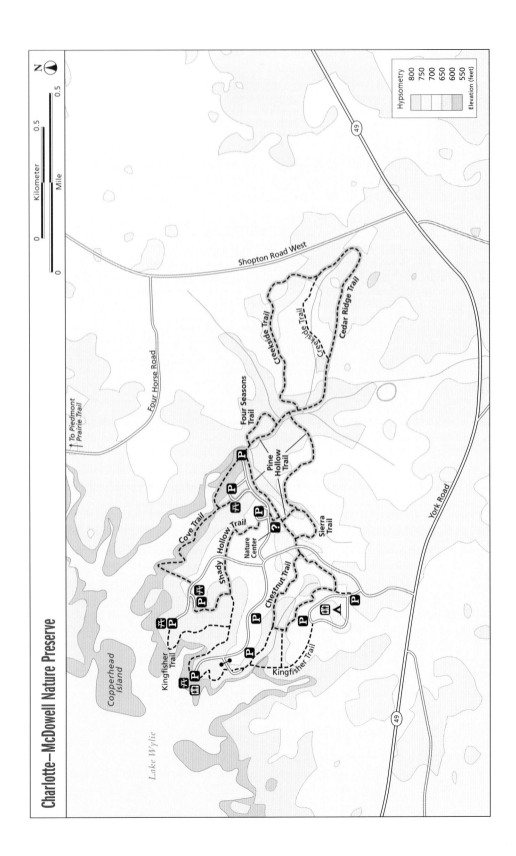

Charlotte–McDowell Nature Preserve

Lake Wylie

Copperhead Island

Kingfisher Trail

Cove Trail

Shady Hollow Trail

Nature Center

Chestnut Trail

Kingfisher Trail

Sierra Trail

Pine Hollow Trail

Four Seasons Trail

To Piedmont Prairie Trail

Four Horse Road

Shopton Road West

Creekside Trail

Creekside Trail

Cedar Ridge Trail

York Road

49

49

N

Kilometer

0   0.5

Mile

0   0.5

Hypsometry

800
750
700
650
600
550

Elevation (feet)

The attractive buildings of Charlotte's "uptown" skyline make quite a backdrop for walkers on the Little Sugar Creek Greenway.

The park's 140-acre prairie restoration area is a unique attraction. The federally endangered Schweinitz's sunflower grows only around Charlotte; it blooms here in September. You'll also see Georgia's aster and the rare prairie dock. Check out the nature center's prairie exhibit and then hike the orange circle–marked rustic park road called the Piedmont Prairie Trail. To reach the trailhead, turn left (east) out of the park entrance on York Road and make consecutive lefts on Shopton Road West and Four Horse Road. Stay straight to the gated junction with Waymart Lane and park in the pull-off. Follow the road east as it soon crosses a power line for a 1.1-mile walk through the prairie to Shopton Road (2.2-mile round-trip) or a 1-mile out-and-back to meadows where bluebirds and quail might also be seen.

46 CROWDERS MOUNTAIN STATE PARK

WHY GO?

As the closest, most dramatic mountain park to Charlotte, "Crowders" lives up to its name. Park attendance has skyrocketed in recent years. Rangers increasingly warn of parking delays on nice weekends—so you might want to have a backup destination or consider visiting off-season or on weekdays. Great mountain scenery and easy access make Crowders worth the extra effort.

A few years ago this park encompassed only two major peaks, but now it spans the entire Kings Mountain Range. The Ridgeline Trail connects Crowders to South Carolina and one of the South's most historic sites—Kings Mountain National Military Park, where the tide of the American Revolution turned. Both the military park and adjacent Kings Mountain State Park have their own great trails and camping (good choices if you need a substitute for Crowders).

This park's major summits are Crowders Mountain (1,625 feet) and The Pinnacle (1,705 feet), both composed of kyanite-quartzite, erosion resistant rock that has left isolated "monadnock" peaks well out in the Piedmont. Summits rise as much as 800 feet above surrounding land.

When it became likely that Crowders and its adjoining peak would be mined for kyanite, local citizens organized to save the mountain; the park opened in 1974. The Pinnacle didn't become public land until 1987. Crowders Mountain State Park then claimed about 2,000 acres. In 2000, another 2,000 acres were acquired that link The Pinnacle to South Carolina's Kings Mountain State Park and National Military Park.

Today the undisturbed 150-foot cliffs of this registered Natural Heritage Area constitute one of the best rock climbing sites in the state outside of the mountains. There's even a bouldering area in the park's newest acreage, accessible from the Boulders parking area near the South Carolina line (where you access the park-linking Ridgeline Trail). Guidelines are posted, but climbers should contact the park office for information on which areas are open and how to register. (No climbing is permitted on The Pinnacle.)

Like other monadnock parks, Crowders is a great place for birding, especially in spring. The park's facilities are modest. A 9-acre lake, with canoes available for rent at the park office (June through Labor Day), offers fishing for bass and bream. A picnic area is located near the lake. Secluded walk-in group and individual family camping sites for backpackers are located about 1 mile from the park office. They're reservable through the park website and available after the

Besides great views, Crowders Mountain State Park's peaks offer hikers a rare Piedmont glimpse of the Low Elevation Rocky Summit plant community most often found in the mountains. VISITNC.COM

park office closes on a first-come, first-served basis for individuals if vacancies exist (just be sure to camp in the site you register for at the sign board). Both types of sites have tent spots, a grill, nearby water, and vault toilets.

On the way to Crowders, consider a stop in Gastonia at the Schiele Museum of Natural History and Planetarium (www.schielemuseum. org; 704-866-6900). It includes a 0.75-mile nature trail. Take the Gastonia exit south on New Hope Road (exit 20/NC 279) to 1500 East Garrison Blvd. The free museum is open 9 a.m. to 5 p.m. Monday–Saturday, 1 to 5 p.m. on Sunday. Crowders' impressive visitor center has a nice museum of its own.

This monadnock state park offers hikes ranging from circuits of Crowders Mountain and The Pinnacle to a short, steep summit hike popular with rock climbers, as well as two easy loops with great birding. There's also a ridgetop route of the entire Kings Mountain Range.

THE RUNDOWN

General location: Near Charlotte

Distance: 1.8-mile round-trip directly to overlook on Backside Trail from Linwood Road access; extend that hike along the combined Rocktop/ Tower Trail, then down Tower Trail to your car for a 3.3-mile circuit. From the park visitor center, a Crowders Mountain summit circuit comprising Crowders, Backside, and combined Tower/Rocktop Trails is 5 miles. A circuit of The Pinnacle on the Pinnacle and Turnback Trails is 3.7 miles. There are two easy loops of less than 1 mile each, and the Ridgeline Trail hike from Boulders Access Area near South Carolina state line to The Pinnacle and visitor center is about 8 miles.

Difficulty: Easy for Fern and Lake Trails; moderate to strenuous for The Pinnacle and Crowders Mountain hikes.

Maps: USGS Kings Mountain, Gastonia South, and Grover. Download a trail map at the park's website (see below); state park map/ brochure available at the park office.

Elevation gain: Negligible for Fern and Lake Trails; about 810 feet for Pinnacle Trail; 870 feet for Crowders/ Rocktop Trail circuit; 735 feet for Backside/Tower Trail circuit

Water availability: Water is available at the park's developed facilities.

For more information: Crowders Mountain State Park, 522 Park Office Ln., Kings Mountain 28086; (704) 853-5375; ncparks.gov/Visit/parks/ crmo/main.php. Kings Mountain National Military Park; nps.gov/ kimo/index.htm. Kings Mountain State Park; southcarolinaparks.com/ kingsmountain/introduction.aspx.

FINDING THE TRAILHEADS

Take I-85 south of Charlotte to exit 13 and turn left onto Edgewood Road (SR 1307). In 0.7 mile turn right onto US 29/74. Go 1.8 miles and turn left onto Sparrow Spring Road (SR 1125). In 2.5 miles turn right (this is where the Crowders Trail crosses the road), continuing on Sparrow Spring Road. In another 0.6 mile, turn right into the park and take the first right to reach the Sparrow Springs access—park headquarters and trailhead for the Pinnacle, Turnback, and Crowders Trails (GPS: 35.213492 / -81.293689). Bear left inside the park and use the first lot on the left for the Lake Trail (GPS: 35.209181 / -81.294327) or the second lot on the left for the Fern Nature Trail (GPS: 35.209230 / -81.296012).

To reach the Linwood Road access for the Backside and Tower Trailheads, turn left off Sparrow Spring Road 0.4 mile from US 29/74 onto Linwood Road at a golf course. Go 1.6 miles to a junction and turn right. The next right is trailhead parking (GPS: 35.240953 / -81.269423).

To reach the Ridgeline Trail at the Boulders access area, leave I-85 at exit 5 and go left (south) on Dixon School Road for 1.1 miles. At the major crossroad, go left onto Bethlehem Road (SR 2245) for 1.5 miles. Bear right in Dixon Gap onto Van Dyke Road and immediately turn into the parking area contact station and restrooms (GPS: 35.170508 / -81.365108).

THE HIKES

The white diamond–blazed Crowders Trail and red circle–blazed Rocktop Trail combine with sections of the Backside and Tower Trails to make a 5-mile circuit over the Crowders Mountain summit.

Leave the park office on the road-width Pinnacle Trail and turn right for Crowders Mountain through hardwood forest. At the junction between the park entrance road and SR 1125, the trail crosses the intersection, enters the woods, and then splits, with the Crowders Trail slabbing left and Rocktop going right. On the right at 2.5 miles, the Crowders Trail intersects the orange hexagon–marked Backside Trail from the Linwood Road access (the quickest, most crowded route to the peak). Pause here at the bench to be sure about this junction. If you are climbing to the top and plan to return this same way—be sure you remember to turn left here at the bench. Despite every intersection in this park being marked by signs and a "you are here" map perfectly oriented to the terrain, many hikers turn right, away from the visitor center, and find themselves at the Linwood access with a long roadside walk. Turn right on the Backside Trail and in 0.25 mile reach the summit at about 3 miles. Impressive views reach east to the skyline of Charlotte. You may see rock climbers on the faces. Continue this circuit by taking the combined Rocktop/Tower Trail past the antennas on Crowders' crest. Go right on the red circle–blazed Rocktop Trail where the blue squares of the Tower Trail go left at 3.4 miles to the base of the Backside Trail above the Linwood parking lot (the shortest circuit over the summit; 2.6 miles).

Continue along the ridge on Rocktop among memorable views and plentiful Virginia pines, a dwarf tree only 3 to 6 feet high. The trail descends the leading ridge and winds to its junction with the Crowders Trail near SR 1125 at about 4.5 miles. Retracing your steps to the trailhead, the circuit is about 5 miles.

The quickest way to the Crowders Mountain summit is up the backside—hence the Backside Trail's heavy use. This is the preferred access for rock climbers. From the parking area, head up the gated, road-width Tower Trail (the vehicle route to summit communications towers) and then turn right on the Backside Trail. It's steep in spots, so be prepared to huff and puff. The trail intersects the Crowders Trail at about 0.6 mile just below the cliffs (that junction I cautioned you about above). At the summit view, the round-trip up and back the Backside Trail is about 1.8 miles.

A better plan than going up and down the popular Backside Trail is adding the Tower Trail to create a 2.8-mile circuit. It's not as long or time-consuming as the Crowders/ Rocktop circuit. From the summit, head 0.4 mile southwest down the combined Rocktop/Tower Trail and turn left at 1.3 miles on the Tower Trail. The gradual, 2-mile descent takes you back to your car at about 3 miles. For an easier climb, reverse direction up the less-crowded Tower Trail and go down the Backside Trail.

To tackle the park's highest peak, make a circuit of the Pinnacle and Turnback Trails. Facing the visitor center/office, head left of the building and bear left on the orange circle–blazed Pinnacle Trail where Crowders Trail goes right. The path gradually rises right and then left around and up the leading ridge of The Pinnacle.

At just more than 0.5 mile, a trail dual-blazed with red squares and blue diamonds drops off right to group and individual family backpack sites. At the family sites, the trail splits (blue heads right for groups) before crossing a power line. The best backpack sites are from #5 (the best) to #10.

Continuing up the prominent ridge, the trail dips and the white triangle–blazed Turnback Trail heads left at about 1 mile. The Pinnacle Trail rears up very steeply and then slabs left on a more gradual but still challenging ascent. (Here the Ridgeline Trail to Kings Mountain takes off left.) The main trail eventually hops out at ridgetop rocks with fine views of Crowders Mountain, northern countryside, and the park's highest summit at 1.7 miles. Be careful if you scramble around up here; it wouldn't be hard to slide off a cliff.

Anywhere on this summit you may notice the blackened evidence of fire. These park-set, low-intensity blazes are crucial to the maintenance of this rare community—the

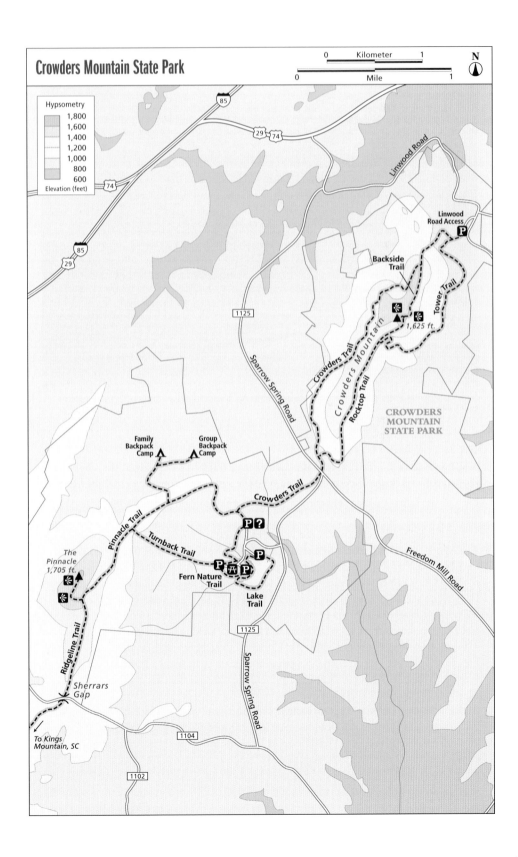

Crowders Mountain State Park

Kilometer
0   1

Mile
0   1

N

Hypsometry

1,800
1,600
1,400
1,200
1,000
800
600

Elevation (feet)

85

29 74

Linwood Road

Linwood Road Access

P

Backside Trail

1125

Tower Trail

Crowders Trail

Crowders Mountain

1,625 ft.

Rocktop Trail

CROWDERS MOUNTAIN STATE PARK

Sparrow Spring Road

Family Backpack Camp

Group Backpack Camp

Crowders Trail

Pinnacle Trail

P ?

Turnback Trail

P

P

The Pinnacle 1,705 ft.

Fern Nature Trail

P

Lake Trail

Freedom Mill Road

Ridgeline Trail

1125

Sherrars Gap

Sparrow Spring Road

To Kings Mountain, SC

1104

1102

North Carolina's state parks are a best-kept secret for backcountry campers. This is a typical quiet site.

low-elevation rocky summit—and its shallow-soil plant communities of bear oak and eastern turkeybeard.

On the descent, turn right on the aptly named Turnback Trail. Lower down, Turnback briefly combines with the Fern Trail. Where Fern goes right, take a left at the sign back to the office parking area for a 3.7-mile circuit. Up and back, the Pinnacle Trail is a little shorter—4 miles.

The 0.8-mile, red hexagon–blazed Fern Trail and the 0.8-mile, blue circle–blazed Lake Trail can be hiked as separate loops, but embrace the park's TRACK Trail and hike them together. Start by the visitor center on the Turnback Trail, and the park's two family-friendly loops can become one easy 2.1-mile stroll. The Fern Trail gains its name from ferns along the stream, so be sure to grab the TRACK Trail guide *Finding Ferns* at the trailhead brochure rack. Scenery on the Lake Trail often includes wildflowers, canoeists, and anglers. Access trails also lead from the first two parking lots by the lake.

From Crowders Mountain State Park, the exciting new red triangle–blazed Ridgeline Trail links the Pinnacle Trail to Kings Mountain National Military Park and Kings Mountain State Park, both in South Carolina. Near the state line, the trail passes Crowders Mountain's Boulders access parking area at Dixon Gap—a great starting point for an 8-mile hike that includes The Pinnacle if you drop a car at the Crowders Mountain Visitor Center. Not far from the Boulders parking area (see "Finding the trailhead"), the path crosses Bethlehem Road in Dixon Gap at a sophisticated pedestrian crossing and then climbs past Boulders Overlook. Running the ridge across two 1,200-foot peaks, the trail drops to a second light-equipped road crossing in Stepps Gap (NC 161/York Road) and then passes a gate. Ridgeline crosses another nearly 1,300-foot summit before descending

From the piney, fire-tinged palisades of The Pinnacle, the Ridgeline Trail follows the Kings Mountain Range into South Carolina.

to a pedestrian crossing of Pinnacle Road in Sherrars Gap. Climbing up a sharp ridge, the route joins the Pinnacle Trail at about 6 miles. Tag The Pinnacle, and it's about 2 miles down to the visitor center for an 8-miler. If you start at the visitor center, just be sure not to accidentally hike off to Pinnacle Road—it's a long haul back up.

Starting with an overnighter at Crowders Mountain's campsite, it's possible to back-pack to Kings Mountain State or Military Park and spend a second and even third night. The Ridgeline Trail intersects a 16-mile blue-blazed backpacking loop through both South Carolina parks where there's camping at a state park campground and isolated trailside sites. Just be sure to let Crowders' rangers know your car will be unattended at the park while you camp in South Carolina.

COAST

47 NAGS HEAD WOODS ECOLOGICAL PRESERVE

WHY GO?

Nags Head Woods is a triumph of preservation—an undisturbed woodland that is an essential anchor for North Carolina's migrating barrier islands. In 1974 Congress named the forest a National Natural Landmark, and portions of the woods have been owned or managed by The Nature Conservancy (TNC) since 1978. The Town of Nags Head was an early supporter of the idea to protect the woods. The town leased acreage to TNC, helped the group acquire another 400 acres, then dedicated 300 acres as a nature preserve.

Nags Head Woods straddles the border between the towns of Nags Head and Kill Devil Hills, where northern and more southerly plant species meet. Abrupt drops from high dunes to watery ponds and swamps further enhance the unique mix of habitats. The Conservancy crows that this is one of only three Mid-Atlantic maritime deciduous forests on the East Coast. The other two are nearby, at Kill Devil and Buxton Woods, but Nags Head is the biggest and most diverse, with more than 550 plant species and the most species of breeding birds, mammals, and amphibians of any place on the Outer Banks. With many trees 300 to 400 years old, and the oldest live oak in the forest thought to be 500, Nags Head Woods offers a near-pristine barrier-island wilderness. A coastal forest like this, where beeches, oaks, hickories, and maples grow, requires a substantial freshwater table and a layer of topsoil. That formed at Nags Head Woods because the 60- to 70-foot dunes that parallel the beach sheltered the site from salty winds, spray, and ocean overwash. The forest's large freshwater aquifer accounts for its thirty-four ponds, many located along trails.

The history of these forests is rich. Woodcutters from New England were dispatched south in the 1790s to cut the live oak for the USS *Constitution* and sister ships. That one of these ships still exists, and that cannonballs bounced off its sides, is testimony to the strength of the wood. Sadly, in 1797, after the wood for the warships was harvested, Congress turned down the chance to designate a forest preserve. Nags Head Woods is a glimpse of what might have been.

The fragility of the forest dictates that hikers (and hunters—yes, that's permitted) stay on trails. Even leashed pets can use only four of the seven paths. Visitor center hours are 9 a.m. to 5 p.m. daily, but staff activities can change that schedule—so check ahead. Luckily, trails are open daily from dawn to dusk. Hiking is free, but a donation is appreciated. The Nature Conservancy is an international, private nonprofit organization that maintains the largest system of private nature preserves in the world. (Consider joining TNC and supporting its work.)

Seven trails explore this 1,111-acre maritime forest preserve in the northern Outer Banks. A short nature trail and a fully accessible trail are near the visitor center, but a circuit of the Sweetgum Swamp and Blueberry Ridge Trails is the premier nature walk on North Carolina's barrier islands. Out-and-back hikes lead to the edge of Roanoke Sound.

THE RUNDOWN

General location: Northern Outer Banks

Distance: 0.25 mile for the Center Trail; 0.5 mile for the ADA Trail, a unique accessible trail built in 2012; 3.75 miles for the Sweetgum Swamp/Blueberry Ridge circuit; about 1.5 miles for two hikes to the sound

Difficulty: Easy for the shortest trails; moderate for others; moderate to strenuous for the longest circuit, especially in summer heat

Maps: USGS Roanoke Island and Manteo. Download TNC's hiking brochure by searching for "Nags Head Woods" on the Conservancy's home page (see below). A variety of great brochure/guides can be downloaded here.

Elevation gain: Numerous changes in elevation over dunes, up to 80 feet

Water availability: No drinking water on trails. Water and restrooms are available at the preserve's visitor center and the Nags Head Town Park trailhead.

For more information: Nags Head Woods Ecological Preserve, 701 West Ocean Acres Dr., Kill Devil Hills 27948; (252) 441-2525; nature.org. Dare County visitor site; outerbanks .org.

FINDING THE TRAILHEAD

Go north on US 158 from Kill Devil Hills to milepost 9.5 and turn left onto West Ocean Acres Drive. Exiting the residential area, the road turns hard right; parking is on the immediate left, 1 mile from US 158 (GPS: 35.989820 /-75.664478). To reach the Roanoke and ADA Trailheads, go left out of the preserve office to the stop sign. The ADA Trail is straight across the intersection. Turn right for the Roanoke Trail, 150 feet on the left (where the Discovery Trail leaves the road right).

The preserve's Town Trail starts at Nags Head Town Park. From US 158 at milepost 11, turn west onto Barnes Street. Go about 0.4 mile (road becomes Health Center Drive), almost to the end of the road, and turn left into the parking lot. The trail starts at a covered signboard on the right side of the lot (GPS: 35.977213 /-75.647376).

THE HIKES

Trails at this Nature Conservancy preserve offer a wonderful interpretive opportunity. Various brochures on the preserve's website interpret the entire preserve, and there are many insightful interpretive signs throughout the trail system.

Five of seven trails begin from the preserve's visitor center. The Center Trail is a 0.25-mile nature trail that ventures across a bridge from the visitor center and crosses two others as it makes a loop. The brief walk can take half an hour if you really involve yourself in how this microclimate works.

The 0.5-mile Discovery Trail starts at a trailhead on West Ocean Acres Drive; just walk out of the visitor center parking lot, go left a short way, and turn right through the fence. The trail makes a short loop and wanders dune ridges to a fishing pier on a pond. There's a spur out to Old Nags Head Woods Road. If you take that spur, the Roanoke Trail (1.5 miles round-trip) begins at a trailhead to the left and across the road. That extends your

Nags Head Woods may be a maritime forest, but scenery ranges from woodsy and intimate to expansive vistas of Albemarle Sound from sand dune summits. COURTESY OF THE NATURE CONSERVANCY

Discovery Trail hike through thick woods bordered by salt marsh to the sandy edge of Roanoke Sound.

The Sweetgum Swamp Trail branches left about halfway through the Center Trail. The 2.25-mile, red arrow–marked trail creates a more than 1-hour hike. The trail reaches a power line and follows it for about 600 feet, then turns left into the forest on a faint logging road where pink lady's slipper orchids can be seen in spring. Various ferns dot the wood's ecosystem, including royal, cinnamon, and Virginia chain ferns and, in the ponds, the tiny aquatic mosquito fern, which floats. Spanish moss and longleaf pine reach their northern limits here. So do the green orchid and the nonvenomous yellow-lipped snake.

The trail continues over dunes and past seasonal ponds and turns right off the old logging road (which continues straight ahead). The path has now grown into an intimate trail. The trail enters its center loop, where the Sweetgum Swamp Trail crosses a number of old dunes on steps, showcasing loblolly pine, sweet pignut hickory, and southern red oak. There's also sassafras, dogwood, American holly, and blueberry bushes. In the wet flats between the dunes, sweet gum grows along with red maple and black gum, more often seen far from the coast. Notice any brown pine needles? An occasional wind-blown coating of salt spray from the east causes this salt burn, the same kind you notice along Blue Ridge highways where snowplows spray road salt onto evergreens. This salt-resistant vegetation shelters less-tolerant deciduous trees.

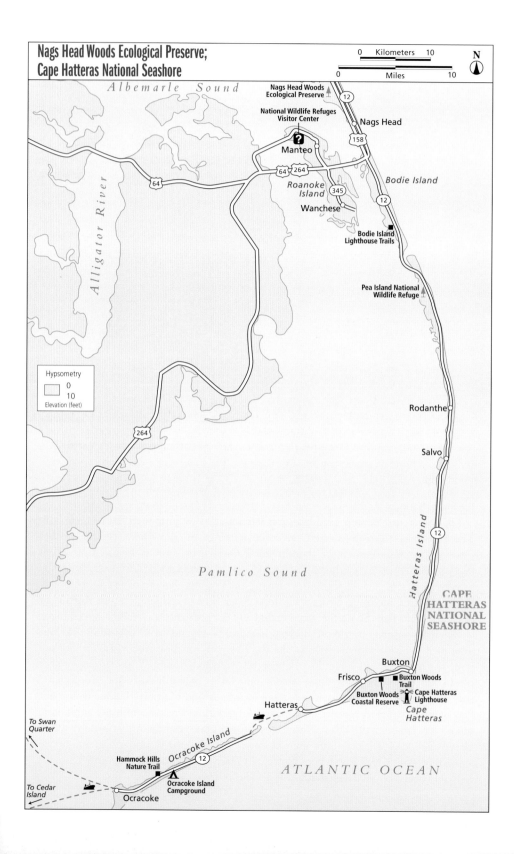

Nags Head Woods Ecological Preserve;
Cape Hatteras National Seashore

0   Kilometers   10

N

0   Miles   10

A l b e m a r l e   S o u n d

Nags Head Woods
Ecological Preserve

National Wildlife Refuges
Visitor Center

Nags Head

12

158

Manteo

Bodie Island

64 264

64

*Roanoke
Island*

345

12

Wanchese

Bodie Island
Lighthouse Trails

A l l i g a t o r   R i v e r

Pea Island National
Wildlife Refuge

Hypsometry

0

10

Elevation (feet)

264

Rodanthe

Salvo

H a t t e r a s   I s l a n d

12

P a m l i c o   S o u n d

CAPE
HATTERAS
NATIONAL
SEASHORE

Buxton

Frisco

Buxton Woods
Trail

Buxton Woods
Coastal Reserve

Cape Hatteras
Lighthouse

*Cape
Hatteras*

Hatteras

To Swan
Quarter

Ocracoke Island

Hammock Hills
Nature Trail

12

Ocracoke Island
Campground

To Cedar
Island

Ocracoke

A T L A N T I C   O C E A N

The path crosses a bridge over a freshwater pond, wanders between two others, and skirts two more. The depths of these ponds fluctuate dramatically with the seasons—from 3 feet deep in winter and fall to nearly dry in lean years. The ponds attract a variety of herons, and during spring and fall bird migrations they are an important stopping point in a landscape dominated by sand and salt. The trail surmounts a wooded dune and descends stairs onto an open sand flat among pioneering plants called sand binders and species such as woolly beach heather, here at its southern limit.

Back in the forest, the trail reaches the Blueberry Ridge Trail, which branches south at an orange arrow. Head back on the Sweetgum Swamp Trail along a ridge crest between two ponds, then rejoin the old logging grade back to the visitor center. Or continue on the Blueberry Ridge Trail, a 1.5-mile, orange arrow–blazed trail that branches into its own loop to encircle a pond. The trail stays largely on a ridge but descends to pond level and crosses a bridge over a wetland to offer some of the preserve's most scenic sights. Back at the Sweetgum Swamp Trail, hike the section you've yet to hike for a total walk of 3.75 miles back at the visitor center.

The newest trail at the preserve is the ADA Trail, built in 2011 and named for its sponsor, the Americans with Disability Association. This fully accessible trail is a gem. Fund-raising was spearheaded by Ed Mays, president of the North Carolina Handicapped Sportsmen. The trail is nominally intended to permit hunting and fishing for the disabled, but it's a great experience for anyone with mobility challenges. The 0.5-mile hike features many interpretive signs, zigzag sections of boardwalk, a great view over the marsh, and a bridge and pier on the pond for fishing.

The Nags Head Town Trail begins at Nags Head Town Park, with its playground, restrooms, water, picnic tables, and pavilion. Take the trail roughly southwest to Roanoke Sound. On the way, it traverses all of the woods' different habitats, including the power line and a woods road. It first crosses an area of dunes and then enters the forest before terminating beside a small strip of salt marsh on the shore of the sound for a 1.6-mile round-trip.

48 CAPE HATTERAS NATIONAL SEASHORE

WHY GO?

North Carolina's Outer Banks are among the top island destinations in the East. Cape Hatteras National Seashore, the first such seaside park in the nation, makes up the bulk of this 80-mile island chain that arcs 35 miles out into the ocean. NC 12 is the two-lane road that bisects these narrow, often less than 1-mile-wide islands. The drive is embraced by oceanside dunes and marshes that mesh with the watery horizon of Pamlico Sound on the west and the Atlantic Ocean on the east.

Most hikers reach this premier barrier island by heading south from the touristy northern Outer Banks. Where signs mark the entrance to federal lands, development suddenly disappears. Just south of the Cape Hatteras National Seashore boundary at Whalebone Junction (where US 64 meets NC 12 on Bodie Island), Bodie Island Lighthouse has a nice birding trail and a longer path around a dike—the man-made reinforced barrier that surrounds wetlands being managed for wildlife.

Pea Island National Wildlife Refuge is next—a 6,000-acre parcel on the northernmost 13 miles of Hatteras Island. It includes a nearly 26,000-acre area of Pamlico Sound closed to hunting for migratory waterfowl. This is just one of nine nearby coastal wildlife refuges. If the refuges are your destination, be sure to stop as you cross Roanoke Island on your way to the Outer Banks and take in the interpretive exhibits at the new National Wildlife Refuges Visitor Center in Manteo (https://www.fws.gov/ncgatewayvc/).

Until the 1930s the Banks were a wide, flat area of sand that was frequently washed over by the sea. The Civilian Conservation Corps (CCC) changed that with artificial dune systems, and the Pea Island refuge took shape as a series of man-made ponds surrounded by dikes. Today, fields of annual grasses are sown in this area as food for waterfowl, and many other active management efforts support and monitor wild users of the refuge.

The area got its name because snow geese foraged there for the seeds of beach pea, a seaside plant with pink or lavender flowers. They are among many birds sighted here, as are piping plovers, twenty-five species of ducks, tundra swans, peregrine falcons, and many more. Birding on the Atlantic Flyway is among the best in the nation. In Pea Island National Wildlife Refuge, the North Pond Trail is a birder's paradise. The total number of birds here exceeds 365 species. Among other wildlife you'll find loggerhead sea turtles. Pea Island nests are thought to produce most of the males for the species because of the sand temperatures prevalent here at the turtle's northern range.

Farther south, the road skips past tiny towns such as Waves and Avon. The farther south you go, the quainter the towns become. One, Salvo, got its name (according to legend) during the Civil War, when a passing Union sea captain noticed no name for the village on the map and ordered, "Give it a salvo anyway." Salvo was scrawled on the chart, and a post office with that name opened in 1901. Between the villages you'll revel in refreshing seaside wilderness. All along these barrier islands, you'll find campgrounds, nature trails, picnic areas, lighthouses, historic lifesaving stations, and shipwrecks. The area is rich in history and natural heritage.

Buxton Woods, on Hatteras Island near the Cape Hatteras Lighthouse, is one of many Outer Banks "woods" being actively protected on public and private land. From Nags Head Woods on the north to Bald Head Woods on the south, new state programs and public environmental groups are working hard to save the last of the maritime forests. On Hatteras Island, the national seashore's Buxton Woods Trail can be complemented with longer hikes on state lands.

Hatteras is probably a corruption of the Algonquin word meaning "area of sparse vegetation." According to the Buxton Woods Trail's interpretive signs, archaeological evidence reflects that ancient human life on the island owed much to a sizable forest that sheltered humans and wildlife. Despite the nearby Federal salvo mentioned above, the town claimed to be the true capital of North Carolina during the Civil War. As in the mountains, Union sentiment was strong among "Bankers."

Farther south, at the end of the island, a free ferry crosses over to isolated Ocracoke, the southernmost part of the national seashore. The 13-mile drive down the island passes more marsh grass–lined inlets and coastal dunes and one of the East's highest-rated beaches. The Hammock Hills Nature Trail is just across the road from the campground.

From Ocracoke Village, a treasure of a tiny settlement with sandy streets and great restaurant sunsets across the sound, toll ferries go west and south on two routes to the mainland, each a more than 2-hour cruise—definitely the best way to get to the island (https://www.ncdot.gov/divisions/ferry/Pages/default.aspx). The Ocracoke Waterman's Association runs its own fresh fish market (Ocracoke Seafood, 252-928-5601), *the* primo source for local fare whether you're heading for campground or condo. Private shuttles across Ocracoke Inlet reach the next island, Portsmouth, where the Portsmouth Village "ghost town" is a wildly wonderful and unique Outer Banks hiking experience in Cape Lookout National Seashore. The Cape Hatteras Seashore also hosts the Mountains-to-Sea Trail, where hikers walk the beach for miles to or from the trail's coastal terminus at Jockey's Ridge State Park.

There are cautions for Outer Banks hikers. Ocean breezes on the banks keep you cool (and can even permit comfortable summer camping), but sunburn can creep up on you. Bring sunscreen and a hat. In addition, insects can be a challenge, on the beach as well as in marshy areas. If you plan to hike in the warmer seasons, definitely use repellent.

Many sections of the beach are open to four-wheel-drive vehicles, but driving on the dunes is forbidden everywhere. Check with rangers to learn about seasonal beach-driving regulations.

The area offers great hikes in Cape Hatteras National Seashore and Pea Island National Wildlife Refuge. The Bodie Island Lighthouse Trail and Pea Island's North Pond Wildlife Trail are perfect for observing waterfowl. Buxton Woods Trail is a maritime forest path that borders a freshwater marsh (with other trails across the marsh). Ocracoke Island's Hammock Hills Nature Trail explores a diversity of forested dunescapes beside a saltwater marsh.

THE RUNDOWN

(See map on page 326.)
General location: Outermost Outer Banks
Distance: From 0.5 mile at Bodie Island Lighthouse; as short as 1.2 and as long as 5 miles for the North Pond Wildlife Trail; 0.6 mile for Buxton Woods Trail; 0.3, 1.5, and 3.9 miles for hikes in the Buxton Woods Coastal Reserve; 0.8 mile for Hammock Hills Nature Trail
Difficulty: Easy for all, except moderate for Buxton Woods' trails. Summer heat ups the ante.
Maps: USGS Oregon Inlet and Pea Island for Pea Island National Wildlife Refuge; USGS Buxton and Cape Hatteras for the Buxton Woods Trail; USGS Ocracoke and Howards Reef for Hammock Hills Nature Trail. Download area orientation maps and some trail maps at the websites below.
Elevation gain: Negligible
Water availability: No drinking water on the trails. Nearby restrooms

and facilities run by the managing agencies are the best bet for water, as are beach vacation-area businesses.
For more information: Cape Hatteras National Seashore, 1401 National Park Dr., Manteo 27954; (252) 473-2111. Ocracoke Island NPS Visitor Center (at the ferry terminal); (252) 475-9701. A variety of information brochures and a seashore map can be downloaded from the seashore's website: nps.gov/caha. Pea Island National Wildlife Refuge, c/o Alligator River National Wildlife Refuge, PO Box 1969, Manteo 27954. Pea Island Visitor Center; (252) 987-2394 (audio tour available). Brochures, including an Outer Banks Bird List and a trail map, can be downloaded at the Pea Island website: www.fws.gov/refuge/pea _island/. Buxton Woods Coastal Reserve: nccoastalreserve.net/web/ crp/buxton-woods; https://mountain stoseatrail.org/

FINDING THE TRAILHEADS

Bodie Island Lighthouse (GPS: 35.818621/-75.564431) is a right turn 6.6 miles south of the US 64/NC 12 junction east of Manteo, 2.5 miles north of the Herbert C. Bonner Bridge at Oregon Inlet, and 9 miles north of the Pea Island National Wildlife Refuge Visitor Center. The North Pond Wildlife Trail starts at the Pea Island Visitor Center, 4.1 miles south of the southern end of the Bonner Bridge on the west side of NC 12 (GPS: 35.716577/-75.493528). Salt Flats Wildlife Trail parking is 1.5 miles north of the visitor center on the west side of NC 12.

The Buxton Woods Trail is on Lighthouse Road, the spur to the Cape Hatteras Visitor Center and Cape Hatteras Lighthouse. From NC 12, 32 miles south of the Pea Island Visitor Center or 11.8 miles east of the Hatteras Island Ferry terminal, turn into the spur road and pass the lighthouse left turn. The trail begins in the picnic area parking lot, just beyond on the right (GPS: 35.252821/-75.528595).

The easiest main trailhead for the Buxton Woods Coastal Reserve is on Water Association Road, 8 miles east of the ferry terminal on the south end of Hatteras Island or 3.7 miles west of the Lighthouse Road spur from NC 12 to Cape Hatteras. Drive 0.7 mile on Water Association Road and park at the turn where Great Ridge Road goes right (GPS: 35.249183/-75.584404). The trail exits the outside of the curve. The Hammock Hills Nature Trail, on Ocracoke Island, starts on the west side of NC 12, about 3 miles north of the village and across from the campground (GPS: 35.125482/-75.923797).

THE HIKES

The Bodie Island Lighthouse Trail and the dike that surrounds the wetland make nice birding hikes, and each provides awesome perspectives on the lighthouse. Left of the lighthouse, take the boardwalk to cross marshy wetlands, span a creek, and reach a view deck near the water's edge. Retrace your steps whenever you want.

Pea Island's North Pond Wildlife Trail is the quintessential wildlife-viewing route. Numerous viewpoints and a two-level observation tower provide hikers with mounted binocular spotting scopes (and they're free to use!). The surrounding wetlands are basically an avian eatery—they're planted to provide food for waterfowl. This is a highly managed environment, where roads and dikes accommodate agency vehicles and make this trail wheelchair accessible (one is available for loan at the visitor center).

Start the North Pond Trail at the end of the lot opposite the visitor center. The center has a year-round information kiosk, restrooms, a small visitor contact station, and a bookstore. The refuge's passionate volunteers, many memorialized on the trail's plentiful benches, answer questions and offer scheduled activities and birding tours (call or check the website in advance for details).

The wheelchair-accessible interpretive path crosses a boardwalk and follows a paved path under wind-stunted trees. The first observation platform with spotting scopes is at 0.2 mile. The path follows a dike west on North Pond with two view platforms jutting south over New Field Pond. At about 0.6 mile the trail terminates on the western shore of the refuge at a two-story tower overlooking Pamlico Sound. The lowest raised platform is wheelchair accessible. Both levels have scopes. Backtrack from here for a 1.2-mile waterfowl-watching hike, even if you've forgotten your own binoculars.

Or follow the edge of North Pond north on an unpaved refuge road (not accessible) until it reaches Eagle Nest Bay and then turns east. There's another observation deck at 2.5 miles (round-trip, just more than 5 miles back to the visitor center). This tower is the end viewpoint for the Salt Flats Wildlife Trail, 0.2-mile or 0.4-mile round-trip from its trailhead via NC 12 (1.5 miles north of the visitor center). You could make a circuit from the North Pond Wildlife Trail to NC 12 via the Salt Flats Wildlife Trail and walk the roadside back to the visitor center (a 4-mile round-trip), but roadside safety might suggest just going out and back from the trailheads.

The Buxton Woods Trail near the Cape Hatteras Lighthouse is a coastal foray into the largest maritime forest on the North Carolina coast. The trail leaves the picnic area and crosses a dune to undulate down into the forest surrounding a wonderfully secluded

Elaborate viewing towers include mounted spotting devices on the North Pond Trail at Pea Island.

freshwater marsh. These ponds are called "sedges," and they're evidence of the aquifer that lies below. This is Jennette Sedge, named for a local family.

The trail splits into a long, narrow end loop with boardwalk. Near shore, you're likely to see coot, heron, white egret, ibis, ducks, rail, and osprey. This forest and marsh burned all the way to the beach in 1954. Today's woods include loblolly pine, American hornbeam, bald cypress, yaupon (an evergreen holly that yields a caffeine drink when cured), live oak (some hung with Spanish moss), and the dwarf palmetto (*Sabal minor*), with its fanlike leaves.

Be cautious in summer near the marsh or rainwater ponds between wooded dunes—water moccasins like to sun there. You also might see "Russian rats": the coypu, or nutria—a web-footed, aquatic South American rodent introduced by a hunting club in 1941.

To really see Buxton Woods, head to the other side of the sedge (by car!) to the 1,000-acre Buxton Woods Coastal Reserve. This is a best-kept-secret island backcountry with miles of hiking (but no camping), part of a ten-site coastal preservation program created by the North Carolina General Assembly in 1989. It includes Bald Head Woods and other maritime forests and estuaries. The program focuses on preservation, education, and research. A few trailheads here are easy to reach, but it can be a mini-adventure motoring sandy roads to isolated starting points (four-wheel drive required).

The Lookout Loop Trail is a 0.3-mile hike that lies west of the national seashore trail. The modest wooded dunes of that trail rise to monsters here. The path wanders up and down around the crest of a major dune peak, at more than 56 feet, probably the highest on the island. Bushwhack paths go off in many directions. There's a good view over Jennette Sedge. The trail is closed much of the winter during hunting season (game includes deer).

The easiest way to get to this hike is to walk Old Doctor's Road from a signed parking spot on the south side of NC 12, 2.4 miles west of the national seashore spur road to Cape Hatteras and 9.7 miles east of the ferry terminal. In a passenger car, pull into the sandy road with some speed and park left on the firm roadside (GPS: 35.263314 / -75.564082). Hike straight back on this pleasant sandy lane (bearing right at the first V intersection). Pass another sandy road right (Tunnel Road) and go straight where less-sandy Flowers Ridge Road comes in from the left. Not far ahead on the left, at about 0.7 mile, the trail goes up a bank to trailhead signs. Straight ahead is a parking turnaround for those who choose to drive their four-wheel-drive vehicles (a side trail joins the loop from there). The round-trip hike from NC 12 is just less than 2 miles.

An easier way to get to this parking area is to avoid Old Doctor's and come in on Flowers Ridge Road. It's the first signed road right on the spur road from NC 12 to Cape Hatteras. Just wander west, bearing left eventually onto a sandy woods road, and take a left at the junction with Old Doctor's to the trail. This end of this route is less sandy (not *un*-sandy), so a nice little adventure nonetheless.

The best hike of Buxton Woods is a 3.3-mile loop from Water Association Road (see "Finding the trailhead") that can include the loop trail. Enter the woods and go right at the junction on the West Trail past palmettos. At 0.2 mile go left on the Boundary Trail (it hugs the reserve boundary). At 1.4 miles go left on the Sedge Trail back to the main dune ridge. Go left again at 1.8 miles on the Ridge Trail (or see option below), which follows the big dune, then turn right onto East Trail to the end of sandy Tunnel Road (where East Trail continues 0.4 mile to NC 12). At the Tunnel Road junction, about 2.4 miles, take a left onto North Trail. The trail jogs left on the way to follow a very scenic dune line—all wooded of course—back to the West Trail junction and your start at 3.4 miles.

In the above hike, where you went left on Ridge Trail, it's easy to include the Lookout Loop Trail and add 1.5 miles to the walk (4.9 miles total). For this option, stay straight 0.2 mile past the Ridge Trail on Sedge Trail and turn right onto Tunnel Road. At 0.4 mile turn right again on Old Doctor's Road to the Lookout Loop Trail and hike the loop. Retrace your steps, or walk Tunnel Road to North Trail.

A great short loop from Water Association Road starts on West Trail as above but turns right on Boundary Trail at 0.2 mile. As you near the Piney Woods Trail (about 0.5 mile), you're again hitting the island's highest dunes. Turn right onto Piney Woods at 0.6 mile, then right again onto Great Ridge Road at 0.9 mile. You'll pass a gate at 1.1 miles and reach your car at 1.5 miles.

Ocracoke's Hammock Hills Nature Trail is the perfect complement to the island's nationally award-winning beaches. It wanders through a variety of habitats for 0.8 mile to the marshy edge of Pamlico Sound.

The trail begins in scrub thicket and splits into its loop at a boardwalk beside a small freshwater branch of Island Creek near NC 12. This surface accumulation of freshwater sustains the salt wind–stunted forest. Go right; the trail parallels the highway through a pine needle– and forest-covered dunescape. Prickly pear cactus grow in sunnier, sandy spots. Leaving the dunes, the path swings left and down into pine forest and more thicket

An emerging maritime forest creeps across the dunes beside the Buxton Woods Trail.

to a viewing platform on the sound-side edge of the saltwater marsh. Saltmeadow hay, above the highest tides, and black needlerush and salt marsh cordgrass, which grow below, wave in the breeze below the deck. The gull-like black skimmer swoops low and uses its large lower bill to scoop fish from this fertile marsh, the perfect nursery for fish and crustaceans.

Swinging away from the marsh, reenter the pine forest, where low cover protects rabbits, black racers, skinks, mice, and tree frogs from owls and the northern harriers often seen circling overhead. This is an earlier stage of maritime forest growth than you'll find at Buxton Woods and Nags Head Woods—the reason Ocracoke supports no large mammals.

Back at the deck, go right to retrace your steps to the parking area.

49 CAPE LOOKOUT NATIONAL SEASHORE

WHY GO?

Established in 1966, Cape Lookout National Seashore protects the southern Outer Banks, one of the few remaining natural barrier-island ecosystems in the world. The park comprises three major islands that run 56 miles southeast from Beaufort Inlet to Cape Lookout and northeast to Ocracoke Inlet (the start of Cape Hatteras National Seashore).

Southernmost Shackleford Banks has high dunes and a stand of maritime forest. The more northerly Core Banks and Portsmouth Island are a wild, low-lying landscape of shrub thickets, tidal flats, dunes, and, on the Core and Pamlico Sound side, salt marshes. This ever-changing landscape is fragile and beautiful, requiring special care from those who visit. Ferries to the park depart from Beaufort, Harkers Island, Davis, Atlantic, and Ocracoke. Ferries from Davis and Atlantic transport four-wheel-drive vehicles, a managed means to reach points of interest. Motorists should get the latest information in advance and stick to approved routes to avoid threatened species, nesting loggerhead turtles, shorebirds, and sea oats, all protected by law.

Though isolated, the sparse public facilities at the Core Banks ferry-accessible sites are visited by about 500,000 people a year. First stop should be the main visitor center at Harkers Island. Be sure to take the self-guiding trail brochure and hike the 0.8-mile Soundside Loop Trail behind the visitor center. It leads along the shore through a maritime forest to an end loop where a side trail reaches a marsh and Core Sound Overlook. Two side trails link the Soundside Loop to two other loops, the longest about 0.4 mile around Willow Pond, a natural area behind the Core Sound Waterfowl Museum and Heritage Center (coresound.com), a worthwhile stop just one parking lot away from the national seashore's visitor center. Besides Harkers Island, the lighthouse complex on Cape Lookout is also very popular.

Recreational opportunities on these islands include astoundingly scenic oceanside hiking and backpacking from any boat- or ferry-accessible landfall. Undeveloped beach camping is permitted. There's also superb marsh and surf kayaking (the park requests that a float plan be filed), fishing, swimming, and seashell hunting. All that said, the weather and elements can be unrelenting. High winds, heavy rain, flooding, voracious hordes of mosquitoes and withering sun can make life miserable. Visitors cope by being prepared (windproof tents with long sand stakes, hats with fine-mesh insect netting, sunscreen). ***Best tip:*** Visit when the weather and the bugs are at their least troublesome. October, March, and April are good. Pick your weather window.

Wander down the sandy streets of abandoned Portsmouth Village for one of North Carolina's most unusual hiking experiences.

Portsmouth Island is on the North Core Banks, and the main attraction is a fascinating now-uninhabited Outer Banks village. Five-mile-wide Ocracoke Inlet separates Portsmouth from the tourist island of Ocracoke. Founded by the North Carolina colonial assembly in 1753, Portsmouth debuted just thirty-five years after the pirate Blackbeard (Edward Teach) was slain by a raiding party sent by Virginia's governor. Blackbeard often sheltered just across the inlet on Ocracoke in an area still called Teach's Hole. World War II enemy submarines lurked there too.

Portsmouth Village got its economic impetus as a transshipment point for goods through Ocracoke Inlet. To reach North Carolina ports such as New Bern, Washington, and Bath, seagoing vessels had to transfer goods to boats with shallower drafts in a "lightering" process that made the town the Banks' largest settlement by 1770. A storm dug a deeper channel through Hatteras Inlet in 1864, and trade shifted there. The hospital closed; then the Civil War drove most residents to the mainland. The customs office closed due to lack of trade. Fishing and processing shipwrecks became dominant occupations. In 1894 the Portsmouth Island US Life-Saving Service Station opened, but it was decommissioned by the Coast Guard in 1937 after a major hurricane. The school closed in 1943, the post office in 1959. The last residents moved out in 1971.

Luckily, a walk through Portsmouth Village still reveals the life-style of the long-gone "Bankers." The 250-acre village was listed on the National Register of Historic Places in 1979; today the federal government protects what remains, in part by leasing the structures to organizations and individuals who maintain and restore them. A few buildings are open to the public, among them the Theodore and Annie Salter House visitor center (with flush toilets and exhibits), the church, school, and life-saving station (with history displays).

Explore the village of Portsmouth, including its eerie open buildings, or wander to the ocean (taking note of flooding at high tides).

THE RUNDOWN

General location: Portsmouth Island, Outer Banks

Distance: About 1.5 miles for a hike through the village; about 3.4 miles for a trip through the village to the beach and back

Difficulty: Easy for walking; difficult for access, isolation, and possibility of challenging weather or insect conditions (avoid midsummer)

Maps: USGS Portsmouth is highly recommended, as are navigational charts and the national seashore's strip map. Download a Portsmouth Village interpretive map/brochure at the national seashore's brochure website (the page has a variety of leaflets): nps.gov/calo/planyourvisit/brochures.htm.

Elevation gain: Negligible

Water availability: Bring all needed drinking water.

For more information: Cape Lookout National Seashore, Harkers Island; (252) 728-2250; nps.gov/calo; e-mail: calo_administration@nps.gov

FINDING THE TRAILHEAD

Informal beach hikes and backpacking trails can be reached via ferries that connect these islands to the mainland; see the seashore website for recommended ferry services and schedules.

For Portsmouth Island, the easiest access is from Ocracoke Island in Cape Hatteras National Seashore, just to the north. To reach Ocracoke Island itself, take either of two atmospheric, more-than-hour-long toll ferry rides from Cedar Island, north of Beaufort, or from Swan Quarter, near Washington and Bath. If you drive down the popular Outer Banks vacation area of Dare County, a short ferry ride reaches Ocracoke from Hatteras Island. To get over to Portsmouth, contact longtime operators Austin Boat Tours (252-928-4361 or 252-928-5431). There is a per-person fee for the round-trip (less for children), with a minimum of three people for a 4-hour stay on the island. Guided tours are also available.

From farther south, vehicle access is possible from lodging at the NPS-managed Long Point Cabin Camp, 17 miles south of Portsmouth Village. Reservations are available through recreation.gov. For ferry transportation to Long Point, contact Morris Marina Kabin Kamps and Ferry Service in Atlantic; (252) 225-4261; portsmouthisland.com.

THE HIKE

The North Carolina state road map marks historic Portsmouth Village with a circle that symbolizes a population of 2,000 residents. In the case of this ghost town, that's 2,000 too many!

Many Outer Banks hikes lead to across-the-water sunsets. This one's on Ocracoke Island, a favorite jumping-off point for ferry rides over to Portsmouth Village on the Cape Lookout National Seashore.

From nearby Ocracoke, Portsmouth appears as an immaculate handful of uninhabited buildings sprouting from rich green reeds and meandering saltwater channels that Bankers call creeks even though they carry no freshwater.

Land at Haulover Point Dock and wander into "town," where preserved Outer Banks architecture stands eerily quiet. You'll notice how villagers captured fresh rainwater on their roofs and funneled it into cistern storage systems. You'll see small outbuildings where islanders prepared meals when the heat of cooking would have turned homes into saunas. You'll see tiny "cool houses," doghouse-size structures where fresh food stayed cool. No doubt these houses contain planks from the dozens of ships lost off the coast.

Portsmouth Island has become increasingly popular since the first edition of this book was the first North Carolina trail guide to include it back in 1996. The Salter House visitor center is open seasonally, June through September (check with the park for hours and the possible availability of interpretive activities). Or create your own tour. Pick up interpretive brochures from the visitor center or website and wander the village.

Continuing on the main road, the old US Post Office is on the right. Past it, a right turn leads to two cemeteries, the Jody Styron and Tom Bragg House, and the isolated T. T. Potter house on the edge of the marsh. (Download a handy history guide to the village's old houses at the seashore website above.) A left near the post office takes you past houses along Doctor's Creek. Near Ocracoke Inlet, the Henry Pigott House was home to the last male resident of Portsmouth, whose death in 1971 prompted desertion of the island.

Cape Lookout National Seashore: Portsmouth Village

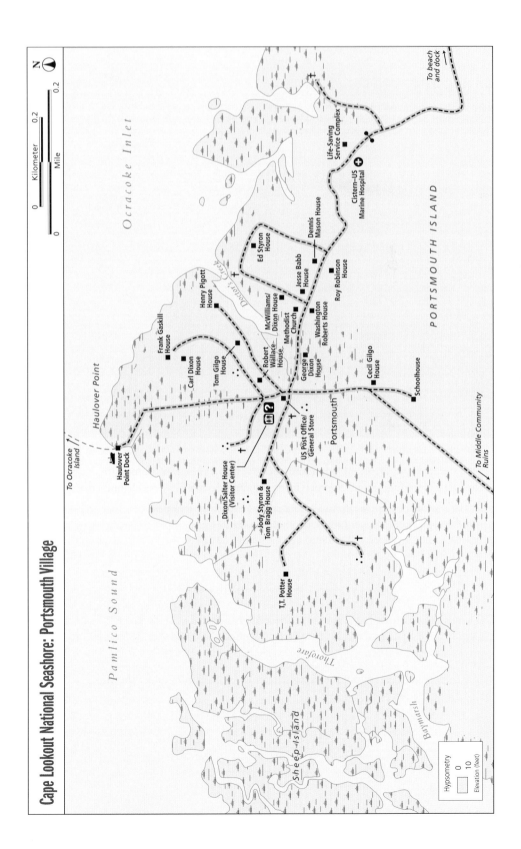

N

Kilometer
0   0.2   0.2

Mile
0   0.2

Ocracoke Inlet

Pamlico Sound

Haulover Point

To Ocracoke Island

Haulover Point Dock

Doctors Creek

Frank Gaskill House

Henry Pigott House

Carl Dixon House

Tom Gilgo House

Robert Wallace House

McWilliams/ Dixon House

Methodist Church

Ed Styron House

Dennis Mason House

Jesse Babb House

Washington Roberts House

Roy Robinson House

Life-Saving Service Complex

Cistern–US Marine Hospital

To beach and dock

Dixon/Salter House (Visitor Center)

Jody Styron & Tom Bragg House

US Post Office/ General Store

George Dixon House

Portsmouth

Cecil Gilgo House

Schoolhouse

To Middle Community Ruins

T.T. Potter House

Sheep Island

Thorofare

Baymarsh

PORTSMOUTH ISLAND

Hypsometry

0

10
Elevation (feet)

Hot season backpack camping on Portsmouth Island or anywhere on the Cape Lookout National Seashore can be challenging for man or his best friend. During cooler times of year with the right weather, the rewards are out there for the well prepared. VISITNC.COM

Back at the post office, the main trail turns left and another path continues straight to the Cecil Gilgo House and the schoolhouse with its big cylindrical cistern. A right out there reaches the ruins of "the middle community." Back at the main trail, pass Doctor's Creek and cross the final bridge into the largest expanse of Portsmouth at a Methodist church. Step inside and it looks as though a service is about to begin.

Go left beyond; a looping side trail to the marsh passes the Jesse Babb House, McWilliams/Dixon House, and Ed Styron House before returning to the main path by the Dennis Mason House. Continue to the beautifully restored US Life-Saving Service complex on Coast Guard Creek. Opposite that, a brick cistern built in 1853 marks the site of the island hospital.

Beyond the Life-Saving Station, a gate bars all but authorized vehicles from the village. Camping is prohibited in the village but permitted on the beach. Past the gate, a road left reaches the Wallace Channel dock in 1 mile. Another road crosses the flats to the dunes and the beach about 1.2 miles away. If you walk to the beach, remember that although these tidal flats are dry under a south wind, they can be covered by more than 12 inches of water with high tide and/or a north breeze—which, be aware, is why these routes are marked with posts.

50 CROATAN NATIONAL FOREST

WHY GO?

Croatan's 160,000 acres compose the only true coastal national forest east of the Mississippi River. This unique region is far more than a bog-filled piney woods baking at the back door of the popular Crystal Coast vacation area. This is one of North Carolina's most scenic, distinctive natural areas, and great trails make it accessible.

Sadly, in late 2018, Hurricane Florence pummeled the forest. Two feet of rain and 100 mph winds did $17 million in damage, much of it to waterside recreational facilities. At press time a year after the storm, disaster funding had yet to address the worst damage when another hurricane hit. The trail descriptions below remain much as they were in the third edition with the expectation that most hikes will be reopened as they were. However, that may not apply to the uppermost end of the Neusiok/Mountains-to-Sea Trail. The Pine Cliff Recreation Area trailhead has seen substantial shoreline erosion, the trail's three backpacking shelters were destroyed and many trail boardwalks were moved out of position. Best bet for the latest news on repairs may be the Friends of the Mountains-to-Sea Trail website (https://mountainstoseatrail.org/, check "Trail Updates" for Segment 16). The Friends' latest book or pdf guides will always contain the latest information on the entire MST and the Neusiok (including how thru-hikers can detour around the damage). Also see the Croatan National Forest contact information below.

The forest's summer regime is buggy, snaky, hot, and humid. Some people like that. But don't sweat it if you don't. The cooler months of the year (excepting hunting seasons) are an awesome time to discover the area. There's lush greenery year-round, and the nearby shores of Emerald Isle and Atlantic Beach are often as attractive then as in summer. December and March are perfect if you want to get into the deeper woods (there is no hunting then).

The ecosystem stands out for its pocosins, an Indian word that means "swamp on a hill." Five large freshwater lakes at the highest part of the forest feed a vast area of poorly drained, acidic blackwater bogs that are home to unusual dwarf wetland vegetation and swamp cypress (the ubiquitous protruding "knees" help the roots breath). The Croatan's nearly impenetrable watersheds ooze slowly, but many just seem to sit there, providing wet, green "gene pools" that sustain the area after frequent forest fires—an integral part of the ecosystem. The USDA Forest Service torches parts of the forest each year in prescribed burns to enhance habitat. One of the interesting aspects of hiking here is passing in and out of fire-blackened areas—or between green and black where the trail delineates the

The neatest feature of the Neusiok Trail may be boardwalks across lush green wetlands.

limits of a fire. On the Neusiok Trail, hikers often hear the tinkle of metal tags nailed to trees as fireproof blazes.

Wildlife is plentiful. Species run the gamut from deer and black bear to turkey and quail. The lakes, swamps, and marshes are home or way station for bald eagles, ducks, geese, egrets, peregrine falcons, owls, woodcocks, the endangered red-cockaded woodpecker, and more. Turtles are everywhere. This is also home to the cottonmouth moccasin, eastern diamondback rattlesnake, and American alligator—but all are inactive and rarely seen in winter.

The sounds and sights of wildlife are everywhere. Wings flapping and water splashing—or even rippling—are evidence of animals slipping away almost unnoticed. Those sounds alternate with "the sound of freedom": US Marine Corps jets and cargo planes coming and going into the base at nearby Cherry Point.

The Carteret County Wildlife Club is passionate about this area, and the group is a pivotal local trail partner for the forest service. They deserve national accolades for creating the spectacular Neusiok Trail, and the North Carolina Coastal Federation is doing wonderful work at Patsy Pond.

Four great hikes in eastern North Carolina's only national forest include three nature trails. Cedar Point Trail explores a tidal marsh; Island Creek Forest Walk wanders through a rare, coastal virgin forest; Patsy Pond probes a pocosin and pine savanna; and the stunning Neusiok Trail is the coast's longest backpacking path.

THE RUNDOWN

General location: Croatan National Forest, south of New Bern, west of Beaufort, and north of the Crystal Coast islands of the Bogue Banks

Distance: Loops of 0.6, 1.8, or 2.5 miles for the Cedar Point Trail; 0.7, 1.7 miles and more for the Patsy Pond trail; 0.6 and 2.7 miles for the Island Creek Forest Walk; and about 21 miles for the Neusiok Trail (overnighters can be as short as 6.6 miles).

Difficulty: Wheelchair accessible for Cedar Point Trail; easy for most others. The Neusiok Trail is moderate due to length. In high summer, it can be difficult due to environmental challenges.

Maps: USGS Swansboro for the Cedar Point Trail; USGS Cherry Point and Newport for the Neusiok Trail; USGS Pollocksville for the Island Creek Trail; USGS Salter Path for Patsy Pond

Elevation gain: Negligible for Cedar Point Trail and Patsy Pond; 50 feet for Island Creek Trail; varies by section on Neusiok, but with gradual grades

Water availability: Water is available at the Cedar Point recreation area, which includes restrooms, a campground, boat landing, and picnic area. For the Island Creek Forest Walk, pick up water in nearby Pollocksville or at the closest national forest facilities, Fisher's Landing Picnic Area or Neuse River recreation area. For the Neusiok Trail, water is available at both the Pine Cliff Picnic Area and Oyster Point Campground trailheads, as well as from hand pumps at each of the three shelters. You can drink from the area's blackwater streams. The water is clean, despite the tea color of tannic acid. Filtering and purifying are required.

For more information: Download the national forest's *Recreation Guide*, brochures, and maps at www.fs.usda.gov/nfsnc (click through to the Croatan for a list of links to literature). Croatan National Forest, 141 E. Fisher Ave., New Bern 28560; (252) 638-5628; e-mail: croatan@fs.fed.us. Campsites at Cedar Point can be reserved by calling (877) 444-6777 or visiting recreation.gov. Campgrounds at Cedar Point and Oyster Point are open year-round. For Patsy Pond, download the North Carolina Coastal Federation's trail map brochure under the "Visit Special Coastal Places" tab at nccoast.org.

FINDING THE TRAILHEADS

For the start of the Cedar Point Trail, go north from NC 24, 3 miles east of Swansboro, on NC 58 (south crosses to the Crystal Coast beaches). Turn left onto SR 1114, 0.7 mile north of NC 24. In 0.5 mile turn left onto FR 153A; park on the right at 0.8 mile, where the road terminates at a boat landing (GPS: 34.691912/-77.086559).

The Patsy Pond Nature Trail is on the north side of NC 24, 5.5 miles east of the NC 58/24 junction, across the highway from the North Carolina Coastal Federation office (GPS: 34.719001/-76.963447).

The Neusiok Trail starts on the south at the Oyster Point Campground and in the north at the Pine Cliff Picnic Area. To reach the Oyster Point Campground trailhead, go to "downtown" Newport (1 mile from US 70) and turn east onto SR 1154. In 7 miles turn right onto FR 181 (Oyster Point Road) to the trailhead in 1 mile (GPS:

34.760913/-76.761556). Get to the Pine Cliff Picnic Area from US 70 in Havelock by driving 5.3 miles east on NC 101. Take a left on NC 306 (Ferry Road). From there, the Neusiok Trail crosses NC 306 at 2 miles at a small parking area on the right (just past a new housing project). In 3.3 miles turn left onto unpaved Pinecliff Road and the Pine Cliff Picnic Area trailhead at 1.4 miles (GPS: 34.938795/-76.822060).

The Island Creek Forest Walk starts in a parking area on the north side of Island Creek Road (SR 1004), 5.5 miles from US 17 in Pollocksville to the west, and 8.3 miles from US 70 near the airport south of New Bern (GPS: 35.027098/-77.136272).

When finding Croatan trailheads, watch traffic. The locals fly down these forest roads.

THE HIKES

Cedar Point's Tideland National Recreation Trail is not to be missed. It's one of the best interpretive trails in the state. And bring your kayak. After you've hiked the land trail, a water trail permits you to easily explore the adjacent channels when the tide is up. The path's boardwalk bridges were rebuilt after Hurricane Fran to arch above the water and permit paddler passage.

The trail explores the rich estuary where Dubling Creek meets the White Oak River and Bogue Sound across from the maritime town of Swansboro. A mix of fresh and salt water nurtures beautiful marsh grasses that wave in the breezes and stir in the rising and falling tides. This is a wonderful trail for birders; many other types of wildlife are also visible, from tiny sand crabs to deer. Best of all, the entire ecosystem is explained with some of the best interpretive signage to be found anywhere.

The double loop trail leaves the parking lot and branches. Either direction, the first, smaller, loop has benches and is suitable for wheelchairs. To the right, it wanders the edge of the marsh to a trail junction. This smaller loop goes left, crossing a boardwalk to an island. Take a left at the junction there; a long boardwalk leads back to your car for a 0.6-mile hike.

Start the same way for the longer loop, but now go right where you first went left. Cross boardwalks and small bridges along the marshy edge of higher woods, then go left across a long bridge to the shore of Dubling Creek and a viewpoint side trail. Beyond the next big bridge, there's another side viewpoint. At the second major junction, turn right to go back to your car, at about 1.8 miles. Or continue on the connector to the smaller loop. Take the connector twice to make a figure eight for a 2.5-mile walk. Be sure to take binoculars and possibly a picnic for a viewpoint bench.

The Patsy Pond Nature Trail explores a scenic area of longleaf pine savanna and four natural ponds—Patsy Pond being the largest and most distant. Grab a brochure at the roadside—the trail's twelve stops tackle such macroecological topics as the formation of the ponds; their carnivorous plants; the local pocosins, or "raised bogs"; and the uses of various plants by colonial settlers and Native Americans. The Croatan's longleaf pine forests are home to the endangered red-cockaded woodpecker—Patsy Pond contains a colony. The longleaf pine forests require fire to germinate, so the forest service uses prescribed burns here to help renew the scenic open savanna understory. Other wildlife includes egrets, reptiles, ospreys, flying squirrels, deer, and bears.

The trail's shortest, 0.7-mile, green loop visits two of the tannic acid–darkened ponds. Add the longer blue loop to create a 1.7-mile figure eight through the sandy forest south of Patsy Pond. A longer yellow trail encircles Patsy Pond, adding another 1.9 miles.

The Cedar Point Tideland Trail is one of North Carolina's best interpretive trails. Fine facilities mesh with superlative scenery.

The trail is a partnership between the national forest and the North Carolina Coastal Federation (NCCF), the state's largest nonprofit coastal preservation organization (252-393-8185). Be sure to stop in at the NCCF offices just across the highway from Patsy Pond Nature Trail (3609 NC 24), and consider supporting their work. The office has a museum, nature store, and lending library. If you're heading out to the Crystal Coast beaches across the sound, pick up (or download) the interpretive brochure for the NCCF's Hoop Pole Creek Trail in the city of Atlantic Beach. The 1-mile out-and-back trail explores a 31-acre maritime forest and estuary that juts into Bogue Sound. The path leads to a picnic spot and has a side spur to a marsh view. It starts at the Atlantic Station Shopping Center with plenty of parking at the trailhead (GPS: 34.701492 / -76.751886). Download the thirteen-stop interpretive trail guide at the NCCF website.

The Neusiok Trail, named for an early local Indian tribe, was coastal North Carolina's premier backpacking trail and hope endures that post-hurricane rebuilding will return it to that status (see above for more). In early 2020, just the northern part of Neusiok from Pine Cliff was closed to NC 306 (with a reroute in place) and the southernmost two shelters were open. The long route winds through terrain favored by insects and snakes, but focus on the dry, cool winter season. This trail rewards with beautiful stretches of cypress swamp and pocosin, longleaf pine savanna, and hardwoods. Plentiful winter greenery includes lush pines, palmetto, ferns, and evergreen species such as fetterbush.

This unusual tree stands out on the hike to Patsy Pond.

Three small shelters (best used for cooking; tents are recommended for sleeping) make Neusiok appealing for out-and-back overnighters. Nevertheless, it's a challenging end-to-end walk. During the October–November and January–February hunting seasons, wearing blaze orange is a must. That makes December and March the time to trek the Neusiok. This white circle–blazed section of the Mountains-to-Sea Trail is also marked with fireproof metal tags. Years of work had made this the time to hike Neusiok. Even then, and after the trail is reopened, hikers should expect some blowdowns and muck.

From the Oyster Point Campground (fifteen sites/water), a handy overnight camp if you're spotting a second car at Pine Cliff, the trail leaves left of the restroom. It winds along the edge of Mill Creek, emerging for a short distance to follow the FR 181 access road, then reenters the woods. The trail crosses Mill Creek Road at about 1.5 miles. The first shelter, Blackjack Lodge, sits in a piney grove at 2.6 miles. (The water pump needs to be primed with water in jugs at shelter; be sure to refill the jugs when you leave.) Turn left onto FR 124 at about 4 miles and hike 0.5 mile. Then go right off the road, through open woods and boggy areas, to exit at 6.4 miles onto FR 169. Turn right there for another road walk, this one nearly 2 miles. At about 8 miles, turn left on FR 147, then shortly turn right, leaving the road to pass a sinkhole and cross a boardwalk section. Be careful to notice the blue-marked trail on the left to Dogwood Camp Shelter at about 10 miles. The trail crosses NC 101 at about 11 miles. There's another boardwalk at 12.6 miles and then NC 306, with trailhead parking, at about 13.8 miles.

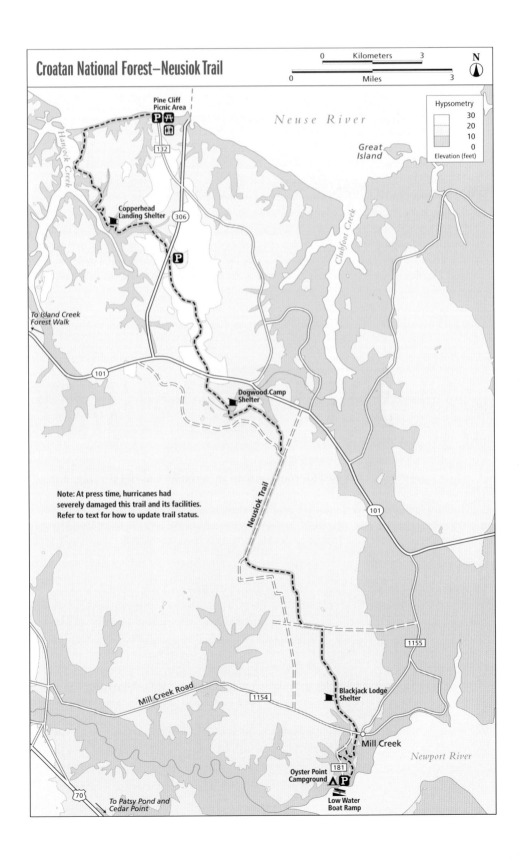

Croatan National Forest–Neusiok Trail

0 Kilometers 3
0 Miles 3

N

Hypsometry
30
20
10
0
Elevation (feet)

Neuse River

Great Island

Hancock Creek

Clubfoot Creek

Pine Cliff
Picnic Area

P A

132

Copperhead
Landing Shelter

306

P

To Island Creek
Forest Walk

101

Dogwood Camp
Shelter

Note: At press time, hurricanes had
severely damaged this trail and its facilities.
Refer to text for how to update trail status.

Neusiok Trail

101

1155

Mill Creek Road

1154

Blackjack Lodge
Shelter

Mill Creek

Newport River

Oyster Point
Campground

A P

181

Low Water
Boat Ramp

70

To Patsy Pond and
Cedar Point

The ease of spotting a car here and at Pine Cliff makes the northernmost section a nice 6.6-mile overnighter with a shelter in the center. The first part of this Neusiok section alternates between swampy areas with boardwalks to pine- and hardwood-forested bluffs. The third shelter, Copperhead Landing, above Cahooque Creek, has a nice waterfront view at just under 17 miles. A boardwalk bridges more swampy terrain before you reach the bank of the Neuse River at 19 miles.

The bluff-top trail has been battered by storms; you could just walk the beach where cypress knees protrude from the sand. Here, blackwater drainages ooze to the edge of the sand just short of flowing into salt water. This is a "cargo cult" section of trail. I actually saw a sailboat crushed to pieces among the shoreline trees. The Pine Cliff Picnic Area and parking are about 20.4 miles from Oyster Point.

From Pine Cliff or the roadside parking slip on NC 306, it's an easy overnighter to the Copperhead Landing shelter.

The Island Creek Forest Walk explores a rare coastal virgin forest. Cypress trees were logged extensively in the Croatan. This trail is the best place to see the impressive old trees with their protruding knees. Island Creek is also geologically unique. The 8-square-mile drainage is underlain with the Castle Hayne marine limestone formation. The alkaline rock neutralizes normally acid soil, supporting diverse plant communities. Along the

Neusiok's freshwater ponds creep within sight of salt water.

The metallic sound you could hear on breezy days along the Neusiok Trail might be the metal tags of fire-proof blazes on trailside trees. You'll often see them paired with MST blazes.

creek the limestone crops out in scenic bluffs surrounded by cypress. (Again, this section will be closed in 2020. Check ahead.)

The main hike is a 0.6-mile streamside loop with fifteen numbered posts and a related brochure available at the district ranger station on US 70 south of New Bern (or request it by e-mail). That trail is part of a longer, more adventurous "user-maintained" network that follows the stream past the best scenery and loops back a few ways following informal spray-painted blazes. The basic loop is easy, and the longer loops are not difficult to find (but turn around if the trail seems obscure to you).

To enjoy the big-cypress scenery upstream of the formal trail, bear right beyond post 7 on the informal path—one of many that expand this hike. Stick with the creek past the first left, then just retrace your steps to return and finish the interpretive loop. You can leave the trail upstream at the first left mentioned above, or farther beyond as it makes a loop back where both trails intersect and run together. If you then bear left where a trail goes right, take the first hard left turn after that; what's called the Natcy Trail reconnects to the formal nature trail (where a right reaches your car). It's not hard to find your way around a loop that can be as long as 2.6-plus miles, but be aware, these are not formal forest service trails.

51 BALD HEAD ISLAND

WHY GO?

Environmentalists balk at being too positive about upscale private islands, but Bald Head is a rarity. The exclusive resort is flanked by an extensive, well-preserved virgin forest of trees up to 300 years old, the state's best example of mature maritime forest where live oaks spread their massive, wind-gnarled crowns.

The public can spend the night here—many of the island's homes, condos, and some inn rooms can be rented—which gives guests temporary access to Bald Head Island Club amenities (golf course, tennis, swimming pool, marina, a fine dining room). You can also spend the day on the island—just for the cost of a ferry ride. There are no cars on Bald Head Island, so an electric shuttle meets the ferry. Thereafter you roam the island in an electric golf cart or ride a bike (both for rent, or bring your own bike) down narrow, Caribbean-style roads under a forest abuzz with cicadas and the feel of the subtropics.

Bald Head Island's Cape Fear is one of the most treacherous parts of the Graveyard of the Atlantic, first named in 1585 when a mariner wrote that "we were in great danger of a Wracke on a breache called the Cape of Feare." It's home to Old Baldy, the oldest lighthouse on the North Carolina coast (1817), just a five-minute walk from the dock. Visitors can climb the light, explore a museum and campus of historic structures and site of a Civil War fort, and even engage an island history tour (910-448-1472; oldbaldy.org).

The Bald Head and Smith Island complex is home to an amazing diversity of birds and wildlife, all watched over by the nonprofit Bald Head Island Conservancy.

A more modern lighthouse was razed in 1958, and the lighthouse keeper's residence and lifesaving structures are now restored and serve as the campus of the Bald Head Island Conservancy. The facilities house interns, and researchers engaged in monitoring the after-dark nesting habits of endangered loggerhead sea turtles and other wildlife. The conservancy's bookstore and gift shop is called Turtle Central, and the group's naturalist-led outdoor experiences are a great way to encounter the island.

The most developed interpretive path is the Kent Mitchell Nature Trail beside Bald Head Creek. Four other trails explore the nearly 200-acre Bald Head Woods Coastal Reserve in the center of the island (see Buxton Woods for another coastal reserve).

Enjoy a short nature trail on a spectacular but private barrier island plus additional hikes in the maritime forest. Public access is available for the ferry fee.

FINDING THE TRAILHEAD

To reach the ferry from US 17 south of Wilmington, take a left onto NC 87 South. At NC 87's junction with NC 211, go left on Howe Street and proceed into Southport. Do not follow the signs to the North Carolina state ferry to Fort Fisher; instead turn right onto West Ninth Street to Indigo Plantation, 1.7 miles from NC 211. Take Indigo Plantation Drive to its dead end at the Bald Head Island ferry terminal. Day visitors are charged for parking, the ferry ride, and any cargo, such as a bicycle, surfboard, or canoe. No-frills tickets are available.

Bicycles and golf carts are for rent near the island ferry terminal for your ride along Federal Road. The trailhead is on the left, about 1.5 miles from the dock, just past the junction with Muscadine Wynd. The first Bald Head Woods trailhead is about 0.4 mile beyond on the right (GPS: 33.856785/-77.979472), the second on the right about 0.5 mile beyond that (GPS: 33.851821/-77.972966), and another near Bald Head Island Conservancy. The two trailheads for the Creek Trail are on the left, just past the first trailhead on the right and before the second right-side trailhead.

THE HIKE

The Kent Mitchell Nature Trail immediately crosses the first boardwalk to the three tiny islets that the trail wanders over in 0.6-mile loops. These three small hammocks barely rise above the tidal ebb and flow of surrounding marshy wetlands. This is the preserved home of more than a third of the animal species listed as endangered in the United States. Birds include bald eagles and red-cockaded woodpeckers. There are also otters, raccoons, alligators, and bobcats. Bring binoculars. The islands sprout quiet, warm, and semitropical amid the expanse of black needlerush, the tubular marsh grass that grows where freshwater mingles with salt water. Benches, perfect for birding, are located in a few spots on the trail. Insect repellent and sunscreen are essential between May and October.

On Bayberry Island, the subtropical cabbage palm, state tree of Florida and South Carolina, is everywhere at its northern limit. A smaller plant at ground level is the dwarf palmetto, which never grows to tree size and reaches as far north as Cape Hatteras. Signs direct hikers counterclockwise around the trail. Cross a boardwalk to Palmetto Island, then take the next left over the boardwalk onto Live Oak Island. Another trail along Federal Road reaches the largest live oak on Bald Head Island.

At the most distant end of Live Oak Island, a side trail leads left to a bench. From here the view includes a historic nearby boathouse and Smith Island, the larger landmass of which Bald Head is the southernmost part. The marsh grasses you see from here are mostly saltmeadow cordgrass and smooth cordgrass.

Some subtropical plants reach their northernmost limit on Bald Head Island.

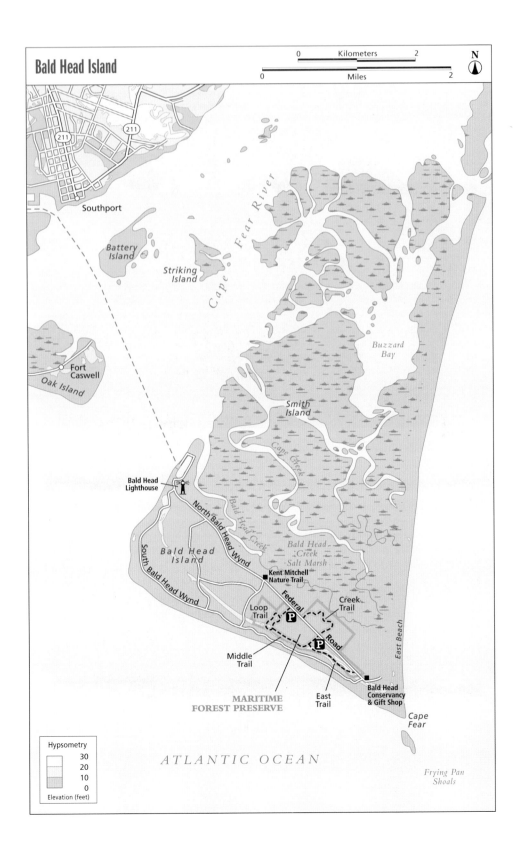

Bald Head Island

Kilometers
0   2

Miles
0   2

N

211

211

Southport

Battery
Island

Striking
Island

Cape Fear River

Buzzard
Bay

Fort
Caswell

Oak Island

Smith
Island

Cape Creek

Bald Head
Lighthouse

North Bald Head Wynd

Bald Head Creek

Bald Head
Island

South Bald Head Wynd

Bald Head
Creek
Salt Marsh

Kent Mitchell
Nature Trail

Federal

Loop
Trail

P

Creek
Trail

Road

Middle
Trail

P

MARITIME
FOREST PRESERVE

East
Trail

Bald Head
Conservancy
& Gift Shop

East Beach

Cape
Fear

ATLANTIC OCEAN

*Frying Pan
Shoals*

Hypsometry

30
20
10
0

Elevation (feet)

Families will follow TRACK Trail markers like this to insight and exercise on many of the interpretive paths listed in the Trail Finder.

Back on Palmetto Island, the trail goes left where red cedar predominates near a third bench at the tip of the island. Cross a small boardwalk back onto Bayberry Island and go left on the last loop around Pine Island to see loblolly pine and Spanish moss. Back on Bayberry Island, go left and then take another left across the boardwalk to Federal Road.

About 0.5 mile past the nature trail on Federal Road, two trailheads lie to the right. From the first, take the 0.4-mile Loop Trail that includes Timmons Oak, a giant of the forest. From the end of the loop, the Middle Trail parallels Federal Road southeast through the woods about 0.6 mile to the next parking area. Not far from that trailhead, the East Trail zigzags 0.5 mile to south Bald Head Wynd near the conservancy campus. Across Federal Road from the first trailhead, the Creek Trail runs the edge of the marsh for 0.7 mile before reaching its eastern trailhead just across the road from the Middle Trail parking slip. For an impressive, almost 1.5-mile hike, leave your golf cart or bike at the Loop Trailhead, walk down Federal Road, and go left on the Creek Trail. Cross Federal Road to hike the Middle Trail back to your ride at the Loop Trail.

APPENDIX: TRAIL FINDER

INTERPRETIVE NATURE TRAILS/WHEELCHAIR-ACCESSIBLE TRAILS
"(H)" indicates accessible for those in wheelchairs.

The relative interchangeability of these paths reflects the fact that the best interpretive trails are often very level and either paved or otherwise surfaced and passable with wheelchairs.

- Balsam Nature Trail, Mount Mitchell State Park, p. 138
- Biltmore Campus Trail, Cradle of Forestry, Pisgah National Forest, p. 167
- Cascades Trail, Blue Ridge Parkway, p. 55
- Cedar Point Trail, Croatan National Forest (H), p. 343
- Chestnut Oak Nature Trail, Hanging Rock State Park, p. 215
- Densons Creek Nature Trail, Uwharrie National Forest, pp. 294–95
- Eno Trace Trail, Eno River State Park (TRACK Trail), p. 255
- Fern Trail/Lake Trail, Crowders Mountain State Park (TRACK Trail), p. 320
- Figure Eight Trail, Blue Ridge Parkway (H), p. 73
- Flat Rock Self-Guiding Loop Trail, Blue Ridge Parkway, p. 107
- Forest Festival Trail, Cradle of Forestry, Pisgah National Forest, p. 167
- Frances Liles Interpretive Trail, Schenck Forest, Raleigh, p. 273
- Guilford Courthouse National Military Park trails, Greensboro, p. 232
- Hammock Hills Nature Trail, Cape Hatteras National Seashore, pp. 329–31
- Hemlock Nature Trail, South Mountains State Park (trout stream ecosystem) (H), p. 287, 289
- Horne Creek Trail through Horne Creek Farm, Pilot Mountain State Park, p. 213
- Joyce Kilmer Trail, Joyce Kilmer Memorial Forest, Nantahala National Forest, p. 198
- Kent Mitchell Nature Trail, Bald Head Island, pp. 350–51
- Mount Mitchell Summit Tower Trail (H), see Balsam Nature Trail, p. 138
- Nags Head Woods ADA Trail, Nags Head Woods Ecological Preserve (H), p. 323
- Oak Rock Interpretive Trail, William B. Umstead State Park (TRACK Trail), p. 270
- Patsy Pond Trail, Croatan National Forest, p. 343
- Rhododendron Trail, Mount Jefferson State Natural Area (TRACK Trail), p. 52
- River Trail, South Mountains State Park (TRACK Trail), pp. 291–92
- Roan Mountain Rhododendron Gardens National Recreation Trail (H), p. 13

- Rock Garden Trail, Hanging Rock State Park (H), p. 214
- Salem Lake Trail, Winston-Salem (TRACK Trail / H), p. 225
- Spruce-Fir Nature Trail, Clingmans Dome Road, Great Smoky Mountains National Park, p. 21
- Tanawha Trail to Linn Cove Viaduct, Blue Ridge Parkway at Grandfather Mountain (H), p. 92
- Three Rivers Trail, Morrow Mountain State Park, p. 304
- Wiseman's View Trail, Linville Gorge, Pisgah National Forest (H), p. 122
- Woods Walk, Grandfather Mountain, p. 102

WATERFALL HIKES

- Cascades Trail, Blue Ridge Parkway, p. 55
- Crabtree Falls, Blue Ridge Parkway, p. 134
- Bard Falls, Harper Creek area, Pisgah National Forest, p. 117
- Big Laurel Falls Trail, Nantahala National Forest, p. 28
- Boone Fork Trail, Blue Ridge Parkway, p. 68
- Elk River Falls Trail, Pisgah National Forest, p. 85
- Glen Burney Trail, Blowing Rock, p. 82
- Graveyard Fields, Blue Ridge Parkway, p. 172
- High Shoals Falls Loop, South Mountains State Park, p. 287
- Hunt Fish Falls Trail, Harper Creek area, Pisgah National Forest, p. 111
- Indian Creek Trail, Hanging Rock State Park, p. 218
- Linville Falls Trails, Blue Ridge Parkway, p. 122
- Looking Glass Falls, Forest Heritage Scenic Byway (US 276), Pisgah National Forest, p. 167
- Lower Cascades Falls Trail, Hanging Rock State Park, p. 219
- Middle Falls/Lower Falls Trail, via Stone Mountain Trail, Stone Mountain State Park, p. 39
- Mouse Creek Falls, Big Creek Trail, Great Smoky Mountains National Park, p. 189
- North Harper Creek Falls, Harper Creek area, Pisgah National Forest, p. 112
- Sliding Rock, Forest Heritage Scenic Byway (US 276), Pisgah National Forest, p. 161
- South Harper Creek Falls, Harper Creek area, Pisgah National Forest, p. 117
- Stone Mountain Falls, Stone Mountain Trail, Stone Mountain State Park, p. 36
- Tom's Branch Falls/Indian Creek/Juney Whank Falls, Great Smoky Mountains National Park, p. 195
- Tory's Den and Falls, Hanging Rock State Park, p. 217
- Upper Cascades Falls Trail, Hanging Rock State Park (H), p. 219

- Upper Creek Falls loop, Harper Creek area, Pisgah National Forest, p. 117
- Widow's Creek Falls, Stone Mountain State Park, p. 37

FAMILY / KIDS' HIKES / KIDS IN PARKS TRACK TRAILS

Beyond this list, consider interpretive nature trails, especially those with disabled accessibility for the very youngest hikers.

- Appalachian Trail from Carvers Gap to Round Bald, near Roan Mountain, p. 9
- Beech Tree Trail, Elk Knob State Park (TRACK Trail), p. 59
- Bethabara Greenway Trail, Winston-Salem, pp. 223–25
- Big Laurel Falls Trail, Nantahala National Forest, p. 28
- Boone Fork, Price Park Picnic Area, Blue Ridge Parkway (TRACK Trail), p. 68
- Cloudland Trail, Roan Mountain, p. 89
- Eno Trace Trail, Eno River State Park (TRACK Trail), p. 255
- Fern Trail/Lake Trail, Crowders Mountain State Park (TRACK Trail), p. 320
- Flat Rock Nature Trail, Blue Ridge Parkway, p. 107
- Great Woodland Adventure Trail, Chimney Rock Park at Chimney Rock State Park (TRACK Trail), p. 159
- Hickory Nut Falls Trail, Chimney Rock Park at Chimney Rock State Park, p. 159
- Hutchison Homestead TRACK Trail, Stone Mountain State Park, pp. 36–37
- Lake Daniel Park Greenway, Greensboro (TRACK Trail for hiking and biking), pp. 235–36
- Nat Greene Trail, Greensboro Watershed Trails, p. 231–34
- Natural Garden Trail, North Carolina Arboretum (TRACK Trail), p. 156
- Oak Rock Interpretive Trail, William B. Umstead State Park (TRACK Trail), p. 270
- Pine Hollow Trail, McDowell Nature Preserve, Charlotte (TRACK Trail), p. 312
- Price Lake Trail, Blue Ridge Parkway (TRACK Trail for hikers and paddlers), p. 70
- Profile Trail, Grandfather Mountain State Park (TRACK Trail), p. 103
- Quarry Trail, Morrow Mountain State Park (TRACK Trail), p. 104
- Rhododendron Trail, Mount Jefferson State Natural Area (TRACK Trail), p. 52
- River Trail, South Mountains State Park (TRACK Trail), pp. 291–92
- Salem Lake Trail, Winston-Salem (TRACK Trail for cycling but great for hiking), p. 225
- Tom's Branch Falls/Indian Creek/Juney Whank Falls, Great Smoky Mountains National Park, p. 195
- Whiteside Mountain National Recreation Trail, p. 203

BEGINNER BACKPACKING TRIPS

- Appalachian Trail: Overmountain Victory Trail to Overmountain tent sites, p. 9
- Crowders Mountain State Park, p. 315

- Deep Creek Trail, Great Smoky Mountains National Park, p. 195
- Eno River State Park, Fanny's Ford Trail campsites, p. 253–54
- Grassy Gap Fire Road (or other loop routes) to Basin Cove campsite, Doughton Park, Blue Ridge Parkway, p. 47
- Graveyard Ridge Trail from Graveyard Fields Trail, Blue Ridge Parkway, Shining Rock Wilderness Area, p. 168
- Morrow Mountain State Park, p. 303
- Neusiok Trail, Croatan National Forest (Copperhead Landing shelter in winter), pp. 342–43
- Tanawha Trail to Nuwati Trail, Grandfather Mountain, p. 92
- Uwharrie/Dutchman's Creek Trails, Birkhead Mountains Wilderness, and Uwharrie and Woods Run Trails circuit, Uwharrie National Forest, p. 293
- Widow's Creek Trail, Stone Mountain State Park (short, steep climb at start), pp. 37–38

BEST WILDFLOWER WALKS

- Appalachian Trail: Yellow Mountain Gap to Hump Mountain, p. 8
- Craggy Gardens trails, p. 147
- Lake Trail, Crowders Mountain State Park (TRACK Trail), p. 317
- Oconaluftee River Trail, Great Smoky Mountains National Park, p. 191
- Pump Station Trail, Eno River State Park, p. 254
- Rhododendron Gardens National Recreation Trail, Roan Mountain, p. 87
- Rhododendron Trail, Mount Jefferson State Natural Area (TRACK Trail), p. 52
- Shady Hollow and Cove Trails, McDowell Nature Preserve, Charlotte, p. 312
- Grandfather Mountain area, on Tanawha Trail between Wilson Creek and Rough Ridge parking areas (p. 92), and Profile Trail (p. 101).

BEST BIRDING HIKES

- Bodie Island Lighthouse Trail, Cape Hatteras National Seashore, p. 320
- Bog Garden, Greensboro, p. 218
- Buxton Woods Trail, Cape Hatteras National Seashore, pp. 329–31
- Cedar Point Trail, Croatan National Forest, p. 343
- Grandfather Trail, Grandfather Mountain (ravens), p. 99
- Hammock Hills Nature Trail, Cape Hatteras National Seashore, pp. 329–31
- Kent Mitchell Nature Trail, Bald Head Island, pp. 350–51
- McDowell Nature Preserve, Charlotte, p. 311
- Nags Head Woods trails, Nags Head Woods Ecological Preserve, p. 323
- North Pond Wildlife Trail, Pea Island National Wildlife Refuge, pp. 330–31
- Patsy Pond Trail, Croatan National Forest, p. 343

HIKE INDEX

ABOUT THE AUTHOR

Randy Johnson has lived in the Southern Appalachians most of his life and has written widely for national newspapers and ski and travel magazines, often on the topic of North Carolina's outdoors. He is the author of *Southern Snow: The New Guide to Winter Sports from Maryland to the Southern Appalachians*, a 2019 second edition of his 1986 "cult classic," and the award-winning *Grandfather Mountain: The History and Guide to an Appalachian Icon*. His other books include recent editions of FalconGuides *Hiking the Blue Ridge Parkway*, *Best Easy Day Hikes Blue Ridge Parkway*, and *Best Easy Day Hikes Great Smoky Mountains National Park*. For nearly twenty years he was editor-in-chief of United Airlines' magazine *Hemispheres* ("world's best inflight magazine," 2007).

Skiing the Appalachian Trail on Roan Mountain. PHOTO BY ROBERT BRANCH

Randy proposed and implemented the trail management program at Grandfather Mountain in 1978 that stabilized public access to the private mountain, reclaimed historic trails, built the Cragway, Nuwati, and Profile trails, and helped lay the groundwork for the mountain's designation as a United Nations Biosphere Reserve. He was a trail design consultant for the Blue Ridge Parkway's Tanawha Trail on Grandfather and helped mesh the system of trails found on the mountain today in Grandfather Mountain State Park and on the Parkway. He's currently the task force leader for the Grandfather Mountain portion of the Mountains-to-Sea Trail and a member of the Grandfather Mountain State Park Advisory Committee.

Randy has hiked and skied all over the world and is a member of the Society of American Travel Writers, the North American Travel Journalists Association, and the North American Snowsports Journalists Association. Randy invites you to visit his website (randyjohnsonbooks.com) to offer your thoughts and suggestions and to see special features relating to his books.